KT-545-539

± c

0

16. NOV

-2

R

CLXX

Book No 0101577

30109 001015778

The Encyclopedia of GLASS

CLXX

The Encyclopedia of GLASS

Edited by PHOEBE PHILLIPS

PP/H HEINEMANN

A Phoebe Phillips/Heinemann Book

First published in Great Britain 1981

William Heinemann Ltd
10 Upper Grosvenor Street
London W1X 9PA
LONDON MELBOURNE TORONTO
JOHANNESBURG AUCKLAND

© Phoebe Phillips 1981

All rights reserved. No part of this
publication may be reproduced, stored in
a retrieval system, or transmitted, in any
form or by any means, electronic,
mechanical, photocopying, recording
and/or otherwise without the prior written
permission of the publishers.

This book may not be lent, resold, hired
out or otherwise disposed of by way of
trade in any form of binding or cover
other than that in which it is published,
without the prior consent of the publishers.

This book is sold subject to the Standard
Conditions of Sale of Net Books and may
not be resold in the UK below the net
price.

434 98200 8

Photoset by Tradespools Ltd,
Frome, Somerset
Printed and bound in the United States
of America

BEXLEY LIBRARY SERVICE
ACC No. N37818
Bk H. J.
- 1 FEB 1982
P £20.00
Cl No. 748 PH + 666.19
PH

Contents

Contributors and Consultants

Joseph T. Butler
Oscar Feldman
Paul V. Gardner
Gabriella Gros-Galliner
Paul Hollister, Jr
Ada Polak
Phelps Warren
Roy Youngs

With such a multi-faceted book, it is
impossible to name everyone who has
generously donated time and effort in
helping us with information, research,
pictures and advice. Nonetheless we wish
to pay especial tribute to Tessa Clark,
designer Harry Green, Nancy Dunnan, Mary
Y. Ischi, Corning Glass, the Cinzano
Collection, Pilkington Brothers, Dartington
Glass, The Glasshouse, Thomas Goode &
Co., Derek Davis, Packwood House Museum,
museum staff and private collectors all over
the world, and the staff of the Victoria &
Albert Museum in London.

List of Colour Plates

Introduction

Glass is, above all, a world of light, shifting and changing with every new discovery and additional piece of research. The exploration of the past goes on, and scholars and experts add to our knowledge every year. As a result, we know our work is far from complete; it can only be a beginning, a personal expression of the delight and enjoyment that I and my colleagues have shared with glass lovers everywhere.

The Encyclopedia of Glass has been designed to show the enormous range and the unique qualities of glass. It is a world-wide survey of this extraordinary material, as part of our background, and our heritage, over the past 3,500 years.

Countries are arranged chronologically so that the story of glass and its manufacture can be followed from the earliest ancient Egyptian sand-casting in the eighteenth dynasty, through the innovation of blown glass, and Roman manufacturing kilns, to the establishment of the famous glasshouses of the great Venetian empire, on the island of Murano (still a major tourist attraction).

Blown and cut crystal developed rapidly in England, and at the same time, Bohemian glassworks specialised in coloured, painted and gilded tableware of all kinds. In the nineteenth century American pressed glass manufacturers used a mechanical process to create an entire art form. Paperweights in France were a delightful, if minor, craze. Art Glass, the Arts and Crafts movement, and Art Nouveau brought decorative forms and iridescent shadows to the popular market. From the early twentieth century glass began to reflect fashion every few decades – Art Deco, Depression and war-time utility glass, stark Scandinavian designs with discreet engraving, and finally, today, the studio glass made by individual artists in their own workshops.

It is very important to remember that all these periods overlap, with no clear-cut divisions between countries or even factories; glassworkers have always been travellers, and the techniques of the glasshouse share a common ancestry. For that reason, we have placed each country or area in its period of major influence to the glass world, but the history within each country may cover up to 2,000 years.

We also believe that it is impossible to understand any craft without understanding the skills involved. For that reason, the techniques of glassmaking are a major part of the book, covering many aspects from simple glassblowing and the chemical properties of glass formulae, to the manufacture of light bulbs.

Many new pieces are photographed and described, selected from private collections and small dealers to help readers to appreciate the areas that can still be explored for their own collection and enjoyment. The dimensions of the pieces are given in inches and centimetres. Measurements that were originally in centimetres have been rounded up or down to the nearest eighth of an inch.

Since any single book cannot be more than an overview of an extremely complex subject, there is a wide and exhaustive reading list, the longest in any book for the general reader. Over 600 titles are included, together with major museum, and private but viewable, collections and leading glass journals. We hope that, inspired by even a brief look at some of the many kinds of glass, readers will go on to find out more about individual artists, techniques, and national traditions.

Finally, there are all the many pleasures we are lucky enough to have today.

Two-dimensional modern flat glass can be so magnificently clear that you cannot see it at all; or stained, layered, flashed, and coloured every tint in the spectrum. Glass in windows of all sizes can be made to let in every ray of sunlight, or shut out even the merest glimmer of starlight; it can be formulated to keep out ultra-violet rays, or double-glazed for heat and sound insulation; sand blasted for all-over surface texture, or delicately engraved with snowflakes. Church windows may be designed to inspire us to quiet reflection. Mirrored glass ceilings recall the great Paris brothels of the nineteenth century.

Three-dimensional glass can be equally versatile. Vitrified dishes go happily from freezer to oven and back again, and grace the same table as a fragile crystal decanter. Little lampwork figurines can be bought for pennies; antique paperweights are rare and unbelievably expensive. Glittering chandeliers and sconces recall Viennese ballrooms and the elegance of velvet and lace; strings of glass beads fringe a pop-star blouse over a pair of jeans. Huge carboys are suitable for complete indoor gardens, or will transport chemicals by the hundred-litre; tiny iridescent perfume bottles hold a quarter-ounce of scent in airtight seclusion.

Glass is, indeed, a world of complete visual experience.

PHOEBE PHILLIPS

Collector's Guide

Page 9
Selection of glass, from the Roman period to the present.

Pages 10 and 11
Detail of a mosaic enamel plate.

Left
Scene in a Majorcan glasshouse.

The newly enthusiastic glass collector is lucky enough to be confronted with such a wide choice that a mixed sale of glassware can have an almost numbing effect. A catalogue may feature a group of small darkish bottles, of irregular shapes and unknown purpose, next to a six-foot high chandelier gleaming with cut crystal facets and decorated with riotous flowers in every shape and colour. In the older-style auction houses, a sinuous Art Deco lamp can be numbered just before a group of Roman wine jars; neither benefits from the comparison.

A good collector, like a good auction house, will learn to co-ordinate certain kinds of glass to give a sense of order and development to the display; in the one case to benefit the eye, and for the pleasure, of the owner, in the other to show the best qualities of each piece and increase its value.

The first task for the novice is to narrow the possibilities, starting in the best local museum if it has a reasonably good glass department; a wide-ranging book will help to fill in the gaps.

Choices will often be based on personal background – for the collector interested in history, the development of glass as a craft is both exciting and rewarding. A particular period will show many of the characteristics of other art forms during that time; the history of colour technology can take you from Egyptian yellow stripes to the iridescent purple of the Art Nouveau decades; commemorative inscriptions and engraved designs reflect almost every aspect of life, and range from lovers' marriage cups to pieces produced for political campaigns. You may become fascinated by techniques, or enchanted by tiny lampwork animals and toys, or paperweights, or the moving and impressive qualities of stained glass. Even a theme as simple as variations on a wine-glass stem can include simple facets, bubbles, lacey twists, twisted dragons – and numerous modern examples, some of which can be almost cartoonlike in character.

A very small collection can still reflect a personal concept about art and decoration, just as even a tiny room can have a focal point of some kind. Remember to go outside your 'theme' now and then to keep a sense of discovery and excitement, and a delight in the unexpected. A careful progression through the ages, or through the major techniques of glassmaking, could result in a collection that is more suitable for a classroom, unless it is unbalanced by those wonderful, totally different, glasses which pleased your eye and your heart. As you grow in knowledge and understanding your tastes may change, and the fundamental basis of your collection may shift from tableware in pressed cranberry glass to modern glass sculpture, but those unplanned purchases, bought with love and inspiration, should always remain a joy to look at and a very special piece of magic.

Ancient and Middle Eastern Glass

The glass generally referred to as 'ancient' is pre-blown glass of all kinds, and Roman blown glass.

Pre-blown glass is difficult to find and extremely expensive in relation to its size and level of craftsmanship. Early Egyptian sand-core bottles are quite small and often somewhat crude in workmanship; the best undamaged pieces are properly destined for museums, although a few are

sometimes available from specialist dealers, or in archaeological rather than glass auctions. One or two of the lovely little fish or palm-tree bottles would make a very attractive starting point for the historically minded collector. These artefacts of a much earlier civilization must be cleaned and stored carefully – go to an expert for advice on care and maintenance.

Enough undamaged Roman glass is available for even the modest collector to build up quite a range of styles and patterns that are charming, and sufficiently varied to be interesting. The most common objects are small bottles blown in moulds. Some have figurative designs, such as masks and leaves, others have geometric patterns; the occasional inscription is sometimes a Roman form of advertising. The finer pieces are almost always bought for museums. More everyday wares were once inexpensive enough to escape the attentions of forgers, but this is no longer the case. It is important to look closely at museum collections, photographs and markings. Roman glass has usually been found buried in the ground, with a higher or lesser degree of iridescence caused by the action of the minerals and chemicals in the soil. That lovely sheen is actually flaking off the surface of the glass. Although the glass was originally light and bubbly, flaking has often reduced its thickness even more, and the pieces are generally very light and extremely fragile. Keep them carefully housed out of reach of young fingers or boisterous animals, and preferably in a glass-fronted cabinet which will be unaffected by extremes of heat and cold. You can buy special stands to keep the round-bottomed flasks upright, or make them yourself from simple pieces of wood and wire. Roman glass was made in very large quantities, and fragments can be recovered, almost by the trowelful, in many parts of Europe where there were settlements or military cantonments. For the beginner, a few fragments bought very cheaply can provide a good education in assessing weight and quality of workmanship; and fragments of the more expensive kinds of luxury glass can be very helpful in understanding how mosaic bowls and double-walled discs were made. Once you begin to buy whole pieces, avoid anything which is badly damaged unless it is so rare that it will retain its value no matter what its present state.

Production fell sharply in the West after the collapse of the Roman Empire, and glass of this period is quite rare. Most known pieces have been found in the course of archaeological excavations, and intact examples will be mainly in museums or major collections. In the Middle East production continued at a reasonably high level. The most likely finds were probably brought back as 'souvenirs' by European and American travellers during the nineteenth century; the control of antiquities throughout the world was very much less effective then than it is today. Likely survivors are carved pieces like seals or scarabs which were not easily damaged, and which in many cases were protected by metal mounts. There are also pieces such as the Um weights and measures, moulded in glass during a period from about 600–750 AD; while these are historically very interesting, especially to students of Arabic script and culture, they are curious rather than beautiful.

The Fifteenth to Eighteenth Centuries

From the fifteenth century on, glass was once again made in sufficiently large quantities to provide more scope for collecting. Winged stem goblets, beakers, cups, dishes and decorative pieces can still be found in reasonable condition, and at prices which are at least occasionally feasible. Soda glass is light compared with potash and lead glass, and most pieces weigh much less in the hand than their appearance would indicate. Damaged pieces lose quite a lot of their value, but unusual examples can be sold for high prices. This period has become an open hunting ground for forgers. During the nineteenth century some extremely active copiers were at work in Bohemia and Venice, where 'traditional' styles were made for the tourist trade. Colour is a clue to replaced or repaired stems. Most early colourless glass was grey or yellow in tone, and too clear a colour should indicate modern work. Try to buy from a reputable dealer who is willing to describe a piece in writing.

Once into the eighteenth century, the collector has a much wider choice. Techniques and styles differ widely enough to offer an almost endless number of permutations.

Bohemian glass was noted for its fine wheel engraving. Brilliant colouring was one of the major Bohemian skills, often in two or even three layers, and almost always substantially made. So you may choose to specialise in Bohemian coloured glass, with an emphasis on engraving, or on engraved glass, or the various kinds of cased glass. Perhaps you would prefer a subject; local scenes or city buildings originally designed for the tourist trade, or brightly enamelled figures and flowers on single flasks and bottles – similar examples were made in America for the German-speaking settlements.

Aspects of Collecting

As a matter of common sense, consider your geographical location. Collecting American pressed glass cup plates in Paris will not give your acquisitive instincts too much scope, although Chinese snuff bottles are fairly easily found there. At the same time, it is frustrating to be confined to a kind of glass you dislike simply because a local factory has flooded the market for a century or more. As with most interests, it may be a question of compromising with your purse, your home, the amount you can afford to spend on travelling, and, of course, your own personal tastes.

There are compensating factors. Catalogues and letters can keep you in touch with dealers and other collectors throughout the world, and vacations can sometimes be planned with particular goals in mind. The world is small today, and getting smaller.

In early days, the glassworkers travelled, and many ideas and techniques are found in different places in slightly different forms. If you are enraptured by Venetian winged stems, try looking for unusual stems of all kinds. If fine French paperweights are too expensive for anything more than a once-in-a-lifetime purchase, concentrate on modern paperweights – a remarkable number of young glassmakers today are working within traditional patterns but contributing their own individual designs. If Roman scent and oil

flasks are too rare, collect Victorian scent bottles which are easy to move, fairly safe from accidental damage, and which can be stored and displayed in a drawer.

Paperweights

Paperweights are eminently collectable – they are easy to show off, pretty to look at, and, because they were once produced in such quantity, easy to find for copying purposes. Because of this they call for a special warning to collectors – particularly applicable now when the price of French weights in the classic period is astronomical, and modern weights by the best new paperweight makers are also becoming expensive enough to be worth forging.

The most common fault in an otherwise genuine weight may be re-grinding. Old weights could become chipped or cracked, and re-grinding, while it would restore the pristine roundness, devalues the weight, and changes the technical effect since it removes a layer of the covering glass, which may destroy its magnifying qualities. There should be a reasonably heavy layer of clear glass all around the central motif, and the profile from the side should narrow down to nothing. Sometimes re-grinding will actually make the outer row of canes disappear altogether, or at best may break into the base to show a vertical shelf.

Facets have also been added from time to time to conceal damage or chipping. Learn which kind of faceting is appropriate to each factory – some forgeries were detected because they had clover cut facets from the New England factory superimposed on copies of a Baccarat type pansy. Never cut or grind down a weight yourself – you may think it will improve its appearance but it will lessen the value immediately, and may prove an easy forgery for the next buyer who may think he has found a rare and more expensive example. Occasionally, as happened in the 1930s, the factories

themselves made 'copies' from old moulds and using traditional styles. It is more difficult than one would imagine to copy accurately the verve and panache of the old examples. Studying the collections which are usually to be found in most major cities (see page 296) will help to distinguish the classic factories, and the specialised literature list gives both rare and commonplace examples.

Finally, there is the commercial aspect. There has always been a good market for fine paperweights, and the prices of some of the best French examples have skyrocketed to un-dreamt-of heights. Collectors who cannot afford to mortgage their lifetime earnings on one piece have begun to look around for modern weights which are increasingly valuable, and have discovered glassmakers all over the world who are interested in trying out new skills and new effects. For both customer and craftsman, paperweights are an ideal choice. The nineteenth-century cheap novelty has become a very special form of modern glassmaking.

Repairs and Copies

Follow the general rule of buying the best you can afford and be very careful about spending considerable sums of money until you are experienced enough to know what to look for. On the whole, damaged pieces should be avoided except, as noted before, when the piece is rare enough to keep its value, or if you want it in order to study a special technique or type of metal. Chipped feet are not as bad as chipped bowls, but grinding down is common. The sharpish edge will be smoothed out, and feel rough to the touch. The foot should extend beyond the diameter of the bowl for necessary stability and an unusually small foot may mean a repair which must be taken into account. Chipped rims can also be ground down, but they are usually more obvious; the glass thickens slightly where it has been re-heated after

grinding. Breaks in the stem are easier to spot. Now that prices are rising rapidly you will occasionally find that a bowl has been set on a stem, of the same period perhaps, but not the original. This kind of repair is quite common on colour twist stems which are sufficiently valuable when whole to encourage replacement. One clue to the alert collector is a difference in colour between the glass of the bowl and the stem: very little antique glass is completely colourless. Unfortunately in the nineteenth century many old styles were revived and the market was flooded with colour twist stems and wheel-engraved goblets of dubious quality.

Pressed glass made with fine quality glass may be extremely valuable in its own right. Unhappily, it has become a fertile source of original material for the copier, although not always for fraudulent purposes. Appreciation of past craftsmanship has led to renewed popularity for traditional patterns. When these are copied for the open market, some find their way onto collectors' shelves as genuine antiques. Most reproduction houses now include some sort of mark or variation in the mould to distinguish their legitimate copies from outright fakes. All the more reason to learn as much as you can about your chosen field and to keep up with latest developments through the clubs and societies which have been formed by enthusiastic collectors.

Cut glass has other problems. Early Bohemian glass was made of potash rather than lead, and has neither the weight nor the sparkle associated with fine quality lead glass. Early lead glass often has a smoky or greyish tone with an almost greasy feel to the surface. Later, decolourizers became more effective, and sometimes when a piece such as the nozzle of a candlestick has been replaced, you can see the difference in tone quite clearly. The blue tone which is supposed to indicate Waterford glass is a figment of the imagination – much early eighteenth-century glass is slightly tinted.

All hand-cut pieces should have crisp detail and sharp edges. Pressed glass copies can be distinguished by two qualities – slightly soft outlines, left when the molten glass contracts slightly in the mould, and the perfection of the pattern. The first can be disguised to some extent by sharpening and finishing the piece at the fire, but the perfect pattern cannot be hidden. Very few cutters ever achieved absolute and total perfection. They were working at the wheel with the surface covered in abrasive, and in reverse – the pattern being cut was always on the side away from them. So whatever their skill, there was always a slight difference in the depth of a scallop or the width of a diamond. The radiating arm of a star, especially at the central point, was a weak point for many cutters. This is one case where copybook perfection is not an encouraging sign.

Attribution

As a general rule, be very wary of over-confident assertions about factories and individual craftsmen. Of course there are some well-documented sources, especially for pieces which were made in this century. But older glass is very hard to identify with complete assurance. Glassmaking is in any case a matter of teamwork; pieces were seldom signed except by the decorator, and even then it was almost always a workshop mark rather than a personal initial.

Coloured glass can give a few more clues. Certain factories were known to produce special colours, but many common names like Bristol blue are generic – blue glass was made in many English and American factories during the same period. Historians of the past were all too quick to establish a provenance for vanished glasshouses such as Stiegel's at Manheim in Pennsylvania. Today we are much more cautious, and even fragments of a pattern found on site excavations may indicate only that such a glass might have been made there, not that it must have been. We also know that factories copied each other's most popular patterns with impunity. Of course elaborate tests can be carried out with laser beams and so on for potentially museum-standard pieces, but most of us have to rely on common sense and our own knowledge.

Researching into pattern books and catalogues, especially those of the nineteenth century, can help to narrow the field of inquiry. Any glasshouse which still maintains its old records is usually extremely helpful in giving collectors access to information. However, if the pattern was mass-produced, finding it in the catalogue will be only an indication, not evidence, that it was made at a certain place. The attribution of one-off hand-blown pieces is even more difficult. Natural variations make it almost impossible to prove a particular origin. Nonetheless, regional differences and characteristics do occur.

Many dealers began as collectors or have become collectors, and have been willing to spend considerable time and effort in trying to trace particular pieces. It is worth every effort to persuade specialists with years of experience behind them to share some of their knowledge. Experienced dealers have seen too many fakes to be easily fooled, and heard of too many strange and wonderful discoveries to be overly cynical about a trunkful of Roman mosaic bowls which have been stored in the local pawnshop for fifty years or more. When you can, buy from such an expert; ask questions until you learn to distinguish what you want, not only for the pleasure of sharing your enthusiasm but simply as a practical matter. A good businessman will advise a long-term customer carefully and sensibly. Remember that a little knowledge can be a fragile thing. You are more likely to make a bad purchase at a lonely village shop which you will never see again than with the man around the corner who knows his reputation depends on local customers like yourself.

Collecting is a pleasure and an art in itself, not an exercise in logistics. It should enrich your life and delight your brain. Learn to respect the medium as well as to understand it, for glass is the last and greatest product of the alchemist's laboratory: from sand and fire and everyday ingredients, he has created light.

Part One
History

Ancient Glass

The craft of glassmaking has kept many of its secrets, so it is not surprising that the home of the first glassmakers is still a matter for inspired guesswork, based on the few sparse facts that are available.

The first known use of glass is a green glaze on a string of beads, and the oldest glass object is a small moulded blue amulet. At one time they were thought to be Egyptian, perhaps made around 3000 BC. So many of our arts have strong Middle Eastern influences that the deduction was not surprising, particularly since the objects had been recovered from Egyptian sites. Today most scholars would suggest that both these and some later finds were actually made farther east, in western Asia, somewhere in the region of Mesopotamia. However simple these very early finds may appear, the craftsmen had obviously learned their trade well, because later Asian levels have turned up some remarkably sophisticated work; one beaker was made of tiny circles of mosaics fused together on a baked-clay core. (The zig-zags of yellow, dark red, white and black are a reminder to all paperweight collectors that the use of *millefiori* rods goes back at least three and a half thousand years – it is only the name which was coined in the nineteenth century.) The Mesopotamians seem to have had a flourishing glass industry by 2000 BC, manufacturing beads and other simple objects in fairly large quantities, with the occasional finely moulded piece for a royal customer.

Egyptian Glass

During the reign of King Tuthmosis III (1501–1447 BC) in the Eighteenth Dynasty, Egypt invaded and conquered part of western Asia. Their first glass factory was found dating from that period, with at least three known objects marked with Tuthmosis' royal cartouche. It certainly suggests that one of the spoils of war may have been at least a single group of skilled glass craftsmen; or perhaps the craftsmen came voluntarily with Egypt's victory – glassmaking is a trade as well as an art, and to prosper it needs a settled and relatively wealthy market.

Egypt was a synonym for luxury and culture in the ancient world, and although the Mesopotamian glasshouses continued to flourish, it was the Egyptians who required and paid for the finest skills and the most perfect materials. So either by conquest or for money, the new glasshouses established a reputation for beautiful workmanship, especially in the use of brilliant colours, and during the next four hundred years, 1400–1000 BC, trade flourished. Glasshouses were built in many cities and probably in some of the settlements around the Aegean Sea and on the island of Cyprus. No doubt future excavations will add more to our practical knowledge of this early period.

The shapes of such small early pieces are quite varied. There are perfume and oil bottles and tiny jars, some with up to four handles, and most with tiny mouths – for the contents must have been expensive and had to be protected from evaporation in the warm climate, and against accidental spillage. There are animal and fish shapes, and the ubiquitous column representing a palm tree. Amulets and scarabs were used like jewellery for personal decoration, as well as for religious protection. Beads in varied tones were made

Right
Cabinet knob of dark blue with yellow and white edge, turquoise centre. Egypt; c 1500 BC; diam 1¾in (4.5cm).

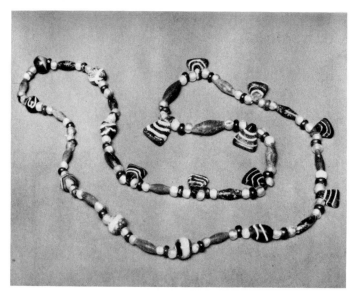

Left
Jug of light blue with yellow and white and dark blue designs, marked with the name of Tuthmosis III. Egypt; 1550–1450 BC; ht 3½in (8.8cm).

Below
Necklace of turquoise, blue and white beads. Egypt; c 1500 BC; length of triangular striped pendant ⅝in (1.5cm).
The Egyptians loved jewellery of all kinds, and glassmakers fashioned beads, combs, rings, and especially necklaces of their favourite blue and yellow colours.

Far left
Jug or oinoche of translucent
dark blue with opaque yellow
and light blue trails. Rhodes;
c 450 BC; ht $3\frac{7}{8}$in (10cm).

Left and below
From the top : an alabastron; a
round aryballos; a fish-shaped
bottle (length $5\frac{1}{2}$in, 14cm); an
amphoriskos.
Below : A palm-tree column
bottle.
A thousand years separates the
fish and the palm tree (*c* 1500
BC) from the later bottles made
during the period of Greek
influence around the 6th and
7th centuries BC. The shapes of
the nature-loving 18th Dynasty
gave way to the influence of
Hellenic pottery, but the
decoration remained
remarkably consistent, and the
wares were all made by the
same core-formed method with
combed and marvered trails.

as well as armlets, earrings and hair pins. Sometimes mock gems of glass were mounted in gold together with real stones in the same setting.

The Egyptians loved bright colours and the glassmakers must have experimented for many years, happily taking advantage of other trading developments to serve their own purposes. Turquoise, for example, was an obvious favourite and a whole new range of bluish-green tones depended on minute quantities of copper in the glass mixture. When the Egyptians discovered a source of ore in the Sinai, they built a number of copper-smelting plants, and these would have provided the glass furnaces with cheap and plentiful supplies. Sometimes, when the atmosphere in the furnace was not right, the copper would produce a deep wine-red glass – a fact also exploited by the Chinese to tint clay for pottery and porcelain ware. Iron and manganese were used to obtain a deep black tint, although finely ground silver was also used to make black. Manganese alone, and in larger

Above
Two-handled jug with
rectangular handles, ground
from a block of raw glass.
Nimrud; *c* 715 BC; ht 3⅛in
(8cm).
An early form of casting started
with a block of glass roughly
shaped by a mould; it was
fired, cooled and then ground
to the finished shape. The
object could then be cut,
polished and sometimes
decorated with gold or jewelled
inlays. This bottle is one of the
first known examples of this
method.

Above
Plaque; cast, inlaid with a
sphinx in black outline and
with traces of blue paint.
Nimrud; 7th century BC;
ht 1¼in (3.3cm).
Small plaques had been used
for centuries, sometimes
assembled from small sections
of thinly sliced coloured rods.

quantities, produced softer tones of brownish-purple and violet, often used in simple trails on a plain white ground, and true blue was made with the forever useful cobalt.

Another example of economic practicality was the use of antimony to make an opaque white. Fairly large quantities were needed, and it should have been simpler and easier to use tin oxide in minute proportions, which has the same effect. The Egyptians imported both minerals from Assyria, but the tin was more expensive and harder to find, and they needed all the supplies for the bronze foundries. So antimony became the standard white agent. The Romans, who had large and inexpensive shipments of tin, continued to use antimony for their white glass, even for luxury work like the Portland Vase. Perhaps this is only an example of how traditional methods continue within a conservative craft.

Yellow was the pride of Egyptian glasshouses, and rightly so – their brilliantly opaque and glowing yellow glass has never been surpassed, even by modern craftsmen like Frederick Carder and Louis Tiffany. The most likely source was antimoniate of lead, which was used in Assyria to make a yellow glaze for brick reliefs; it would have been easy to import the antimoniate with the other ingredients.

Tools and Techniques

It is important to remember that almost all pre-blown glass looks rather like pottery – often opaque or, at the most, translucent. Transparency is something associated with all 'glassy' objects, but it is essentially a quality of blown glass, which did not develop for another thousand years. Until then the products of glass manufacture remained very much the same: core-built bottles and jars, carved and cut boxes and adornments, engraved ornamentation and moulded objects of all kinds. Many of the tools and techniques would be familiar to any modern craftsman: the ingredients were melted in an open pot, the core-built pieces were mounted on a metal bar used exactly like a pontil rod; or moulds were filled with liquid glass and allowed to cool; or the glass was poured into rough blocks, cooled and powdered to a fine frit, which was then packed into shaped moulds, re-fired until it liquefied, and re-cooled. Even a cutting wheel was used, although most pieces were polished or cut with abrasives such as powdered gemstones and fine emery, and a great deal of elbow grease. One of the distinctive decorative patterns is the use of trailed coloured rods, spun onto mostly core-built pieces while the glass was still warm, marvered on a slab of stone until the trails sank into the surface, and then combed with a fine metal instrument up and down across the lines to make the parallel equidistant curved bands of festoons which look delightfully fresh and cheerful. Such combed festoons have been used by almost every decorative glassmaker since then, including the Venetians, the Nailsea-type factories, and the makers of Art Glass in nineteenth-century America.

During the period after the Eighteenth Dynasty had ended, Egypt herself was racked by civil unrest and continual strife. All the arts suffered, including glassmaking, and for five hundred years or more the Delta Kingdom went through its own Dark Ages. Finally prosperity and trade returned, and, seemingly intact, the great glassworks of

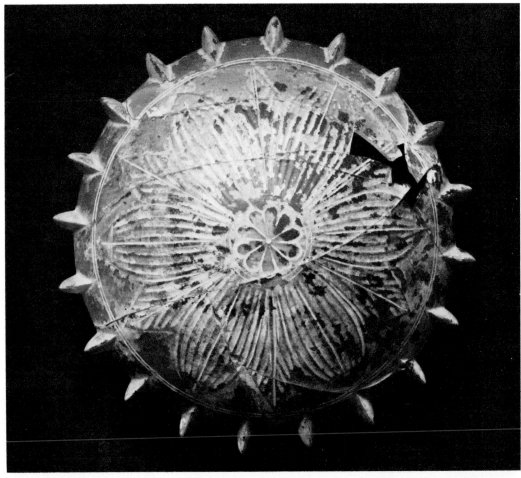

Right
Bowl of transparent glass, cast in a two-piece mould, cut and ground to the final shape. Canosa, Italy; 3rd century BC; diam 8in (20.5cm). A magnificent bowl, whose design is appropriate to any period. The Alexandrian workshops where it may have been made were particularly famous for their wheel cutting; the rosette pattern cut into the base, and the bosses around the edge in relief are typical of their very best work. The pattern could be easily adapted to modern crystal of the 20th century.

Right
Alabastron of many coloured bands. Sidon (now Lebanon); 2nd–1st century BC; ht 4⅜in (11cm).
Although clear and cut glass was beginning to dominate the Roman period, some of the more complicated core-formed methods were not only retained but greatly improved. This alabastron was made from separate bands, including some with gold foil between layers of colourless glass. These were cast on a core, manipulated to give the wavy effect, and finally ground and polished. There are a number of these gold-banded glasses, which form the last real link with core-formed Egyptian glass, until the solid glass techniques were revived at the end of the 19th century.

Alexandria grew even more famous and certainly more skilled than before. Egypt again became the cultural and artistic centre of the East and experienced a revival which lasted well into the Christian era, surviving the domination of Rome, as well as the exploitation and turmoil which followed the Mohammedan Crescent.

Syria, and especially Damascus, had also acquired a reputation for glassmaking and it was almost certainly there that glassblowing was developed. There is no way of knowing how it came about. The method was quite unlike any method employed before in glass or in any other material, but that one invention was enough to create an entirely new and unique substance.

With the onslaught of the Roman armies, life changed drastically for the Middle Eastern craftsmen, as the glass trade in particular was pulled relentlessly into the mainstream of Western civilization.

Caesar came to the market places of Egypt and took back bowls and goblets, and finally the men to make them. Those who stayed went on producing beautiful objects for the privileged few, and waited patiently for the invaders to leave.

Many of the Syrian glassblowers went with the Roman armies, too, travelling to the capital, and then to the provinces, perhaps to settle finally on the Rhine or in the Seine valley. With them they carried their skills, their knowledge, the old moulds and the new blowing pipes, to create a part for themselves in an empire that might have lasted forever, and did last another four hundred years.

ATLANTIC OCEAN

Ireland

England

Holland

Belgium

E. Germany

W.Germany

France

Switzerland

Aust

Portugal

Spain

Corsica

Rome
Ita

Sardinia

Si

Algeria

Morocco

Tunisia

L

U.S.S.R.

Glassmaking areas during the Roman Empire. The objects shown were found in the areas indicated, but may also have been made in other parts of the Empire.

oland

kia

ngary

Romania

goslavia

Bulgaria

BLACK SEA

Albania

Greece

Turkey

Syria

Lebanon

Cyprus

Iraq

Israel

Crete

Jordan

MEDITERRANEAN SEA

Alexandria

Saudi Arabia

Egypt

The Roman Empire

It has previously been accepted for the past century at least that the Romans were something less than important to the world of art; that the Roman Empire was merely a kind of super-efficient conduit, a distribution network through which the Western world was lucky enough to inherit the great philosophical and cultural inspiration of Greek ideals.

The result has been a rather low estimate of Roman values and especially their appreciation of art, with a correspondingly high opinion amounting almost to superstitious awe of the Hellenic world.

For those who regard the art of glass as one of prime interest, this attitude has had its own irony, for the Greeks seem to have been almost totally uninterested in glass as an art form, regardless of their achievements in sculpture and pottery.

So our awe and well-merited admiration has had to focus on the pre-Roman artisans of the Middle East, on the great workshops of Alexandria and the glassblowers of Syria, which left the Romans just where they were – in the transport business.

W. Thorpe, one of the most fascinating and idiosyncratic writers on the history of glass, described the ordinary Roman collector as being 'without any real sensibility to glass. They were card-indexers and ritualists, good at bits and parts. They behaved bittily themselves, and they made others do the same . . .' Something of the almost contemptuous scorn for an older nation of shopkeepers, perhaps?

If historians have learned anything at all in the past decades, the most important lesson is that traditional assumptions are seldom as simple as we used to think. The Greeks were not all golden; those Utopias were for a very privileged élite only; the fiercely independent city-states spent more time fighting uselessly and destructively among themselves than fulfilling their own promises; and the Hellenic attitude towards women, foreigners and ordinary people, would have them condemned by any modern open society.

At the same time, we have seen a growing appreciation of the part Rome played on what would today be called the international stage; their willingness to learn and adapt can be seen as an admirable quality in itself, instead of merely a lack of inner creativity. Their recognition of the need for basic stability for all their citizens throughout the provinces would earn them more credit today than many theoretical

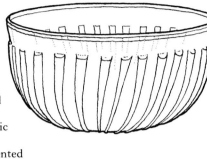

Right and below
(both pages)
The well-known ribbed bowl (*above right*) was made in streaky 'gemstone' and mosaic versions as well as in clear glass. The Romans experimented with the first free-blown glass (*below, from left*) making individually formed small objects, including beautifully balanced pieces such as the trailed jug fifth from the left. But their great contribution towards the glassmaking industry was the use of glass blown into moulds, creating duplicated wares with often complicated detail, quickly and cheaply. The drawings on the opposite page are all of mould-blown wares made *c* 100–300 AD.

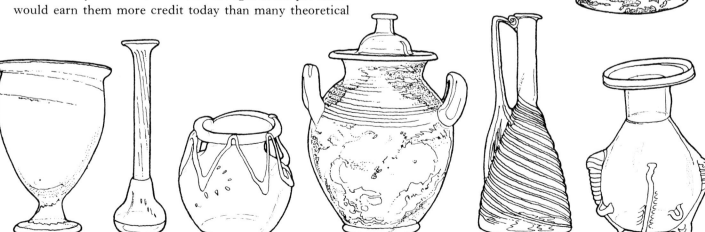

Right
Drinking bowl with everted
plain rim, standing in a simple
bowl with flared sides and a
folded rim on a ring base. Late
Roman; 3rd–4th century AD;
diam of bowl 5½in (14cm).

Above
Bowl of greenish glass with
heavy iridescence. Roman;
3rd century AD; ht 2⅜in (6cm).

Right
Beaker in amber glass, mould
blown with figures standing in
arches. Possibly made in Sidon;
c 100 AD; ht 4⅞in (12.5cm).
The four classical figures may
be the four seasons – Hermes
with his caduceus for autumn,
Diana for winter, Hercules
bearing a young calf for
summer and Hymen for spring.

dialogues. The Greeks may have invented the words for democracy; the Romans at least tried to make them work.

In that light, perhaps we can look at one aspect of Roman culture – its encouragement and support for the glassmaker and his trade. Whatever the individual artist's achievements – in the past, or working with the sculptural vocabulary of modern studio art – it's surely fair to say that glass, like ceramics, is firmly rooted in craftsmanship rather than fine art. The pragmatic Romans took a luxury product for the very rich, and continued to create magnificent pieces for show and display. But they were also able to see the possible benefits for their ordinary citizens and subjects. In the end, the very ordinary-ness of ordinary Roman glass is our greatest heritage.

'Gemstone' Glass

Long before the Romans came to the Middle East, there was a flourishing trade in gemstone bowls. Carved out of streaky gems and semi-precious stones, these pieces were greatly prized by the Egyptian court and by the entire Oriental world. In 61 BC there was an exhibition in Rome of such work, brought home by Pompey and other Roman soldiers as part of the spoils of war. The exhibition was an enormous success, and that precious and intelligent combination of the right product for the right market suddenly materialized. The originals were too costly for anyone but the highest aristocracy, but the Alexandrian craftsmen had been making glass imitations in small quantities for a long time – many Egyptian necklaces and ornaments were set with an apparently random collection of stones and glass, side by side. Now, with the right backing and support, together with a steady source of customers, 'gemstone' glass became available to any reasonably comfortable Roman household.

There are basically two forms of these multi-coloured pieces: streaky and mosaic.

The streaky versions are usually a mixture of two or more different coloured glasses, often blue and white, with yellows, reds and greens. All the colours are opaque or translucent – transparency was not really required or wanted – and the glass was randomly patterned, almost identical to our splashed and spattered end-of-day mixtures from the nineteenth century. Occasionally special attempts were made to imitate a particular stone, so the pattern was much more subtle, similar to the marbling effect in natural stonework.

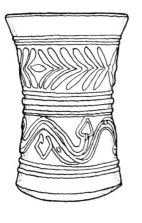

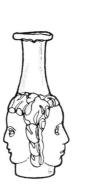

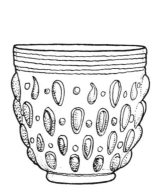

Left

The Portland Vase in dark blue moulded glass, overlaid in white which has been cut away in cameo relief. 1st century AD; ht 9½in (24cm).
The vase was probably intended as the funerary urn of Alexander Severus (*d* 235 AD) but that is still conjecture. It is perhaps more related to sculpture than to glass, its basic shape simple even stolid, while the carvings have been responsible for an entire family of descendants in Wedgwood ceramics and the work of John Northwood and others in 19th-century England. The cameo work is undoubtedly the finest example of its kind that we know and, together with the Lycurgus Cup (page 35), indicates the truly remarkable technical achievements of cutters working in cold glass.

Right

Small pieces from the early period of the Roman Empire: an alabastron with Egyptian-influenced trails; a small rounded bottle in a quilted modern pattern; the remaining two pieces free blown. All 1st–2nd century BC to 1st–2nd century AD; ht of quilted bottle 3in (7.6cm).

Many bowls may have been mould pressed with heavy ribbing on the base, which was possibly slightly twisted as the glass was removed. Alternatively, they may have been sagged into the moulds. Well-designed examples with natural-looking streaks and fire-polished rims were probably made in Rome or Alexandria for the better end of the trade; others are obviously Roman end-of-day cheaper products, either made by lesser craftsmen or possibly blown in one of the outlying districts for the local citizens who nonetheless wanted the latest fashion in urban living.

Once considered very rare, a number of such bowls and goblets have turned up in various sites occupied by the Roman armies. They may have been imported as gifts for native chieftains or possibly as reminders to homesick commanders that the luxuries of life were not entirely beyond recall. Other glasses were made into much more elaborate items, carefully coloured so as to be almost indistinguishable from one of the more precious stones, and then carved into elaborate patterns with intaglio and/or cameo reliefs. Some precious examples were often mounted in gold and set with real jewels. The basic shape might be mould blown, as in

the Portland Vase, but the blowing was almost unimportant and was merely a way of achieving the right shape so that the real work of carving and designing could be carried out on the cold, relatively thick glass.

The second, mosaic, version was made of fragments, and probably originated in the craze for this type of work during almost the whole of the Roman period. Some early glass mosaics are very like enamels with fairly simple designs on solid backgrounds. The patterns are again imitations of stonework, and to begin with they have no feeling of glass as a material; it is all too opaque and heavy.

But the Roman market was beginning to understand and appreciate the real qualities of this new material (*pace* Thorpe) and this led to the manufacture of thin coloured rods which were allowed to cool, then fused together in regular patterns, cooled once more, and cut into tiny slices like a stick of rock. These early examples of *millefiori* were then used in many different ways. Some were merely pressed into place in a round mould for marbles or some kind of game piece; different coloured slices would be used for a set of six or three balls. Another popular technique was to lay the

Left
Beaker with flared top in amber glass, trailed in amber and opaque turquoise. Persia; *c* 3rd century AD; ht 5½in (14cm).
Alexandrian workshops declined rapidly towards the end of the Empire, and the work of different areas became more varied. Persian glasshouses began to develop the graceful lines which are so typical of Islamic design. The trails on this elegant beaker suggest Arabic calligraphy rather than the older looped patterns of Egypt.

Above
Dish with broken rim, made of sections of a cane or rod with an opaque white spiral and opaque turquoise centre on a clear dark blue ground. Other sections are cut from gold foil (sandwiched between clear glass layers) and plain coloured rods. Late 3rd century BC; diam 11¾in (30cm).
An early example of mosaic which already includes complicated canes and gold foil pieces. The sections were fused within a mould and the dish was polished when it had cooled.

Page 30
Beaker, mould blown. 1st century AD; ht 2¾in (7cm). Moulded beakers have been found in many parts of the Empire. This example with its victor's wreath may have been a ceremonial gift to an athlete or soldier.

Page 31
Two bowls of 'gemstone' glass, the top streaky, the bottom mosaic. Both mould pressed, with added rims. These are fine examples of early *millefiori* work. 1st century AD; diam of top bowl 2⅜in (6cm), bottom bowl 2⅝in (6.6cm).

slices together in a mould of the required shape and then heat the mould until the pieces fused together to make a solid cup, bowl, plate, etc. Or the pieces in the mould might be covered with a thick layer of colourless glass and then fused so that there were clear spaces between the roundels.

It is said that Nero paid 6,000 sesterces for just such a goblet, and although gold and silver objects might be melted down to pay for armies and clean water, a mosaic plate from the court was carefully saved and treasured – and then copied! Such was Roman appreciation and Roman practicality at its best.

Carved and Cut Ware

Differences in style can be quite amazing; the outline of the Portland Vase is quite simple, the shape is sturdy rather than elegant, and the glass has lost all its feeling as a material; the carving is all, and the delicate cameo work could have been equally effective in shell or ivory. The Lycurgus Cup, on the other hand, is deliberately shaped and treated so that the glass itself becomes an important part of the art form. Although when lit from the front it appears to be agate or perhaps a jade of some kind, when lit from behind it glows with an amber red which is positively alive. The carving is so detailed and complex that the figures seem to spring out of their background, and although only the one colour is used, the feeling is much more glassy than the cameo work on the Portland Vase.

Another kind of carving, which the Romans adored, is a variation of the Cup – the glass is extremely thick to begin with, in either one or two layers, and the carving is even more three-dimensional with areas cut away behind the design, so that with the exception of tiny 'pegs' left attached to the surface, the design almost floats around the cup. Because the glasscutters were called *diatretarii*, we have come to call these fragile and extraordinary pieces *vasa diatreta*.

Most Roman cut glass was much plainer and much more straightforward: cups and bowls decorated with flat hexagons, circles, diamonds and so on, cut on the wheel. These were often in clear glass, and patterns foreshadow the simplicity of those cut into tumblers and bowls from the first era of English and Irish glasscutting, *c* 1750–90.

Blown Glass

In spite of all these complex and beautifully glowing pieces and the shining example of their carved cameo work in our museums, the greatest contribution the Romans made to our understanding of glass was much simpler, and much more accessible. Some time during the one hundred years before the birth of Christ, the Syrians had learned to exploit the art of blowing. It was still quite new during the height of the Empire, and many of its qualities were not really exploited until much later in history. But all at once here was a material that was clear, malleable when hot but rigid when cold, easy to clean (the Romans were obsessed with cleanliness compared to previous civilizations, and their real love of glass may have been spurred on by the fact that it could be hygienically cleaned in a way impossible for wood or earthenware), able to keep out the weather and let in the light. Roman bath houses were glazed with thin sheets of marble – and thin sheets of glass.

The wonderful flexibility of blown glass also became quickly apparent. Instead of the time needed to make and cut or carve elaborate cups and bowls, blowing and mould blowing were immediate manufacturing processes. Wine glasses, fruit dishes, commercial storage jars, could all be blown in minutes and cooled in hours. Small or large, tall or short, dimpled or plain – no material before or since has been so versatile.

These everyday objects themselves are varied and individual, often interesting and sometimes breathtakingly perfect. As the centuries wore on and blown glass became a real expression of art, the craftsmen became more skilful and their audience more demanding. As early as a century after Christ, the jugs became rotund at the base, with a long stretched-out neck and handle, sometimes swirled, sometimes decorated with trailings and threadings. Tiny jars were studded with moulded diamonds, bowls were decorated with two-coloured rings and marvered loopings. Early Christian symbols have been found with gold-leaf designs scratched and rubbed away and encased between two layers of clear glass.

Glass Marketers: A Roman Legacy

The glassblowers who moved through the countryside and built temporary workshops and kilns continued to influence local cultures throughout the so-called Dark Ages, but to begin with these craftsmen needed the Romans as much as the Romans needed their glass. They brought their skills with them, but they changed and adapted to what was wanted there and then. Needing to be linked to an appreciative audience they became willing and active participants in creating new forms and providing pleasant additions to ordinary life.

The citizens of the far-flung Roman Empire included traders who filled ships' holds profitably with tightly packed square jars, instead of unstable round-bottomed versions that wasted space and required extra straw padding; and army providers who realized that the ingredients for glass could be found within reach of almost every campsite throughout the Empire. These were the true Roman innovators as much as the actual blowers. They grasped the meaning of what this completely new source could bring, and they exploited the possibilities enthusiastically.

Blown-glass artefacts from the Roman period are, on the whole, not as impressive-looking as the carved and cut works of art for the aristocracy, but viewed as part of history they are perhaps much more impressive than anything else in or out of our museums. Ennion left his name for eternity in a mould-blown piece, others carved their moulds to include advertisements: 'Jason make – lest you forget'. They blew to create hundreds of thousands of similar bottles for the export trade; they blew free form to make little cups and tiny bottles of exquisite simplicity; they added spiral ribbing to bottles in local green glass; they blew beakers and round-bottomed cups, dippers and phials; they made jugs and platters for the table and glasses for their wine. Every corner of the then known world could be supplied with glassware at an almost disposable cost. Indeed, we know from fragments in middens and rubbish heaps that pieces were thrown away

almost undamaged when they could have been repaired relatively easily – for it was cheaper and easier to buy a new glass. Local furnaces, however, were encouraged to do repairs for the better pieces, and also to make domestic wares for soldiers stationed abroad. The provincial glassblowers did not need a relatively rich community; they built their furnaces, cut down enough forest to fire them for a season, found more or less suitable sand, and, when the local fuel was gone, moved on to another place to build another furnace for another group of customers.

The Romans did more for the glassblower than just provide roads and ships; they created stable trade routes, appreciated and paid for the finest artistry, provided the luxury market with what it wanted, and the ordinary market with what it needed.

Glass is part of our lives, adding substance and beauty to our surroundings; it is a reflection of our everyday world, one of our most precious inheritances – and it has come to us through Rome.

Left

Ewer of thin glass with cut decoration in simple panels of cross-hatching. Persia, possibly Nishapur; 7th century AD; ht 6⅛in (15.7cm).

As the Roman Empire disintegrated flourishing communities of glassworkers in the provinces and Asia Minor gradually adapted to local preferences. Persia and Mesopotamia had known of cut glass manufacture probably from as early as the 8th century BC, and, as the Roman trade fell away, craftsmen turned to other markets – some pieces were certainly exported to Japan in the 6th and 7th centuries AD. This ewer is a perfect example of two cultures combining to produce an extremely elegant piece: cutting on clear glass with a Romanic shape popular in metalwork at least five centuries earlier.

Right

The Lycurgus Cup, carved from a thick blank probably mould blown, mounted in gold. 4th century AD; ht 6¼in (16cm).

The Lycurgus Cup is the culmination of Roman achievement in glass carving. The figures illustrate a story about Lycurgus, King of Thrace. They are carved in relief and then cut away, attached to the background only by small bridges of uncut glass. This process, called *diatreta*, is extremely rare. The cup is also important to glass historians because of its colouring. Olive green when lit from in front, the cup becomes translucent reddish purple when lit from behind, perhaps because of a small quantity of gold in the glass. This use of shaded colouring is one of the few early examples we know, and the technique was not exploited again until the Art Glass of the 19th century.

The Middle East

After the collapse of the Roman Empire, many of the glass-workers in the Middle East continued to supply their own people with glass for their needs and requirements. For a time the period of confusion and war interrupted the production especially of luxury glass, but under the Sassanian emperors, during the sixth century, glasscutting again began to improve and delight the lives of the rich and cultivated Persians. The objects that belong to this period display a variety of techniques and a craftsmanship which is truly remarkable.

Some of the techniques were already in common use during the Roman period – concave cutting, applied ornamentation, and mould blowing. The finest and most spectacular examples seem to have been the wheel-cut bowls, some of which were sent to Japan in the following period and have happily been preserved intact. The facets were usually carefully cut all over the bowl, and simple globular flasks were also made, probably dating back to fairly late in the pre-Islamic period.

In the course of the seventh century, the Islamic banner unfolded over just those countries where glassmaking had become a major and flourishing industry – Egypt, Syria, Mesopotamia and Persia. After the Arab armies gained supremacy, they established their capital in Syria, but until the more settled conditions of around 750 and the choice of Baghdad as the capital, glassmaking seems to have come to a halt. Then, as the Islamic creed became a unifying culture for a very wide and diverse area, glassmaking grew again in skill and importance, but this time with a distinctive Islamic flavour and a recognizable style.

Wheel-cut glass returned to favour and was made in many parts of the Islamic world, especially in Persia. The most unusual style was one in which the entire surface was ground away leaving the pattern in relief. The earliest examples date from the ninth century, but later finds are really exquisitely worked, with very thin walls which must have cost the cutter weeks of anxiety as the bowl neared completion. There is also the well-known beaker of perfectly simple flaring shape, with an overlay of green glass which has been almost entirely cut away except for the figure of a hare.

A famous group of seven glasses, known as the Hedwig glasses, have been ascribed to Egyptian factories, but recent Russian excavations are said to have turned up fragments on the site of an old glass factory in White Russia. Since the glasses are certainly different from other known Islamic pieces, it is a possibility that these are some of the earliest known examples of Russian glass.

Applied Decoration

Lustre was and is typical of much Islamic art, both on pottery and glass. The overall designs in rich colours which are so often found on Moorish pottery might well have been tried on glassware, although only a few fragments so far have been found.

Gilding and enamelling are equally appropriate, and much of the later Islamic glass has been gorgeously decorated in the most beautiful opaque enamels. Many travellers will immediately think of the glowing mosque lamps and ewers, in traditional metal shapes, which are obviously made of glass.

Below
Bottle of greenish colour with red swirled decoration. Possibly Sassanian; 3rd–4th century; ht 4⅜in (11.2cm).

Left
Flask in greenish glass, cylindrical in shape and cut all over. Possibly Sassanian; 5th–6th century; ht 8¾in (22.3cm).

Simple shapes were made in Syria, Persia and Mesopotamia. The globular body and small neck on the bottle, and the hexagonal facet cutting on the tall flask, were both derived from earlier patterns.

Left
Flask with oval-cut facets and
flared neck. Persia, possibly
Nishapur; 9th–10th century;
ht 5⅞in (15cm).

Below
Dish cut with U-shaped
grooves. Persia, possibly
Nishapur; 9th–10th century;
diam 6⅛in (15.5cm).

These two glass pieces were
made during the revival of
Sassanian traditions, but they
are linked to later techniques
and shapes which were to
become part of Islam.

Above
Flask with very long neck and
rounded body; trailed rings at
the top are the only decoration.
Syria; 4th–5th century;
ht 14⅛in (36cm).
The long neck is characteristic
of Islamic shapes, sometimes
straight, sometimes more
elaborate and curved.

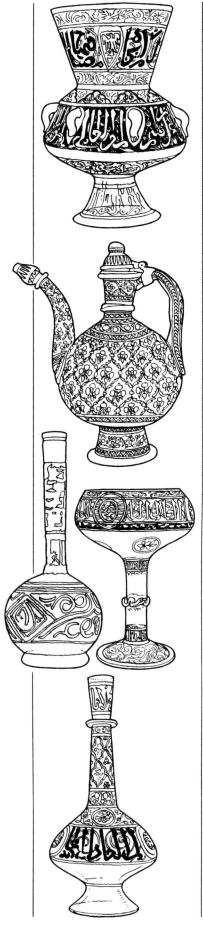

Left
Various Islamic shapes showing the rich decoration which often covers the entire glass in a veritable carpet of gilding and enamelling. The long necks and the curved spout are typical.

Below
Pilgrim flask flattened on one side, completely covered in enamelled painting with gilded additions. Aleppo, Syria; *c* 1250; ht 9in (23cm).
This beautiful and remarkably decorative piece is an example of the splendour of Islamic painting, here adapted to the story of Alexander on his travels through the Middle East. The enamelling uses eight colours.
The beaker on the opposite page was probably made at the same workshop.

These were probably made in Syria, at least during the earliest period up to 1400, and later in Persia, when richly decorated pieces were known right until the end of the Mughal period.

Pilgrim flasks, footed bowls and rose-water sprinklers seem to have been fairly common until the eighteenth century, although the latest examples are probably from India.

An interesting comparison for colour and overall impression is a Huqqa bowl made *c* 1700 in India, of imperfect deep green glass gilded with poppy sprays. The effect is startlingly similar to a Bohemian tumbler of the same period. The civilized world was becoming smaller, and influences and artefacts being made some nine thousand miles apart share a common heritage.

An interesting development has been the re-growth of the Middle Eastern glass industry, especially in modern Iran and Israel. The Iranian pieces are very much in the Islamic tradition, although modern techniques are now substituted for some of the time-consuming processes which make old pieces so valuable and hard to replace.

The Israeli industry has developed along very different lines, reviving the Alexandrian tradition of swirled and coloured glass in purples and greens, and combining this with delicately blown pieces of distinctly modern shape. As skill and expertise are gained by both countries, it may well be that an entirely new art will grow that is based firmly within the region of the great glassmaking centres of the past.

Above
Dish of brownish glass, gilded and enamelled, with the figure of an angel. Persia; 16th century; diam 5½in (14cm). Damascus was raided by the Persian Empire in 1400, and many of the glassmakers were sent back to the Persian capital. Syrian glass never quite recovered.

Left
Vase of opaline glass. Israel; 20th century; ht 11½in (29.2cm).
The modern revival of glassmaking in Israel often adapts traditional Middle Eastern shapes and uses a very light, soda-lime glass. There is seldom any added decoration.

Left
Beaker in blown amber glass. Syria; *c* 1250; ht 4⅜in (11cm).
The enamelled and gilded design of fishes and eels is beautifully executed, in this case leaving the clear glass as a perfect and delicately tinted background.

Northern Europe

A contrast with Roman skill in creating a comfortable way of life is the low point that glassmaking and other arts reached when the Empire began to disintegrate and the outlying provinces were left to fend for themselves.

As the Romanized civilization disappeared, and invaders came from all directions to reap what was left of Roman treasures, glassmakers were cut off from their trading base in the capital. Left on their own in wooded settlements and deserted outposts, it must have seemed a very bleak future indeed. Some areas were better off than others. The farthest outposts were in trouble, certainly – glassmaking probably stopped almost entirely in England until the tenth century – but the Romans had left a strong centre around the Rhine, and what is today known as the Seine-Rhine district

Right
Beaker with almond bosses in pale bluish-green glass, highly iridescent. Romano–Syrian; *c* 100 AD; ht 5⅜in (13.7cm). One of the early mould-blown beakers in a very unusual colour – most known examples are pale amber or brownish. The mould mark at the base is clearly visible on the left. It is thought that these almond-bossed glasses were blown in an openwork mould so the bosses could expand as intended. An example has been found with a silver case cut away to allow the bosses to show. These bossed goblets became very important in the northern area, and are related to the style of early claw-beakers.

Left
Bottle, blown in a square mould. *c* 100 AD; ht 3¾in (9.5cm). Though this bottle was found in England it was almost certainly made somewhere in Rome. Square-sided, flat-bottomed bottles were an efficient way of storing quantities of liquid. The Roman garrisons in the north would have found these sturdy containers easier to handle than the traditional round *amphorae*.

Left
Beaker in amber green with a
defined waisted shape and
rounded base. Late Frankish
period; *c* 650 AD; ht 4⅝in
(11.7cm).
Most Frankish glasses had
rounded or pointed bases (see
drawing at right) which made
them unstable. Intact
specimens generally come from
undisturbed graves, and few
have been dated later than
c 700–750 AD when the Franks
gradually stopped burying
possessions with their dead.

Right
Claw- and cone-beaker shapes –
two of the best-known
Frankish glass types from the
Seine-Rhine district.

Below
Bottle with trailed and flattened
decoration. Cyprus; *c* 150–175
AD; ht 6⅛in (15.5cm).
These 'snake' trailings became
popular as 'merrythought' jugs
made during the Frankish
period.

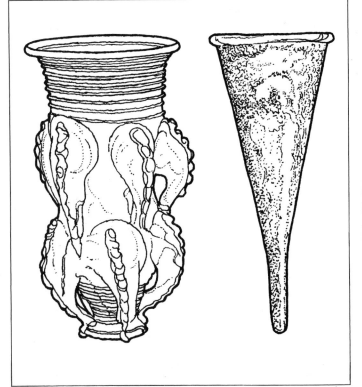

Above
Bowl with cut engraving of
Actaeon and Artemis. Romano–
Germanic; 1st or 2nd century
AD; diam 4¾in (12cm).
The rim of this bowl has been
knocked off (or perhaps it had
become cracked and was
ground away) and the edges
smoothed at-the-fire.

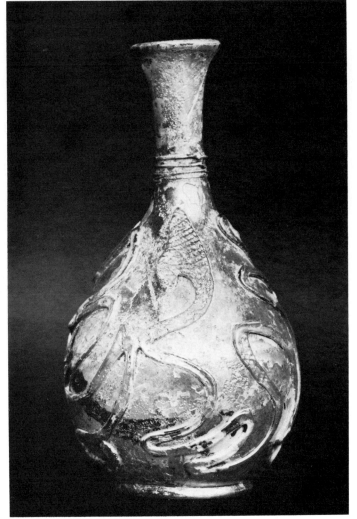

continued not only to make glass, but to refine and improve
both the material and design throughout this period.

In some ways it is immediately comprehensible that the
first skill to disappear would have been that of the Alexandrians, who made their wares for the luxury market.
Cutting and carving retreated to Egypt and the Middle East,
to consolidate and continue there throughout the medieval
period and well into the eighteenth century. The newer, and
flexible, Syrian blown glass was another matter. With the
fast manufacture of everyday objects, the blowers had
brought glass to the comfortable rather than the rich, and
found a lucrative and hitherto untapped market. Those
craftsmen who had emigrated to the northern provinces
were not about to go home with the retreating armies. The
Seine-Rhine glasshouses served a surprisingly large area;
there were miles of wooded forest, good quality sand, and
river transport to reach the towns.

During the transition period (third to fourth century to
the sixth century) there was a great deal of trading still
going on between Syria and Europe. The absolute statement
that this or that glass was made in Syria, Egypt, the Rhineland, or even Russia, is usually very difficult to justify. It is
generally a matter of shape, concentration of finds, fragments
at furnace sites, and comparisons with other similar pieces.
Typical is a honeycomb shape with an unusual deep round-
bottomed bowl, *c* 350 AD. Quite a few have been found in
and around Cologne, and they could well have been a
speciality of the Seine-Rhine houses – but others were found
in France, Hungary, Yugoslavia, Sicily, Russia, and Syria
itself. Northern Europe is only one, very likely, origin.

Another very special glass, this time unique, so far as we
know, is a bottle, pierced with four spaces like a dovecote,
with tiny opaque white and blue doves flying in and out.

Left
Flask in the shape of a barrel, in colourless glass, with yellowish opaque threading, and small dolphin handles. Germany; late 1st–2nd century AD; ht 5⅜in (13.8cm).
A number of barrel flasks have been found dating from the early medieval period, and although they seem to be slightly awkward to handle, they may have had some significance which we do not understand. This one certainly was made with care and attention to detail.

Left
Helmet-shaped flask; white body with green base and blue ribbed design. Romano-Germanic; 3rd century AD; ht 4in (10.2cm).

The 'dovecote' was made in the same Seine-Rhine area, and it points to a re-evaluation of this part of the Dark Ages for many who visualize the period after the collapse of the Empire as a total disintegration of all the arts, except perhaps in the monasteries. Glass (with the exception of stained glass) was a very secular craft.

The two main styles during this period are the cone-beaker and the claw-beaker; both could be skilfully made in the forest glasshouses. The cone is simply that: an extension of the original smallish tumbler, which was gradually elongated and developed a dozen or so variations, narrow at the base and widening at the top.

Finally, the foot itself disappeared into an elongated cone like an English hunting cup, a beaker which cannot stand by itself, but has to be emptied while still in the hand. Almost all cones are decorated simply with trailings, round the top in a widish band, then up and down on the base.

The claw-beaker is more obviously an Oriental invention, probably starting with the Persian or Roman silver-cased tumblers which were inflated within a mould that had regular holes cut out so that the glass would expand into the bosses. The claws were, at the beginning, merely bumps which were decorated with additional trailings to make them stand out even more and curl over.

Through the centuries the claw-beakers also showed a lengthening and narrowing at the base, so that the later examples are almost without feet, although they never became totally unstable like the cones. The trailed decoration is very similar – threading around the base, applied milled or pincered streaks on the claws, and sometimes trailings over the whole bowl, claws and all, wrapped round from the foot to just under the rim.

Another common shape is the bulbous jug, with a long narrow neck and applied, squared off, or rounded handles. This was usually decorated with ribbing, either wide or narrow, sometimes swirled. One rather delightful variation

Left
Jug with single handle in dark yellow green, cut all over the body in rows of geometric design. Egypt; c 350–400 AD; ht 12⅜in (31.5cm).

Above
Flask with internal tubes made of greenish glass. Northern area; 4th or 5th century AD; ht 4½in (11.5cm).
Perhaps this was a kind of early puzzle glass.

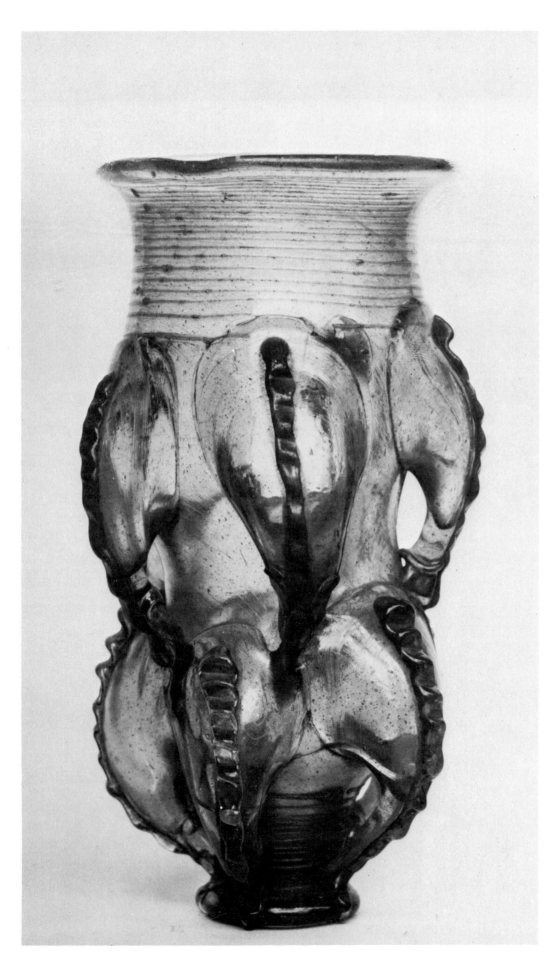

Left
Beaker of tapering form in green with heavy drawn-out claws and trails in dark blue. Seine-Rhine manufacture, found in County Durham; late 5th–early 6th century AD; ht 7½in (19cm).
The body was made then cooled enough to hold its shape, and the claws applied as warm blobs which, under pressure from re-blowing, melted the wall and were blown out into attached bubbles. These in turn were manipulated with tools to form the claws, folded down and finished off.

Right
Beaker of cone shape, in green soda glass, with many seeds or bubbles. Seine-Rhine manufacture, but found in a grave in Kempston, Bedfordshire, England; late 5th–early 6th century AD; ht 10¼in (26cm).
One of the loveliest beakers ever found, the Kempston beaker is justly famous for its elegance and finely detailed trailing. At this period, northern glasshouses were still using the old formulae based on soda and the *barilla* plant; potash glass, called *Waldglas* or *verre de fougère*, was not developed until *c* 1000 AD.

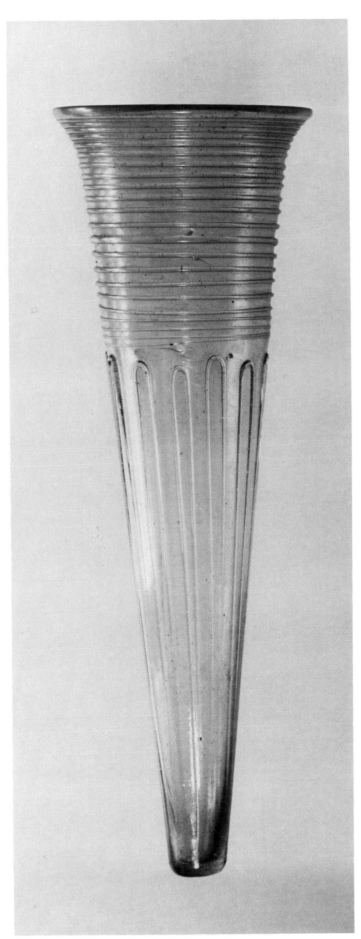

has a chain handle of interlocking threads.

A jug form is occasionally found with a very tiny spout, which obviously was suitable for sprinkling rose water, or dropping oil onto the hands or for use in some ceremonial ritual. And, of course, there are the 'merrythought' bottles, round and squat, mostly earlier in date. They have the same trailings around the rim, and a rather wildly untidy heavier trail over the body.

There were many other individual shapes including jugs and bowls, 'bobbin' bottles and round palm cups that show a greater appreciation of free-blown form and decoration.

We should be wary of making too many hasty judgements about the northern civilization and its glass, which seemed clumsy and crude to experts steeped in the skilful moulded and carved perfection of the Roman period.

It is perfectly true that the very elaborate work disappeared, and it is also true that in general the shapes of this period can be catalogued in a relatively small number of types, instead of the hundreds of forms in use before. But many of those forms had been moulded, and individual pieces have little originality. The claw-beakers and cone-beakers are all unique.

Then again, the glass itself was less than perfect, often pitted with seeds and discoloured and streaked with impurities. But the fairly simple greens reflecting the forest and its resources were to develop into the controlled and impressive range of greens and ambers used during the end of this period (*c* 1000–1400 AD). The type was called *verre de fougère* in France, where the alkali was made from bracken, and *Waldglas* in Germany and Bohemia, where the potash was obtained by burning beech and other woods.

And yet anyone who believes that the earlier pieces were necessarily crude should look again at the Kempston beaker. Its glass, its form and its decoration are sophisticated and skilfully made – it needs no apology.

Finally, there is the recurring myth of isolation, and a general lack of travel and communication between settlements. This does not seem to be borne out by the latest research. The Seine-Rhine glasshouses, like the later Venetian houses, were established and well-known manufacturers of a product which was much in demand throughout the European trading area. Their work turns up in excavations as far apart as Ireland to the west and Russia to the east. Somehow they travelled from one place to another, and in considerable numbers, too. Undoubtedly, there were considerable dangers – confused and continual political wars, supplies interrupted by raiding parties and sieges. And glass-workers were competing in the open commercial market, not protected by Church patronage. It was unlikely to have been an easy life; the glass of the period reflects the problems, but also the future, of this very secular craft. If the arches and elongated shapes of the cone-beakers have seemed to remind some modern writers of the lines of Gothic architecture, as drinking vessels they were a commitment to ordinary people, and the requirements of everyday life. Glass-blowers were never monopolised or even encouraged by the Church, and they remained outside the rise of medieval Christianity and its effect on European civilization.

Stained Glass

Although stained glass is usually regarded as an ecclesiastical art, particularly associated with Christianity, its history goes back a very long way, almost as far as the making of glass itself. It was influenced and encouraged by a number of related techniques which were used in domestic and secular settings as well as in a religious context.

The Development of Mosaics

During the very first period of recorded history, the use of small fragments in varied colours to build a picture or a pattern was part of most civilizations. The Babylonians set seemingly dull forms like sun-baked bricks in staggered rows to catch the light at different angles, and chequerboard designs in marble or stone are almost as ancient. As architecture developed, smaller scale patterns became more appropriate for the rooms in which people lived, and the objects they used in everyday life. The wealth of Egypt and its neighbours was reflected in the time and effort they spent to embellish even the smallest object. Patterns and paintings previously simply drawn on the walls were transferred to furniture, to vases, clothing and utensils. Paint would have been impractical on any of these surfaces, and precious stones, metals and bits of glass were used to build the design. Jewellery, with its gleaming gems set in a tracery of metal combined two interesting ideas – the use of small dots of colour to create a pattern or picture, and the effect of reflected light set within a matt framework.

The first glass mosaic dates back to the fifteenth century BC; roundels of different colours were set in a mould to form a zig-zag pattern around a beaker. The glass of this period was opaque; otherwise it would have been easy to see its relation to stained glass windows with borders of roundels in many colours.

Mosaic work continued to develop, and Roman villas were famous for floors and walls set with hardstones in many colours to make pictures of the gods, the seasons, and scenes from everyday life. Glass mosaics added brilliant colour, especially when the small tiles, or *tesserae*, were made of gold foil sandwiched between two layers of clear glass. Glazed windows were used occasionally, although whether the frames were filled with sheets of glass or thin sections of marble or stone is questionable.

When the great Byzantine era of church building began, mosaic work became a dominating feature, used by architects and craftsmen for illustrations to inspire the faithful. When the Dome of the Rock was built in Jerusalem (691 AD) mosaics covered the arches, the columns, the niches and the framework of the building – in short, every available surface.

Window frames were usually filled with a complex tracery of carved wood or stone, and small sections of coloured glass were sometimes set in the tracery to add their glowing colours to the polychrome effect.

The Byzantine Empire may well have established trading routes to Adriatic Italy at a very early period; in any case, by the time the great churches at Ravenna and Torcello were built, a flourishing group of glasshouses in the Venetian area were making glass tiles for their mosaic walls.

In the south windows were heavily restricted by the need to shut out the harsh sunlight. It was the church builders of Germany and France who first seem to have recognized the need for more light in the interior. Perhaps they also saw in travellers' stories of the windows in Byzantine churches a way of combining two requirements: physical, in the sense of protection from the cold and damp; spiritual, in the creation of atmosphere as well as pictorial reinforcement of biblical teaching.

When these needs combined with technical skill in making sheets of coloured glass, the great period of ecclesiastical stained glass began.

Early Stained Glass

There are early references in texts and manuscripts to glazed windows, in Tours during the fifth century, and later in Sunderland, but there are no visual records to show what those windows looked like, or exactly how they were made. A few fragments of plain glass are neither denial nor confirmation.

Only a few centuries later, there were at least three churches in the Frankish area which had sophisticated and carefully designed windows with remarkable painted detail – Lorsch and Augsburg in Germany, and Wissembourg, now in Alsace. These early designs are clearly developed from mosaics. Illuminated manuscripts show the same straight-backed, formalized subjects set against monumental backdrops. They sit or stand in serried rows, pointing with elongated fingers to significant details, or special inscriptions.

These very early examples were part of the changing church architecture. The light inside the church was still severely limited by the need for heavy stone walls and few unprotected openings. But it must have been enough to give the glaziers considerable experience in handling the problems and characteristics of windows of different exposures.

One of the immediate discoveries for anyone who takes the trouble to look at the same window from inside and outside a darkened interior is the effect of halation: the light seems to expand when viewed from inside, making the lead or stone dividing lines much thinner, and creating a halo around each window. This effect is particularly strong with plain glazed windows, but it affects coloured glass as well. Many early churches with fairly heavy stone-mullioned windows nonetheless appear filled with radiant light inside. By the time Augsburg Cathedral was built, in the eleventh century, craftsmen were highly professional, and skilful in the use of all such techniques.

At this period, and for much of the medieval era, glaziers were attached to local monasteries, although they were probably considered lay artisans. The Bishop of Auxerre rewarded his glaziers with a prebendaryship. Glassmakers had also settled in England near Chiddingfold, making window glass for the church. Few records exist of the individual glaziers who worked on a particular building; they were only some of the whole communities of craftsmen and artisans who designed and built the great cathedrals and churches which began to rise all over northern Europe.

Windows of the Gothic Era

The Gothic period saw the great flowering of this particular aspect of Christian art. From St Denis near Paris, the effective use of glass spread throughout France, England,

Right
The Hezekiah panel. Figure
from the south west transept
of the South Window,
Canterbury Cathedral,
England. *c* 1213–1220;
63in × 29in (160 × 74cm).
A genealogical figure of
Hezekiah (*Ezec hias*).
A great problem in dealing
with very early glass is the
amount of restoration and
repair that is often needed.
Too often the result of intensive care has been to remove
the patina of centuries, and
sometimes some of the glass
surface; occasionally there is
even a visible change in the
colour. This panel with its
rich jewel colours has been
cleaned and treated by a
special workshop set up in the
Canterbury Cathedral
precincts specifically to work
on the building's substantial
amount of glass. It seems to
have benefited from its
treatment and the detail of the
flowered scrolls and roundels is
quite beautiful – similar to the
William Morris designs some
650 years later.

Left
Panel of stained glass; one of a pair from the Gothic period. *c* 1425; ht 45in (114.3cm).

Right
Detail from the Annunciation Window originally in St John the Baptist, Worcestershire, England. *c* 1340; ht 60in (152.4cm). The iconography of stained glass is a study in itself. These two examples of early windows are full of beautifully detailed symbolism, as well as lovely intricate patterns on the dresses and backgrounds. Note that many glasspainters used similar images throughout the great period of religious dominance – the hands of the main figures are in identical positions, and the roundels on the border of the Worcestershire example are repeated in the bed drapes of the Gothic period panel.

and Germany. Architecture grew softer, with a more fluid, naturalistic line, and the stained glass windows of the thirteenth century fit comfortably into the new style with more relaxed figures and flowing drapery, and a correspondingly fluid relationship between the pieces of glass and their particular piece of the jigsaw. In the Jesse Tree window in Chartres Cathedral, the use of chips of brilliant colour is remarkably intricate and subtle, the whole divided first into rectangles with the framework of iron, but then into an amazing tapestry of blues, reds and greens, each figure and detail shaped and outlined in gracefully irregular leading, details painted sparingly, the whole a marvellously rhythmic flow from top to bottom.

Because of their very individual contributions to the story of stained glass, it is worth while looking at two cathedrals in detail: Chartres, and the Duomo in Florence.

Chartres Cathedral remains today one of the most impressive accomplishments of man's dedication to God. It was built in the thirteenth century, replacing five earlier churches which had testified to the piety and religious fervour of the local population.

The town was a trading centre and a place of pilgrimage (the Virgin's cloak or tunic had been a gift from the Emperor of Constantinople to Charlemagne, whose grandson Charles the Bald had given it to the city in 876) but above all it was a source of pride to the citizens. They contributed time, money and materials whenever fire destroyed their cathedral – the last time in 1194. During the final re-building the fervour was even more intense – the previous cathedral had been largely destroyed but the cloak remained unharmed and it seemed that Chartres had been given a very special sign of the Virgin's blessing.

The entire Christian world responded with an open hand, and in less than a hundred years the new Chartres was re-dedicated. Most of the windows – 172 of them – had been

glazed between 1215 and 1240. The oldest three complete windows date from the twelfth century, as do four panels in the revered Blue Virgin Window (*Notre Dame de la Belle Verrière*) – making 176 windows in all. A stupendous job for a modern studio equipped with every technical advantage – an incredible achievement for a team of artisans working without any way of knowing what the work would look like when the glass was in place. Their ability and self-confidence must have seemed like a miracle in itself.

The all-pervading effect in Chartres is blue – blue for most of the windows in the ambulatory, blue for the frames of the round windows in the aisles, and a sombre blue for the twelfth-century lancet windows beneath the west Rose.

A very special aspect of Chartres is the number of guilds and tradesmen who contributed enough money to commission windows with the symbols of their profession. Although the artists were anonymous, the donors did not intend to be unrecognized, and many of the most magnificent windows include a small image of a shoe, a loaf of bread, or a wheelwright at work.

Chartres Cathedral is a synonym for near-perfection, that coming together of community devotion, available money, and artistic brilliance which lit up the Christian world. But there are still other examples of Gothic windows – Bourges, Sens, Auxerre, Assisi, Ravenna, Canterbury, York, Winchester, and Fairford, to name only a few.

As the centuries passed, the style and purpose of the windows changed as well. The early windows are fairly static in subject matter, depicting saints and symbols in an architectural niche or framework. During the fourteenth century, the more naturalistic imagery of the Gothic period was used to create softer lines and more human posture. By the sixteenth century, in smaller buildings like Fairford in Gloucestershire, the story-telling element was very strong, and gospel stories also served as what would be today called visual aids, very much in fashion.

Detail of faces and figures was growing more and more naturalistic. The Italian glaziers since the time of Giotto kept to the tradition of humanistic effects – designers were much more concerned with the realistic appearance of

Left
Panel of two men, with
domestic scenes above.
Switzerland; c 1600; ht 42in
106cm).
The detail shows two men in
the local dress of guards and
soldiers, with marvellous
plumed hats and elaborate
ceremonial spears. Domestic
scenes inset around the figures
include one of a man weaving
cloth while a woman holds
what seems to be a skein of
wool. Many of these Swiss
domestic panels were imported
into England and America
during the craze for stained
glass in the 19th century, and
they remain one of the few
accessible antiques that a
private collector can buy and
display. One museum houses
its collection in a specially
built room, but most private
owners hang them in front of
a plain glass window, or inset
them into the window itself.
Today there are many forgers
of these secular panels, but the
detail on the painting is usually
crude and rather simplistic.

Above
An illustration of a medieval
scene by the American artist
Will H. Bradley; c 1896.
Such medieval scenes were
meat and drink to the Neo-
Gothic stained glass artist –
the heraldic outlines and
symbols were particularly well
suited to stained glass panels
such as those made by the
Pre-Raphaelites.

figures than were the craftsmen of the north. Gradually this solid pictorial approach became more and more popular, and the stained glass window became a kind of translucent canvas for the painter instead of a medium with its own glassy qualities.

The cities of the Renaissance were prepared to pay handsomely for the finest painters of the day to decorate their churches. During the fifteenth century, the great cathedrals of Italy were filled with frescoes and paintings; the windows were regarded as simply a different kind of surface. The designs were sketched out by men who were often sculptors, goldsmiths, architects or painters, then completed by skilled glaziers. Uccello, Ghiberti and Donatello are the most famous names, but it was Lorenzo Ghiberti who contributed most. He designed three of the famous *occhi*, or eye windows, high in the dome of Florence Cathedral, the Duomo, and many of the lancets, as well as the doors of the adjoining Baptistry. Inside, the Duomo is very like an art gallery; colourful with elaborate frescoes, sculpture of many kinds, even false windows of mosaic; and, of course, the brilliantly coloured glass, alive with people and landscapes, with naturalistic saints and the flowing draperies of Renaissance art.

Story-telling had become the focus for the window design, rather than a delightful addition to an essentially glassy kaleidoscope, and reached its apogee in the nineteenth century, when windows were conceived as either medieval re-workings, or glass pictorial canvases which illustrated a dramatic moment in time – the stained glass equivalent of 'When Did You Last See Your Father?'.

Another kind of window had evolved alongside the richly coloured examples which we all know. Towards the end of the thirteenth century simple painting in sepia and black tones on plain glass had become more and more popular, sometimes combined with small medallions or roundels in isolated splendour.

The reason for these designs is not entirely clear, but it may be simply that as the interiors grew more and more elaborate, with carved woodwork and painted canopies, decorated ceilings and beautifully detailed statues, it became necessary to allow more light to enter so that the congregation could appreciate its surroundings. The enormous height of the new cathedrals would mean that no one without a telescope would be able to see the top half of many of the windows, so the designs were concentrated in the lower half, leaving the surrounding space as geometric patterns in lead and clear glass.

Then too, with the Reformation and the Puritan influence, the rich colour and elaborate imagery of the great cathedral windows would have seemed almost heretical. Many early windows were destroyed or damaged beyond repair during this period, and contemporary churches often had totally plain windows, their only decoration achieved with leading. Since the glass was still quite irregular both in content and surface, the window would nonetheless have an amazing amount of individual shading, and the effect could be both tranquil and very moving in an austere way.

Eighteenth and Nineteenth Centuries

By the eighteenth century, the rational architect had begun to concentrate on secular buildings rather than on churches. Coats of arms were set into the windows of aristocratic homes, and even religious windows had a light, almost lacy appearance. In northern Europe this trend was strong enough to make the painted and decorated window, complete with a charming domestic scene and a heraldic panel or two, absolutely vital for the stylish house owner.

Gothic and the Neo-Gothics

In the nineteenth century stained glass suddenly grew important again. The Neo-Gothic interest, and the whole medieval cult, ensured that traditional scenes and figures could be ordered from the catalogue in assorted colours to suit every occasion and site. The Pre-Raphaelites applied their talents to thousands of small chapels and churches throughout the countryside and at their best they returned to the idea of glass as a medium of its own, with those special qualities of light reflection which make stained glass such a unique art form. The worst effect was the purely pictorial influence already mentioned, which destroyed the validity of the medium, and used windows only as canvases lit from behind, playing down the leading as much as possible, and relying on the painting to create emphasis and form.

The Gothic revival sparked off a popular interest in the partial or total 'restoration' of all kinds of buildings in Europe and America. Architects called for more and more church windows, panels, home skylights, fanlights, and so on, but there were far too few craftsmen capable of undertaking such fine work. Mass manufacturers of sheet glass rose to the bait, turning out mediocre copies of every kind of medieval kitsch.

Chemists, and makers of better glass, began to experiment with various kinds of metals and colourings until they achieved a good standard of 'antique' glass, and, from the 1870s onwards, the general appearance of both secular and church glass improved enormously as the insipid sepias and cloudy yellows of the eighteenth and early nineteenth centuries were superseded.

William Morris

The equally insipid painting also disappeared as the Arts and Crafts movement, spearheaded by William Morris, began to assert itself. Its followers were concerned with the quality of contemporary life, and the amenities which they felt had been destroyed by the industrial revolution and machinery. Stained glass was an ideal medium for expressing their beliefs, still made by artists and craftsmen working together. Many of the early windows designed by Edward Burne-Jones for Morris and Company reflect their delight in the dim but rich colours so perfectly attuned to the stained glass palette, and in the pictorial aspect of quiet, domestic scenes and natural beauty.

Then too, for the first time since the Middle Ages, stained glass became part of everyday life, although the emphasis was much more secular. Even the smallest suburban home might aspire to a door panel of flowers or a bouquet, a bathroom window decently obscured with a floating swan, or a few pseudo-medieval windows with leaded diamonds in dirty pinks and greys. The same themes were used in more affluent homes by better artists and with more expensive glass, so there is a wide field for the collector; many of the best manufacturers issued catalogues and pattern books to help identification.

Although Morris and his firm were partly responsible for the renewed interest in stained glass art, Burne-Jones' designs were essentially in the antique tradition. It was the Art Nouveau artists such as John La Farge and Louis Comfort Tiffany who were rather more innovative.

Tiffany and Art Nouveau

By the 1880s, Tiffany had begun to experiment with many kinds of opalescent and marbled glasses, and the new Art Nouveau style with its sinuous lines and curving flower stems was perfectly attuned to the flexible leading and fragmented colours of stained glass. Wisteria, lilies, peonies, roses and lilies of the valley climbed and twirled across windows, lampshades, ornaments, boxes, and screens in almost every fashionable home; before Art Nouveau declined thousands of stained glass objects had been made in Tiffany's factory and other workshops. This is another fertile field for the collector, although the Art Nouveau period has become immensely popular, and work is correspondingly difficult to find, and increasingly expensive.

The Later Arts and Crafts

On the other hand, the Arts and Crafts movement, with its sturdier patterns and simpler lines, never achieved quite the same mad popularity. However, it remained influential for many years. In Scotland, Charles Rennie Mackintosh was the leading figure, and his designs for the Willow Tearooms in Glasgow included windows, panels, and magnificent stained glass doors. Their muted colours and linear abstract leading lines are still significant as a direct influence on many modern glass artists.

The Contemporary Scene

During the two World Wars, the craft suffered from lack of craftsmen and, of course, the bombings which destroyed so many churches. But after the 1950s, another resurgence of interest in stained glass joined forces with technical achievements and new materials to create a substantial school of young artists in Europe, particularly in Germany and the United States, as well as in France and England.

Modern Germany

In Germany, a school of glaziers and stained glass designers has been thriving since the Bauhaus days before the Second World War. Johann Thorn Prikker was born in Holland, but he lived and worked in Germany most of his life, and was undoubtedly the best-known and most influential artist in the pre-war development of modern stained glass. Many of his pupils went on to span the period between the Cubist movement and the post-war years. Anton Wendling and Georg Meistermann are among the best known.

Since the war, there has been a whole group of innovative and exciting glaziers/designers. They have been employed by many architects who have used stained glass in new and old churches, and very imaginatively in secular buildings of all kinds – schools, office complexes, theatres, and so on. The use of enamel over- or under-painting has largely died out even for church windows, and artists have concentrated on designs with lead lines and coloured glass, sometimes with acid etched, engraved or sand-blasted details.

Johannes Schreiter is another prominent designer whose cool restrained windows are masterpieces of subtlety, with complex but slender abstract leading patterns, and tones of grey, green, blue, and even black and white. There is an overwhelming atmosphere of serenity in his work, even when the windows take up whole walls, or, as in the case of the chapel of the Johannesburg convent in Leutsdorf, a whole room.

Ludwig Schaffrath creates a very different type of wall, in addition to his leaded windows, with slab glass, an inch or more thick, inserted directly into concrete. This technique, called *dalles de verre*, has been particularly successful in some of the more experimental buildings in France and the United States.

A more recent use of stained glass is in small compositions which are intended for table or window-sill displays, or slightly larger panels to be inserted in windows or interior walls. The work of Hans Gottfried von Stockhausen has been of great influence on the younger generation, since he teaches glass design in Stuttgart – Ada Isensee is one of his ex-students, and both have made a number of restrained panels in stained glass, using large pieces in rich colours with white, and some etched textural decoration.

France

In France, rather like Britain, stained glass reached its height of splendour in the medieval period when the great

Gothic cathedrals were being built. Through the intervening centuries the quality of stained glass windows steadily declined until the second half of the twentieth century. However, many Post-Impressionist painters in France were influenced by the symbolism and atmosphere of religious buildings – Georges Rouault's work was always affected by the pictorial potential of black lines and rich simply coloured shapes – and great windows have been designed and supervised by Georges Braque, Le Corbusier and Fernand Leger. The most recent examples are the many windows designed by Marc Chagall for the Lincoln Centre in New York and the Jerusalem windows in Israel. Chagall's work is the most important commissioned by a new patron of stained glass. The Jewish religion had traditionally forbidden the use of graven images, but in the past decades synagogues have incorporated many beautiful, sometimes magnificent, windows by contemporary artists including Ben Shahn.

England in the Twentieth Century

For a long period after the decline of the Arts and Crafts movement, stained glass in England was mediocre in both quality and quantity. In the 1920s and 1930s the Irish school continued to turn out some highly competent artists under the direction of Sarah Purser, who died at the age of ninety-three still running her studio and encouraging artists such as Harry Clarke and Evie Hone. Evie Hone's work was particularly imaginative and greatly influenced the younger generation of British stained glass workers.

Immediately after the Second World War a number of churches had their damaged windows replaced, but the most prominent project was the re-building of Coventry Cathedral. For this great and moving symbol of Britain's survival, the authorities chose a team of artists: John Piper, who painted the designs, and Patrick Reyntiens who made the glass and the windows. The dominating window, an abstract design in brilliant yellows surrounded by blues and reds, takes up the entire curved baptistry wall. The transfer of Piper's watercolour abstracts into rectangular panels of glass set within the arched concrete wall is a masterpiece of instinctive craftsmanship.

Since Piper's influential work, a group of younger workers has begun to explore stained glass techniques. The most prominent is Brian Clarke, who took on the mantle of the German and French schools; although their influence has declined, his very distinctive style is still linked to the clear geometric subtleties of the Ludwig Schaffrath and Johannes Schreiter schools in Germany. Nonetheless it is

Right
Panel designed by Brian Clarke, University of Nottingham, England. 1977; ht 19ft 8in (5.9m).
In some modern work, the symbolism has become abstract, with the emphasis on pure colour and pattern rather than meaning. Clarke's work has become more individual, although the influence of his stay on the Continent is still important; this particular window has something of the spare lines of a Japanese screen, akin to the work of several American artists. He has also made windows for private clients and churches.

true to say that English stained glass has a long way to go before modern painters and craftsmen make British stained glass a force on the world scene.

Contemporary America

New schools of stained glass artists have been most successful in the United States, where the whole concept of studio glass has revolutionized many of the old craft techniques. The West Coast of America has been particularly fruitful for glassworkers; the climate seems to encourage the use of experimental work in many kinds of buildings, as well as in churches and office blocks which have traditionally been the mainstay of the stained glass studios.

Types of stained glass have also changed. While leaded panels and windows of various kinds are still pre-eminent, many artists are using the *dalles de verre* technique of slab glass embedded in concrete, cut and laminated acrylic sheets, and fused glass where different colours are laid together side by side, or in layers, and heated until they are firmly melded. Fused glass in particular can give a rich, double-strength quality to the colours which blend around the edges of the individual pieces, which are not separated by leading; sometimes the attached pieces are also faceted making an extra reflecting surface. This technique also utilizes different qualities and textures of glass more easily, since without leading there is no real restriction on the surface and thickness of individual pieces.

Another important contribution to modern glasswork has been the non-glass backgrounds of many artists who have never worked before in craft shops or glasshouses, and therefore bring a very different approach to stained glass. They are willing to try all kinds of materials, creating some remarkable compositions of unusual complexity: glass tubing; resin epoxy for the surrounds, sometimes textured with sand and pebbles; lapidary saw work to create curves and circular shapes; three-dimensional objects; welded metal framing for the glass pieces; and, most recently, some very unorthodox surface patterns which have been printed or etched with X-rays, photographs, silk-screen prints, etc.

In addition to the amazing variety of materials, it is true to say that American architects and private clients have been exceptionally open to new and exciting sites for panels, windows and free-standing sculptures. Shops and restaurants are using glass to create the right atmosphere, with natural or artificial light sources behind panels and walls, floors and entire ceilings.

Interior and exterior doors are the perfect canvas for imaginative and inventive panels (one of the earliest sets of stained glass doors was made by Charles Rennie Mackintosh in Glasgow in 1904), and can be completely made of glass or have smaller panels inset into wood or metal. Stained glass is also used as space and room dividers. Clerestory windows take on an entirely new look, as with those by Vincent O' Brien for the Air Force Chapel in Colorado, while a food shop can include images of hamburgers and milk shakes in its stained glass store front. A ski lodge has small alpine badges incorporated in its windows, while a huge office building in Florida is completely enclosed in a *dalles de verre* rectangle of pre-cast panels.

Private customers abound, using glass for hallways, bedroom and hall windows, skylights, shower doors, bathrooms, and display pieces.

Paul Marioni's 'Dali', a portrait of the artist, includes inset lenses to give the appearance of motion, eyes made of two-way mirror insets, and a tiny doorway which has two silver hands as doorknobs. It's only fair to say that Marioni began as an English and Philosophy graduate, a car repairer, and a tenor sax musician – a typical example of the Californian craft scene. Not all American artists are so experimental – Peter Mollica specialises in traditional leaded stained glass (including the restrained use of simple, clear and frosted plain glass, and black framing) while Kathie Stackpole Burrell's dreamy nature studies bring a tranquil air to the windows of a nunnery. James Hubbill also uses stained leaded glass, but it is often set directly into moulded concrete walls and ceilings to create particular atmospheric conditions in restaurants, as well as in bathrooms like underwater grottos, and bedrooms in his own home.

Another group of artists concentrated on smaller scale, more sculptural, effects. Henry Halem has created particularly subtle effects with sand blasting, and coloured glass panels with decorative shapes and patterns marvered into hot glass.

Robert Kehlmann, writer turned glass artist, has been very influenced by the modern German school, and has written a major article on Ludwig Schaffrath. His work in the 1979 exhibition of glass organized by the Corning Museum of Glass was opaque white leaded glass with appliqués and insets in subtle grey and blue tones, while Peter Mollica included two small panels of completely colourless glass with simple grids of leading.

In complete contrast, Richard Posner's panel, 'Another look at My Beef with the Government', uses many colours of leaded glass, sand-blasted decoration and a photographic transparency. Narcissus Quagliata is one of the many women who have taken up stained glass (Janet Jansen is another), and her work is particularly rich in imagery and inclusions of X-rays, lenses, mirrors, etc.

These new studio workers have added immeasurably to our appreciation and understanding of stained glass as a completely modern medium. The best continue to work in churches and public buildings creating monuments for the future, but they have all inspired ordinary people with the remarkable and thrilling effect that stained glass can have on even a small room in a simple home. In their hands, the future is full of hope for this most traditional of glass arts.

Right
The drawings show the many different outlines and shapes of stained glass windows over eight centuries. Here in black and white, it is much easier to see the enormous importance the leaded lines play in creating the desired imagery and design. The earliest window (*top right*) and one of the most modern (*centre right*) both use the lightest leading, while both the traditional mother and child in the centre row and the radiator cover by Frank Lloyd Wright (*bottom row, third from left*) use areas of entirely solid black lead to emphasize important features.

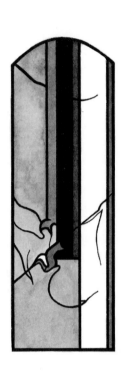

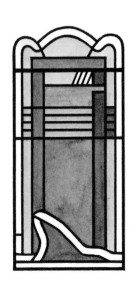

Venice

In theory, Italian glass should mean glass made anywhere on the peninsula, or inside today's national boundary. In fact, to most people Italian glass means Venice and the island of Murano. The growth of Venetian glass is a long story, encompassing its beginnings in Roman times and ending with the new interest in modern design which has only recently begun to appear in the Murano workshops.

Rome had encouraged trade as well as being a source of craftsmanship and technical achievement. The satellite towns which were known as glassmaking centres during the height of the Empire did not include furnaces in northern Italy as far as we know, although a settlement at Aquileia, east of what is now Venice, was reported to have glassworkers who escaped from the barbarian invasions during the fifth century, and fled to the remoter region around Venice.

During the medieval period the centre of glassmaking shifted unmistakably to the north, to the Seine-Rhine area in particular. The Syrian tradition was in full flood during this period, with its plastic line and malleable hot-glass decoration at the fire and a correspondingly low interest in colour and cutting.

The Romano-Alexandrian talents were left for the moment on the fringes of history. On the fringes, but not extinct. In the Middle East, glass was being made and cut, coloured and painted, even if in smaller quantities than before, and it was obviously not going to be kept out of Europe forever. The Catholic Church had played its part in the dissolution of Rome, and now it made good at least one loss by reuniting in mosaics the Eastern and Western crafts. Churches in Constantinople and throughout all the Byzantine Empire were filled with tiles and painted pictures; the Romans had loved mosaic floors and walls, the Egyptians adored brilliant colours and gold jewellery. Combine all these tendencies and the great glittering mosaics with gold backgrounds begin to fill the new cathedrals of Europe and especially the buildings at Ravenna and Torcello.

Early Tile-making

Recent excavations have proved that glass *tesserae* were being made in the Adriatic region in large quantities to cover the walls of many cathedrals in northern Italy. There the vague memories of a flourishing blown-glass industry could become a reality, and although much investigation remains to be done, it is clear that the revival of glass tilemaking had a vital effect on re-introducing the art of glassblowing. We do not yet know who these first Venetian glassmakers were, and how they arrived, although the histories of families like the Aldobrani suggest they came from the Middle East. We cannot draw too strong a distinction between Egyptian and Syrian influence because by this time anyone involved in glass must have absorbed some ideas and traditions from both cultures. Nonetheless, the first known Venetian goblets are coloured like jewels and, albeit somewhat crudely, enamelled with jewel-like dots and fish-scale patterns.

The records are sparse; a 'Domenica' is named as a glass-worker in a document of 962, a medieval text has a picture of a glasshouse in operation (*c* 1040) and then suddenly a few hundred years later there are references to a glassmakers'

Right
Goblet of clear glass, with transparent dark blue folded foot, and enamelled dot and fish scale rim on bowl.
c 1500; ht 4⅞in (12.5cm).

Below
Bowl, blown in a mould and ribbed; painted in chestnut brown lustre. Egypt; *c* 1150; ht 3⅜in (8.5cm).

Left
Detail from a mosaic, showing the Empress Theodora. San Vitale, Ravenna; *c* 600–800 AD. The small *tesserae* were made at many early glasshouses. Excavations at Torcello in Italy have revealed fragments of many kinds of *tesserae* and early mosaic wares.

Left
Goblet with clear bowl applied with opaque white trailings and rings. The stem and folded foot are blown in *lattimo* and clear glass. *c* 1600; ht 6½in (16.5cm).

Right
Goblet of opaque turquoise and dark blue, enamelled with fish scale patterns, which also enclose medallions with gilded frames. Late 15th century; ht 4⅞in (12.3cm). The brilliant colou.s are reminiscent of sand-core Egyptian work, but the shape is wholly Renaissance.

Right and below
Goblets of clear *cristallo*, both with lightly enamelled bands around the rim of the bowl. *c* 1500; ht 5¾in (14.6cm). Two examples of the delicate use of plain glass.

guild, complaints about the number of fires in the city, and finally in 1292 an ordinance which forbade the glasshouses to remain in Venice because of the danger to the other buildings and to the inhabitants. The entire guild was banished to the island of Murano, within the Venetian lagoon.

The Muranese Monopoly

Undoubtedly there was, as always, a political reason for the move as well as a humanitarian one. The prosperity of the glass guild must have made the government realize that if they could only keep a monopoly on this new and apparently very appealing art, they would be able to keep all the trade which the glasshouses provided both in importing their supplies and sending out their products. Control is always easier on an island. On pain of death, no craftsman could leave Murano or even teach a resident foreigner any of the trade secrets without express permission and that was seldom granted. The men were almost prisoners, and whatever the intentions or the reasons behind the regulations they worked well enough for the next few centuries. There were always some men who managed to get away, of course, but until the decline of the industry in the eighteenth century, most of the blowers were content to stay at home. As the fifteenth century developed, the texture of the glass itself became more obvious. The northern flexibility in trailed glass, as well as growing trade with Damascus affected the static quality of the early period. In any case, the chemists had been at work and the glass had been refined and clarified continually until it was almost transparent, and certainly clearer than anything yet produced. There is no real evidence to say who actually invented what they called *cristallo*, but the mixture became the great leap forward for the entire guild. It was in use by the end of the fifteenth century, traditionally due to the family of Barovier, or one of the other families which created so much beauty, sometimes over hundreds of years and generations of craftsmen.

Whatever the source, the Venetian guild saw to it that once discovered, the formula was kept in Murano, and this new glass together with the increased skill and artistic sense of the glassblowers meant that within a very short period Venetian (or Muranese) glass was considered to be the finest made in the Western world.

Major Source of Wealth

Cristallo is particularly well adapted to fantastic shapes and thinly-blown pieces; it is remarkably ductile, easily worked when hot, and gives a light and fragile appearance. It is also too thin for cutting or engraving with anything heavier than a diamond point. Glass cutting lost its popular appeal for a while and the blowers of Murano became the most important workers in what was a very important industry and one of the major sources of Venetian wealth.

Still, the multi-coloured murrhines were as popular in the fifteenth century as they had been with Pompeians, and Venetian lampworkers saw no reason to disregard their customers' wishes. They began to make lighter, more delicate, versions of Roman work, and developed the use of sliced *millefiori* canes that would find its ultimate expression in nineteenth-century French paperweights.

The canes were carefully assembled from coloured rods

laid in different shaped moulds, heated and pulled until each rod was no thicker than a pencil. When it was cool, thin slices were cut, and these were arranged in the desired pattern. The old Roman method of gluing together the round canes and then heating them until fused was still useful, but it limited the shaping process. The Venetians experimented and improved the technique, embedding the slices in clear glass which could then be expanded into any shape, and finished off as required. Many small murrhine pieces were regarded as precious jewels, and were mounted in silver or gold to set off their colourful appearance and protect the glass from rough handling or accidental breakage.

While they were experimenting with colour, the Venetians found that it was possible to make a particularly opaque white with a milky almost opalescent glow. They called this *lattimo*, or milk glass, and it was used to make white beakers and cups as well as being interspersed with clear glass in broad panels.

The plain blues and turquoises of the early years had become more sophisticated, and many of the jewel and gemstone glasses made at the height of the Venetian supremacy recall the exquisitely reproduced imitations of natural stones popular during the Roman period. However, the Venetians had learned to blow even these marbled glasses thinly and the aventurine and chalcedony bowls are remarkably beautiful and left simple and unadorned. An opaline glass falls somewhere between the two – it has a lovely rainbow tint and a milky opalescent surface, but blown very thin into ribbed and moulded shapes it couldn't possibly be mistaken for carved opal. By 1500 *cristallo* was obviously more important than any of the coloured glasses, and the glassblowers had also developed favourite devices and decorative effects to be used alone or together. Goblets were almost always on a flaring stem with a flat base to the bowl, gadrooned around the edge, swelling from the base to a generous rim.

Many of the cups had covers decorated to match, with jewel-like spots of enamel paint in geometric designs on the feet, around the rim and sometimes over the whole glass. Trailing was becoming important, too, as it had been in Syria and the north. Threading was not very common except for a ring or chain of interlocked threading which was often around jugs or under the raised rim of a plate or *tazza* (a

Right
Twin bottle in the shape of
open-mouthed birds on a
swirled knop stem and folded
foot. *c* 1600; ht 11in (28cm).
Possibly used for vinegar and
oil, or some herbal mixture.
Note the dark colour of the
glass and the many seeds and
striations.

Left
Three goblets, one with cover,
showing the gradual change to
simple shapes from the late
15th to the early to mid-16th
century; ht of covered cup
9½in (24cm).
With the development of
clearer and more transparent
cristallo, the need for heavy
overpainting in enamel grew
less important. Pure 'white'
glass with only self-coloured
diamond point engraving
showed off the craftsmen's
ability.

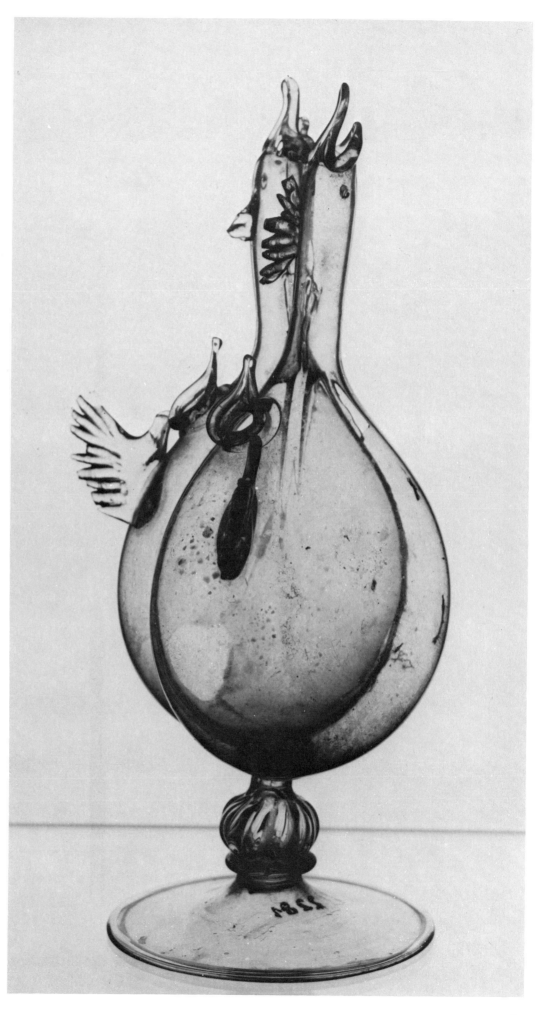

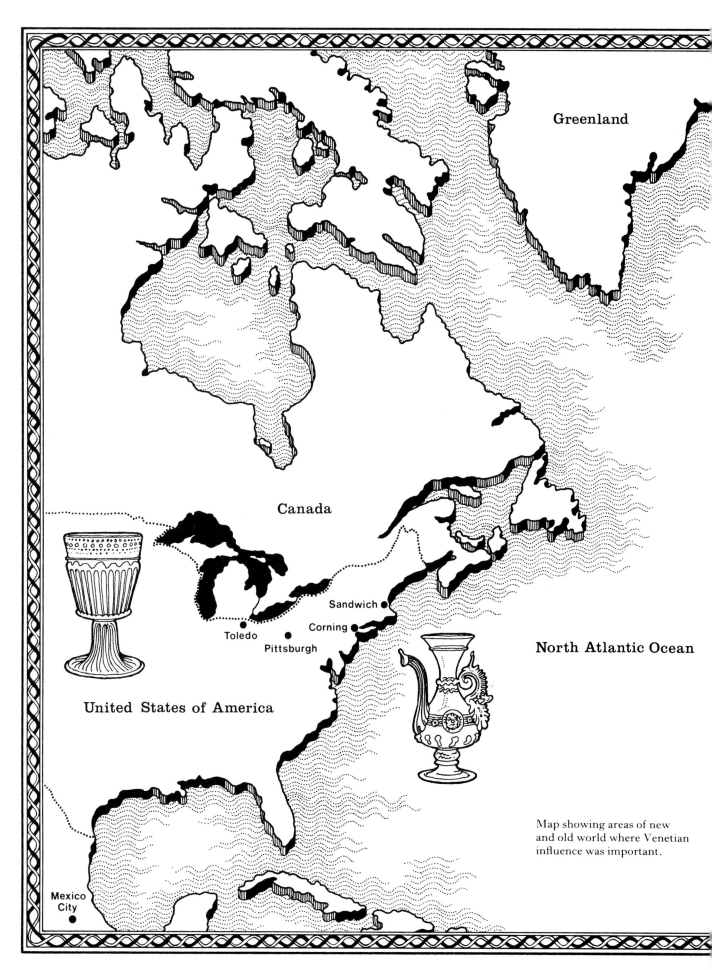

Greenland

Canada

Sandwich ●

Corning ●

Toledo ●   ● Pittsburgh

North Atlantic Ocean

United States of America

Map showing areas of new
and old world where Venetian
influence was important.

Mexico
City
●

Far right and right
Later in the century the glass shapes became more fantastic, incorporating Roman and Oriental designs. (Compare top drawing with photographs right and below.)

Below
Vase with flared neck and scroll handles in dark blue. Late 15th century; ht 9in (22.9cm).

Above
Jug and cover with handles scrolled as serpents, engraved with simple floral design in diamond point. Early 16th century; ht 7½in (19.2cm).

Right
Flared beaker pattern moulded in diamonds. 16th century; ht 5½in (13.9cm).

66

cup or serving plate on a foot). *Lattimo* was drawn out into thin threads and used instead of trailing to make lacy patterns within the glass. This particular effect seems to have been a source of great enjoyment for the blowers. The first rather simple threads of white laid on in straightforward lines became more and more complicated, using two or three different threads in crossed-over patterns like a network. The English adaptation during the eighteenth century used the *lattimo* threads mainly for simple stems; the Venetians worked their *lattimo* threads into fantastic designs and used them for the entire body of the glass, blown and tooled into curves and elongated bowls. There are dozens of versions with or without other colours, air bubbles and moulded details, but actually Venetian pieces of the sixteenth century are far simpler and more attractive than many of the complex attempts at a later stage.

Another use for the *lattimo* threads was within the stems of the winged glasses, a series of goblets and wine glasses made mostly during the late sixteenth and seventeenth centuries. These have bowls of varying shape, almost always in clear glass, a foot with a folded rim, usually quite simple, and then a fantastic stem which is likely to resemble something like entwined dragons or the wings of a double-curved angel. As the years passed these stems became more and more extravagant, with pinched extra wings, milled and patterned side pieces and generally an air of delightful dotty uselessness and instability. Confectionery glass, perhaps, but today hard to find without damage to the delicate stem.

A kind of shell was also a favourite shape, balanced on a stem, with a curved and coiled, rather long and narrow top, curling up on one side. These are derived from a rock

Above
Ewer with basin in rib-moulded clear glass. 16th century; ht 13¾in (34.9cm).
A marvellous piece which needs no decoration but its fine *cristallo*. The shapes are reminiscent of the Roman period.

Left
Dish with swirled ribbing and enamelled decoration; nef, or fantastic boat shape with reticulated glass netting topped with a horn. Both 16th century; ht of nef 13in (33cm).
Used as a centrepiece, sometimes to hold knives and forks, or less commonly as a salt or spice cellar, nefs were made in Venice and in *façon de Venise* glasshouses, mainly for aristocratic patrons. Because of their fragility very few survive intact.

crystal shape which was commonly used during the same period and revived later in Bohemia.

The Venetians never forgot that they were traders and many lamps and glasses were made for the Middle Eastern market, sometimes with inscriptions and mottoes in Arabic. One such mosque lamp of traditional design, which is badly damaged, has an inscription which indicates that it was made for Sultan Queit Bey, who ruled from 1468–96. This proved irresistible to a forger in the 1930s and he produced a perfect undamaged version, complete with inscription.

Early Venetian glass was highly decorated in some way, and usually with enamel painting. Designs were geometric and jewel-like. They were painted with extreme delicacy, and sometimes in incredibly tiny detail. Gradually more and more of the glass was left clear, and the painting that remained was of the highest quality.

In the sixteenth century, a number of stylistic patterns became apparent. The *cristallo* was refined and improved and very few pieces were painted in all-over patterns, although there are still a number of medallions and figurines which decorate tall cups and the centre of large platters.

Towards the end of the sixteenth and throughout most of the seventeenth centuries the Venetian glassmakers used the

Left
Goblet in the Venetian style, *c* 1880. As a warning to collectors even the fragile elaborate dragon-stem goblets have been copied. This particularly successful attempt was made by C. F. A. Muller. One mistake was in the total clarity of the bowl – even the best 17th-century *cristallo* was uneven by comparison.

Above
Straw-toned bowl with ribbed border, the flattish rim with enamel decoration. 16th century; diam 16in (40.6cm). *Cristallo* was exceedingly fragile, so the rims of bowls and dishes were folded to prevent chipping.

Right
Covered goblet with cup, ribbed and moulded in clear glass, central knop in amber. 17th century; ht 7⅝in (19.4cm).

Left

Tazza and bowl. Late 16th–
early 17th century; diam of
tazza 10⅜in (26.3cm).
Flat *tazze* were always popular,
and at this time clear chain
trailing often replaced enamel
decoration. Chains reappeared
in Ravenscroft glasses in
England, and in Cains'
American glasshouse.

Below
Beaker with flared rim and
enamel decoration of figures
from the *Commedia dell'Arte*.
c 1575; ht 7½in (12.2cm).

Left
Decanters of clear glass with
blue frilled trailings, and
copper-tinted prunts. Ht 15in
(38.1cm).
Modern glassmakers continue
old skills – these decanters
were made recently in a
traditional style, perhaps as
copies to complete a set.

Page 70
Goblet of looped *lattimo* glass
on a hollow-blown stem with
winged handles, and a simple
folded foot. 17th century;
ht 6½in (16.6cm).
Later customers demanded
colour and fantasy as well as
skill – this goblet is fairly
simple by comparison with
some of the more elaborate
examples. Many winged goblets
were not intended for ordinary
use but were made as
presentation pieces.

Page 71
Beaker with enamelled
decoration and the figure of
'The Marianne'. Dated 1798;
ht 4½in (11.4cm).
Cristallo was far too thin to be
cut or engraved, so inscriptions
were often painted.

soft ductile quality of their glass to the utmost, and many of
the most fantastic designs and shapes come from that period.

Many of the new pieces were made to be much more
delicate and fragile, on thinly-blown narrow stems with cup
bowls or a rounded base, but often with a very wide lip. The
cups or chalices are almost always unadorned, relying for
their effect on perfect balance and simplicity of form. Others
are made with *lattimo* spirals or a *reticello* network over all
the glass, the only decoration on simple and straightforward
shapes. Larger vases and baskets still had a central flared
stem and a flat-bottomed bowl, but the bowl itself was likely
to be quite high, of plain clear glass and with a clear cover,
the decorative finial almost the only frivolous touch. The
'boat' shape on a stem makes its appearance with rigging and
much detail, and sometimes a spout at the prow, obviously
used to drop rose water or perfume on to one's hands.

With demanding and extravagant patrons simplicity was
forgotten. Hollow stems were mould blown into extraordinary shapes; bowls and cups were made with a variety
of decorative finishes, like the crackling and frosting used to
make 'ice' glass; diamond point engraving became even
more popular and was used to decorate the entire piece,
much as enamel painting once was; and even the bowls
curved and curled over the rims, with or without strips of
lattimo and pastel prunts.

A pair of tankards, mounted in pewter, are probably from
Liège, but the use of *lattimo* shows how convoluted even
simple stripes can appear when the shape is just that little
bit exaggerated. The whole output of the Venetian colony
became a little frenzied, perhaps in a natural reaction to the
growing influence of other countries and other kinds of
glass. For years there had been a great many complaints
about the fragility and thinness of Venetian products, particularly when shipped abroad. John Greene, a glass merchant in London, wrote a very modern note of complaint
to his supplier about the number of breakages and he was
only one of many hundreds of traders all over Europe.

Right
Two winged pieces, both clear glass with coloured handles. Early 17th century; ht of goblet 16¾in (42.5cm). Stems and handles became more and more elaborate, often grafted onto basic Islamic shapes.

Below
Boot in *lattimo*-striped glass with prunts. Early 17th century; ht 8⅞in (22.5cm). Both the pieces on the right, and the boot, may be *façon de Venise*.

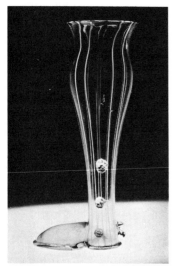

Above
Winged goblet with twisted stem and pinched 'ears'. Late 17th century; ht 6¼in (15.2cm).

Right
Pieces made with opaque white decorations. Perhaps *façon de Venise* or Liège. Ht of covered cup 13⅛in (33.3cm).

Over the years too, more than one craftsman, in spite of all the decrees and all the penalties, had slipped away to become his own master in another city, and by teaching the secrets of Venetian glassmaking helped to spread knowledge and expertise throughout Europe. There were centres in Altare, Genoa, Antwerp, Liège, Spain and even in London. At first, the blowers would duplicate the exact styles and patterns they had been used to making, but naturally as time went on they would adapt to local tastes and local preferences. Their pieces are sometimes very difficult to distinguish from Venetian-made ware, and have come to be called *façon de Venise*. Some can be assigned for reasons of style or inscription to a particular area, but many pieces could have been made almost anywhere in the emigré colonies. In England, the interest in coal-fired furnaces and the lack of wood as a fuel was creating a whole new approach to glassmaking, and by the time Ravenscroft had worked up his new formula with lead oxide, the Venetian monopoly was in pieces, and the great period of Venetian achievement was nearing its end.

In England, glass of lead was perfected during the final years of the seventeenth century, and as the pieces remained stable, and crizzling disappeared, the new glass was considered a success for both George Ravenscroft and the English glassmakers. The Bohemians had also been experimenting with potash as well as lead and both new glasses were stronger and more durable than the fragile soda glass of *cristallo*. In addition, the fashion was moving towards cut and wheel-engraved styles, suitable for lead glass but almost impossible to use on soda glass, which lost its basic quality of ductile flexibility when it was blown as thick as was necessary for any but the lightest wheel engraving. Within twenty or thirty years, exports of Venetian drinking glasses in any real quantity had practically ceased.

Nonetheless, Murano was hardly abandoned and continued to make many other useful objects and various kinds of novelties. Chandeliers were a new Venetian idea, reputedly first made at the workshops of G. Brioti, who had a furnace at Murano and a workshop in Venice as well. A contemporary comment by Carlo Gossi refers to Brioti's 'magnificent clustered (lights) for illuminating the rooms of great lords, the theatres and even the streets on festive and joyous occasions'. Outdoors, the towering confections of pastel-tinted glass and swags of flowers must have looked unbelievably impressive; many have twisted columns to conceal the framework, flowerheads by the hundreds, beaded chains, leaves and petals wired to shimmer in the warm currents of air created by the burning candles.

The Venetians were always ready to adapt and modify: they eventually returned to the classical designs which were being popularized in England and the Low Countries. They made plain dishes in milk-white *lattimo* to imitate porcelain, with restrained landscapes and scenes in russet and polychrome tones. Simple decanters and candlesticks were cut in the Bohemian manner and engraved with sprig designs and painted with pastoral scenes. They also continued to make huge quantities of beads and mosaics, jewellery, and decorative objects.

Above
Beakers with painted scenes of the birth of Christ. 18th century; ht 5in (12.6cm). Realistic painting was never a strong point of Venetian glassware. These scenes are more professional than earlier examples.

Below
Mule in clear glass with blue glass decorations. 17th–18th century; ht 4⅛in (10.4cm). Glassworkers have always seemed fond of animal shapes. All are grotesque and amusing, and may have been given to children of the gaffer.

Above and top
Two goblets of the late 17th century. Ht of top goblet 10¼in (26cm).
Decorations became complicated and over-fragile as the Venetians and their related *façon de Venise* fellow workers tried to compete with the new heavier glass of England and Bohemia. Goblets became so elaborate that they were often impossible to hold, even for a ceremonial drink.

Right
Vase of opaque green glass in the form of a shell. 17th century; ht 8½in (21.5cm).
An elegant shape, very Oriental. The mould-blown vase is delicate but reasonably sturdy – although the handles seem a little stiff.

Massive centrepieces of fountains and birds were matched only by elaborate tabletop settings with arches, parterres, garden urns and benches, etc, all laid out with architectural model-type exactitude. Glasspainting had never lost its appeal, and it was revived as the natural decoration for plain simple shapes. Most of the paints were enamel but some oil paints were used. Large presentation dishes had first been made during the Renaissance. They were probably kept for ceremonial occasions as the oil would have quickly washed off.

Religious groups of figures were also made, some for use at home, others obviously for use in a church or in a nativity scene for public display.

Silver patterns were copied for candlesticks and tableware, cut with overlay and engraved throughout in the traditional Bohemian manner. Many of the workshops went on making traditional goblets and plates, particularly the armorial designs which had once been so sought after in the sixteenth century and which now were copied and changed slightly for the new nobility who liked the idea of a crest even if they had no real coat of arms.

Clear *tazze* and tall covered goblets of classic simplicity were still showpieces for craftsmen who wanted to continue practising their difficult art.

Special Venetian Techniques

A particular form of glassmaking craftsmanship, as extraordinary as it was difficult, was 'knitted' glass, usually called reticulated glass.

In essence it is very similar to the openwork patterns made in milk or *lattimo* glass which was pulled into spiral lace columns within the stems, or spun flat into the bowls of cups and goblets. However, reticulated glass is almost always composed of clear threads, knitted together. It was used to form the rigging of ships in miniature models and can be seen to perfection in the body of a vase, and cover, decorated

blow-pipe; the rods of clear glass are softened and fused to an already finished base. The rods are then drawn into threads and woven around a mould until the desired shape is covered with the openwork threads. Finally the rods are clipped off and the ends bent back to form the scalloped rim; the whole is left to cool upside down until the glass has hardened and the mould can be slipped out. The cover is made in the same way: the finial is suspended above the lamp, the rods are attached, woven around a greased mould and finally clipped off and bent up to form the scallops. The process resembles the making of spun sugar, and the finished article is rather like that sticky, sweet confection.

Mirrors

Mirrors were an important part of Venetian manufacturing and there are records of looking glasses being made in the sixteenth and seventeenth centuries, although there are no surviving pieces that we know of at present.

By the eighteenth century, Venetian mirrors, although very expensive, were highly regarded by the public because they were blown instead of being cast and ground flat as the

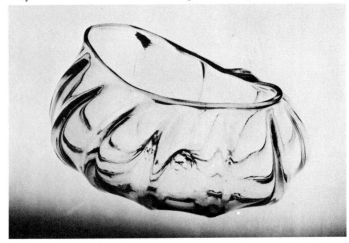

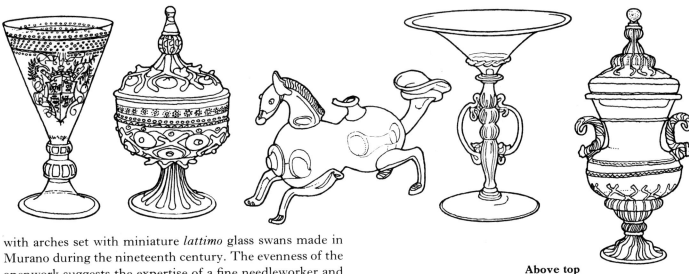

with arches set with miniature *lattimo* glass swans made in Murano during the nineteenth century. The evenness of the openwork suggests the expertise of a fine needleworker and the source word in Italian (*reticello*) is the term for network, although today *reticello* itself is taken to mean clear glass with a decorative mesh of white opaque threads in various patterns beneath the surface or within a column.

Reticulated glass is made at the lamp rather than with the

Above
Some typical Venetian details which are still being copied and adapted by glasshouses all over the world.

Above top
Bowl of ribbed glass. Late 17th century; length 4½in (11.5cm). Swirled ribbing shows off the improved *cristallo* glass which by this period was clear of almost all impurities.

Left

Chandelier. Late 18th century; ht 48in (121.9cm).
A much smaller version than the relatively restrained chandelier on the far left, this is relatively restrained and was perfectly suitable for comfortable family homes of the growing middle class.

Above

Chandelier with festoons and bubbles in multi-coloured glass. 18th century; ht 70⅞in (180cm).
Palazzos had large, elaborately decorated reception rooms, the only appropriate settings for the equally elaborate chandeliers which need at least 14ft (4.3m) ceilings to look their best.

Above right

Bowl with gold foil centre. 19th century; diam 4⅝in (11.8cm).

Right

Opaque white sprinkler with metal top, probably for the Middle Eastern market. 18th century; ht 10⅞in (27.5cm).
The painted design was intended to attract a new market, as Western buyers seemed to prefer the more fashionable Bohemian and English glassware.

French and Spanish mirrors were. The thin glass was silvered and then set into metal or wooden frames. Perhaps because large pieces were difficult to obtain with the blown method, the Venetians developed a style of framing their looking glasses with smaller cut pieces of mirror arranged in whatever way pleased the customer. These surrounds usually covered the wood frame completely and often had pieces of blue glass interspersed with the clear ones. Many pieces were engraved and the edges cut into notches so the whole effect was one of lightness and glitter. Candleholders attached to the sides reflected back the light and added to the festive appearance. The same principle was applied to furniture, often inlaid with pieces of blue or mirrored glass painted with classical scenes or left alone to appear like lapis lazuli and rock crystal. A set was apparently made for the then Sultan of Turkey in 1777, but there is no record of what happened to it.

Portrait Millefiori

These special effects used in various kinds of paperweights and other *millefiori* articles were first made in Roman times – there were then quite distinctive mosaic patterns made as eyes, faces and animal shapes, but in general the smaller rods were crudely made and simple in outline. During the mania for paperweights which swept France and Italy during the mid-nineteenth century, there were two or three Muranese factories which specialised in making unbelievably subtle and complex portrait rods with up to four different shades of flesh tones to mould the face, and correspondingly ornate details of costume surrounding the head. The finished rods, drawn out to *millefiori* size, were used in weights and in bracelets, the bases of bottles, and knobs for cabinets, doors and even the tops of walking sticks.

Miniature Mosaic

This form of mosaic had been popular in Italy ever since the first Roman floors and frescoes, but the nineteenth century as usual added technological ingenuity to a traditional idea and with the revival of classical and archaeological patterns in the early part of the century, the renewal of glass mosaic was only a matter of time. The original pieces were made out of chips of precious stones, lapis, turquoise and marbles of various kinds, quartz, agates and so on. These were still used for the finest furniture inlays, but tiny chips,

often knocked off in the course of making the larger pieces, could be used for miniature mosaic. This was particularly suitable for the classical jewellery which was suddenly the latest fashion. Such small chips were distressingly irregular, and the art of glass *tessera* was revived in miniature to adorn the necks and wrists and ears of women dressed in up-to-the-minute styles. The tiny glass squares were set in roundels or oblongs, designed to make up classical motifs: Greek vases and masks, Roman swags and so forth. Florentine and chased gold mounts were used to great effect and the scope of the miniaturists was limited only by their tiring eyesight.

Towards the end of the century, floral bouquets, just like the patterns on Berlin needlework, had replaced the classical themes and a long necklace of twenty roundels might have twenty different bouquets. The most common shapes were various sized ovals and roundels, especially for single flowers and portraits. Oblongs were usually retained for the classical scenes still occasionally made. Such pictures were also inlaid in furniture, mounted on silver cups, around the base of tiny ornaments such as thimbles, perfume bottles and so on. Souvenir ornaments were also popular, with scenes from the Borghese Gardens or framed classical statues.

The Nineteenth and Twentieth Centuries

For most glass collectors, the period from the late eighteenth century to the early twentieth century is a fairly unhappy era in Venice. Imagination seems to have drained away following years of originality and taste. Of course, there were beautiful things produced during that time, but in general the reputation of Venice suffered enormously, and the craftsmen were reduced to making endless copies of banal novelties for souvenir shops. The best pieces are perhaps small and inventive 'toys': little scent bottles, inlaid with *millefiori* canes or striped with *lattimo* designs, cosmetic jars and perfume bottles, carved rosaries and strings of beads in every conceivable colour and pattern. Simulated pearls had always been one of the chief Venetian glories, and may well have seemed the major economic one. They were particularly pearl-like and glowing, and with a soft sheen that couldn't be matched elsewhere. Happily for Murano, the fashion for ropes of pearls remained the sign of any up-to-date woman, and dresses were decorated with seed pearls, lit up with sequins, embroidered with paste jewels and fringed with crystal. The passion for needlework worked at home was responsible for pillows embroidered with glass beads, slippers marked with beaded and jewelled monograms, and more fringes on lampshades and curtains. The better kinds of tableware still to be found included epergnes with hanging baskets for fruit and sweetmeats, four-tiered cake stands, glass fruit and animals to set in groups on a tabletop.

A notable aspect of Venetian glass is that many families have been connected with glass and glassmaking for generations. Vincenzo Zanetti, writing from *c* 1850 to the 1880s, described his family's century-long association with the craft, and how it encouraged the revival of pride and craftsmanship in the best Venetian tradition. A number of Muranese factories turned out magnificent copies of sixteenth- and

Above
Mirror with clear and blue glass frame, cut and engraved. 18th century; ht 47¼in (120cm). During the 18th century mirrors used in the home became very popular.

Right
Teapot of opaque white glass painted in a crude floral design. 18th century; ht 5¼in (13.4cm). As a complete contrast to the large chandelier, teapots were made for ordinary families to take home as souvenirs.

Right
Goblet of *latticino* glass, the stem a moulded lionhead knop. Late 19th century; ht 7¾in (19.7cm).
At the end of the 19th century, interest in antiquities gave an added impetus to a revival of Venetian glassmaking, and many Murano houses copied old bowls from the Christian era (but usually got the figures and inscriptions wrong). At the same time, they adapted the older Venetian designs to simpler, more modern shapes.

Right
Deep amethyst sculpture in
lead glass, set on a slate cube.
Salviati; c 1960; ht 14in
(35.5cm).

Below
Sculpture 'Cartoccio', mould
cast in clear lead glass.
Designed by A. Barovier, made
by Barovier and Toso; 1972;
ht 6⅞in (17.4cm).
These two modern pieces show
the way Venice is adapting to
contemporary ideas while
renewing some of the old
traditions. The amethyst
sculpture recalls the deep
jewel colours of 15th-century
goblets; the ripples and
bubbles of 'Cartoccio' have
a strong affinity with the
swirled bowl on page 77.

Above
Two goblets from a suite of
tableware, designed by Salviati
and manufactured c 1955. Ht of
tall goblet 7in (17.6cm).
The mass-production necessary
to run an economically viable
glasshouse in the 20th century
has meant that even the hand-
blown glasses still being made
in Venice by one of the leading
factories must make their
effects with more easily blown
patterns.

Right
Wine glass with lampworked
swan as stem. c 1965; ht 5in
(12.6cm). One of the better
'souvenirs' made in Murano.

seventeenth-century glass (see the pair of decanters illustrated on page 72).

The modern factories which have contributed so much to
the renewal of Venetian glass were beginning to make themselves known in the 1920s and 1930s. Paolo Venini (1895–
1959) began by making the old traditional glass, but in 1926
he started employing new designers and experimenting with
unusual finishes and techniques. Today Venini & Co. is still
in the forefront of commercial glasshouses. A design by
Laura Santillana, Paolo's granddaughter, was shown at the
1979 exhibition organized by the Corning Museum.

Other leading factories are Salviati & Co., founded by
Antonio Salviati in c 1859, and Barovier & Toso, established
in 1936 by descendants of two ancient Murano glassmaking
families. Both combine the best Muranese traditions with
modern commercial techniques. They experiment constantly, employing young designers, and working with
porcelain and pottery companies to produce integrated or
matching products for the table; and are willing to attempt
anything from cut glass taps to delicate chandeliers.

The new Murano glass has become an integral and vital
part of the concept of interior art and design, a notable
achievement that is recognized throughout the West.

Spain and Portugal

There are no real traces of a native glass industry in Spain and Portugal until around 100 BC when the Roman armies and trading ships brought their expertise to the Iberian peninsula.

There were probably imported artefacts from the newly prosperous workshops of Syria and Alexandria as well as the first northern products from Gaul and the Rhineland. As the Romans established military encampments and civilian settlements, glassmaking would also have been needed in order to provide, at the very least, repairs and replacements, and then gradually more and more wares for the increasing home demand.

The glass found in Iberia cannot normally be distinguished from other Roman provincial wares, except by the type of alkali, the necessary flux in the batch of ingredients. Some sort of soda or potash is always required to help the sand to melt, and it can be obtained from a number of sources. Throughout the Mediterranean region, workers collected special plants which grow in the salt marshes, dried them in the sun and then burnt them. The ashes contained a high proportion of a carbonate of soda, and a smaller proportion of lime. As the glass industry prospered, it was obvious that the plants of the Spanish salt marshes were particularly rich in the required ingredients, and freer from impurities than many other varieties. The ash has been known since Roman times as *barilla*.

Early Developments

During the centuries of Roman rule Hispano-Roman glass was made in all the usual forms: moulded bottles, simple drinking cups, plates and mosaics, bowls and ointment jars, grave furnishings, and containers of all kinds. The colours were the normal range of this era: various shades of green, which could be cleared by using manganese in minute quantities, cobalt blue, topaz and browns made with antimony, and the amethysts and purples that come from the addition of larger quantities of manganese.

As the Empire fell apart, the Visigoths moved down the peninsula and gradually displaced the Roman influence. From the fifth to the eighth centuries, the Visigoths remained in control of most of Spain, but in spite of the popular belief that all culture ended when the Romans left, glassmaking certainly continued, albeit at a lower level of expertise. The earliest written document about local glassmaking dates from this period, when the then Bishop of Seville, St Isidore, wrote in detail about manufacturing methods in Spain, Italy and Gaul. He described quite accurately the various kinds of ingredients, the method of melting batches to obtain liquid 'metal', the craft of blowing and shaping, and even the process necessary to clear the impurities in the ingredients in order to provide a colourless transparent glass.

There are very few pieces which can accurately be dated to this period, except for a few simpler glasses, an early Christian paten with a moulded fish, a few examples of cloisonné jewellery, with cut pieces of coloured glass set in metal, sometimes alone, but more often with precious stones.

The Moors were the next invaders, and they brought with them the finest examples of craftsmanship for their reigning caliphs, in the form of pottery, mosaics, lustreware, velvets and silks – all the luxuries that the courts of the East made

Left
Decanters. Spain; c 1820; ht 12¼in (31cm).
The long and narrow necks are in the Moorish tradition, though the delicate gilding shows Bohemian and Venetian influences.

Above
Flask with threaded ornamentation. Almeria, Spain; 16th century; ht 6⅝in (16.7cm).

Below
Three elaborate Iberian shapes showing a very strong Middle Eastern influence.

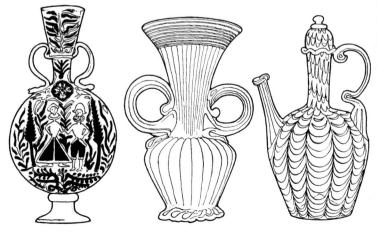

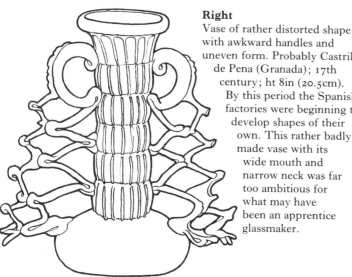

Below

Spanish glass of the 16th to 18th centuries delightfully showing off the craftsman's firm belief that anything is possible. Glasses like this one must have given great pleasure to the glassblowers as well as their customers.

Above

Vase with two handles in clear glass, enamelled with figures and foliage. Barcelona; c 1590; ht 9¼in (23.5cm). Enamelling at Barcelona often resembles Venetian painting of the same period.

Right

Vase of rather distorted shape with awkward handles and uneven form. Probably Castril de Pena (Granada); 17th century; ht 8in (20.5cm).

By this period the Spanish factories were beginning to develop shapes of their own. This rather badly made vase with its wide mouth and narrow neck was far too ambitious for what may have been an apprentice glassmaker.

famous – and, of course, glass and glassmakers. Certainly by the thirteenth century there was much documentary evidence mentioning the glassmakers of Almeria and Malaga, Murcia and the whole of the Castilian region.

Spanish *barilla* became an important export; Venice took huge quantities from the port of Alicante to feed its hungry furnaces on the island of Murano. When rival manufacturers tried to lure Venetian craftsmen to settle in their cities and train native blowers, they often specified that the new masters would be supplied with the finest ingredients for their craft, including boatloads of *barilla*.

The Eastern influence seems to have pervaded Spain so completely that it persisted throughout the following centuries. Even the winged Venetian handles were grafted on to basically Moresque shapes, and the use of Syrian threading was complemented with overall enamel and gilt decoration on flat areas. Even after the Christian armies defeated the Moors in the eleventh century and re-established Western control over Spain, *vidre de Damas*, or glass in the style of Damascus, retained its reputation and desirability, and was eagerly bought and carefully preserved by members of the wealthy aristocracy.

In the thirteenth century, many Islamic glass craftsmen settled in the Iberian peninsula, especially in Almeida (Portugal) and Barcelona. In 1324 the authorities closed down the glasshouses in Barcelona because of the risk of fire. But towards the end of the fifteenth century, glassmaking started there again.

At that time Barcelona and Cataluna were the centres of the native glassmaking industry. Their products were well known throughout Iberia and even highly regarded in Italy itself, being held equal to the wares of Venice by a number of writers and travellers. Many of the typical Spanish shapes, like the *porró* and *cántir*, had already evolved from Middle Eastern originals, and there were decanters, water sprinklers and jars of all kinds, covered dishes and vases, salt dishes and bottles, goblets and cruets. Unfortunately there are very few whole pieces left, since life in Spain during the entire period was a series of wars and sieges, temporary truces and recurring pitched battles.

It was not until the sixteenth century that the peninsula became relatively quiet, and then, as if they had been waiting for the chance to develop, the craftsmen of the Catalan region in particular took up the challenge, and for the next few hundred years produced glass that was of the finest quality and design.

The Sixteenth and Seventeenth Centuries

In 1503, a lady-in-waiting to Queen Isabel wrote a remarkably detailed inventory of some of the Catalan glassware given to the queen by King Ferdinand. Lady Violante de Albion obviously loved the pieces she described so vividly; they were made of many colours, especially blues and purples, enamelled in different styles, gilded and flecked with gilt, ornamented with threadings of opaque white, yellow, and green, wrought into fantastic shapes of animals and birds, inscribed with mottoes and proverbs, painted with coats of arms, all-over patterns and landscapes. There were glasses and goblets, vases, bowls, wine jars, candlesticks,

Right
Cántir of greyish glass.
Cataluña; 18th century; ht
10⅜in (26.4cm).
By the mid-18th century a
number of unique Spanish
forms had developed.
This *cántir*, with its carrying
handle rather impractically
topped with a bird, its thin
drinking spout, pincered
prunts, *lattimo* stripes and
embedded canes of *millefiori*,
would seem to add up to a
truly horrific pastiche. In fact
the *cántir* is charming, with a
sense of whimsy and fun all too
absent from the northern
tradition of glass.

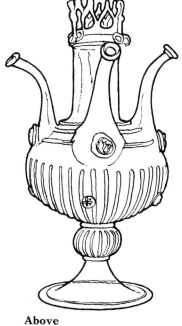

Above
Almorratxa. Barcelona; late
16th century; ht 10¼in (26cm).

86

Left
Dish of shaped form, moulded, wheel cut and gilded. La Granja; late 18th century; ht 6⅝in (16.8cm).

Below
Bottle in opaque white with red and blue striations, winged handles (one broken). 18th century; ht 5¼in (13.3cm). An echo of *façon de Venise*.

plates, jugs, trays and salts, and a four-spouted jar which was clearly a rose-water sprinkler, an *almorratxa*, adapted from the East.

The court continued to support the glass industry, and the craftsmen of Barcelona were highly regarded as fine workers and expert blowers, although they were primarily working in the Venetian fashion, then at the height of its reputation. Venetian originals were imported into Spain and must have been useful models, but the local product was up to the competition; Philip II and his wife owned both Venetian and Barcelonian glasses in almost equal quantity. The only time the annual glass fair was cancelled was in 1599, during the mourning period after Philip's death.

Venice held sway as the major source of design, but some characteristically Spanish and Oriental elements were retained. The Syrian love of all-over enamel decoration was an important aspect of Catalan glass, long after the Venetians had lost interest in painted wares. Such patterns often covered the entire surface, so that the clear glass underneath was almost hidden. Green, gold and white are the dominating colours, the patterns are foliage and flowers, scrolls and initials, scenes and figures, trees and birds. Frosted glasses were also made, mostly in Venetian styles. Strangely enough, although Spanish glass is often associated with over-decorated and flamboyant shapes, most of the glassware was simpler and more direct than the Venetian models. There are no winged stems, or fantasies of piled-up, spun glass decoration. Stems are usually simple hollow cones or inverted balusters. The Syrian tradition still had an effect – compare the flaring rim of the Catalan goblets with the Syrian beakers of the sixth century. The excessively thin Muranese glass was replaced by sturdier walls and simpler details, and by a more comfortable 'feel'.

There were factories outside Barcelona. Some were in the province itself, some in Tarragona, Gerona, Lerida and the Rousillon district. The guilds were generally quite powerful, although sometimes, as in Valencia, a local industry prospered apparently without any official organization. Alicante continued to supply *barilla* to the rest of the European glass factories, and local furnaces made ordinary domestic and medical ware in fairly thick, crude but satisfactory glass.

The Eighteenth Century

During the eighteenth century, the great Catalan tradition began to die away and the shapes became more and more pedestrian. Even the glass itself seems to have been less well produced, with a greyish, uneven tone. Spanish forms were emphasized: the *cántir* or *cántarro*, a closed jug with a ring handle and two spouts, one for filling the jug and one for pouring the wine into the drinker's mouth; the *porró*, which has the same purpose as the *cántir* but has a long open neck and one attenuated spout; the *almorratxa* or rose-water sprinkler; and the *botijo*, a water-jug with a round body, a short spout and overhead loop handle.

The Catalan glassmaker, Ventura Sit (*d* 1755) left Cataluna sometime during the 1720s, and built a glass furnace near San Ildefonso, near the palace of La Granja, south-west of Segovia. He specialised in making large panes of plate glass for windows and mirrors, and gradually his

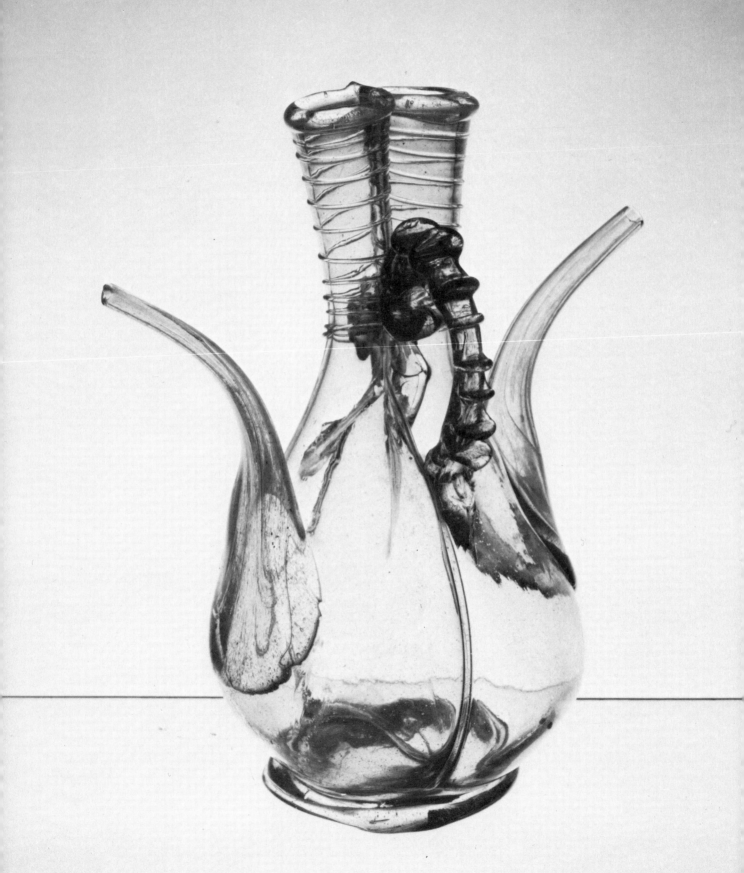

Left
Double cruet in green glass
with double spout, and trailed
decoration; winged handle.
18th century; ht 6⅞in (17.4cm).
Venetian and Roman
influences were still affecting
new pieces with styling more
appropriate to a much earlier
period.

Right
Tumbler in opaque white glass
enamelled in blue green.
Probably La Granja; mid-18th
century; ht 3¾in (8.2cm).
Small, delicate and fresh-
looking with the charm of
French glass of this period.

technique and ability impressed the royal family so much
that he was given a site on crown property. The mirrors were,
by all contemporary accounts, the finest and largest produced in any Spanish glassworks. Molten glass was poured
into brass frames, which moved slowly into an annealing
oven before grinding and polishing. Larger frames gradually
came into use, and a mirror found in the 1820s was so large
that it could reflect the entire shape of a man on horseback.
Other ingenious devices ensured that the grinding and
polishing could be carried out mechanically, before quick-
silvering took place to make the mirror backs.

La Granja's reputation for mirrors was not quite matched
by their other products, although their glassmakers produced
good quality crystal and chandeliers, cut and gilded in the
French and English fashions which had superseded the old
Venetian forms. They made tumblers and decanters, condiment sets, chandeliers and lamps. By the mid-eighteenth
century the glass factory had separated from the La Granja
mirror workshop, and was known as Réal Fábrica de
Cristales. Sigismund Brun from Hanover worked almost all
his life there, from 1768 until after 1791. It was he who
probably perfected the technique for firing gilt. Surviving
pieces are still bright and unworn, often adding lustre and
charm to engraved and cut decoration. Blue and white
glasses were also made, decorated with flowers and scrolls in
the neoclassic design in many coloured enamels.

Covered jars with two handles and a globular base were a
distinctive design, and at their best when decorated freely
with multi-coloured garden flowers.

Economic difficulties beset the factory which had always
been subsidized by royal patronage, and when in the 1800s
the Irish-English fashion of high quality, deep-cut lead glass
was all the rage, the less-than-perfect Spanish glass lost its
popularity. When the king withdrew his patronage in 1809,
the factory was sold to a private company and the last remaining period of Spanish craftsmanship was over.

Left
Decanter of plain glass,
beautifully engraved and gilded
in a floral spray. Probably La
Granja; late 18th century;
ht 12¼in (31cm).
Simple shape, simple engraving
– the result is perfect, proving
that at its best La Granja
produced beautiful elegant
glassware.

Germany and Bohemia

The term 'German' with reference to glassmaking covers all German-speaking countries, including Austria, Bohemia and Silesia. So large an area naturally gives rise to variations in the history of glassmaking within different regions.

In the second and third centuries Roman glass was imported in considerable quantity into German lands, shipped along the Rhine, Danube and, if expedient, the French rivers of the Rhône and Meuse. The Rhinelands probably imported their glass directly from Rome or the Roman glasshouses of Cologne and Aix-la-Chapelle (Aachen); Bohemia and eastern Slovakia may have been supplied by Aquiliea.

During the decline of the Roman Empire, glassmaking in the Rhineland areas managed to survive under the auspices of Syrian craftsmen. The best of these migrated to Altare in the ninth century and glassmaking became a localized craft. Small glasshouses began to settle in the forest areas of Germany and they produced *Waldglas* (forest glass), a thick bluish-green glass with many impurities, bubbles and striations, made from a potash derived from the ashes of beechwood. The first shapes to be mould blown were plain, ovoid, handleless palm cups. Later, around the fourteenth century, the Syrian-inspired decoration of applied prunts was exploited in the form of the *Nuppenbecher* (prunted beaker) with its variations of the *Igel* (hedgehog) with pointed prunts, and the *Krautstrunk* (cabbage stalk). A peculiarly Bohemian adaptation is a tall flute-shaped glass with almost the entire surface covered with applied raised dots.

From the *Nuppenbecher* evolved the most important of Rhenish vessel forms, the *Römer*, which has survived to this day. The *Römer* is a drinking glass of generous proportions with a large ovoid bowl, a hollow stem with applied prunts and, traditionally, though not in the earliest stage of development, a spun foot produced by winding glass threads about a wooden cone. Later a hollow-blown foot appeared on some examples. The sixteenth and seventeenth centuries saw a great flowering of the *Römer*, particularly in the Netherlands, and the traditional green tint of the glass was deliberately retained.

Another style which developed during the same period as the *Römer* was the *Kuttrolf* or *Angster*. This slow-pouring vessel, descended from the Syrian sprinkler, was in the shape of a bulbous flask with a long, inclined neck consisting of several intertwined tubes.

Waldglas survived for a long period, into the seventeenth century. Medicinal and chemical glasses and mortars for domestic and pharmaceutical use continued to be made in the thick green glass, but the glass was blown thinner for drinking vessels, which became increasingly larger in capacity. The *Maigelein*, a low drinking cup derived from the earlier palm cup, developed a high kick in the base by the fifteenth century and was found in a variety of mould-blown patterns. During the sixteenth century a number of different glass shapes were developed: the tall narrow *Stangenglas* on a hollow foot, the *Humpen*, with a high kick and applied foot ring, and the tankard. The tall *Passglas* (a type of *Stangenglas*) had horizontal rings which indicated the different levels to which each man had to drink as the glass was passed round the table. A variation of the *Passglas*, popularly termed the *Bandwurmglas* (tapeworm glass), shows a modification of the applied rings in the form of a rising spiral trailed around the entire surface of the vessel.

Stained Glass

The term 'stained glass' covers all coloured glass, usually referring to windows which may be coloured in the pot, stained on the surface, or painted and fired. The thirteenth and fourteenth centuries were the great period of European stained glass, although plain window glass was also produced in great quantities. The earliest church windows were influenced by Byzantine mosaics, made of glass *tesserae*.

The windows in Augsburg Cathedral (c 1065), representing single monumental figures of the prophets, are considered to be among the earliest German stained glass. The expanding influence of the Church resulted in a continuing growth of monastic life with established monasteries representing the cultural and erudite centres of the surrounding community. Schools of glasspainters sprang up in these areas, in Cologne, and particularly near Lake Constance, where the Dominicans had founded a large monastery. Many of the friars were trained glasspainters, and since the monasteries had close links with foreign establishments and there was a lively exchange among clerics and members of the brotherhood, the style and design of stained glass must be traced to foreign, predominantly French, inspiration. These influences are modified by absorption of local characteristics and by adaptation of designs from known illuminated manuscripts – a fundamental source of inspiration in stained glass painting. Such prolific interchange of ideas and journeying to and fro affected glassmakers and glasspainters alike. The Paderborn church records cite two fifteenth-century glasspainters, the Dominican friars Fra Bartolomeo di Pietro of Perugia and Jakob Greisinger from Ulm, who left Germany to found a school of glasspainters in Bologna. Paderborn was known in the eleventh century because a monk there, Theophilus of Helmershausen, wrote his *Diversarum Artium Schedulae*, one of the earliest descriptions of, and recipes for, making and staining glass.

In Bohemia, stained window glass was certainly produced from the thirteenth century onwards, and possibly earlier. Some of the most interesting stained glass windows are at Kolin, near Prague, in the church of St Bartholomew. They

Right
Beaker. Frankish; 6th century; ht 6½in (16.4cm).
Northern and European influences were often combined in the same piece. This beaker, in olive green, has a conical foot and slightly flared lip. The body is decorated with trailed and marvered threads.

Left

Left, small tumbler decorated with flowers and a baroque building. *Centre*, flask with copper top, the figure of a man, and decorated borders. *Right*, marriage glass with inscription. All mid-18th century; ht of small tumbler 7in (17.7cm).
Mid-European decoration in bright enamelled colours was typical of simpler German tableware in all the Bohemian countries and in 18th-century America; compare with Bride's Bottle on page 269. Figures, inscriptions and, to a lesser extent, country scenes were popular. The glass is usually of only middling quality with many seeds and striations.

Page 92

Left, beaker with blown and moulded bosses and a high kick base. *Right*, *Humpen* with a heavier, slightly irregular shape; the surface has been crackled in imitation of Venetian ice glass. Both German; 17th century; ht of *Humpen* $10\frac{1}{4}$in (26cm).
As Bohemia developed, Venetian influence competed with the sturdier forest tradition. Both these glasses are representative of this trend.

Page 93

Goblet and cover with elaborate engraving; the stem shows the high relief *Hochschnitt* quite clearly. Silesia; *c* 1730; ht 11in (28cm). Elaborate wheel engraving could be used in the heavier potash-lime glass when the soda glass, beloved of Venetian makers, proved too thin.

date from the last quarter of the fourteenth century and show the influence of earlier miniature painting from illuminated manuscripts. Bohemia and Silesia favoured the Premonstratensian and Cistercian Orders, far more restricted and severe than the Dominican Brotherhood. Nevertheless, the monasteries with friars from France and Flanders concentrated not only on agricultural labours but also on arts and crafts, with small workshops producing church windows and also domestic and ritual vessels. Further glassmaking centres are recorded at Kosice (Kaschau) in eastern Slovakia, and at Kolosvar (Klausenburg) in Transylvania at the Benedictine monastery. Particularly remarkable is the application of Byzantine-inspired mosaic work on a grand scale, which is to be seen at St Vitus's Cathedral of the castle at Prague.

Above
Stained glass roundel. 15th century.
Early panels of German stained glass show strong lead shapes which usually outline the main figure. Glass pieces were still fairly small, and thinner leading was used to support large areas.

Right

Goblet with horizontally ribbed bowl. Hall, Austria; c 1575; ht 11¼in (28.5cm).

Below

Goblet, *façon de Venise*, enamelled. Probably Liège; c 1600; ht 6¼in (15.8cm). Decorated Venetian glass was the predominant influence on hundreds of German glass-houses. The Hall goblet is much simpler, and almost 20th-century in its strong outline and shape.

This representation of the Day of Judgement on a gigantic scale – 102 yards (85 metres) square – was ordered in 1370 by the Emperor Charles IV for the southern portal, and was executed by Venetian artisans.

The seventeenth century brought in the baroque style. Gilt statues in carved robes with voluminous folds, intricate and graceful ironwork and lavishly painted stucco ceilings and walls expressed a new splendour which overshadowed the noble and austere beauty of the stained glass window. Stained and painted glass remained fashionable, though no longer as windows, but in the form of stained glass panels and panes, to be inserted into a plain glass window or to be hung against the window for colourful effect. Later the glass picture came into being with some of the finest work emerging from the Augsburg school. The frequently religious themes remained with the glass picture into the eighteenth and nineteenth centuries, when its status changed from that of genre painting to functional representation of the icon, particularly in the eastern Slovak regions. Glasspainting is a field of many aspects with widely differing styles and quality, equally embracing sophisticated grandeur and rustic folk art.

Engraving and Cutting

During the late fifteenth and early sixteenth centuries, fuel costs in Germany rose sharply due to the expansion of the native mining industry, in which wood fuel was used in smelting. Many of the small scattered glasshouses moved east to Bohemia and Silesia where wood was in plentiful supply. As in France, the large landowners and the nobility did not hesitate to seize any chance of a profitable business venture. Glassmakers were induced to establish their glass-houses on feudal forest land, with promises and the granting of a variety of privileges. By the early sixteenth century, about forty established glassworks existed in Bohemia alone. At this time the Venetian influence was prevalent, Venice having started exporting glass to German lands as far back as the thirteenth century and having established 'glass routes' in the fifteenth and sixteenth centuries. Vienna, Cologne and Dessau had established Italian-initiated glass-houses, and Saxony, Bohemia and Silesia made attempts at reproducing *latticino* glass, though neither very elegantly nor successfully. The seventeenth-century Venetian winged glasses were ably imitated and called *Schlangenpokals* and *Flügelgläser*. They were largely produced in Italian-established glasshouses at Liège, Altare, Antwerp, etc, and exported to Germany.

The most interesting results in Venetian-inspired diamond engraving were produced at the glasshouse in Hall, in the Tyrol (established 1534), during the last quarter of the sixteenth century. These glasses, particularly when in the form of large covered goblets with hollow-blown baluster stems, show engraved decoration in the hatched Venetian style which has a great affinity with the vessels produced at the same period in Jacopo Verzelini's Crutched Friars Glass-house, and attributed to the hand of Anthony de Lysle. It seems that a link may have existed between Hall and the Verzelini glasshouse.

Diamond engraving had proved one of the most suitable forms of decoration which could be applied to the thin and

Far left and left
Green, covered goblet in
cylinder shape, 1650s; bulbous
covered goblet in clear glass,
c 1580. Both engraved in
diamond point. Both Austrian;
ht of green goblet 9in (22.9cm).
Similar presentation pieces
were made in many *façon de
Venise* houses.

Above
Römer of green glass, heavily
prunted on the stem with
gadrooned foot rim. *c* 1620;
ht 7⅞in (20cm).
By the 17th century many
German shapes were
developing. This *Römer* shows
a return to the northern style of
Waldglas, away from the fragile
Venetian influence. The prunts
and sturdy shape still appear.

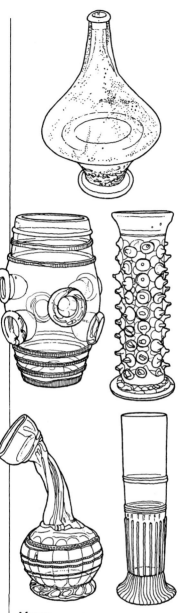

Above

Most 16th-century glassworkers
were quite international. Many
common decorative motifs were
used in Germany and
throughout the world: simple
blown bottles, milled rings,
thick-set prunts, twisted
Persian-necked bottles, and
delicate lines of *latticino*.

Right

Puzzle glass. *c* 1650; ht 9½in
(24.1cm).
These syphon glasses were
Venetian in origin, but
particularly popular in
Germany for convivial
drinking parties.

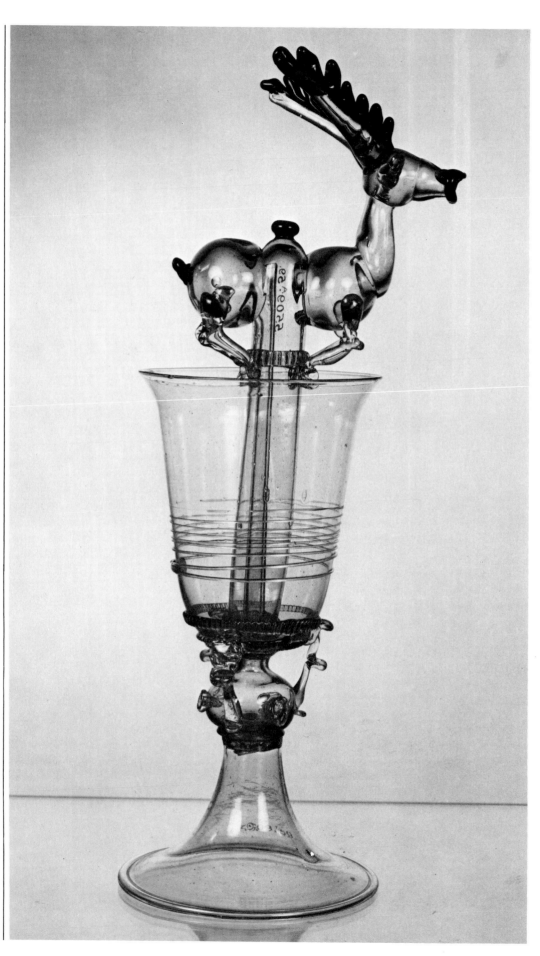

Left
Green glass *Krautstrunk* decorated with strawberry prunts and milled ring. 17th century; ht 5⅞in (15cm). The elaborately elegant and decorative fantasy piece, and this solid shape, illustrate the different influences at work.

Above
Rock crystal nef with elaborate figures and engraving. 16th century; ht 7½in (19cm). Carved and engraved pieces in rock crystal were the height of fashion in the late 16th century.

brittle Venetian *cristallo*. However, at the beginning of the seventeenth century, Caspar Lehman (1570–1622), Royal Lapidary to Emperor Rudolf II at Prague, began to apply his lapidary art – the art of wheel engraving – to the medium of glass. The court of Rudolf II was one of the most glittering in Europe, and the art-loving monarch invited the finest artists to contribute to this splendour with their creation of precious and ingenious works of art and artefacts. At this period, Bohemian rock crystal carvings in the Italian Renaissance style, set with precious jewels, enamelled and mounted in gold, were at the height of fashion. Mining however was costly, and the mineral not inexhaustible. Glass seemed a perfect substitute, and with Lehman's accomplished lapidary techniques, Bohemia stood at the threshold of becoming the world leader in glass cutting and engraving. *Cristallo* was too thin to be carved in the manner of rock crystal, and the robust potash-lime glass was not developed successfully until about 1670. However, from the very few pieces by or attributed to Lehman, it seems clear that his early attempts were made on flat panels of glass with shallow, matt cutting and the occasional use of the diamond point, and that his work was extremely competent. The Perseus and Andromeda panel is one of a number attributed to his hand; the only signed piece, the Armorial Beaker dated 1605, shows a similar broad baroque treatment of the figures.

Lehman obtained a monopoly for glass engraving in 1609, and upon his death this passed to a talented pupil, Georg

Schwanhardt (1601–67). Schwanhardt's contribution to the art lay in extending the technique by polishing parts of the engraved design, resulting in a far more lively and brilliant pictorial representation than had been seen hitherto. He was also the first to use a polished diminishing lens on the reverse side of a glass object. The hazards of the Thirty Years War prompted Schwanhardt to move to the free city of Nuremberg and there, with the assistance of his sons, Georg and Heinrich, he laid the foundation for an important centre of glass engraving. Followers of Schwanhardt, such as Hans Wolfgang Schmidt (1676–1710) and Hermann Schwinger (1640–83), an accomplished engraver of lively naturalistic scenes and figures, continued in Schwanhardt's tradition by applying both matt and polished cutting with the occasional use of the diamond.

Several of Lehman's pupils moved to other parts and established workshops with new pupils. Caspar Schindler settled in Dresden, Johannes Benedikt Hess in Frankfurt. One of the last engravers in the best tradition of the Nuremberg school was Georg Friedrich Killinger, who died in 1726.

Armorial devices, landscapes, portraits, panoramic views and hunting scenes are found on glasses of this period. The typical Nuremberg shape is a tall covered goblet (*Deckelpokal*), relatively thin blown with a hollow inverted baluster stem, a knopped stem, or a stem combining both these features, interspersed with several pairs of flat collars or mereses. It is an elegant and important glass with a cover which may have matching engraved decoration and an

elaborate finial complementing the stem features. Many of these vessels have survived, though not always with the cover, and since the engravers frequently added a signature, the identification and attribution of related work is greatly facilitated.

Bohemian glass decoration, in the meantime, developed in another direction with two major developments in the technology of glassmaking. In about 1700, water power began to be used for driving the cutters' lathes. (Prior to this, an assistant turned the wheel by means of thong and handle.) In conjunction with this powerful cutting technique came the perfection of a more robust glassmetal. A number of glassworks were experimenting in the development of glass-metals, but the most successful during this period was the potash-lime metal; lead-containing crystal glass was perfected at a later stage. From the Silesian and Bohemian glasshouses emerged a cutting technique in high and low relief, akin to the Renaissance rock crystal treatment, which also influenced the form of the vessels, particularly the boat and shell shapes. Less well balanced were the baroque designs of glasses and goblets with covers. The stem grew thicker and was shortened, incorporating plastic relief and scrollwork. The foot and other parts of the glass frequently included cut palmette designs and the bowl was decorated

Left

Footed bowl engraved with a laurel leaf wreath around the centre, flowers and fantastic animals around the rippled rim, and the arms of Trolle. *c* 1725; ht 6½in (16.5cm).

18th-century shapes were simpler, but still descendants of old favourites; compare the bowl (*left*) with the rock crystal boat on the previous page. As wheels developed power and control, subtle shading and delicate touches were introduced – the horn of the unicorn is quite clearly defined and the trees behind him have a three-dimensional effect. Bohemia soon became known for its fine wheel engraving – and continued to lead the glassmaking world in that field for two centuries.

Right

Stangenglas, brilliantly enamelled and decorated with coats of arms and the double eagle. Early.18th century; ht 12⅞in (32cm).

The *Stangenglas* was another hybrid, often elaborately decorated, but still a practical, capacious drinking glass. These presentation pieces were very colourful, relying on a palette which included yellow, red and black – all striking colours, used with a lavish hand.

Right

Zwischengoldglas beaker. The body is decorated with three rows of flowers alternating silver and gold, the base of the glass with a band of silver foliage. Within the bottom of the glass is a further decoration in silver, of a bounding stag. The internal glass body is rounded, but the exterior is faceted with vertical flutes. *c* 1700; ht 3⅛in (8cm).

The use of double walls to enclose silver and gold decoration dates back to Roman times but the 18th-century Bohemian makers brought the art to its finest height.

with engravings of landscapes or pastoral scenes and figural motifs which heralded the charm of the rococo period. The style of Bohemian glass tended to be tall and elongated in direct contrast to the squatter form of the Silesian glass.

One of the foremost Silesian engravers in the high relief technique (*Hochschnitt*) was Friedrich Winter of Petersdorf whose brother, Martin, worked at Potsdam and may well have been instrumental in influencing early Potsdam glass forms which, in their ponderous design, relate closely to their Silesian counterparts.

Enamelled Glass

Bohemia was also the centre of the craft of enamelling glass in the late sixteenth century. This, too, was derived from the Venetians, as was the fragile soda glass used for enamelling. The designs, however, were in peasant style, hearty and robust, covering the glass in bold colours, and the fashion for this kind of glass steadily grew. Trade guilds and fraternities met for organized drinking contests and glasses were suitably enamelled with emblems or coats of arms. Trick glasses of all types – in the shapes of women, bears, boots and hats, for example – were very popular at this time and were used in drinking bouts.

Popular recurring motifs were the imperial double-headed eagle (the *Reichsadler*) – showing the arms of dukes, electors, etc, belonging to the empire; the *Kurfürsten-humpen* (Electors' Beaker), picturing the electors of the empire in their regalia and frequently on horseback; the ages of man; apostle glasses and glasses decorated with biblical scenes, and a great variety of pictorial representations of a more personal nature – wedding celebrations, birthdays, ceremonial events. A large group of these glasses are attributed to the glasshouses in the Fichtelgebirge and are of a pale greenish hue. A distinct category of *Fichtelgebirge-glas* is represented by the large-size *Humpen* enamelled with important sites of the locality – the Ochsenkopf mountain with its symbol of an ox head, and the four rivers springing from it, the Eger, Saale, Main and Naab.

Bohemia, Bavaria, Franconia, Saxony, Thuringia and the Tyrol were some of the most prolific producers of enamelled glass. Often cold-applied and treated with a fixative, the decoration is colourful, charming and frequently rather naive. A primitive, rustic style and poor spelling may point to individual decorators working locally, away from the glasshouse.

The rediscovery of producing a cobalt blue transparent glass, attributed to Christof Schürer in the late sixteenth century, resulted in a very distinctive Bohemian glass colour which looked most effective when enamelled in a brilliant orange red. This was used to make, among other glasses, a bulbous, pewter-mounted tankard, a special feature of the Bohemian drinking vessel of that period.

The best quality enamelled glass, perhaps, came from Saxony, which specialised in decorating small-size beakers with attractively coloured coats of arms. Large numbers were made for the Dresden Court Brewery (*Hofkellerei* glasses).

In the mid-seventeenth century a sophisticated enamelling technique was developed by the Nuremberg porcelain and glass decorator, Johann Schaper (1621–70). A *Hausmaler*, or 'home painter' who worked on undecorated ware bought from factories, his technique was derived from his work in stained glass. He used *Schwarzlot*, which is black or can have a sepia effect, almost exclusively for his portraits, figures and landscapes. His favourite vessel was a cylindrical short beaker – often with a cover – on three ball feet. Signatures are often present, usually as initials.

In the same medium, but of later rococo charm, is the enamelled work of Daniel Preissler (1636–1733) and, more prolifically, of his son Ignaz Preissler (*b* 1670). The Preisslers worked at first in Breslau and then on the estate of Count Kolovrat in the Bohemian town of Kronstadt. Preissler's *Schwarzlot* enamelling is frequently highlighted by red enamel and gilding. Delicate garlands of leaves, branches and flowers with interwoven grotesques and figures, and the frequent inclusion of chinoiserie motifs were the Preisslers' favoured themes, although their work is also associated with more heroic pictorial representations and heraldic emblems.

Several *Schwarzlot* painters enamelled glass at this period, and most of these belonged to the group of *Hausmaler* who decorated both glass and porcelain. Signatures are not always present, particularly in the case of the Preisslers who may, perhaps, be associated with work signed 'Preussler'. The Preusslers were a large family of glassmakers, proprietors of the Zellberg (Bohemia) glassworks.

Important Glasshouses and Techniques

During the second half of the seventeenth century the economic and commercial status of artisans had stabilized and glass decorators emerged as a group divided into distinct guilds of engravers, cutters, enamellers, painters and so on. The earliest glassmakers' guild was established in 1661 by the glasshouse owner Count Kinsky of Chribska (Kreibitz).

Despite the havoc of the Thirty Years War, the glassmaking industry had recovered fairly quickly, and this was partly due to the fact that many of the small glasshouses were located in remote forest regions and constantly on the move. By the last quarter of the seventeenth century, the home-produced glass supply outstripped the demand of the impoverished population, and it was at this point that the Bohemian glass industry began to organize glass export on a commercial basis. The path to this venture was paved by the exploits of travelling glass salesmen, who were also trained in engraving and painting. The best known of these was Francis Kreybich from Kamenický Šenov, in whose diaries we read that during the years 1683 to 1721 he undertook thirty journeys which included Russia, Poland, Hungary, Germany, Turkey, Italy, England, Denmark and Sweden. He remarks that when he visited London in 1688, six glassworks were already established in that city and that, although business was poor, nothing similar to his painted and enamelled ware had as yet been seen on the market.

By the end of the eighteenth century, the glass industry had established agencies in fifty-four European cities and in six cities overseas. These export organizations were run on strict and almost monastic lines. Youngsters were sent abroad at an early age and given more responsible posts later. Gambling and drinking in public were forbidden, and members were only allowed to marry after a certain age.

Above

Small glass. Austria; 18th century; ht 6¼in (15.8cm). This was undoubtedly used to hold small quantities of potent liquid and could be chilled without breaking.

Left

Panel from glass window, engraved on the wheel. Made for Abraham Stabli, Switzerland; *c* 1792; ht 6⅞in × 4⅝in (17.4cm × 11.7cm). A change during the 18th century was the increasing use of engraved and stained glass panels in houses rather than in churches.

Right

Tankard, simply engraved except for the elaborate building – one of a group showing scenes of French châteaux. 19th century; ht 5in (12.7cm).
Tall goblet, ruby flashed with heavy flute-cut base and diamond edgings. Bowl with cut base and masonic decoration. 19th century; ht 8in (20.3cm).
Bohemian glassmakers were the first to exploit the beautiful colour and richness of ruby glass. Although copied later by many other countries, the Bohemian factories originally made the finest range of colours, and exported them all over the world.

Left
Four *Römers* of different
centuries and different glass, all
following a northern tradition
of prunt and trail decoration.
Left to right :
Blue-green glass with conical
foot with trails and a ring below
a flattened merese. The bowl
has been engraved with a vine
and leaf border. Germany;
early 19th century; ht 6¾in
(17.1cm).
Clear pale green glass, on stand
with open stem, strawberry
prunts and trailed conical foot.
A milled ring under a tallish
cup bowl. Germany; late 18th
century; ht 6¼in (15.8cm).
Dark green glass. Flat foot with
marvered trails and an open
blown stem with lionhead
prunts. Probably English; 19th
century; ht 6¼in (15.8cm).
Mid-green glass, on low stand
with trailed foot and open
blown stem with raspberry and
milled prunts. Milled ring
poorly finished under incurved
bowl. German; late 17th
century; ht 6½in (16.5cm).

Astute business acumen, the excellence of a brilliant glass-metal and first class decorative techniques combined to achieve a world monopoly for the Bohemian industry. The great glass centres of Kamenický Šenov, Turnov, Jablonec and Nový Bor are still producing fine glass and glass jewellery today. It is interesting to note that during the first half of the eighteenth century one of the great Venetian mirror-makers, Giuseppe Briata, was so concerned about Bohemian competition in the production of mirrors and crystal chandeliers, that he worked for three years in a Bohemian glass factory disguised as a porter, to discover their secrets. On his return he took out a patent to make glass and mirrors by the Bohemian method.

Ravenscroft's development of crystal glass in England encouraged foreign glasshouses in similar experiments, and one of the first to do so was the Lauensteiner Hütte (near Hamelin) in the principality of Calenberg, founded about 1700. Their process was not particularly successful and early Lauensteiner glass is affected by crizzling, a misfortune which also befell early Potsdam experimental glass. Lauenstein produced some impressive goblets, tall, with a domed foot which may bear a signature on the ground-away pontil mark under the base: a lion rampant and the cipher C, for Calenberg.

Several German glasshouses produced good engraving and excellent cutting. One of the best engravers of this period was Franz Gondelach (1663–1726), the court glass engraver working at the Kassel glasshouse. His work is distinguished by outstanding techniques in *Hochschnitt* (high relief) and *Tiefschnitt* (intaglio), and several of his goblets are decorated with the portrait of his patron, the Landgrave Karl of Hesse-Kassel. The eight-pointed star, found under the base of some Kassel glasses, is associated with Gondelach's work.

The Potsdam glasshouse was founded in 1674 by the Elector Friedrich Wilhelm of Brandenburg, who engaged his protegé, the able Johann Kunckel (1630–1703) as chief chemist. As a glassmaker, Kunckel was far ahead of his time and produced some extremely interesting results during his many experiments. He is best known for his *Goldrubinglas* (gold ruby glass) of a beautiful deep red colour perfected by multiple firing and necessitating the addition of gold in the form of a chloride. However, this process proved too costly to be commercially viable and the gold was later replaced with copper. Potsdam also produced excellent wheel-engraved glass of a deep green and deep blue colour and, as already mentioned, employed Martin Winter, and Gottfried Spiller (1663–1728) whose speciality was the superb intaglio engraving of the human body.

A remnant of the Venetian technique is the inclusion of red spirals in the stem and finial of some eighteenth-century Bohemian luxury glass, which may be additionally decorated by applied or inserted *Goldglas* medallions on red lacquer grounds. Kunckel's treatise on the art of glassmaking, *Ars Vitraria Experimentalis*, forecast a revival of antique *Zwischengoldglas* techniques, and this decoration was applied in a special group of glasses made in Bohemia *c* 1720–45, usually seen in faceted beakers and more rarely in tall covered

Above and below
These covered glasses for ceremonial and presentation purposes were always a speciality of German and Bohemian glassworkers.

goblets. In this technique, gold foil or silver foil is enclosed between two glass vessels, one fitting precisely into the other, the inner one having a lip which joins tightly, about $\frac{3}{8}$in (1cm) down, onto the outer vessel, which is shorter than the inner beaker by exactly that amount. In the faceted beaker, the base of the outer vessel is cut out, the base of the inner vessel decorated by metal foil, and the cut-out disc tightly replaced to cover the decoration. The gold foil is engraved with a fine needle and the design occasionally augmented by coloured lacquer. Typical rococo scenes of hunting or pastoral interest with elegantly clad figures are usual decorative motifs, but there is also a group decorated with coats of arms and monastic emblems. The latter has led to the assumption that this delicate work was produced by artisan monks.

Between about 1690 and 1710, there appears a rare variation of the *Zwischengoldglas* beaker, in the form of a plain, uncut, cup-like vessel in which the foil covers the entire surface of the inner beaker and the outer vessel is painted to resemble marble or chalcedony. Usually both the beakers are of equal height and the join can be seen at the top, which may be disguised by gilding.

At Gutenbrunn in Austria, a refinement of the *Zwischengoldglas* technique was developed by Joseph Mildner (1763–1808). Mildner was a talented artist and his *tour de force* was medallions, often miniature portraits, fitted into the wall of the glass. Mildner glass is found in the form of beakers and tankards, and they were produced in clear colourless crystal as well as milk glass and ruby glass. He painted not only on glass and porcelain but also on parchment, and developed a technique of enclosing the parchment miniature within a glass matrix, duly inscribing the name of the sitter, the date and his signature on the reverse. Mildner fancied himself a poet and occasionally added a naive motto or poem.

A delightful group of salt cellars also falls within this category of glass decoration. Moulded with additionally cut scalloped walls, they are oval and measure about $3\frac{1}{8} \times 2\frac{5}{8}$in (8 × 6.5cm). The base is hollowed out to be fitted with an oval glass disc which is decorated in the form of a portrait medallion, surrounded by an engraved, gilt, oval frame, all on a red lacquer ground. These salt cellars usually come in pairs, and probably represent a wedding gift. Each bears the portrait of a lady or gentleman, facing each other. More rarely, the decoration consists of flower bouquets. They date from about 1800, or a little earlier, and are probably of Austrian, Bohemian or German manufacture.

After the Napoleonic Wars

The ravages and deprivations caused by the Napoleonic wars forced harsh economies upon impoverished nations. The glittering grandeur of the Empire style gave way to a decorative concept of comfortable simplicity, particularly affecting interiors and the decorative arts. This was the age of the middle class and the Biedermeier style reflected this. The *Sturm und Drang* period of German literature, with Schiller at the helm, called for new enlightenment, for liberty and freedom and the brotherhood of all men, but the man in the street turned away from political argument and the accent was on the home, the family and the pleasant

Above
Zwischengoldglas beaker with portrait and foot ring. J. Mildner; *c* 1792; ht 4½in (11.4cm).

Left and above
Ceremonial goblet of white glass with gilded and enamel decoration. *c* 1785; ht 12½in (31.7cm).
Another form of very popular Bohemian decoration – the gilded swags and wreaths, and the neoclassic shape are all intended to show off the two portraits. This was probably a marriage goblet.

Left
Covered goblet with *Zwischengoldglas* decoration. *c* 1760; ht 10½in (26.6cm).
As the piece on the left shows, double-walled glasses were made in traditional covered goblet forms, which were popular for most of the century. The beaker (*above*) has a very different design – its absolutely classic shape relies entirely on the inserted medallion and rim for decoration.

Left
Annunciation glass. *c* 1815; ht 5¾in (14.6cm).
Bohemian engravers specialised in elaborate scenes – often secular but occasionally religious, as in this example. Other glasses depict *The Last Supper* and *The Adoration* and were used in religious ceremonies. The flute-cut foot and waisted bowl are also typical of the neoclassical style which was so universally admired in Europe during the Napoleonic period.

Right
Goblet on heavy stem. *c* 1800;
ht 8in (20.5cm).

Right
Waisted tumbler with *Zwischengoldglas* scene of a village
church. *c* 1800; 3¾in (9.4cm).

Right
Tumbler with a landscape
rimmed with flowered swags
and a marriage inscription.
Gottlob Samuel Mohn. *c* 1809;
ht 3⅝in (9.1cm).

Right
Tumbler with map of Leipzig.
Samuel Mohn. *c* 1813; ht 5½in
(14cm).
During the first quarter of the
19th century, decorated
beakers were made by many
glassworkers, usually to special
order as souvenirs of a holiday
or a special occasion. The
Mohn family were among the
most famous.

aspects of nature. This sentimental trait underlines the intimate and romantic character of the nineteenth-century Biedermeier period, one of the most delightful and rewarding for the collector of German and Bohemian glass. Appealing colours of soft pink, bright turquoise and milky white enhance simple glass forms and an endearing charm exudes from the applied decorative themes of historical and family portraits, panoramic views of cities and buildings, mottoes and protestations of love, affection and, above all, fidelity.

A fine feeling for the sentiments of the period is best heralded in the exquisite work of Samuel Mohn (1762–1815) of Dresden and his son, Gottlob Samuel Mohn (1789–1825). Samuel Mohn decorated both porcelain and glass, and his earliest works were the delightful silhouette portraits applied to porcelain cups. Soon, however, the Mohns transferred their talents to the medium of glass. At first they continued in the same style, painting silhouettes, portraits and dedicative inscriptions on rummer-like goblets and plain beakers in colourless or milk glass, but with additional painted decoration in delicate transparent enamels. This technique, which the Mohns proudly acknowledged to have revived, was derived from stained glass painting, a hardly surprising application since Gottlob Samuel Mohn had been engaged in this technique for many years, particularly at Franzensburg Castle in Laxenburg. The Mohns' later work includes pictorial representation of great variety including panoramic views and subjects of romantic, allegorical and patriotic nature. Signatures in full or initials and dates are frequently present, but specimens rarely come on the market. The son,

Right
Heavy goblet, wheel cut and engraved over yellow and pink stain with silvered overlay. *c* 1830; ht 8in (20.3cm). Bohemian cut glass reached the height of its popularity from 1825 to 1860. It was usually stained in reds or yellows, and sometimes, as here, in a combination of the two.

Below
Marriage glass, cut and engraved in yellow stained glass. *c* 1825; ht 5¼in (13.3cm). The dove carrying an olive branch presumably brought a peaceful life to bride and groom. Marriage glasses were made with leather cases to protect them, and many have survived.

Above
Ranftbecher, blown and cut with band of beads. 1820–40; ht 5in (12.8cm). An unusual combination. The beads give the appearance of embroidery imitating the bright colours and floral patterns of contemporary Berlin needlework.

Below
Engraved and ruby-stained glasses with scenes of hunting, animals and landscapes. The central *Ranftbecher* is engraved in the style of E. Hoffman. *c* 1840–60; ht of stemmed goblet 6¾in (17.1cm).

Gottlob, settled in Vienna in 1811 where he greatly influenced the most prolific of transparent enamellers, Anton Kothgasser (1769–1851), with whom he had already worked earlier on the Laxenburg windows. The Mohns' and Kothgasser's glasses represent one of the most delightful aspects of art glass of the period.

By about 1814, the cylindrical Empire beaker took second place to a new glass form, the *Ranftbecher*, a trumpet-shaped vessel on a cogwheel base. This was the type of glass favoured by Kothgasser, and was usually additionally embellished by a yellow stain (silver nitrate) and cut decoration. Kothgasser was exceptionally skilful and versatile, and his subjects range from panoramic views and portraits of well-known personalities to allegorical representations and motifs or illustrations from the animal or plant world. Signatures appear in full or as initials A.K. when present. Among a number of his followers are C. von Scheidt, a colleague of the Mohns, Andreas Mattoni in Karlsbad and C. F. Hoffmeister of Vienna.

In contrast to these aesthetically pleasing forms, cutting and engraving assumed exaggerated importance with a great variety of patterns often covering the entire surface of the glass. Nevertheless, some of the finest engraving was produced during this period by individual artists, in particular by Andreas Mattoni and his pupil, Ludwig Moser, in Carlsbad, Franz Anton Pelikan of Meistersdorf, the Simms of Jablonec and Karl Pfohl, known for his spirited engraving of horses. The growing popularity of Bohemian spas encouraged visitors to obtain lasting mementoes, and glass artists frequently settled in these spas during the season.

Dominik Biemann (1800–57) was undoubtedly one of the most gifted and accomplished engravers of his time. Born and trained at Neuwelt Harachsdorf, he studied at the Prague Art Academy and settled at the fashionable spa of Franzensbad. His beakers, goblets and medallions, engraved largely with portraits of local and visiting personalities, almost always in profile, represent everything that is best in the Biedermeier style. His work is signed with several versions of his surname or with initials.

An important contribution to glassmaking was made during the first half of the nineteenth century with the introduction of new colouring techniques developed in Bohemian workshops. From 1826 onwards ultramarine was applied in glassmaking, resulting in hues from the palest blue to almost black. The hitherto unfashionable green gained new impetus with the development of a uranium glass – *Annagrün* and *Annagelb* – introduced by Josef Riedel's Dolny Polubny factory, and named after his wife, Anna Maria. Production of these fluorescent green to yellow shades began during the 1830s and ceased there *c* 1848. An opaque variety was the Chrysoprase alabaster glass.

A true black opaque glass was patented in 1820 as Hyalith by its inventor, Count Buquoy, owner of a Georgenthal factory in southern Bohemia. Buquoy also produced a sealing-wax-red glass. Hyalith appears in exceptionally elegant Empire-style forms, decorated by gilding which frequently includes chinoiserie motifs.

An imaginative and dynamic personality among glassmakers was undoubtedly Friedrich Egermann (1777–1864). He had studied glassmaking from all aspects – glassblowing and painting in Kreibitz, pottery and painted decoration in Meissen, and a chemical knowledge had been acquired from a pharmacist friend. He finally settled and established his workshop in the glass centre of Haida. Egermann's Lithyalin – a marbled opaque glass, predominantly red but also produced in other colour nuances – was the most interesting of his developments and was patented in 1828. Early Lithyalin may be semi-transparent or combined with a transparent red or green lining or casing. The marble effect is so ingeniously arranged that the parts decorated by cutting show up patterns of incredible intricacy and beauty. Occasionally, Lithyalin glass is decorated by gilding. Signatures are extremely rare and frequently obliterated, if present. Gold topaz, a beautiful, deep, yellow stain was another important development of Egermann's workshop, and finally, after a great many experiments, Egermann produced a ruby stain, achieved by the substitution of the costly gold with copper.

By the mid-century, cased glass was produced in a great variety of colour combinations, frequently with additional enamelled and engraved decoration. There seemed no limit to the ingenuity of the glass manufacturers and a revival of earlier techniques resulted in both excellent, but also poor and cheap looking, glassware. The increasing demand for all kinds of souvenirs and spa glasses in the ruby and yellow stained metal encouraged the mass-production of acid-etched and poorly lacquered glass, and Bohemian novelty ware flooded European and overseas markets. At the other

Left
Engraved portrait by Dominik Biemann. Bohemia; 1834; diam 3¾in (9.5cm).

Above
Perfume bottle in blue and opal glass with enamelled and gilt decoration. *c* 1840; ht 3¾in (9.5cm).
A delicious fancy, the 'egg' in its eggcup may have been an Easter present like its jewelled Fabergé counterparts.

Left
Jug; Hyalith glass, gilt and engraved. Bohemia, attributed to glasshouse of Graf von Buquoy; *c* 1830; ht 5in (12.6cm).

Left
Covered bowl in Lithyalin, blown, cased, cut, gilded. Bohemia, possibly from F. Egermann; *c* 1830–40; ht 3⅝in (9.2cm).

Right
Goblet of heavy colourless
glass with a top layer of yellow
stain, the foot very elaborately
cut with stars and raised
diamonds. *c* 1840; ht 7in
(17.7cm).
This magnificent goblet shows
the quality of the best
Bohemian cutting at this time.
The portrait is as detailed and
full of expression as the most
delicate miniature painting.

Above
Simple *Ranftbecher*, in ruby
glass cut in octagonal panels.
c 1840; ht 5⅜in (13.6cm).

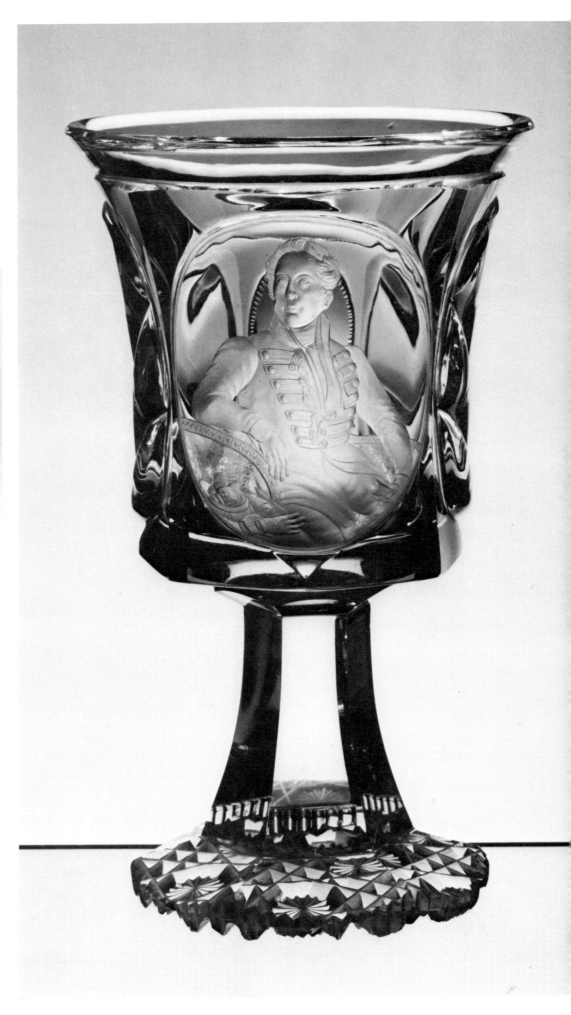

Left
Most German glassmakers
continued to use and adapt
comfortable and capacious
forms right up to the modern
period. Only Art Nouveau
influence, at the turn of the
century, inspired the totally
different, fragile, iridescent
glasses shown in the first two
drawings.

Right
Tobacco or powder box with
separate inner lid, superbly
engraved with a foliate base
and a delightful country
scene on the cover. Mounted
in gold which is also engraved.
Early 19th century; ht 4½in
(11.4cm).
In spite of their reputation for
rich and varied colour,
Bohemian engravers also
worked with delicacy and
precision on the finest clear
crystal.

end of the scale, a number of excellent craftsmen left their native soil and brought their knowledge and skill to glass centres abroad.

The Art Nouveau movement drew a great response from the glass industry. The Viennese Louis Lobmeyr, an enterprising industrialist and glass designer, who founded a studio at Kamenický Šenov in Bohemia, brought together some of the best Bohemian and Austrian craftsmen and designers, to produce attractive functional glassware in a contemporary mood. In contrast, Lobmeyr also devoted a great deal of effort and ingenuity to the revival of individual Art Glass based on earlier traditional techniques and glass forms, including *Schwarzlot* painting, enamelling and gilding. More significantly, Lobmeyr appears to have been the first to show iridescent glass at the 1873 International Exhibition in Vienna, where it was greatly admired and copied by Thomas Webb in Stourbridge. Louis Comfort Tiffany, in turn, perfected his iridescent glass, aided greatly by information obtained from Stourbridge.

The Austrian glasshouse of Johann Lötz Witwe in Klostermühle (1836–1932) must be considered one of the most vital exponents of Jugendstil Art Glass. The factory was best known for its successful adaptations of Tiffany-inspired iridescent glass and was greatly helped by engaging one of Tiffany's ex-employees. Under the direction of the founder's grandson, Max Ritter von Spaun, it expanded the development of original glass compositions, metal overlay and metal mounts to enhance their complicated patterns. The factories of Graf von Harrach, Joseph Pallme König, Bakalowitz und Söhne in Vienna and Adolf Zasche in Jablonec, developed similar glass textures and the usual absence or rarity of signatures make definite attribution extremely tentative.

One of the most able designers of the period was Kolo(man) Moser of Vienna (1868–1918), founder member in 1897 of the Wiener Sezession, a union of radical Viennese artists, and founder, together with Josef Hoffmann and Fritz Waerndorfer, of the Wiener Werkstätte in 1903. Moser produced designs for Lötz, Bakalowitz, Meyr's Neffe and Rheinische Glasshütten Köln-Eberfeld. Ludwig Moser und Söhn (established 1857) of Karlsbad are still active today, and have always employed first class cutter-engravers. A speciality were coloured, predominantly amber or violet vases, facet cut and with a surrounding band of relief gold. Signatures may read Moser, or Moser Karlsbad.

Some more important Lobmeyr pieces may be signed, usually with two capital Ls in geometric arrangement. Lötz signatures vary. They may read 'Lötz', 'Loetz Austria' or Lötz Klostermühle may appear in the form of a symbol: two crossed arrows within a circle and four stars, with or without the signatures.

The Gräflich Schaffgotsch'sche Josephinenhütte at Schreiberhau (established 1842), an important Silesian glasshouse, developed fine ruby glass. In 1923 it merged with that of Fritz Heckert of Petersdorf, a well-known producer whose antique reproductions were often mistaken for authentic pieces. The company is still producing fine glass today.

The Silesian glasshouse of Fritz Heckert employed some excellent artist designers during the Art Nouveau period. Established in 1866, its earliest efforts were directed towards the reproduction of medieval enamelled glass, but it reached a very high standard towards the end of the century with fine quality iridescent pieces and original enamelled decoration based on individual designs by Ludwig Sütterlin and Professor Max Rade. A signature in the form of initials is usually found on the base of the vessel.

The reproduction of Roman and German medieval glass was brought to a fine art by the Rheinische Glasshütten, Köln-Ehrenfeld. Enamelled glass in the Venetian or early

Left

Wide-necked vase of lustred gold glass with silver design. Lötz, Austria; c 1900; ht 9in (22.9cm).

In 1873, at the International Exhibition in Vienna, Lobmeyr exhibited the first iridescent glass made in commercial quantities during the 19th century. By 1878 every metallic hue conceivable was made, and objects ranged from 'bronze' looking like buried metal at least 5,000 years old, to fragile balls piled high in bowls, resembling nothing more than a froth of soap bubbles. The Johann Lötz Witwe factory was probably the best known of all the Bohemian manufacturers who specialised in this very attractive glass. In particular it was famous for its adaptations of Tiffany-inspired iridescent glass. Many pieces were exported to the United States.

Page 114

Above, three double-walled glasses with elaborate gilt and painted decoration. Possibly 19th-century copies; ht of tallest glass 6¾in (17.1cm).

Below, one of the most difficult techniques is the insertion of gold foil decoration between layers of molten glass. The early Roman disc (diam 2⅝in, 6.5cm) inspired its 19th-century copies, each centred in a bowl.

Page 115

Wine glasses. *Left to right*: Hock glass, pale green stem with four knops, bowl engraved with vine leaves. England.
Ruby cased goblet, cut and gilded with cut and fluted knop and stem. Bohemia; ht 8in (20.3cm).
Champagne glass with fine bowl on stem, moulded hollow turquoise knop. Venice.
Amethyst cased bowl with thumbprint cutting and fluted stem. England.
All late 19th to early 20th century.
Fine tableware often copies traditional shapes and colours, but stems are usually more slender than the original forms and decorations simpler.

Above
Nuppenbecher. Blown by R. G. Ehrenfeld, Cologne; c 1886; ht 8½in (21.6cm).
An old tradition, revived with surprising delicacy around the turn of the century.

Above
Scent bottle in opaque turquoise glass, moulded and polished. Czechoslovakia; c 1930–60; ht 7⅝in (19.5cm).

seventeenth-century German technique and style was a speciality of this glasshouse and was produced in enormous quantity. Despite excellent workmanship it can be purchased quite cheaply on occasion and may be considered an attractive, well-made curiosity. The factory closed in 1937.

During the 1890s, Meyr's Neffe in Adolf nr. Winterberg, southern Bohemia (established in 1814) produced a very attractive series of glasses decorated in the Islamic style after designs by Franz Schmoranz. Meyr's Neffe were closely associated with Lobmeyr and the Wiener Werkstätte and since 1922 have been merged with Ludwig Moser and Söhne of Karlsbad.

An unusual series of Art Nouveau glasses were designed and made by Professor Karl Köpping (1848–1914) who worked in Berlin. They are in the form of delicately modelled flowers with thin tall stems, but are less practical than his elegant and well-balanced drinking glasses.

The Württembergische Metallwarenfabrik, founded in 1853, still exists today. From about 1907 they employed the very talented cutter-engraver Wilhelm von Eiff (1890–1943), later professor at the Stuttgart Kunstgewerbeschule, who developed techniques of glass etching with electric tools. Much influenced by Tiffany, they produce exciting coloured crystal and lustre glass – 'Ikora-Kristall' and 'Myra-Kristall' are some of their developments and their mark is WMF.

The Staatliche Fachschule in Zwiesel (Bavaria), founded in 1904 for the furthering of neighbouring glasshouses, is today one of the most important glassmaking colleges in Germany and under the leadership of Bruno Mauder (1877–1948) developed a certain affinity with the style of the Wiener Werkstätte. Individually designed pieces may be signed and marked with the initials FZ within a circle.

In post-war Germany two of the top training colleges are at Rheinbach and Hadamar and are run by the state. Most large cities, such as Nuremberg and Stuttgart, have a faculty of glassmaking and design. An important one, at Munich's Akademie der Bildenden Kunste, is run by Professor Gangkofner. In East Germany there are training colleges at Lauscha (Thuringia) and Dresden. The accent now is on colour, free form and glass montage. There is less cutting and engraving.

It is interesting that the German Rosenthal group, concerned primarily with ceramics, have set up their own glass studio in Selb since the war. They produce a small amount of fine quality table glass, often as part of a set of tableware which also includes ceramic and steel. Among their team of freelance designers are Tapio Wirkkala of Finland and the Danish artist, Bjørn Wiinblad.

Today the Czech glassmaking industry is nationalized. Art colleges and factories are flourishing in old centres – Nový Bor (Haida), Kamenický Šenov (Steinschönau), Železný Brod (Eisenbrod), Prague and Jablonec. The standard is high, young artists are engaged in all fields of glassmaking and successfully compete on the international scene. The emphasis is not only on fine engraving but also on form and colour under the influence of such talented personalities as Josef Drahonovsky and Jaroslav Horejc, as well as the Stephen Rath group.

Russia

One of the most interesting facets of Russian glass is its antiquity. Recent excavations at Novogrudok have turned up fragments which would seem to date from the third or fourth century. And these are more than mere slivers of bottle glass. They are of many shapes and sizes, decorated in various ways, gilded, painted and so on, which would also indicate that there was a flourishing industry there some sixteen hundred years ago.

In addition, in 1960 Dr Shelkovnikov of the Hermitage Museum in Leningrad was given some fragments unearthed at Novogrudok which seem to bear a stylistic and composition relationship to the known Hedwig glasses.

These carved glass beakers with geometric wheel cutting are unique in the Islamic world, but since they were found in the Middle East, the type had been assigned to the twelfth century AD and probably to Egypt. The relief cutting is particularly fine, although in a style and manner not found so far in any comparable glass of the period. The fragments from Novogrudok are therefore a particularly exciting find that puts the art of glassmaking in Russia at a very high level and at a very early period.

A considerable quantity of glass was made at Novogrudok and at other sites until well into the nineteenth century.

Not too much remains of this early period, except for a few beakers. In the seventeenth century, at least one known factory was in operation, but apparently making only rather poor window glass and bottles.

A century later, there were a number of other glassworks, including the one best known today founded by the Mal'tsevs. It is a symbol of fine Russian tableware in the same way that Baccarat has become a symbol for fine French ware.

The early period of the Mal'tsev factory is interesting because it was apparently expected to produce decent quality tableware for a relatively sparse middle class, the court being well supplied with glass made in the St Petersburg factory. Much of the production was intended as everyday ware; jugs, glasses, tumblers, plates, and *shtoffs* – special beakers for drinking vodka.

In general, the articles were free blown and rather like the individual pieces made in eighteenth- and nineteenth-century English and American glassworks. Some were merely useful, but others were expressions of a native sense of humour similar to the trick glasses beloved of the Bohemian blowers with an animal somehow inside the glass. The Russian term for this free-form blowing and manipulation at the fire is *gutnaya*.

The factory was known as Gus-Khrusthal'nii, and it became over the next fifty years the leading exponent of Russian crystal, developing an unusual cutting technique which was known as the Mal'tsev facet. By the time of the 1829 Exposition, Gus-Khrusthal'nii was producing goods fine enough to win gold medals for its glass.

Today the Gus-Khrusthal'nii factory makes glassware of every kind, and with all sorts of decoration. A whole group of artists have designed new pieces and worked to find a way of mass-producing fine tableware at a reasonable price. They make cut crystal, wheel-engraved glass, fine-blown hollow ware and glass sculpture purely for decorative purposes.

Below
Goblet of cut and enamelled glass with a hollow stem; decorated with the Russian eagle. 18th century; ht 8¼in (21cm).

Left
Goblet from reign of Nicolas I.
St Petersburg; ht 7in (17cm).
Part of an extensive set of
tableware with the royal coat
of arms: the heavy crystal has
been cut in arched ribs on a
square, star-cut base.

Below
Three small glasses of double-
walled glass enclosing gold foil.
19th century; ht of tallest
beaker 3½in (9cm).

The St Petersburg factory was rather different in both its inception and its history. Peter the Great established the first state glasshouse in the early eighteenth century, closing down its two rivals and calling it the official glass-works. Another factory was built, in 1777, leased to Potemkin, and after his death it reverted to the tzar. This became known as the St Petersburg Imperial Glass Factory, and by the end of the century it was combined with the Imperial Porcelain Factory to serve the requirements of the court and the wealthier courtiers. During its operation under the guidance of the various tzars and tzarinas, including Catherine the Great, St Petersburg made European crystal in the latest fashion, goblets engraved and gilded with the Imperial Eagle, chandeliers to hang in the ballrooms, and other tableware of very fine quality.

In spite of the royal patronage, economic difficulties made it very difficult to run the factory efficiently, and it managed to survive into the twentieth century only to collapse completely during the Revolution.

These two factories represent the different kinds of Russian glassware produced for the various segments of the urban population. But another kind of glass was obviously for the rural people, and especially for the Georgian and southern Russians who were still nearer to the Eastern and Moslem world than they were to the court at St Petersburg. These are generous glass shapes, either open jars or covered bowls, with simple outlines and a beautifully interlaced design of enamel painting that recalls the colours and patterns of Oriental rugs. The gilding and enamels are so thick that it is hard to see at first glance if the pieces are glass or pottery, and it may well be that the rather amateur decoration was done at home by outside workers who decorated the pieces for what was clearly an unsophisticated market.

The majority of these pieces date from the early part of this century, from the reign of Nicolas II, and they are so full of vigour and glowing with colour that they make much of our clear and colourless glass look rather anaemic.

Above
A pair of blue transfer beakers
showing the figures of the tzar
and tzarina, Alexander II and
Maria Alexandrova. c 1856;
ht 3⅜in (8.5cm).
The transfers, together with the
floral patterns on the reverse of
the glass, are in white enamel;
the rims are heavily gilded.

Left
Goblet of cut and engraved
glass, enamelled in black and
gilt, on a wide folded foot;
engraved with the double eagle.
1750; ht 7½in (19cm).

The Low Countries

With rare exceptions, it is difficult to distinguish between early glass made in the various districts of the Low Countries, which include present-day Holland and Belgium.

During the medieval period, the entire area was influenced by craftsmen working in the Frankish tradition, adapted from the late Roman and forest glass designs.

However, during the sixteenth century a number of Italian glassworkers from Murano and Altare settled in Antwerp and Liège to begin making *façon de Venise* wares for the increasingly sophisticated market. The colony in Antwerp flourished, and Jacopo Verzelini lived there for twenty years, leaving only in 1571 to work in London, where he obtained the monopoly for manufacturing Venetian-style glass throughout England.

Documentation from all of the Low Country glassworks is scarce and somewhat unreliable until the 1630s. The countryside was continually troubled by political and religious unrest as King Philip II of Spain tried to hold his empire together.

Right
Decanter with silver cap, neck ring, and vermicular collar, magnificently engraved. Holland; c 1650–80; ht 9½in (24.1cm).

The Dutch and Flemish peoples were divided amongst themselves in many ways, but they were firmly united in their efforts to attain independence from the Spanish government. Philip died in 1598 and in 1609 Holland became independent.

The Seventeenth Century

From then on, as the country settled down, manufacturing and trade began to prosper, with evidence of a growing number of glass factories. There is a record of an Antonio Miotti working in Middelburg at this time, but little else is known of him, except that there was a Miotti family of

Left
Goblet with opaque white *latticino* decoration on the bowl, winged or pincered handles and a wide flat foot. *Façon de Venise*, probably made in Belgium, possibly Liège; c 1575–1650; ht 5¾in (14.6cm). Early *façon de Venise* is very hard to attribute with certainty, but the Belgian and Dutch glasshouses generally produced well-made glasses with good proportions, capacious bowls, and rather simpler stem shapes such as this inverted baluster.

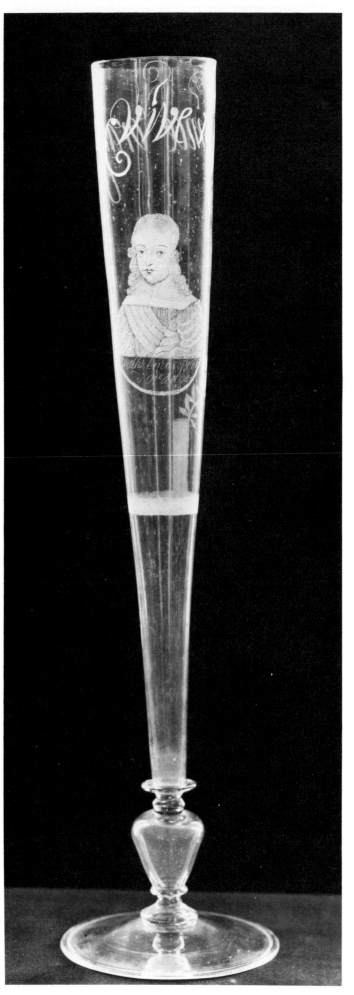

glassworkers in Venice during the eighteenth century who were well known for enamel painting on opaque white glass – quite possibly they were related to an earlier craftsman.

Another name from this period is Anna Roemers Visscher (1583–1651). The first woman artist in glass whose name is recorded in documents, she developed a distinctive style of calligraphic engraving; and working on both green and clear *Römers*, she decorated them with inscriptions, foliage and flowers, in a combination of linear work in diamond point, and stippling. The two styles gave her patterns a special lightness, and signed and dated examples of her work are highly prized. During this period, much of the engraving was done by highly gifted amateurs rather than professional workers – Anna and her sister Maria Tesselschade Roemers Visscher were daughters of a wealthy family, but they both earned fine reputations as inventive and expressive artists.

Holland was becoming the centre of glass engraving – many artists experimented with diamond point and stippling during the seventeenth century, and bottles were a favourite shape, presumably bought plain from the factory in dark shades of purple, blue, green and amber. Another 'leisure artist', Willem van Heemskerk (1613–92) was a cloth merchant by trade, but a glass engraver for pleasure; his bottles were covered with mottoes, verses, inscriptions and quotations from the Bible. He even added his age to the dated signature on many examples.

During the seventeenth century, Liège was growing into a busy city. As an independent bishopric, it escaped most of the political problems which beset Antwerp and Holland. By 1630, the glass trade was firmly established, although there are few known factories with identifiable products from the early years of the century. Two Dutch brothers, Henri and Leonard Bonhomme, opened the Bonhomme Glass Factory in 1638, specialising at first in fine *façon de Venise* glassware for the fashionable market, and supplying England with the elaborately worked openmesh baskets and table decorations which were so popular after the English Restoration. The Bonhommes were commercially successful – they were businessmen, not glassworkers, and they concentrated on running a profitable and efficient organization with branches in other cities which also made inexpensive glassware for everyday use in the sturdy Frankish forest glass. Their prosperity encouraged other entrepreneurs, and unhappily by the mid-eighteenth century the factory had to close.

Left

Tall fluted glass in the true Venetian style, with diamond point engraving of William III. Holland; *c* 1675; ht 6¾in (17.1cm).
Although they experimented with potash and the new lead formulae, glasshouses in Holland continued to make many objects in *façon de Venise* style. This flute clearly shows the bubbles so characteristic of soda glass.

Right

Bottle or decanter in blue glass, with a single neck ring; engraved in diamond point 'B. Boers, 20 May 1699, Warmont'. Ht 9½in (24.1cm). Diamond point engraving could be used as an overall pattern as well as for inscriptions and portraits.

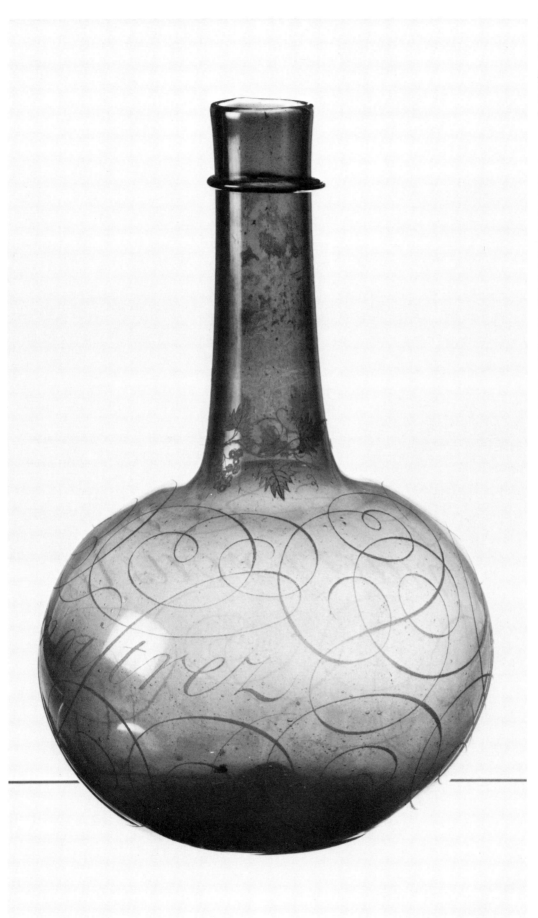

Below
Illustration from a book of
trades. Holland; 1695.
The caption reads 'A clump of
glowing glass is shaped, by
blowing and swift movement,
like supple wax, into a rummer
or a glass.'

Glasblazer.

Een klompje gloeiend glas gekreegen,
Werd door geblaas en snel beweegen,
Gevormd, gelijk het buigzaam wasch,
Tot eene roemer of een glas.

The Eighteenth Century

By this time the Netherlands were considered supreme in the art of engraving. Many well-known decorators continued to develop stippling and fine diamond point as an amateur occupation for gentlemen; Frans Greenwood worked between 1722 and 1745, and although his family were English he settled in Dordrecht and lived there for the rest of his life. His style was particularly suited to fine shading and subtle effect and he was the first engraver to discard linear diamond point completely and concentrate only on stippled diamond point designs. David Wolff worked just after Greenwood, and his stippled scenes and portraits are prized possessions of museums and collectors.

Meanwhile wheel engraving, adapted from Bohemian craftsmen, was developing its own style – Jacob Sang was one of the best-known engravers to work at the wheel at this time.

Most of the decorators worked mainly on clear glass, much of which was made in Newcastle and shipped over to Holland for engraving; the English glassworkers were considered supreme in the production of fine lead glass. The Dutch attempted to make the same formulae but most of their production was unsuccessful, and unstable.

They were strongly influenced by Bohemian craftsmen who settled in the Low Countries throughout the eighteenth century, bringing their potash-based formulae with them.

Above

Goblet with elaborate wheel-engraved scene of barrel-making framed in baroque scrolls; possibly a presentation piece for a coopers' guild. The large bowl is set over two cushion knops, over an inverted baluster stem on a high foot lightly engraved with a wreath of flowers. Holland; *c* 1730; ht 11in (27.9cm).

The engraving may have been done a few years after the glass was made – the stem is an English style, but the relief engraving is Bohemian in character.

Left

Wine glass of clumsy shape, with facet-cut stem; stipple engraved with a double portrait of William V, Prince of Orange, and his wife. Holland; *c* 1759; ht 5⅜in (13.6cm).

Right

Three *façon de Venise* glasses. *Left to right:*
Wide-bowled wine glass with hollow-blown swirling stem and pincered wings on a simple conical foot with folded rim; ht 5½in (13.9cm).
Bucket bowl with heavily gadrooned base over collared and gadrooned stem. The unusual foot has a cushion also heavily gadrooned over a plain base.
Sharply funnelled wine glass with greyish tint; the bowl with applied moulding and tiny prunts over a sharp merese, hollow blown baluster and almost plain foot.
All 17th century.
With the spread of Venetian-trained glassblowers to many areas of Europe, small factories began to reproduce what they remembered of Venetian design. Local preferences and expertise changed the craftsmen's concept, and they gradually evolved a distinctive style that was Venetian in origin but also owed something to the northern countries they adopted as home.
These three glasses, probably made during the same period, show the best of this style – simple clear shapes that are comfortable to hold.

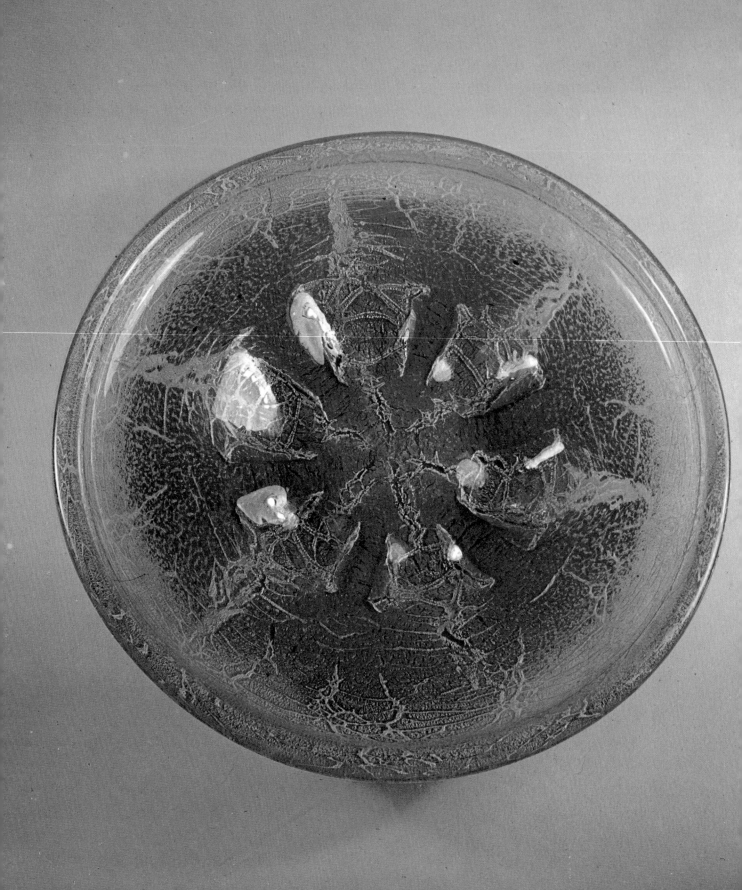

Left

Vase of clear glass enamelled by de Lorm with a dragon in brilliant colours. Royal Dutch Glass Works, Leerdam; *c* 1920; ht 6in (15.2cm).
Leerdam is one of the most interesting centres of modern glass in Europe. Since 1912 it has specialised in the latest technology and design.

Below left, and detail

Vase of white pearl glass, cased in amethyst cut away to form an overall pattern of violets. Val-Saint-Lambert, Liège; *c* 1895; ht 10½in (26.6cm). Val-Saint-Lambert is Belgium's leading glasshouse and one of the best-known makers of fine quality crystal in Europe.

Large quantities of glass novelties were also made, much of it enamelled in Bohemian style. During the nineteenth century Dutch and Belgian glass was generally based on copies of popular designs, and it has few distinguishing characteristics.

Even the prestigious Cristalleries du Val-Saint-Lambert, established in Liège in 1825, was staffed at first entirely with English craftsmen. They made fine lead glass, and quickly established themselves as the leading Belgian factory, a position they have maintained up to the present.

The artistic direction of the factory has changed, however, especially during the past hundred years. The growth of Art Nouveau and the Ecole du Nancy influenced their products considerably, and the emphasis shifted away from England and towards the new flowering of French craftsmanship. Cut and carved glass in many layers echoed the work of Emile Gallé, and many of their delicate floral designs were copied by other factories.

Gradually the clear cut tableware of modern French design became the major style, and variations with engraved and gilded patterns are produced in considerable quantity, and sold throughout the world.

In Holland, the largest glassworks is the Royal Dutch Glass Works at Leerdam. Founded in 1765, its early products were not particularly distinguished although generally of good quality. However, at the beginning of the twentieth century the emerging modern style was encouraged by the number of fine designers and craftsmen who were hired to revolutionize the factory's output. Andries Copier worked there from 1914 to 1970 and was responsible for the establishment of a modern design studio to promote the best developments in commercial tableware as well as one-off studio pieces. Today Leerdam is among the finest producers of superb quality glassware, and it is noted for constantly encouraging young and imaginative artists.

Left

Large platter, mould blown and splashed with orange and gold. Leerdam, Holland; *c* 1920; diam 21in (53.3cm).
A magnificent example of modern Dutch craftsmanship. Holland has had a tradition of glassmaking since the first Venetian exiles settled there. To this day the Leerdam factory creates some of the most exciting modern glassware in the Netherlands.

Above

Two cut glasses in lead crystal from 'Senlis', a contemporary set of tableware. Val-Saint-Lambert, Liège; all modern; ht of tall goblet 6¾in (17.1cm). Today Val-Saint-Lambert is best known for its remarkably fine cut crystal. The shapes are usually graceful, but sturdy enough to be solid and useful as well as decorative. Most patterns are stylised variations of traditional motifs.

England, Ireland and Scotland

During the years of the Roman occupation, the art of glass-making somehow came to Britain, a country which had developed many crafts in settlements and towns throughout the islands, although, as far as we know, glass was not among them.

There are enough fragments of glass bottles, flasks and everyday drinking glasses to make it clear that whether imported from furnaces in Rome or its more northern provinces, or made in local glasshouses most of which have disappeared, glass was cheap enough to be used and discarded without too much thought. There is little evidence of fine glassmaking, however, and almost certainly glass in the villas and temples built by the Romano-British aristocracy would have been imported. Decorative frescoes and small mosaics or inlaid pieces, a set of game pieces with *millefiori* decoration (found at Welwyn), carved dishes and cups, almost certainly came in the ships which travelled regularly through the Mediterranean and across the Channel. Bottles, of course, were a mainstay of trade, the perfect carriers for liquids such as wine and oil. The vineyards of southern Britain, planted by Roman settlers, were obviously producing enough wine to be shipped to outlying military encampments as well as back to nearby bases on the mainland. Small, newly established furnaces would have been perfectly capable of turning out satisfactory containers and simple everyday wares. So that when the Romans finally left Britain the basic craft would have survived, even in a very primitive and practical form. These facts aside, we do not really know exactly how glassmaking started in England, and without new finds are unlikely ever to be sure.

The efficient Romans were to blame for this uncertainty. They were so successful in creating a Roman style all across the known world that glass from all their satellite provinces, including England, shows remarkably similar characteristics.

There is one quite important difference between the fashionable wares of Rome and popular objects locally produced in the trading outposts. Early glassmaking developed in the workshops of Alexandria and the glasshouses of Syria, and the two traditions were very different, although later they were combined within the same glasshouse, and even the same piece. The Alexandrians were much concerned with the oldest kind of glassmaking, solid forms in moulded and cut glass which rely on the jeweller's and stone cutter's art; in the main they concentrated on turning out beautifully carved and gem-set articles of luxury for the sophisticated Roman taste. The Syrians, in contrast, continued the tradition of glassblowing, a flexible and manipulative art that almost certainly began in Syria; moving away from the Middle East, they settled in many of the northern outposts where they created the great tradition which is now known as the Seine-Rhine culture. There were furnaces in many such glasshouses by the second and third centuries, in Lorraine, Trèves, Amiens and Beauvais, Cologne, Mainz, Liège and Namur, and although there may be discernible differences between the French and German products, the fact is that they were remarkably similar, and it is almost impossible to assign them with any certainty to any one region.

Below
Jar of small, squat shape, in dark blue glass with trellis pattern trails and rounded, bevelled edge. Found in Essex, probably Seine-Rhine manufacture; *c* 7th century; ht $2\frac{7}{8}$in (7.3cm).
A tiny jar of blown glass showing the continued decorative use of trails during the entire Frankish period. The jar may have been used for ointments or precious oils, as the bevelled rim suggests a metal mount and perhaps a cover. The trellis chain appears over and over again in glass design throughout the centuries.

The claw- and cone-beakers which the Seine-Rhine Syrians produced to suit the northern European taste have been found in many parts of England, and were obviously valuable treasures for any family. Transport and trade must have been much more an everyday occurrence than we used to think, because the glassware has been found in surprising quantities. The popular impression of the Dark Ages as a primitive period in which tiny villages huddled together without ever seeing or hearing from anyone but those in the nearest settlements is obviously untrue. In spite of the political unrest and continual invasion from the north, with all the disruption and unsettled years, enough glasses have been found to show that trade continued, however intermittently. The known beakers that have survived vary widely in skill and technique; some are clumsy and static, some exquisitely conceived and magnificently executed.

The claw-beaker found at Gilton in Kent and the extraordinary cone-beaker known as the Kempston beaker (Bedfordshire) are probably the most perfect examples. There were other Seine-Rhine products which are both beautiful and practical, and date from an earlier time when the Roman influence was still strong. These are jugs and bottles, almost always with long necks and sturdy handles and very solid bases.

Left
Detail of window showing the 'Three Wise Men' and the 'Star of Bethlehem'. Canterbury Cathedral, England; c 1250. Beautifully simple. Contrast with the example below.

Below
Detail of Continental window of the same period – crowded and bustling. The confusion and noise of battle is almost tangible.

The glass in all of these British finds consists of variations on the *Waldglas* tradition; pale or dark green, sometimes brownish, easily worked, not very clear and with bubbles and impurities. Decoration is almost always self-coloured, the trails and rigaree handles made from the same pot, although very occasionally one comes across a blue or white glass used as decoration.

The northern Seine-Rhine finds seem to die away towards the end of the fifth century and a long silence indicates another period of war and strife which disrupted trade and left the occupying settlements in disarray and unrest.

During the early medieval period, the German invaders threw out many of the craftsmen who had inherited the Syrian trade, and the Seine-Rhine area was left with an inadequate native industry. Workers probably knew the basic factors in glass manufacture, and a few blowing techniques, but were incapable of turning out serious or finely blown work. The Church became the great patron of the period, as the only stable force in an otherwise very unstable world, and it was not interested in beakers or wine bottles, however beautiful. The Church had begun to build, and it wanted windows for its churches throughout the length and breadth of Europe. By 1000 AD a textbook on glassmaking was available concentrating only on windows, and the

Lorraine and Norman glassmakers took up the skill with perhaps a sigh of relief, and left the finer points of domestic manufacture to the future.

In 1225 or thereabouts, a Norman glassmaker, known to us only as Laurence Vitrearius, arrived in England and settled in the Kentish Weald. He built up a prosperous business, supplying both plain and coloured window glass for the new churches which were being built in a vigorous era of construction. In 1240 he was commissioned to supply both his kinds of glass for the new abbey at Westminster. By 1300 his success had resulted in a Royal Charter for the town of Chiddingfold, and for the next few centuries the Kentish Wealden glass industry supplied window glass for many of the chapels and churches of the period. The industry was important and prosperous enough to have salesmen and London agents travelling all over the country to pick up orders and, no doubt, to listen to complaints about late delivery. Two names, at least, remained active for many years, John le Alemayne, and the family of Holmeres.

The factories must have produced some domestic glass, too, although there are only a few fragments that can definitely be assigned to this period: a piece of a jug in rather poor quality *Waldglas*, a small cup of Roman-based design, and what seems to be the remains of a specimen glass – used by doctors to collect and inspect urine. There are also many pieces of what are now described as glass lamps, and fairly common bottles for oils and unguents.

The Sixteenth Century

The Venetians had remained unchallenged as glass producers, partly because their guilds attempted to keep trade secrets by inflicting heavy penalties and severe fines on talkative craftsmen, and forbade the exchange of information with other glasshouses and the emigration of skilled workers. By the sixteenth century even such drastic measures had proved useless – many glasshouses all over Europe were started by renegade Venetians, and throughout the next two centuries continued to find new immigrants prepared to train and teach young apprentices in the traditional Venetian manner. The Low Countries were an important centre for *façon de Venise*, and the industry flourished in many cities, especially Antwerp and Liège. Jacopo (or Giacomo) Verzelini was one of the many young Muranese craftsmen who came to Antwerp; in his twenties he settled down with his family and began to produce the kind of fine tableware in *cristallo* which was sold locally and exported to many western European countries including France and England.

Window glass was also imported into England; the native industry which had been largely based in the Wealden country of Kent and Sussex had died out, while the Norman and Lorraine workmen had established a wide reputation for good quality clear glass sheets for domestic and secular buildings as well as churches. Many of the monasteries and religious buildings were dismantled during the Dissolution, so stained glass artists had almost no patrons at all, but secular building was increasing every year. Windows were growing larger and more elaborate, and the semi-fortified architecture of the past was abandoned in favour of manor houses and comfortable homes with plenty of light, and long galleries that allowed the fashion for walking set by Elizabeth and her courtiers to be followed even during the long, dull winters and wet weather.

However, the prosperous glass industry in France and the Netherlands began to suffer with the rest of Europe as religious and political clouds gathered. Philip of Spain tried over and over again to subdue his Protestant subjects in the Netherlands, and the Calvinists and Huguenots in France were persecuted for their beliefs. The newly Anglican country of England seemed a haven for non-Catholic workers, and a long trail of refugees began to cross the Channel in search of a more comfortable life.

Jean Carré was one of the first to arrive from the Low Countries, and immediately saw the possibilities of establishing a new glass industry; he was ambitious and full of plans for many different kinds of glassware to be made at separate furnaces in Sussex and London. His first venture was a practical one – two furnaces at Alford, in Sussex, for the production of good window glass. Carré started negotiations with the Tudor government and an endless array of official councils and committees, and eventually received his letters patent in 1567 and a manufacturing monopoly;

imports were still allowed. Production began with a work-force of Flemish and Lorraine-trained immigrants.

Almost as soon as the kilns were fired, he began on his next venture, a *cristallo* manufactory in London to make Venetian-style glasses for the table. Carré had noticed that Elizabeth and her court admired the Italian fashions, but the sea trip from Venice was long and hazardous, and prices were high. He had no doubt that a small but rich luxury market existed for the best kind of drinking glasses, and he applied for a monopoly and for a licence to build within the old monastery grounds of the Crutched Friars in London. He obtained the licence, but not the monopoly, and soon the kiln was in production. With this particular furnace there seem to have been more problems with his partners and with the staff, also Flemish immigrants. In 1571 he decided to hire Verzelini to come and manage the *cristallo* house for him with a team of new craftsmen, while he himself was to move into Kent and begin yet another furnace for making ordinary green glass tableware for the growing middle class market. Before that was firmly established, Carré died and Verzelini was left in charge of the Crutched Friars building.

Whatever his individual talents as a glassblower, Verzelini had obviously established a reputation very quickly as a good manager and a friend of England; he was granted the patent which Carré could not obtain, and on far more attractive terms: there was an undertaking, but not an obligation, to train young English apprentices, no suggestions on how he should price his goods and, above all, an absolute monopoly – commercial imports of Venetian-style drinking glasses were forbidden for the next twenty-one years, except by special licence.

Verzelini's glasshouse was in active production for all of this time, except after a fire possibly started by jealous rivals. Unhappily, only a dozen or so examples of his glass have been known to survive – *façon de Venise cristallo* was thin and brittle, so it is probably not surprising that so few remain intact. The glasses themselves, although similar to each other in style, are immediately recognized by the engraving rather than any factory mark. The diamond point engraving is usually attributed to Anthony de Lysle, or Lisle, and it would appear that most Crutched Friars glasses were made to special order; the engraving almost always includes a cartouche with a shield, a quotation, a dedication or a date, and it seems clear that Verzelini's men and the engraver worked together in designing the glass and the decoration, on commission.

The goblets themselves are simple and capacious – it is natural that in London the Venetian shapes took on a practical air not always apparent in the more fragile Venetian fantasies of the same period. Elizabeth's England had a taste for flowery, fanciful ornamentation, but her subjects were also a practical people, and the glasses were comfortable to hold with a pleasant knop on the stem, a wide bowl to fill with claret or sack, a simple foot to stand on the table. The elaboration is in the engraving, with its horizontal bands of circles and ovals, scrolls and flowers, and the occasional hunting scene. The glass, made from

Right

Two goblets, both attributed to the glasshouse of Jacopo Verzelini, and with diamond point engraving probably by Anthony de Lysle. Both date from the 1580s; the bottom example is inscribed 1583; ht of damaged goblet (top) mounted on a wooden stem and foot 8in (20.3cm).

The problems of attribution are mentioned in the text, but the craftsmen who actually made and engraved these glasses were obviously used to working together. The ornate stems with moulded knops held remarkably simple bowls of capacious shape, perfect for scratched decoration in horizontally divided sections. Even when the decoration is a varied landscape, it is set on a horizontal band, and finished off at the base with a row of pointed ovals. The artistic compatibility of all the Verzelini–de Lysle glasses is probably the only record we will ever have of a particularly successful partnership.

barilla imported from Spain, is reasonably clear. All known examples are dated from 1577 to 1590.

Verzelini himself retired from the business in 1590 to live mainly on his Kent estates, but was always affectionately regarded by his colleagues and acted as an arbitrator and adviser until his death in 1616.

There were two sons to take over the glasshouse, but times had changed and so had the political atmosphere at court. Verzelini's success had created jealous rivalry, Elizabeth was granting more and more privileges to favourites, and a Sir Jerome Bowes was given the remaining years of the patent. The Verzelini sons were imprisoned in 1598 with the help of some of Bowes' friends and partners, and Bowes leased the management and most of the profits to William Robson, who controlled the monopoly until the fuel crises of the early seventeenth century.

Meanwhile, the window and forest glass factories had spread throughout England and many new Protestant refugees moved to less competitive regions, wherever raw materials and transport were available. Migration became a way of life for the workers with their temporary kilns, causing local shortages of wood, and enraging native farmers who protested about the 'foreigners' who came and left burnt-out forests behind them.

The Seventeenth Century

The problem of fuel consumption was always a sore point with glasshouse owners. As forests covering the countryside became diminished, many of the royal hunting preserves became bare, and as agriculture developed, fields were cultivated until the entire landscape began to change.

Finally, a Proclamation in 1615 flatly forbade the glassworkers to burn wood in their furnaces, and they were no longer able to manufacture and supply glass.

It was obvious that one of two courses would have to be considered, and preferably both together. The first was to move almost bodily to the new American colonies where, it was said, sand and wood were freely available in huge and seemingly unlimited quantities. The exodus had already begun in 1608, when the first settlement at Jamestown had been established when the London Company had lent money and marketing ability for the new venture. It failed miserably, and there is some doubt as to whether it ever actually made anything but a few trial samples. The next attempt, in 1621, was equally disastrous. The second alternative was to develop a way of using coal as fuel.

The problems were many, and it was clear that a whole new technology affecting the kilns, the pots, and the raw materials would be needed. There were conflicting patents, legal squabbles, and many rival investors clamouring for the fame and fortune that would come with success, not only for the glass industry but in many other manufacturing regions where coal was available and relatively cheap.

There were two particularly important concerns for the glass factories. First, open pots used for the raw ingredients were set inside the furnaces until the glass was molten enough to blow. Every bit of carbon residue in the air settled on the glass, creating seeds and impurities, and affecting the colour and transparency.

Another problem was that of heat: coal burns at a much higher temperature than wood, and the pots which could be used for the old furnaces would disintegrate in the new ones.

The glass industry, guilds, owners and craftsmen alike, lost their sense of security so completely that when Sir Robert Mansell was granted the monopoly in 1623, they were grateful for the lead, and Mansell proceeded to put good business practices into effect. He knew nothing about glass, but a good deal, it seems, about finance and management. He foresaw that the industry could best survive on a national level. He employed potters and chemists to experiment with clays until they found a substance that could withstand the heat, and could be made in a form that would keep the worst of the coal dust off the surface. He organized the transport of coal to the glasshouses, and of finished wares to the shops and markets. He tried new ideas and backed seemingly wild schemes for bottles and other necessary objects. He needed more fuel, so he paid for exploration rights throughout England and Scotland, opening up mines and controlling traffic and investment.

Monopolies were a way of life in the history of glassmaking. In 1610 James I had granted George Hay a patent for the exclusive right to make glass in Wemyss, Fife, for forty-one years. The Wemyss factory never seems to have done very well and when Sir Robert began his rationalization programme, he first took over the glasshouse in 1627, but closed it down after it had proved to be a continual drain on Scotland's limited resources.

Perhaps if Mansell had been allowed to continue, we would have had a National Glass Board today, but the Civil War brought such unrest to the kingdom, and indeed to many settled businesses, that Mansell lost control and the trade was disrupted for at least twenty years. Unfortunately there are no single pieces attributed to Mansell's workshops, but many of the heavy wine bottles and other simple glasses of the period might have been made in his workshops.

The end of the war brought welcome relief, and gradually normal life resumed and the glass industry re-organized itself. Another Scottish Hay opened up a bottle glass factory in Leith. He was obviously interested in outdoing the bottle factories already established, because his petition indicates that he would make a 'superior metal to that of bottles, suitable for ale and clear wine glasses'. By 1696, Leith was obviously a small but flourishing centre of glassmaking, apparently employing about 122 glassblowers, aside from assistants and other members of the groups. Bottlemaking continued to be the main activity of glasshouses throughout Britain.

One thing Mansell had not been able to accomplish was the completion of a new formula for glass which would make a clear, colourless substance, free from crizzling, and much sturdier and more durable than the Venetian *cristallo*. This was really a chemist's problem, and the Company of Glass Sellers were very impressed when George Ravenscroft announced that he thought he could make a better and finer glass mixture. After seeing his work, they offered Ravenscroft a glasshouse at Henley-on-Thames, and the freedom to devote himself to the new marvel. All they required was a

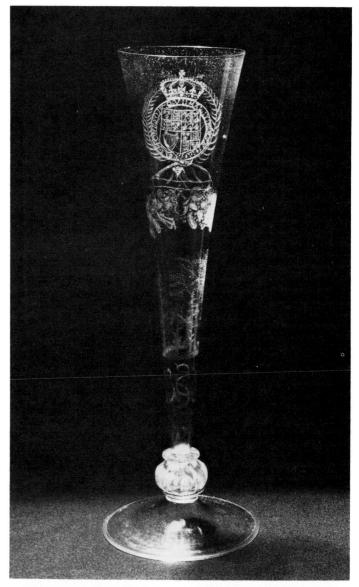

Below
Goblet of early lead glass with bucket-shaped bowl and gadrooned base, multi-knopped stem containing a 1698 coin. Ht 7¼in (18.4cm).

Left
Tall flute glass on moulded knop over a folded foot. Probably decorated in Holland; ht 15⅜in (39.1cm).

Left
Posset cup on flat base with high kick, two handles and a curved spout. Ht 5in (12.6cm). This cup and the flute glass (*above left*) are both made of visibly bubbly glass.
In the 1680s manufacturers were experimenting with new formulae – and many new shapes. The tall flute was very popular in Holland and is much like many delicate, fragile Anglo-Venetian shapes. The posset cup is recognizably English: simple in outline, practical to use, with something of the spirit of the early balusters in its comfortable stability.

promise to market all his wares, provided they were of fine enough quality. In May of 1674, he showed the Company some of his new glasses and received a seven-year privilege to make and develop his new formula. For two years, he worked to remove the crizzling which marked or marred many of his early attempts, although we do not know if it appeared immediately, or only after a year or two had passed. Ravenscroft worked on the difficulties with other colleagues for quite a long time. Finally, in 1677, he seems to have overcome the worst effect, and he was given the right to stamp all his pieces with a seal. Not surprisingly, he chose a raven's head as his mark.

Across the Irish sea the same interest in developing an alternative to the old soda glass was beginning to stir. The new experiments in London with lead oxide made establishing an Irish glasshouse an even more attractive proposition. In Dublin, Christopher and Robert Fitz-Simon became partners with a Patrick Hudson and a Captain Roche, to build the first glasshouse. They seem to have had a great deal of trouble in constructing the actual building, which collapsed twice before completion. The third attempt seems to have been successful, and by the 1700s, Dublin newspaper advertisements were listing the many kinds of newly fashioned drinking glasses which could be obtained from the Round Glass House. Goblets and wine glasses were decorated with engraving, and although some were very crude indeed, a few pieces were good enough to be the work of a very skilled craftsman, either from the Continent or from one of the better glass shops in England.

Below
Beer mug engraved with hops and barley. Ht 5⅛in (12.9cm). Another, later, example of how the heavier weight of lead glass could be enhanced with delicate engraving and two thin trails.

Left
Sweetmeat glass with bucket-shaped bowl and gadrooned base on a hollow simple baluster and a flat folded foot. *c* 1690–1710; ht 4½in (11.4cm). With the new development of Ravenscroft's lead glass the old Venetian shapes gradually became simpler, to show off the clarity and beauty of the new material. Compare the transparency near the rims of this sweetmeat and the goblet (*above left*) with the flute glass and the posset pot on the opposite page. In a very few years the character of glass, and then glass design, changed in England to give an entirely new appearance of almost oily, glowing solidity.

Eighteenth-century Shapes and Styles

As early as 1695, the first baluster-shaped stems were being made; the glass was greyish, still, but held a deep reflected light in its depths. The forms were basically quite simple, and the heavy stems were almost all solid, too, except for the occasional tear (tear-shaped air bubble). The trumpet-shaped bowl developed a heavier base so that it sat fair and square on the stem, and ornamentation was almost always found only in the various combinations of knops, cushions, rings and pad from the base of the bowl to the top of the foot. For many collectors, this early period of English glass remains the most satisfying aesthetically and historically. The new medium was uneven and experimental, with individual shapes and quality of metal rather than the perfect clarity and even forms of nineteenth-century production.

Because of the concentration on stem ornamentation, this period of glass takes its name from the most common derivation, the simple baluster, and goblets are described for the first time mainly in these terms. The groups are: simple baluster, inverted baluster, and pedestal. Various knops include ball, cushion, acorn, egg, cylinder, annulated, angular, etc.

Bowls are usually capacious considering the size of the glass, either as a simple funnel, a trumpet or a lily-shaped bell, and the stems can be found in various combinations. As the quality of the glass improved, the tone and colour showed the rich, almost liquid clarity which distinguishes this period. The grey and yellowy tones gradually disappeared as the new century began and the glass became much more transparent, with fewer seeds or imperfections. It must have been very difficult to adapt the techniques learned with *cristallo* to the new glass of lead, and some glasses show the uneven balance and slightly out of kilter stem one would expect. There was almost no cold decoration during this period. Cutting and engraving was often added later to old glasses, but painting and gilding look peculiarly inappropriate on early balusters, and must have been confined to a few commemorative pieces. Coloured glass is equally rare – the chemists could hardly have been sure enough of their material to try adding cobalt or too much manganese.

As the century progressed, the blowers learned to handle the metal with more skill and ease. The stems became lighter and the bowls thinner. The knops were often teared, or shaped into longer and straighter pieces, and the bases of the bowls became lighter, too. These glasses are sometimes called balustroids, to indicate their transitional character. London had originally been the centre of glassmaking when Ravenscroft was working at Henley, but as knowledge and experience were gained, the other centres of glassmaking in England also expanded.

When the Lorraine glassmakers left the Weald of Kent, they had settled in various towns throughout the country, particularly in Bristol, Newcastle and Stourbridge. At first they made fairly commonplace and ordinary wares, but gradually they came to specialise in certain forms of decoration or colouring. The Newcastle glassmakers were just across the Channel from the fine engravers of Holland, and

Above
Two baluster drinking glasses, both with bell bowls and baluster stems on plain feet. Ht of left-hand glass 7in (17.7cm).
As glassworkers learned to manipulate the new metal, shapes became lighter and more balanced. The left-hand glass is probably *c* 1705, the other *c* 1720.

Left
Silesian stem goblet of octagonal shape and with shoulder stars, decorated with a border of strapwork, foliage and hanging parrots on the bowl. *c* 1730; ht 7½in (19cm). Silesian stems, or pedestal stems, became popular around 1715.

Right
Large goblet with unusual composite stem, a pinched chain trail on the bowl and a plain foot. The top section of the stem has a simple opaque thread corkscrew over a beaded knop and a plain section. *c* 1750; ht 10½in (26.7cm).

Baluster candlestick. *c* 1750;
ht 11in (27.9cm).
The inverted baluster stem
may have been cut some time
after it was first made. The
darkish metal and shallow
cutting suggest an early date.
The nozzle was certainly
replaced, probably about 15 or
20 years later.

Left
Armorial goblet with bucket
bowl and opaque twist stem.
Enamelled with Royal Arms
and motto of George III on
one side, Prince of Wales
feathers and motto inside a
crown on the reverse. Signed
by Wm Beilby Jr. Inscribed
'W. Beilby, Gunt. Invt. and
Pinxt'. 1872; ht 8⅜in (21.2cm).

Page 136
Left to right:
Sweetmeat, moulded bowl and
foot both scalloped. *c* 1740;
ht 6½in (16.5cm).
Light bell bowl baluster.
c 1700.
Three-piece wine glass with
simple funnel bowl, opaque
worm twist stem on a domed
foot. *c* 1760.
Small wine glass with incised
stem and folded foot. *c* 1715.
Tall sweetmeat, honeycomb-
moulded ogee bowl and domed
and folded foot, connected by
an opaque twist stem. *c* 1755.

Page 137
An assortment of green glass:
two decanters, *c* 1775; one
wine glass with air twist stem
and flute-cut funnel bowl; two
doorstoppers, one with 'flower
in the pot' motif, the other with
air beads; small 19th-century
ink bottle of very dark green.
English (except possibly ink
bottle); 18th century (except ink
bottle); ht of wine glass
7½in (19cm).

many Newcastle glasses were sent by boat to be cut and
engraved with border patterns in floral or geometric forms,
armorial designs, and landscapes and figures. Most of the
fine engraving during this period was done in Holland. At
Bristol there was a cheap source of cobalt, and much of their
later work was coloured, so the term 'Bristol blue glass'
became common. In fact, blue glass was made in many
glasshouses throughout the country, and it is really a
generic term rather than an accurate term of reference.

The Round House in Dublin seems to have had a monopoly
– there are no certain records of other furnaces working at
that time. However, it seems quite likely that there were a
number of establishments in the smaller cities or even in
Dublin itself, although these would have made less decorative tableware, and would have been content to produce
window glass, bottles, and a few domestic trifles.

Captain Roche, who had been the partner with an interest
in and a knowledge of glassmaking, died not long after the
two Fitz-Simon brothers, leaving £5 in his will to those
'who cry about glasses and travel into the country'. The
factory was sold in 1760 and there is very little evidence of
what happened thereafter.

In 1714 George I came to the throne, and the house of
Hanover became the royal household. Moulded stems with
straight sides suddenly appeared, often with the letters GR
at the top, or even with the complete motto, 'Long Live
King George'. Gradually the moulded shape became more
decorative, with strong ribbing, and then swirled with stars
or prunts at the pointed shoulders. These have become
known as Silesian stems, perhaps in deference to the background of the king, but there is no real link with Silesian
glass, and the modern term of pedestal stem is perhaps
more accurate.

Another innovation at this period was the introduction of
specialised glasses of all kinds. The earlier simple goblets
that might have been suitable for any kind of drink began to
give way to obviously purpose-made shapes. Small glasses
with narrow bowls and short stems (or no stems at all) were
used for ale – at the time a very heady and powerful drink to
be treated with extreme caution. Open-bowled sweetmeat
glasses were used for the tiny candies and sugary confections
the Georgians loved. The round cup-shaped bowls, usually
on tallish stems, were kept for cider or mead – later engraving
often depicted fruit, grapes, hops or barley.

Tiny bowled glasses on tall stems were kept for cordials
and liqueurs. Very heavy, short glasses with extra-thick feet
are called firing glasses, from the habit of using the base to
bang on the table when the drinker wanted to catch someone's attention at a club or tavern.

A wine glass with a deceptively thick bottom, so that it
contained very little liquid, is called a toasting glass, and it
was often used by those who were required by profession or
inclination to go on drinking toast after toast, and preferred
not to become totally inebriated. There were tankards, of
course, for beer, covered goblets for all kinds of ceremonial
occasions, loving cups for weddings, small syllabub glasses
for the tiny jellies and frothy desserts for the dinner table,
open-cupped salts for the ordinary table, and even tiny

Right
Cordial on incised stem
and domed foot.
c 1740; ht 6¾in
(17.1cm).

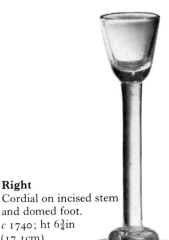

Above
Drinking glass with bell bowl
and air twist stem. *c* 1740; ht
5¾in (14.6cm).
One of the ordinary but
satisfying shapes made during
the 18th century. Air twist
stems are best when straight
and simple.

flat-bottomed glasses on short stems for dressing tables, to hold patches or a few comfits.

As the glassmakers became more and more ingenious, so the number of types and shapes proliferated, until the fashionable household near the middle of the century might have had thirty or forty different kinds of glasses. They were seldom in sets, of course, since the custom of everybody having the same glass did not really become popular until the middle of the 1750s. By this time the moulded stems were almost always confined to sweetmeat and other heavy glasses, the tall balustroids had reached their limit, and the simpler fashion for straight stems with interior decoration swept the old forms away. Bowls were much smaller (taxes were beginning to take their toll of imported wines and sherries) and some of the old Venetian techniques were revived to ornament the new wine glasses. Air twist stems

Above
Two dwarf ale glasses with rib-moulded bowls, very short stems and plain feet. 18th century; ht of left-hand glass 5in (12.7cm).
Wrythen moulding was a favourite decoration for these useful glasses. They were made in many variations and are inexpensive and highly collectable.

Left
Wine glass with trumpet bowl drawn into a straight stem with elongated bubble, on a conical foot. *c* 1740; ht 10in (25.4cm).

Above
Patch stands – two miniatures traditionally made for the dressing table, with everted rims and castellated edges, short stems and domed, scalloped feet. *c* 1740–70; ht of smaller stand 2¾in (7cm).
It has also been suggested that they were used as sweetmeats.

Right
Goblet with matching rib-moulded bowl and foot, straight stem with central and base knops. *c* 1715–40; ht 7½in (19cm).

Far right
Two pedestal glasses. *Left*, the earlier piece with funnel bowl; *c* 1718–20, ht 6½in (16.5cm). *Right*, sweetmeat with an ogee bowl, ringed base and domed foot; *c* 1740, ht 6in (15.2cm). Pedestal drinking glasses were not made after about 1745.

Right and below

Right, sweetmeat with opaque twist stem in complex design, pan-topped bowl with honeycomb moulding repeated on the domed and folded foot. *c* 1770; ht 6½in (16.5cm).

Below, flute glass with mixed air and opaque twist stem and simple foot, the base of the bowl with an annulated ring. *c* 1770; ht 7¼in (18.4cm).

In complete contrast to the glasses on the opposite page, both these examples are unusual, and rare finds for the average collector.

The flute is interesting because of the mixture of twists in the stem: the central cable is opaque, and is surrounded by an air twist corkscrew.

The sweetmeat is particularly rare because of the combination of an opaque twist stem and the honeycomb moulding.

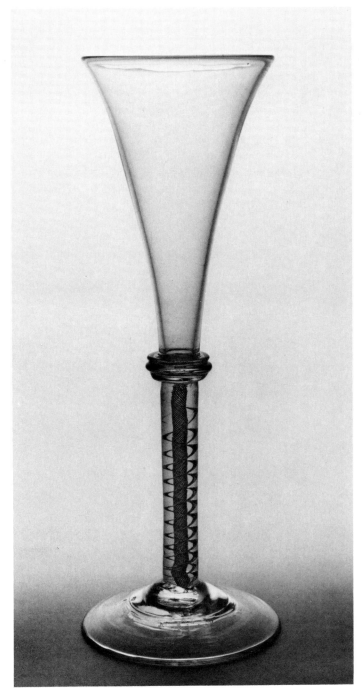

were made in large quantities; bubbles were inserted into the gather which was drawn out and twisted until a long rod was formed. When it cooled, it was cut up into lengths suitable for glass stems. The early air twists were made directly from the gather underneath the bowl, being pulled out and twisted as the blower held the blow-pipe. The bubbles took on a silvery look, and these are sometimes called mercury twists – they should not be confused with mercury glass made in the nineteenth century, where the mercury is used to impart a silvery appearance to the whole glass.

Opaque twists were made in every kind of twist and pattern, and sometimes opaque white canes and air bubbles were used together to make a 'combination' stem.

Sometimes opaque white was combined with coloured canes, in reds, blues or greens, or a combination of all three. These colour twists are extremely rare; they were difficult to make, often became badly damaged over the years, and sometimes a much later bowl and/or foot was added to re-use the original stem.

By the 1750s, the Jacobite rebellions of 1715 and 1745 were responsible for a whole class of commemorative glasses. They were often engraved with the simple motto FIAT (may it be so), and a thistle, a rose and other Stuart mementoes. Sometimes entire verses of the Jacobite anthem were engraved on the bowl. These 'Amen' glasses as they are called are very rare indeed.

With the return to simpler forms, colour became important again, and lovely sets of green and blue and amethyst glasses were made, usually with simple straight stems, sometimes with a central knop, and very rarely with an air twist barely visible. They are almost always small, although there are some larger examples, and the occasional double glass, with a coloured stem and clear bowls.

Engraving was now taking the place of plastic decoration, as the taxes on glass meant that every additional quarter ounce increased the price enormously. English engraving of this period is still fairly crude compared to Dutch.

English and Irish glasses were beginning to show the type of cutting which has become almost a hallmark of late eighteenth and early nineteenth-century tableware. Candlesticks were probably the first to appear with cut edges, almost certainly to help them reflect the light. Drops on chandeliers and edges of mirrors served the same purpose. As wheel cutting developed into a real art, every surface was cut and cut again – stems, bowls, feet, handles – all received the extra special sharpening used to heighten and increase the glittering effect.

Eighteenth-century Scotland

Though the English houses made all kinds of fine glassware, Scotland was more commercial and Leith continued to be the centre of bottlemaking and specialised in producing oversize bottles of sometimes startling capacity. In 1750, a newspaper reported that 'a globular bottle has lately been blown here by Thomas Suymmer . . . containing two hogsheads, and the dimensions are 40 inches by 42 inches. This piece of curiosity . . . is reckoned by all who have seen it to . . . exceed in capacity anything ever done in any glasshouse in Britain.'

Apparently such large bottles were made by using alcohol inside the expanding bulb; the alcohol vaporized and

Above
Set of pan-topped air twist glasses with central knops and plain feet. *c* 1750; ht 6½in (16.5cm).

Right
Jacobite 'reunion' glass with heavy stem, engraved with the thistle and the rose. *c* 1780; 5in (12.7cm).

Below
An enviable collection of glasses all with opaque twist stems and unusual moulded bowls or feet. *c* 1760–80; ht of small glass 4½in (11.4cm).

expanded in the heat causing the glass to expand. By 1777, there were at least seven known glasshouses, and although they were said to be making bottle glass as the main article of manufacture, they doubtless made domestic articles and figures of all kinds for friends and relatives in their spare time, using up the remnants of glass left in the pots at the end of the day.

At least one factory at Alloa was known to have made a slightly more decorative glass, using white opaque loops and streaks similar to some Nailsea trailings. Eventually, under the directorship of Timothy Warren, who had trained at Nailsea and Newcastle, Alloa made clear and coloured glass of high enough quality to be advertised as equal to wares made in Newcastle, and sometimes even stipple engraved with coats of arms and mottoes.

Irish Glass from 1780

The term 'Irish glass' as used here refers to the luxury glass made in Ireland between 1780 and about 1835. Glass was made in Ireland before and after those dates, but it was the product of Irish glasshouses during this period that won world-wide renown and earned Ireland a chapter in the history of world glass.

The beginning date of 1780 is readily arrived at. In that year the English parliament began easing restrictions on Irish industry, including the manufacture of glass, while it continued to levy punitive taxes on the glassmaking industry at home.

Duty by weight had been imposed on glass in England in 1745, 1777, 1781 and 1787. The glass manufacturers watched their trade drop away and although making smaller sizes of glasses helped, bowls, jugs, decanters and so on needed to be of a reasonable weight so that intricate patterns could be cut into the glass.

There were two closely related results of those measures. Irish businessmen with capital noted the competitive advantage given to their country and set about establishing new glasshouses, augmenting those already in existence. In turn, glassworkers in England migrated across the Irish Sea and found ready employment of their skills – in mixing the English lead metal and cutting the unique vessels made from it – in an unencumbered industry.

The transplanted artisans, working with local trainees, created heavier and heavier vessels, cutting them more and more elaborately, in the development of what we today call Irish glass.

This English contribution explains why Irish glass is sometimes referred to as Anglo-Irish glass, and why it is difficult to differentiate between glass made in the late eighteenth century in England and glass of the same period made in Ireland.

But in time vessels were made in new forms – Irish forms. The turned-over rim and the turned-in rim are examples. Others are the oval or boat-shaped bowl and the tall ewer with swan-neck handle, both of which reflect the interest in, and the influence of, classical design. The classic urn form lent itself to candlesticks and to large and small covered jars, the latter most frequently equipped with button finials. Plates and serving dishes had wide flat flanges; the covers

Above
Pair of spirit bottles, probably made for a fitted case (see page 153). c 1775; ht 9in (22.9cm).

Left
Sweetmeat with vandyke rim, flutes, and a flat foot. c 1800; ht 9⅞in (25cm).

Below
Fruit bowl, elaborately cut with bands of strawberry diamonds, laurel-leaf wreath, and flute-cut rim. c 1820; ht 8½in (21.5cm).

Pair of candlesticks with petal-cut *bobêches* and hanging buttons and drops, simple arched pattern and fluted nozzles. Late 18th century; ht 14in (35.5cm).

Below
Fruit bowl with shallow swags separating fine and coarse flutes; a central star and a modified vandyke rim. Late 18th century; diam 11¾in (29.8cm).
The central star has been unevenly cut, and the rim is also uneven. The bowl was probably made by an apprentice or inexperienced cutter.

Above
Two hyacinth glasses, a blank and a finished cut version. Ireland; 1780–1810; ht of blank 6¼in (15.8cm).
An interesting juxtaposition. The blank was blown with extremely thick walls suitable for cutting. The cut is simple, with diamond bands and simple panels. Hyacinth glasses were part of the 18th-century craze for 'scientific' nature – the plant's roots were visible through the glass. Some examples were so heavily cut that observation and study must have been very difficult.

of jars and butter coolers fitted within the rims of the lower vessels, not over them. The large-sized goblets which we often call rummers were also popular and were used for beer, ale, wine or water. The most elaborate pieces had much more brilliantly cut patterns; step cutting positively shone on the table, and strawberry, diamond and other multi-faceted cuts made sure that every surface would gleam and glitter. Standing rims were shaped to one of four styles: the plain scallop, either large or small; the inverted scallop; the trefoil or vandyke rim; and the fan scallop.

By the 1800s the cut glass idiom was reaching its high point of popularity. Engraving was still used but usually in conjunction with at least a simple band of diamond cutting, and shamrocks began to appear with regularity along with the Irish harp and other national symbols which reflected some of the national concerns of the time. By now decanters and jugs were made of really substantial glass shapes. The handles were sturdy and useful, often plain or with a simple edge of cut notches on just one or two of the edges. Patterns were either all-over prunts, combined with step cutting, flutes and milled rings, or more often wide banks of strawberry diamonds over fluted bases. Simpler but sharply cut diamonds all over the surface of small items were also popular, and little salts, fruit dishes, butter bowls and such items had scalloped edges.

There were also many combination forms at this time. Wedgwood-made pottery bases were used for table lamps and candlesticks, ormolu mounted vases were the latest rage, and sets of decanters decorated the sideboards; cruets were arranged on the table, mounted in silver or gilded metal.

Some typical treatments resulted from manipulation of the molten metal, and others from the cutting of the blank vessel. Most of them show an extravagant use of metal, in itself an Irish characteristic. The glassworker in Ireland could be prodigal in his use of metal whereas his counterpart in England, who paid tax on the weight of the ingredients he used, tended to make lighter and lighter vessels.

But there are other means of identifying glass vessels as being of Irish make, in addition to these characteristics. There is, for example, engraving of a topical nature. A jug with an appropriately dated inscription to Belfast's linen industry may be accepted as most likely of Irish origin. Likewise, a plate bearing the coat of arms of an Irish peer, or a drinking glass inscribed to a named Irish military organization, may be considered as most probably Irish. A glass vessel with a silver fitting bearing the mark of an Irish silversmith may with caution be accepted as of Irish make. A history of long ownership within a family will often support Irish attribution perhaps made with reservations on other grounds.

But an infallible sign of a vessel's Irish origin is the name of an Irish glasshouse impressed on its base.

Irish glasshouses used moulds for the bases of jugs, decanters and bowls such as butter coolers and finger bowls. These moulds carried the trade names of the glasshouses using them. Today in museums and private collections, there are varying numbers of vessels, in a variety of forms marked for four glasshouses: Benjamin Edwards in Belfast (1776–1812 for Edwards, Sr); the Cork Glass Co. (1783–1818) and the Waterloo Glass House Company (1783–1835), both of Cork; and the Waterford Glass House (1783–1851). The trade names were, respectively: 'B.

Above
Creamer with turn-over rim. Late 18th century; ht 4½in (11.4cm).
Designs are still simple, but local patterns are beginning to appear. The turn-over rim is an Irish detail – the plain circular medallion is also unusual.

Right
Cut glass condiment holders with hallmarked silver mounts. Ireland; 1787; ht of jug 8¾in (22.2cm).

Left
Decanter of clear glass splashed with colour. Nailsea type; c 1800–25; ht 8¾in (22.2cm).

Right
Scent bottles. *From top left*: Grecian urn in cut crystal with gilt cap; pink-and-white and green-and-white bottles with pinchbeck caps; cameo flask in leaf pattern with silver cap; gilded green facet-cut bottle and pinchbeck moulded cap; clear glass with opaque red threads, glass applicator intact. *Centre*, snail or sea horse of turquoise and white with pincered decoration, cap missing. All English, except urn which is probably French; 18th and 19th century; length of urn 3in (7.6cm).

Edwards Belfast', 'Cork Glass Co', 'Waterloo Co. Cork', and 'Penrose Waterford'. A few other trade names are represented in marked vessels, but they are of persons or companies whose precise role in Irish glass manufacturing or distributing is at present unresolved.

The use of trade names was also adopted by some retailers presumably to indicate designs or patterns made for them, and four shops in Dublin had marks of their own. Francis Collins, Armstrong Ormond Quay, Mary Carter and Son, and J. D. Ayckbowm. Most of the pieces which survive are decanters, and most of the patterns are variations of cutting but occasionally there are engraved designs with vines, shamrocks (of course) and monograms, etc.

Obviously any vessels bearing glasshouse trade names pressed into their bases may be confidently accepted as of Irish make. They may also, with a few notable exceptions, be acknowledged the product of the houses named. The exceptions will be noted below.

Glasshouse style becomes evident by studying the quality of the metal, the forms, and the engraving and cutting of numerous marked vessels. Characteristics of quality, of form, of engraving or cutting appear as 'Belfast' characteristics, or 'Cork' or 'Waterford' characteristics. Once the student is acquainted with these distinguishing traits he may with reasonable confidence – other factors being equal – attribute unmarked vessels to their likely source.

Exceptions to the general rule of identification by impressed bases are as follows. There are instances where vessels marked clearly and in the quality and form of one glasshouse have engraving or cutting styles of another. Thus an impressed decanter marked 'Waterloo Co. Cork' may be found with 'Penrose Waterford' cutting. It is not unknown that a glasshouse would on occasion send its blank products to another house in another city for engraving or cutting. Also, it is historically on record that glassworkers over the centuries have been migratory, moving from glass

Above
Claret jug in classic style, richly engraved with gods and goddesses. c 1850; ht 14in (35.5cm).
Wheel-cut decoration in the Bohemian relief style was all the rage at the Great Exhibition of 1851 in London. This jug, made by J. Green, is very similar to the example from the exhibition catalogue (*right*).

Left
Modern glassmaking shows many influences. This picture shows the various kinds of glass made by one group of glassblowers in London. *From top left*: scent bottles (Fleur Tookey); two vases (Chris Williams); two goblets (Ray Adnitt, Annette Meech); paperweights (three at back by Annette Meech, front weight by Tony Stern, centre left by Jane Bruce); shallow bowl (Fleur Tookey); decanter (Jane Bruce); three vases (Chris Williams); glass sculpture (Pauline Solven); goblet (David Taylor). Made in the Glasshouse, London; 1978–79; ht of top right-hand vase 9in (23cm).

Right
Commemorative goblet beautifully engraved with a sailing ship and the Wear Bridge, Sunderland. *c* 1825; ht 7½in (18cm).
The bridge was opened in 1796, but commemorative glasses continued to be made for many years. This substantial form of goblet continues today, often with club insignia or other kinds of commemorative decoration, since it is particularly suitable for modern presentation pieces.

centre to glass centre, city to city, taking with them personal styles and the styles of previous employers. The student of Irish glass must therefore be on the alert for incongruities which result from these conditions.

Notwithstanding the thirty-six years of B. Edwards, Sr's operation in Belfast, the only vessels bearing his impressed name are decanters. While the form of several reflects Edwards' background in Bristol, England, there is so little unanimity of form among his marked vessels they contribute little to our knowledge of Irish glass. The yield of information is much greater when we study the impressed examples of the other three glasshouses.

The two Cork companies produced glass over a period of fifty-two years. Each developed a distinctive engraving signature and the earlier of the two companies, Cork Glass Co., also developed a distinctive cutting signature. Indications are the Waterloo Co. copied the earlier company's styles. Doubtless when Cork Glass Co. closed in 1818 some of its artisans went to work at Waterloo. Insofar as cut glass is concerned, therefore, attribution of unmarked vessels to Cork cannot be specifically to one or other of the two houses.

Of the four glasshouses represented by marked vessels, the Waterford Glass House is the most fully documented on paper; and, thanks to its surviving impressed cut examples, it ranks first in our knowledge of quality, form and style. Founded by George and William Penrose (an uncle and nephew), it was fortunate in procuring a glassworker from Stourbridge, in England, who assembled and led a team of

Above
Candlestick with engraved and cut lampshade, hanging drops. Late 19th century; ht 16½in (41.9cm).
By the end of the 19th century candles were used for table decoration rather than serious lighting. This simplified candlestick remained popular for decades; copies were made well into the 20th century.

of workmen whose members were qualified in all phases of glassmaking 'from the mixing room to the cutter's wheel'.

Although the Stourbridge supervisor, John Hill, remained in Ireland for only three years, he established a standard of quality which made the Waterford Glass House pre-eminent for fifty years, under Penrose and a succession of owners.

Analysis of the cutting of Irish glass indicates that there are two, quite different styles. At the risk of over-simplification, one might say there is a flat diamond style and a sharp diamond style, each employing its diamonds with an accompanying galaxy of lesser motifs. Tentative attribution has been made to the Cork houses for the flat diamond style and to Waterford for the sharp diamond style. It is possible, however, that future researchers will produce firm evidence that glasshouses in Dublin, Newry or elsewhere also produced vessels in these styles.

The first style makes copious use of flat diamonds in belts or within oval or circular depressions; there are flat leaf festoons, flat hollow facets and alternate prisms. The net effect is soft and limpid; the surface of the vessel is gentle to the touch. The quality of the metal of vessels so cut is uneven and there is a tendency to greyness. Vessels with these characteristics of cutting often show a blue cast, sometimes very marked.

The second style of cutting is attributable to Waterford. Heavy pillar columns are found, sometimes alternating with vertical panels filled with tiny diamonds filling the enclosed space. Prismatic cutting and graceful swags, multi-rayed stars, sharp medium or tiny diamonds in wide fields or single bands; these constitute the Waterford cutting vocabulary. Incisions are deep and the numerous motifs are adroitly disposed in relation to one another.

These characteristics ascribed to Waterford are invariably found in an absolutely colourless glass that is free from specks, striae or other blemishes. Indeed, the perfection of its metal was a continuing purpose of the Waterford house, the legacy of John Hill. Today it is a signature of Waterford comparable to the pillar and arch design and cut swags mentioned above. Contrary to popular belief, Waterford glass does not have a blue tint.

A number of drawings of vessels, in the forms and with the cutting used by Waterford in about 1830, are also of assistance in identifying pieces. An invaluable record of the later Waterford styles, they are preserved at the National Museum of Ireland in Dublin.

The term 'Waterford chandelier' is in such frequent use that no discussion of Irish glass in general, or Waterford glass in particular, can ignore it. Though chandeliers are popularly believed to have been made in Waterford within our period, the present writer knows of no chandelier backed by firm documentary evidence supporting Waterford attribution.

Not all Irish glass was complicated; many of the provincial glasshouses went on making traditional jugs and vases in opaque white milk glass, looped colourless glass, splashed colours in multi-patterns and pressed glass in all sorts of tiny shapes and sizes.

Above
Cut glass scent bottle with sulphide enclosure of Queen Charlotte. Probably Apsley Pellat, Falcon Glassworks, Southwark, London; *c* 1830; ht 3in (7.6cm).
The 19th century was a great period for inventive and decorative glass of all kinds. Apsley Pellat's cameos, made with his crystallo-ceramie process were inserted into glasses, bottles, paperweights, and many different novelties.

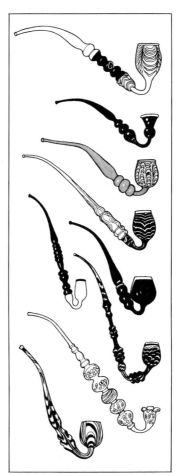

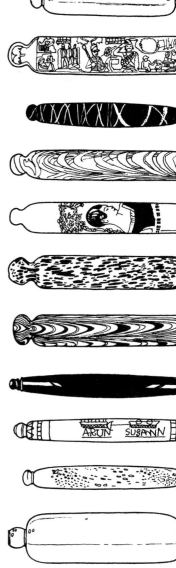

Above
Nailsea rolling pins, with a variety of decorative ornamentation. 19th century; average length 13in–14in (33cm–35.5cm). Some were closed at both ends, some like the bottom example were intended for storing tea or sugar, or even for rolling pastry; these had a stopper at one end. Collage decoration made with decals and cut-outs were often backed with a layer of plaster.

Left
Nailsea pipes in a variety of shapes and looped patterns. Like the rolling pins, they were basically decorative rather than useful, bought as souvenirs and gifts in novelty shops and at fairs.

Steam power was introduced into Ireland in 1818. It enabled the glasscutter to control the revolutions of his wheel with more precision than ever before. He became more and more proficient and his public delighted in the elaborate cut glass he produced. Mechanical perfection and excessive decoration were the result of the cutter's virtuosity and unrefined public taste – and the 'prickly monstrosity' was born. The brilliant colourless metal of a century before was still the substance of the vessel, but the graceful cascading draperies making a scintillating web of highlights were gone. A rigid mesh, mathematically precise, grasped the vessels; stylistically the Irish chapter in glass came to a close.

Irish glass was sent abroad as far away as Portugal, Barbados, Canada and the West Indies, and it enjoyed a reign of affluence and prosperity which was all too soon over.

Below
Pressed glass mantelpiece statues or table decorations. Made by John Derbyshire, Manchester; *c* 1875; ht 6⅜in (16.2cm).
Pressed glass began to take over the cheaper end of the market, and novelties and tableware of every sort proved economical to make and attractive to customers. These figures, of Punch and Judy, may have been fairground prizes like the Staffordshire pottery figures which are now equally collectable.

Left
Pressed plate commemorating Queen Victoria's Jubilee. Sowerby & Co., Gateshead-on-Tyne; 1887; diam 6in (15.2cm). Sowerby's was one of the most successful English pressed glass manufacturers. Although its wares were previously thought of as not worth attention, today's collectors are beginning to discover the charm and skill that were characteristic of its best pieces.

Far left
Nailsea novelties in plain and looped glass. 19th century; ht of lamp (used by lacemakers to magnify their work) 5in (12.7cm).
Nailsea has become a generic term for the pleasant fripperies the Victorians loved, but similar glass was made in many parts of England and America.

The grant of Free Trade for Ireland lasted until 1825. In 1835 the Irish glass industry was hit by its first excise tax and thereafter glass manufacture in Ireland began its slow decline. In the latter half of the nineteenth century glass was still being made in Ireland, notably in Dublin, but the chapter on Irish glass in the history of world glass had come to an end.

Although it is common to hear the tax blamed for everything, there were other factors which must have contributed to the decline. Above all, public taste was changing rapidly, particularly since the introduction (often by their own houses) of mould-blown pressed glass imitations of cut patterns. The interest in delicate colourings and floral engraving was stimulated by the great achievements of Bohemian glasshouses which were exhibited in 1851. Ireland had never produced much coloured glass, and its engravers were almost all imported or relatively unskilled. Ruskin and William Morris were the prophets of the new paradise on earth, and Ruskin's flat statement that all cut glass is barbarous because it conceals the honest quality of the material, must have had some effect, too.

Only one new factory that we know about was established in Dublin during this period, T. and R. Pugh of Dublin, and the owner saw at once where their market was going. Bohemian engravers were hired to decorate blown-glass shapes with clear shapes, and ribbed trailings reminiscent of the snake-thread bottles of the Seine-Rhine period.

Unhappily, by 1899 Pugh was closed down, and it was not until the 1950s that the new industry began again in Ireland with the introduction of a re-organized Waterford company, and other glasshouses all over the country. Some cut glass will always be in demand, of course, but today's Irish glassmakers are able to make modern engraved and clear glass, as well as simplified patterns based on the old favourite designs.

English Pressed Glass

Pressed glass was largely an American invention, although small hand presses had been made in England for years. By the end of the nineteenth century, American techniques had been introduced in England, and many factories in the Midlands installed machinery that turned out a thousand variations on popular Victorian novelties, in a variety of clear and coloured glasses. The presses operated with a plunger and both the insides and outsides of pieces were moulded under considerable pressure. Designs are crisper and more elaborate in detail than the old blown-mould commercial products. Although clear glass lost its brilliance in the process, coloured versions were much more successful and attractive. Some of the best-known makers were T. Hawkes & Co., Rice Harris & Co., and Bacchus & Green,

Top right
Cameo plaque carved with Venus and Cupid. G. Woodall; c 1890; diam 18in (45.7cm).

Centre right
Cameo seal and scent bottle. Late 19th century; length of seal 4¼in (10.7cm).

Right
Decanter in green glass, mounted in silver, designed by C. R. Ashbee and made by the Guild of Handicraft in 1901.

Right
Modern paperweights.
Perthshire, Scotland;
diam of top weight
$2\frac{7}{8}$in (7.2cm).
Traditional skills are being
revived in Scotland, where
Paul Ysart and later craftsmen
have developed flourishing
paperweight factories.

Below
Sugar box or tea caddy, made
of cut glass with silver mounts.
Mark of Joseph Preedy;
1770–75; ht $6\frac{1}{4}$in (15.8cm).

all in the Midlands and all using various formulae of lead glass. Later in the century companies on the Tyneside around Newcastle established themselves by using a cheaper semi-lead glass, and undercutting those in the Midlands considerably as a result.

The most popular period for pressed glass was during the 1870s and 1880s, and the best-known factory was Sowerby's Ellison works in Gateshead. Its peacock's head trademark was impressed into the most extraordinary range of glass novelties, in every shape and form and in a wide selection of colours that was continually being enlarged with plain and marbled patented glasses: marbled blue *sorbini*, dark red *rubine*, a milky opal called *blanc de lait*, etc.

Other successful factories around Newcastle included George Davidson & Co. (trademark a lion on a crown in a circle). In Sunderland Henry Greener & Co. used a demilion rampant holding first a star and later, from 1886 when the factory was taken over, a lion holding a battleaxe.

Decanters and Fittings

The Victorians had a mania for making decorative containers – even cheap hair pomade was sold in highly coloured and today very collectable little pots of inexpensive ceramic ware. Finely cut glass was more desirable: cruets, bottles, glasses, jars, flasks; carefully constructed boxes for travelling and home use, all had their more or less precious mountings. The most sought-after sets are in decanter and spirit boxes and dressing cases.

Decanters were often made in sets of two or four, and fitted into a wooden box. The decanters were often square in order to get the greatest quantity of spirit in the smallest possible area, and tight-fitting stoppers kept the liquid safe during all but the most hazardous voyage. There were often slots for a pair of glasses to be fitted into the top of the box or alongside the decanters. Larger sets had space for wine as well, and the Victorian version of a picnic basket had bottles, at least four glasses, small bottles for spices, lemon peeler and corkscrew – in short everything the gentleman would need.

Travelling boxes were often covered in leather outside, stamped in a simple gilt or blind design, even when the inside was elaborate with carving, velvet casing, and inlay. Much more decorative boxes for the home with marquetry inlay in coloured woods, or metals, and beautifully fashioned locks were popular until the mid-nineteenth century, when the tantalus was invented. This silver 'cage' allowed the full beauty of cut crystal to be shown while a self-locking device kept the decanter safe from over-enthusiastic drinkers, and the fitted case gradually became old-fashioned.

It is not always easy to tell which decanters were made for boxes if the container has been lost, but generally the smaller size bottle, with a square section from base to shoulder, was the most popular shape. Cutting was fairly limited, but the stoppers could be highly decorative. Decanters used in a tantalus were much more elaborate since they were more clearly on display. Matching glasses in various sizes were part of a complete set.

Another kind of decorative box was the dressing case. Although toilet boxes had been used in various forms for

Above

Three 19th-century methods of decoration. *Left*, a small wine glass with gilded swags of flowers; *centre*, a little vase blown in a ribbed and patterned mould; *right*, a bowl with a finely detailed acid-etched design made for a pinchbeck stand for sweetmeats or condiments. Ht of bowl 4⅛in (10.4cm).

Left

Two faces of contemporary glass. *Far left*, a handmade but highly commercial design 'Ring Tree and Necklace Tree' by Frank Thrower, made at Dartington glassworks, Devon; ht 8in (20.3cm). *Left*, a limited edition vase; the base is cut in notched flutes, the body all over in diamonds, with a wheel-engraved relief vignette inscribed 'The Prodigal Son'; made at Waterford, Ireland; ht 13in (33cm).

centuries, the first really large-scale production of dressing and toilet cases took place in the nineteenth century and some of them are miracles of ingenuity and complicated mechanism. They range from simple wooden boxes with two powder glass jars, a brush and comb and a simple scent bottle to unbelievably elaborate outfits, with double or triple tiers of drawers containing scent and rouge jars, powder boxes, pill and beauty patch boxes, cream and lotion jars, a secret drawer for jewellery and a separate tray with folding scissors, needle case, button hook, pen knife, mirrors, mixers and nail files, etc. The little jars and bottles were often made of the finest cut glass, sometimes with an engraved and gilded monogram, silver screw tops and mountings. The date of the mounting is a very useful guide to the date of the glass itself, although replacement fittings must be allowed for. To find such an elaborate box complete with all its tiny jars and fittings is quite a windfall.

Glass Boxes
Small glass bowls, for ointments and lotions, were often rimmed in silver or gilt metal, incorporating a catch at the front and tiny hinges behind. Coloured glass was often preferred for these; gemstone colours are particularly lovely, looking like agate or jade.

Cigarette boxes, a twentieth-century development, were essential accessories in fashionable drawing rooms at one time. Elaborately cut in crystal, or matt-finished with a classic nude, who often also supported an ashtray, draped over the top, they were matched to sets of tableware, glasses, tablepieces, and even cigar boxes. Geometric patterns in stylised designs were followed by the new emphasis on heavy flawless crystal with minimal decoration. Metal mounting was much less popular and most 1930s and 40s boxes have heavy lids which fit fairly loosely, often with a simple squared monogram in a geometric pattern. Colour almost disappeared, except for opaline or milk glass, which also retained the gilt or ormolu banding in imitation of French designs of the 'traditional' kind.

Finally the 1970s revival of studio glass, brought back a fashion for small decorative bottles and boxes, often made with the same brilliantly coloured inlays and enclosures which mark the larger pieces of modern glassware.

Blown Art Glass
The growth of Art Glass in the 1880s changed the products of many English glasshouses. J. Powell & Son of London made glass for William Morris and many designers of the Arts and Crafts movement, and were responsible for some of the finest designs of the late nineteenth, and twentieth, centuries.

W. H., B. & J. Richardson produced some extremely distinctive glass in the 1850s, attractive and reasonably priced with floral enamelled patterns on clear glass. Stourbridge was a centre for makers of fine glass. John Northwood of Stevens & Williams Ltd, who worked on the famous copy of the Portland Vase for three years, developed the technique of cameo cutting, and Thomas Webb & Sons employed decorators and craftsmen with world-wide reputations. George Woodall, one of Webb's carvers, specialised in classical cameo work.

Unhappily, the commercial use of acid etching flooded the market with inexpensive 'cameo' copies, and individually carved pieces became uneconomic. Eventually, most of the English factories returned to the cut glass that had been so popular, and produced various re-interpretations of the best Georgian patterns for most of the twentieth century.

Today English glass is still largely traditional, and although there are individual designers of importance, only one factory really concentrates on modern commercial glass. Frank Thrower's work for the Dartington Co. in Devon is adaptable and responsive to new ideas and consumer demand. The company was the first to produce avocado dishes, and ring and necklace trees.

Modern Scottish Glass
In the past century, Scottish glass has finally achieved its own individual reputation. One of the Leith glasshouses has become Webb's Crystal Glass Co, which has a fine reputation for cut and crystal tableware of all kinds. Another at Perth, the North British Glassworks, renamed the Moncrieff Glassworks from 1864, has become very well known for the production of art glass. John Moncrieff, the owner, employed Salvador Ysart some time in the 1920s and this began one of the most distinctive family traditions in modern British glassmaking. Salvador had come from Barcelona and brought his Continental style and colours to Scotland, but his son, Paul Ysart, has achieved even greater fame as the maker of some of the loveliest paperweights made in Britain today. He worked at Moncrieff until 1961, and then at Caithness Glass and his own factory. His best examples include a cane in the traditional manner with his initials PY.

The Caithness factory itself makes other paperweights today, many of a startlingly modern design but in limited editions, using moon shots, comets and other phenomena as their inspiration. The best pieces are now eagerly sought after as collector's prizes. Caithness has two factories, and it also makes contemporary crystal and engraved glass. Perhaps more than any other glass company it is responsible for the growing interest in Scottish crafts and in studio glass which has produced some interesting and exciting pieces in the last few years.

Studio Glass
A few studios such as Greystan & Monart began to emerge in the 1930s, and today some individual glassmakers, along with other British craftsmen, are attracting a growing public. Their work is still strongly rooted in traditional concepts of functional objects such as drinking glasses and bowls.

Stained glass has certainly developed its own distinctive vocabulary in England, with well-known artists and glassmakers collaborating to produce magnificent windows and murals for churches and other public buildings.

Engraving has also benefited from the renewed interest in individual crafts, and Laurence Whistler's success has inspired many engravers, who work mostly on commission.

For the future, the impetus of the British Craft Centre, and the technical possibilities of small kilns, have raised the standard of individual one-off pieces. However, the quality of design in English commercial glasshouses has yet to match what can be the finest lead glass metal available.

France

The early beginnings of French glassmaking are linked with the expansion of the Roman Empire. The regions of the Seine-Rhine area, always regarded as particularly flourishing, produced early on some well-designed and individual glassware. During the second and third centuries the practical mould-blown bottles appeared, many bearing the intriguing maker's mark of Frontinus. On a more luxurious plane, there were the elegant, tall, chain-handled jugs as well as the notorious, snake-thread glassware decorated with coloured glass threads, a distinct inspiration of Eastern and Semitic influences, brought into the Rhineland by artisans following in the wake of the Roman legions.

After the fall of the Empire, the Roman influence diminished, but there is no doubt that glassmaking continued, particularly in northern Gaul. A glass style developed which spread from Frankish Gaul and the Rhinelands to England and Scandinavia – the Frankish or Merovingian glass made in pale amber or greenish *verre de fougère*. This was a glass made from the ashes of fern or bracken, and which resembled the German *Waldglas*. The domestic glassware corresponded to vessels made in the more utilitarian materials of wood, horn, or metal, and the cone-beakers and drinking horns with applied glass threads show a certain elegance of style. More pedestrian are the ribbed drinking bowls and plain small palm cups, so-called because they were held in the palm of the hand. The most elaborate of Frankish drinking vessels is the claw-beaker or *Rüsselbecher* made from the late fifth century onwards. The complicated technique involves application of the claw to the cooled surface of the beaker in the form of a hot glass blob. The surface softens at the point of impact and the gaffer quickly continues blowing the glass vessel, making a hole at the

Right
Scent bottle with *millefiori* garland centre and basket stopper; *millefiori* paperweights. *Top left*, entwined garland; *top right*, simple garland with facet-cut sides. Both Clichy; diam 3⅛in (7.9cm). *Bottom left*, concentric garland. Clichy; diam 3¼in (8.3cm). *Bottom right*, crown hollow blown. St Louis; diam 2⅞in (7.2cm).

softened site and inflating the blob which is pulled outwards and downwards and the tip pressed to the glass surface one or two inches below.

Glass of this period, between 400 AD and 800 AD, cannot be distinguished by political borders as we know them today, but by regions of historical significance. One cannot easily make any distinction between glass finds in northern Gaul or those from Rhenish tombs on the opposite bank of the Rhine. The so-called Dark Ages or 'medieval slump' in European glassmaking, from about 800 AD to the end of the fourteenth century, may be attributed to several factors, not least to the desire for the establishment of a native industry, coupled with envy and resentment at the success and prosperity attained by foreign artisans and merchants. The result was constraint and harassment of foreign glassmakers, in particular those of Oriental or Semitic origin, with the consequence of a migration of glassmakers during the ninth century. Of particular interest is the group of artisans who settled in Altare, near Genoa, the predecessors of those fifteenth-century Altarist rivals to the Murano glassmakers, who returned to French soil, bringing with them the secrets of Venetian *cristallo* techniques. Additional factors contributing to the dearth of medieval French glass were continuous unrest, wars, pillages and the Norman invasions. Disappointing, too, was the stand of the Church, which discouraged the making of hollow glass, but was instrumental in the great development of stained window glass.

Stained and Clear Window Glass

The concept and inspiration of coloured panes of window glass comes from Byzantium and the Eastern Church, but stained glass in Europe must be described as essentially a Gothic art, as its growth and flowering coincides with the development of Gothic architecture which, in its turn, was conditioned by the growing power of the Church.

Left
Early Romano-Frankish glass on slender foot, the surface iridescent in patches. Ht 3⅜in (8.5cm).
The Seine-Rhine area was the great glassmaking centre after the Romans had left; the Syrian glassmakers who settled there used light soda glass to great effect in small cups and glasses in very simple shapes.

Left
Bottle-vase, carved and enamelled in a design of fuchsias. Emile Gallé, Nancy, France; c 1880; ht 9in (22.9cm).
A small piece, but typical of the best of Emile Gallé's work in exploring technical innovations. The glass is slightly ribbed and the blown bulbous mouth has three openings. The flowers have been etched and then enamelled to produce a subtle, three-dimensional relief. Although best known for his glass, Gallé worked on many kinds of decorative art, including furniture and jewellery.

Page 158
Mosque lamp enamelled in gold, blue, black and white. Joseph Brocard, France; c 1870; ht 10⅛in (25.7cm).
The Islamic influence on European glass continued long after the medieval period. The French, who had cultural and political links with North Africa until very recently, were particularly responsive to Arabic patterns. Brocard, a studio craftsman (working 1860s–90s), made many versions of Syrian lamps, some of which have been mistaken for 13th and 14th-century originals.

Page 159
Small bowl in *pâte de verre* with moth motif. Gabriel Argy-Rousseau, France; c 1920; ht 4in (10.1cm).
Pâte de verre is an old process which was revived by French Art Nouveau craftsmen in the late 19th century. The first pieces were made by Henri Cros in the 1880s; later artists were Emile Gallè, Almeric Walter, Renè Lalique and Argy-Rousseau – whose signature can be seen on this bowl. Soft, subtle colourings and natural forms in low relief were typical of the entire period, and continued to be popular until well into the 1930s.

The technique of making stained glass windows has not changed much since the eleventh century. We have several early descriptions of the technique, notably in the second volume of Theophilus' *Diversarum Artium Schedulae* written in the eleventh century. The basic material was 'pot' metal – a glass mass of a single colour, made from only one pot of colour. The window was built up by tracing the design from a full-size cartoon drawn by the artist, with the lead lines marked and the colours indicated. The individual glass pieces, stained or plain, were then cut to shape by making an outline with a hot iron and cracking the outline by dropping water on to it. The glass was then broken as required and additional cutting was carried out with the grozing iron, a notched, spanner-like tool. Diamond cutting tools were not used in window glass manufacture until about 1500. The sketched design was outlined and shaded in a low viscosity paint mixture of black or sepia prepared from copper oxide and powdered glass, called *Schwarzlot*, which was also used to obtain a variety of decorative effects achieved by scraping and abrasion. When completed, the painting was fused onto the glass surface by annealing, and the individual glass pieces leaded by being set into H-shaped strips of lead or calmes, soldered wherever pieces of lead crossed each other and further secured by cement rubbed into the grooves.

The fourteenth century saw the invention of the yellow stain – a thin film of silver nitrate laid onto the surface of the glass pane and fixed by firing. The result was a brilliant colour which could be varied from the palest yellow to a dark ochre. When applied to panes of pot metal blue, the silver stain produced a bright emerald green. By 1500, an additional colour – *eisenrot* (iron red) – had been developed, and decorative treatment included the overlaying and grinding away of colour films, as well as stippled shading.

An early twelfth-century window at the Cathedral of St Julian, Le Mans, picturing the Ascension, is probably the earliest Romanesque window to feature a group rather than a single figure. Still Romanesque in character are the important twelfth-century windows of St Denis, and some of the magnificent thirteenth-century glass at Chartres. The eleventh-century window style, with single and angular figures, changed characteristically with the advent of Gothic architecture. Representational figures were surrounded by medallions displaying a sequence of the related legend and the spandrels (the space between the medallions) filled in with foliage built up from small pieces of glass. The twelfth century was an important period in the art of miniature painting where some of the most colourful and eloquent work came from the Paris school, and this greatly influenced the pictorial design concepts of stained window glass.

A late thirteenth-century development was the grisaille window for which a larger quantity of plain glass was used. Some of the plain parts were painted in grey or brown enamel with the introduction of just a few pieces of coloured glass in brilliant reds or blues and painted designs of trellis, plants and foliage. The window pattern was either purely geometrical or incorporated subject medallions.

With changes in architectural style, the window grew taller and wider; plain glass was used to a much greater

Above
Head of Christ. Wissembourg, France; 11th–12th century. One of the earliest known examples of stained glass, painted in a beautifully symmetrical Norman style. The first flush of Gothic churches spread from Germany through northern France, spurred by Abbé Suger's new choir at the Abbey Church of St Denis near Paris. The Abbé encouraged stonemasons to create as much light as possible. The result, a hundred years later, at Sainte-Chapelle is known as the 'chapel of glass'. The new style and artistic inspiration gradually spread to Chartres, Bourges, Tours, Auxerre and other places, small and large, throughout northern Europe.

extent and the glasspainters were aiming at clearer colours and more effectively planned compositions. A naturalistic movement emerged during the fourteenth and fifteenth centuries which is reflected in the pictorial entity of the painted window. Architectural and figural representation grew more complex and the border, which was once a decorative trellis and plant surround forming part of the picture, became plain in order to separate the window from the stonework frame, or was even omitted altogether. Some interesting transitional work, with Gothic and Renaissance details side by side, are to be seen in a number of French windows, particularly in some of the Rouen churches, a great centre for stained glass windows. The iconography and architectural history of stained glass merits a huge chapter to itself, and whilst the stained window gained in importance and splendour, French glaziers and French coloured glass were in great demand, with foreign countries relying on French and Flemish techniques.

This applied equally to plain window glass. The crown process, also known as the Normandy method, is probably of Syrian origin and was brought to the West by immigrant glassmakers. It involves blowing a large bubble of glass (the parison), transferring it to the pontil and rotating it freely in front of the glory hole until the required size is obtained. The so-called broadsheet technique, practised by the Lorraine glaziers, is already described by Theophilus in his treatise. By this method, the parison is blown so as to form a long cylindrical bubble which is cut off straight at both ends, cut open lengthwise and flattened. This technique may well have been inspired by the Venetians and did not come into use until after 1500.

Les Gentilshommes Verriers

During the fourteenth century, the glassmakers' craft was raised to a most respectable status, and French glass history presents us with the intriguing chapter of the *Gentilshommes Verriers* – the Gentleman Glassmakers.

Despite much documented evidence, there is still a great deal of speculation about the so-called 'nobility' of French glassmakers, and if the great potter and glassmaker, Bernard Palissy (1510–89), writes: *L'art de la verrerie est noble, et ceux qui y besognent sont nobles* (Glassmaking is a noble art and those toiling at it are noble), then this in itself affirms the ambiguity.

From time to time throughout history, glassmakers have been granted special privileges and exemptions. In France, however, as in Bohemia, the feudal system under which the real nobility held large tracts of afforested land encouraged the setting up of aristocrat-owned glasshouses. As early as 1338, a document drawn up by Humbert, Dauphin of Viennois (the Poitou district), granted permission to a certain Guionet to establish a glasshouse on ducal land, on condition of an annual supply of something like 2,400 glass vessels of various types, all minutely specified. French landowners of noble lineage hoped to establish a profitable glass industry, but these hopes were not always realized. From about 1490 French glassmakers gained the prescriptive right to style themselves *Gentilshommes*, along with privileges of the nobility. The Lorraine glassmakers were the first to adopt

Left
Goblet with tall bucket bowl
moulded with almond bosses
under a plain rim, and
enamelled with white dots;
stem with hollow blown knop
and folded foot. *c* 1500–50;
ht 8¼in (20.9cm).
A magnificent example of
Franco-Venetian glass. The
moulded pattern dates back (see
page 41) and also forward to
the honeycomb moulding of
the 18th century (see page
136).

Right
Goblet. 1600–50; ht 6¾in
(17.1cm). Enamelled
decoration; later diamond-
engraved inscription 'Found in
a hole behind the ivy in Stoke
Curci Castle'. Still very
Venetian in both shape and
decoration.

Above and right
Heavy bowl with rib moulding
on a wide foot, decorated with
thick trails inside. *c* 1500–50;
ht 6¼in (15.8cm).
An unusual bowl in a
traditional Venetian shape, but
much more solid than
cristallo. The thickness gives
the impression of crystal.

Above
Bottle or flask of flecked multi-
coloured glass blown in a
square-sided mould. Late 16th
century; ht 8¼in (20.9cm).
These multi-coloured bottles
were often made from the
glass left in various pots at the
close of work – hence the
common name 'end-of-day'
glass in England (also 'splashed
glass' in America). It has been
a favourite with blown glass
makers for centuries. Because
of its very nature, each piece is
individual and seldom
duplicated.

the right by entitling themselves *Chevaliers*, a qualification which permitted them to carry a sword.

It was usual practice for related families to settle on one estate and, by intermarrying, secure the strength of future glassmaking dynasties. However, the title of *Gentilshommes Verriers* applied equally to some of the impoverished nobility turned glassmakers, and since the profession was not considered to be one which would disgrace rank, a good number of Huguenot noblemen became adept at the art. Persistent efforts to import Italian glassmakers and know-how created the curious situation that many of the glassworkers on feudal estates, particularly in areas along the Loire, were the descendants of those same Altarists who had fled from France to settle in Altare during the Middle Ages.

French rulers took a personal and active interest in the glassmaking industry. In 1552, Henry II set up Theseo Mutio at St Germain-en-Laye, but the venture did not prove very successful. In 1598 Vincent Basson and Thomas Bartholus from Mantua were granted permission to settle at Rouen, to make '*verres de cristal, verres dorés emaulx, et autres ouvrages qui se font à Venise*'.

Little French luxury glass of the sixteenth century has survived. A group of rare goblets and chalices, decorated by gilding and enamelling, testify to Venetian inspiration, but there is a distinct delicacy and simplicity of style which distinguishes the character of these glasses from the Venetian product, and is, perhaps, related to the pictorial design of French playing cards. Made and decorated to order, the best known examples of the work are the two marriage goblets – one in the British Museum and the other in the museum at Toledo, Ohio. Among the rare milk glass vessels is a chalice decorated with a crucifixion, which is in the Wallace Collection in London.

The Seventeenth Century

The glasshouses at Nevers and Paris were set up by Henri IV in 1603, and in 1664 Louis XIV's chief minister, Colbert, sought to persuade Bishop de Bezier, French ambassador to the court at Venice, to recruit some Venetian glassmakers for the French industry. The ambassador replied that he dare not do so for fear of being thrown into the sea. Nevertheless, in 1665 eighteen Venetian glassmakers were bribed to travel to Paris and began to manufacture mirrors in the Faubourg St Antoine, at premises entitled 'Manufactory of Glass Mirrors by Venetian Workmen'. In Tour-le-Ville near Cherbourg, Richard Lucas de Nehou was producing mirrors with the assistance of some Strasbourg workmen who had clandestinely obtained knowledge of Venetian practices. After some difficulties with the Venetians in Paris, Colbert united the two factories and production proved so successful that in 1669 it was possible to prohibit importation of Venetian mirrors.

In 1688, an exclusive right for the manufacture of making large plates of glass by casting was granted to a lawyer, Abraham Thévart, supposedly a synonym for the syndicate formed by the true inventor, Louis Lucas de Nehou, a nephew of Richard. The door of the chapel at Gobain in Picardy is surmounted by an inscription stating that in 1691 Louis Lucas de Nehou invented the technique of casting

Above
Scent bottle made of blue glass and moulded in relief. Probably made at the glasshouse of Bernard Perrot; c 1650–1700; ht 3½in (8.8cm).
The fairly stylised pattern around the fleur de lys and crown is a typical Perrot design – a similar pattern was based on three hearts. Other colours were amber, red and an opaque white. The cap, missing here, would have been silver or pewter.

Right
Jug made of clear glass, with moulded and applied decoration. 1650–1700; ht 9⅛in (23.2cm).

glass and established his factory at the Château de Saint Gobain in 1695. St Gobain is today still the largest industrial glass factory in France. The French monopoly of casting plate glass lasted for over a hundred years until the introduction of a plate glass works at Ravenhead, Lancashire, in 1773. The casting hall of the old building is still standing.

Another claimant to the invention of casting glass was Bernard Perrot or Perrotto (d 1709), who inherited the monopoly of supplying glass throughout the region along the river Loire. Perrot was an enterprising and able glassmaker, active during the last thirty or forty years of the seventeenth century. In his Orléans glasshouse he produced mould-blown vessels of great charm and originality, incorporating figures, motifs of fleurs-de-lys, sunbursts and colonnades and heart-shaped emblems in beakers and scent bottles of predominantly clear white or amber glass. His style is quite unmistakable and thus a collector's delight. Perrot also produced marbled and opaque white glass objects in Venetian-influenced designs, and according to a source quoted in Hartshorne had developed a method for casting glass – '*de faire couler le cristal en table comme des metaux*' as early as 1662. A little later he began to utilize anthracite fuel for his furnaces.

At this time, France imported glassware in large quantities from neighbouring countries. No distinct French style had as yet evolved, and the drinking glasses and candlesticks of French manufacture are difficult to distinguish from glass made elsewhere. It does seem, however, that early French jugs and ewers are designed with a more aggressive pouring lip or spout – more everted, more pointed, and later with a more distinct curve than the foreign product.

An entirely different aspect of glassmaking is presented by the work of the so-called glass enamellers with their *verre filé de Nevers*, produced from the late sixteenth century onwards. This form of glassmaking appears in the shape of miniature models made at-the-lamp – small grotesques representing subjects of classical or, more frequently, religious character, comedy figures and animals. There is a well-known reference, dated 1605, to the little dogs of glass and other animals made at Nevers, which were the favourite toys of the young Prince Louis (XIII). Individual figurines were patiently assembled, frequently by nuns, to form plaquettes or tableaux of astonishing complexity, and small grottoes resembling shrines. Nevers, some 120 miles south of Paris on the Loire, had become one of the most important glassmaking centres, staffed chiefly by Altarist workmen, although their grotesques very much represent a local art, frequently practised by innkeepers. Figurines from Nevers were made of glass threads supported by internal copper wires – unless the threads were too fine. Very thin glass threads – *verre frisé* – were applied for additional decorative effects and the smaller objects, as for instance animal shapes, were made of hollow-blown glass. Single figures were made with a base of trailed *verre filé*, and any figurines found with the stand missing have probably been broken off from a group ensemble. Figurines and groups of enamel glass – the so-called *porcelaine en verre*, were made at Nevers during the eighteenth century and are of much higher artistic merit

Left
A *verre de Nevers* comedy figure in 16th-century costume. 18th century; ht 5in (12.7cm).

Below
Two of a very rare set of 'The Four Seasons' in *verre de Nevers*. Late 17th century; ht 5¼in (13.3cm).
Nevers work is much sought after by collectors. In fact, it was produced in many glassmaking areas including Paris and Marseilles, by lampworkers who bought the rods and tubes direct from the factories. It continued to be made through the 19th century but the quality varies considerably.

Bottle in opaque white glass
with enamelled decoration.
Loire district; 1711; ht 7⅞in
(20cm).
By the 18th century there were
a number of prosperous French
glasshouses, such as St-Gobain
(which is now one of the largest
industrial glass factories in the
world), but the Perrot factory
continued to dominate the
Loire region. Painting of this
period is still very Venetian in
style and execution – charming
and delightful but not really
sophisticated or as expert as
the work of later artists.

Above
Scent *flaçon* in blue glass.
Early 18th century; ht 5in
(12.7cm).
A mounted Perrot bottle with
cap and base intact – even the
ring to attach a protective
chain can be seen on the right.

Above
Pear-shaped jug of purple
glass with elongated lip spout.
Late 17th century or early 18th
century; ht 8in (20.3cm).

Left
Bottle in clear glass with
enamelled decoration. 1729;
ht 10⅝in (26.9cm).
Note the undistinguished shape
and poor quality glass; the date
may have been added later.

Below
Glass jug with a gadrooned base. Early 18th century; ht 9¾in (24.7cm).
The applied decoration under the jug's lip also strengthens a very vulnerable part (compare with jug on page 165, perhaps made at the same glasshouse). Compare too, with pitchers made a century later in the South Jersey area of America (page 184). The reinforced lip does not appear on any known American examples.

Left
A lacemaker's lamp, surmounted by a globe. 18th century; ht 10⅜in (26.3cm).

Above
Glass candlestick with a domed foot. Early 18th century; ht 7¼in (19.6cm).

Below
Double cruet stand with three feet and two large handles. 18th century; ht 3⅜in (8.5cm).

168

than the rustic *verre filé*. *Verre filé de Nevers* continued to be made during the nineteenth century, but was not necessarily produced at Nevers.

Despite these efforts and the systematic encouragement given to the *Gentilshommes Verriers* by the nobility and royalty, France had failed to establish a really prosperous and successful glass industry. Competition from Venice, Bohemia, Germany and the Netherlands was extremely powerful, and although from time to time import duty on glass was considerably increased, this did not prove an effective measure and hollow glassware remained the prerogative of the foreign glassmaker.

French plate and window glass, however, and French-made 'Venetian' mirrors had become a flourishing industry and were exported in large quantities. This did not please some of France's neighbours and certain countries, such as the Netherlands, attempted to stem the flow of French imports by legislation. However, this did nothing to prevent smuggling on a wide scale. More effective were the reformist Lowlands which presented an ideal refuge for the persecuted Huguenots. Consequently, a large number of new glasshouses were established in the northern Netherlands by French Huguenot refugees, and from 1668 window glass began to be manufactured on Dutch soil.

The Eighteenth Century

From 1700 to 1750 glasses were made from *verre de fougère*, with hollow cigar-shaped stems supporting conical bowls in the *façon de Venise* tradition. In 1723 Savary de Bruslon stated that 'finical gastronomes now imagine that wine is finer and more delicious when . . . sipped from *verre fougère*.' By the middle of the century this light metal was replaced by glass in the English or Bohemian style made from soda imported from Alicante in Spain, called *verre pivette* by Fougeroux de Bondaray although the use of this term seemed unclear even in the eighteenth century; and a fine crystal (possibly *verre blanc massif*) which nonetheless compared unfavourably with the common glass of England. Fine lead crystal was not produced until 1772.

From the middle of the century until the Revolution of 1789, upwards of three hundred glasshouses were operating in France, of which about half appear to have been making the green *chambourin*, or *verre de fougère*, even though the period was generally one of decline.

Certain regional characteristics have been noted in eighteenth-century glass: a clear metal comes mostly from the north, a pinkish crizzled metal is possibly from central and western France, and a dark green metal is associated with the south and Spain.

Development of Commercialized Industry

An initiative for the foundation of a realistic French glass industry did not present itself until 1764, when the glass-house of Sainte-Anne at Baccarat was set up due to the efforts of the Bishop of Metz, Monseigneur de Montmorency-Laval. The primary aim of this establishment was to create employment for the impoverished diocese after many months of economic crisis, and this was agreed upon by Louis XV.

After the decision to produce table and window glass, the

Below
Verre de Nevers grotto. 18th century; ht 31½in (80cm). The later Nevers figures were often set into an elaborate grotto such as this, with spun glass clouds, birds, flowers, etc. Unfortunately the quality of the figures is generally poor.

company carried on successfully until 1789, but from then on, until 1802, work could only proceed under the greatest difficulties and when the ravages of the Revolution had brought the factory to a standstill it closed down. It was then bought by Lippmann-Lippmann, a merchant from Verdun, who sold it in 1816, for 862 hectogrammes of fine gold, to Aimé-Gabriel d'Artigues, the owner of a crystal works in Vonêche in Belgium, and the owner and director of the St Louis factory from 1791–97. In 1817 the factory obtained authorization from Louis XVIII to produce lead crystal instead of ordinary (soda) glass, and in 1823 the factory was sold once again to emerge finally, a few years later, as the Compagnie des Cristalleries de Baccarat. Tableware and fashionable colour glass was produced at the factory from 1823, and after the opulence and glitter of the Napoleonic regime, pretty opaline and agate glass in the attractive contemporary Biedermeier style represented a large proportion of the factory output. One of the most sought-after colour shades today is the so-called *gorge de pigeon* opaline, which is frequently found with enamelled or gilded decoration, or mounted in ormolu, and is a soft greyish-pink.

From 1839, Baccarat produced a further innovation in the form of coloured crystal glass and in 1843 there appeared the

first pieces of uranium glass, a response to the slightly earlier Bohemian *Annagrün* and *Annagelb* developed by Riedel. Baccarat named its product '*cristal dichroide*', a colour which has a yellow or green tint depending on the light source. This was followed with the development of a green opaque glass – Chrysoprase, which Baccarat claims to have been the first to produce. Impeccable cutting and polishing is one of the distinctive features of this green glass. Unlike early French glasshouses, Baccarat was not managed by nobility, but excelled in supplying luxury crystal for the royal houses. Particularly beautiful is the glass furniture mounted in bronze and made for the Queen of Spain in 1819 in co-operation with the Paris studio, L'Escalier de Cristal; a crystal candelabra nearly 13 ft (4m) in height for the tzar's St Petersburg Palace in 1903; and numerous table services with fine cutting and gilding for royalty.

Paperweights and Revival of Italian Techniques

Disappointing though France's contribution was to earlier glass development (apart from window glass), by the mid-nineteenth century she was becoming a leader in fashionable and decorative ware of fine quality.

The development of the glass paperweight as an artefact is

Below
Rectangular casket in cut glass, mounted in gold. *c* 1850–80; length 10⅛in (26cm).
French styles of this period were very popular in Russia – this casket may have been made in Paris; or by a French glasscutter working in Russia.

Above
Fingerbowl in semi-opaque turquoise glass with gilt decoration. 1800–25; ht 4¼in (10.7cm).

Right
Vase of opal glass with blue decoration. Choisy-le-Roi; *c* 1845; ht 7½in (19cm).

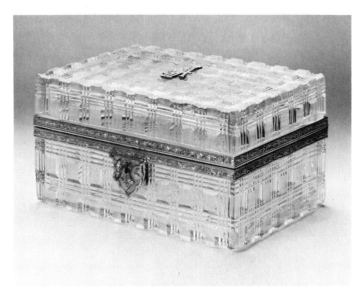

Above
Small ink bottle of pale green, moulded in horizontal and vertical ribs, and with a finely milled ring at the top. c 1860; ht 3½in (8.8cm).

Top right
Butterfly and ribbed clematis; paperweight. Diam 2¾in (7cm).

Right
Butterfly on a filigree ground; paperweight. Diam 2⅞in (7.3cm).

Below
Flat bouquets on a circular plaque, cased and cut around sides and top. Diam 3½in (8.8cm).
All three attributed to the Baccarat factory. c 1845–50.

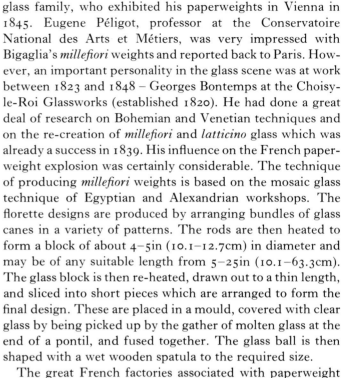

attributed to Pietro Bigaglia, a descendant of an old Murano glass family, who exhibited his paperweights in Vienna in 1845. Eugene Péligot, professor at the Conservatoire National des Arts et Métiers, was very impressed with Bigaglia's *millefiori* weights and reported back to Paris. However, an important personality in the glass scene was at work between 1823 and 1848 – Georges Bontemps at the Choisy-le-Roi Glassworks (established 1820). He had done a great deal of research on Bohemian and Venetian techniques and on the re-creation of *millefiori* and *latticino* glass which was already a success in 1839. His influence on the French paperweight explosion was certainly considerable. The technique of producing *millefiori* weights is based on the mosaic glass technique of Egyptian and Alexandrian workshops. The florette designs are produced by arranging bundles of glass canes in a variety of patterns. The rods are then heated to form a block of about 4–5in (10.1–12.7cm) in diameter and may be of any suitable length from 5–25in (10.1–63.3cm). The glass block is then re-heated, drawn out to a thin length, and sliced into short pieces which are arranged to form the final design. These are placed in a mould, covered with clear glass by being picked up by the gather of molten glass at the end of a pontil, and fused together. The glass ball is then shaped with a wet wooden spatula to the required size.

The great French factories associated with paperweight manufacture are Baccarat, St Louis (established 1767) and Clichy (established 1848 under Maes). Baccarat and St Louis have collaborated since about 1825.

Baccarat began to put *millefiori* weights on the market in 1846 and if dated, they will be for the years 1846–49 – the last year being the rarest. The marks show the year preceded by the letter B and if other initials are present without a date, they most likely represent the workman's signature. In 1848, the factory put out a new line in paperweights – the so-called *sulfures*, enclosing bouquets, flowers, fruit, animals or insects. Shortly afterwards there appeared the sulphides (see page 249) – paperweights enclosing medallions and portraits made of a metallic or refractory material within a clear glass matrix – a process termed *cristallo-ceramie*. Cut and faceted beakers decorated in the *cristallo-ceramie* technique with added enamelling, and vases and *tazze* with *millefiori* patterns were specialities. Baccarat paperweights frequently have additional features such as a star-cut base.

St Louis paperweights may be marked with dates between 1847–49 with the initials SL preceding. Designs and patterns are less conventional than Baccarat, and some of the most sought-after reptile weights were produced by this factory, which also made flower, fruit and *millefiori* weights. A St Louis characteristic is a slightly flattened dome in contrast to the weights produced by other factories. Weights marked with dates later than 1849 are rare and were made for presentation purposes.

Clichy paperweights show a number of distinctive features such as swirl patterns and striking colour cushions of brilliant red, green, blue, yellow, mauve. The letter C, incorporated in the cane pattern, indicates this factory, but it must be remembered that any factory mark on paperweights is rare.

Above
Scent bottles have always been particularly important to French factories; many classic shapes today are designed in collaboration with the great perfume houses. The bottles shown above date from the 16th to the 19th century.

Much sought after are overlay paperweights, which were produced by all three factories. They are made in a variety of colours and have windows cut away to reveal the enclosed pattern. Double overlay weights have an opaque white lining which shows up attractively in facet cutting. Weights were made in several sizes: miniature weights of a diameter $1\frac{1}{2}$–2in (3.8–5cm), standard weights of $2\frac{1}{2}$–$3\frac{1}{4}$in (6.3–8.3cm) diameter; anything larger is termed a magnum weight. *Millefiori* canes showing animal silhouettes were produced by both Baccarat and St Louis.

Paperweights are prized and priced according to rarity of colour and design and may fetch several thousand pounds, particularly if they are specimens not hitherto recorded.

Art Nouveau and Ecole de Nancy

France had by now gained a reputation as one of the most important producers of fine luxury glass with excellent cutting, enamelling and gilding. The distinctive French opaline glass in white and pastel colours, and particularly in a striking turquoise blue, became a fashionable refinement with a place in every home. A cheaper substitute for the opaque white glass was the so-called 'alabaster' or *pâte-de-riz*, in an unappealing greyish-white, with a slightly rough or sticky coarse surface. Most French factories produced opaline, and a large quantity of excellent colour glass was produced by the glasshouse at Pantin, which was originally sited at La Villette under E. S. Monot.

With the Revolution, the old dynasties of French glassmakers had also disintegrated. Official support in the form of competitive exhibitions invited the art and craft industries to display their best efforts to a large public, and individual glassmakers were encouraged to demonstrate their skill and ingenuity in their chosen medium. By the mid-nineteenth century a renewed vogue for Italian-inspired glass techniques resulted in interesting concepts of bright colour contrasts and *millefiori*, striped, spiral and *latticino* patterns as envisaged by Georges Bontemps in his *Guide du Verrier*. These glassmakers were the true forerunners of the most brilliant phase in French glass as expressed by studio work of the Art Nouveau period and epitomized in the ideals of the Ecole de Nancy.

The decorative style of Art Nouveau swept both Europe and America during the late nineteenth and into the beginning of the twentieth century. It was both a reaction against earlier design forms and imitative concepts and an elegant fusion of the primary artistic elements of the mid-century – naturalism and symbolism. In spite of the many sources from which the Art Nouveau movement draws inspiration – the vogue for Oriental art, Chinese and Japanese in particular, and the taste for sombre Gothic forms with accents on fantasy and eroticism – it is a style which is unmistakable and aesthetically satisfying at its best.

The paramount object of the Ecole de Nancy was to further the new principles based on scientific observations of live models. At its head, the leader of the craftsmen and artists gathered at Nancy, stood Emile Gallé (1846–1904), son of Charles Gallé, a designer of luxury faience and furniture. The parental establishment at St Clément-sur-Oise soon expanded with the addition of the mirror factory, part

Right
Glass vase with a square mouth and a large bulbous body; decorated with a floral design in enamel colours. Emile Gallé, Nancy; 1889; ht $9\frac{1}{2}$in (24cm).

Below
L'oignon vase. Emile Gallé; 1900; ht $13\frac{1}{2}$in (34.2cm). Literally translated, this onion vase has a *martelé* decoration on the 'bulb'; its *marqueterie de verre* decoration was developed by Gallé and involved pressing another motif, usually of a different colour, into the glass surface.

of Madame Charles's inheritance, and the production of table glass.

Emile Gallé's earliest efforts are seen in faience of the typical Provençale style decorated with charming and naturalistically sketched designs, and in elegant pieces of inlaid marquetry furniture. His philosophy courses at Weimar in 1862, and his subsequent training, undertaken at his father's advice, at Meissenthal in glass and pottery making were complemented by botanical studies and experimental laboratory work. When Gallé returned to work in his father's factory, he found a kindred spirit in the personality of a gifted designer, Victor Prouvé, with whom he was able to share his ideals and ambitions. This relationship was briefly interrupted when Gallé, filled with romantic visions and fired by patriotism, volunteered to fight in the Franco-German war, from whence he returned unscathed. From then on, Gallé decided to devote his entire life to expressing the beauty of nature in his very personal, lyrical language; and in the fluid and luminous substance of glass he found his ideal medium. Once he had made the decision to become a glassmaker all his efforts were directed toward the realization of this dream.

In 1874 the factory at St Clement was transferred to Nancy. Here Gallé's early work was confined to the decorative enamelling of what were not always gracefully designed vessels in clear white, amber or bluish glass. Some of this work is quite splendid, particularly when the subject motif is of historical or heraldic significance. However, it is in the creation of exciting and unusual glass effects that Gallé's imagination is virtually boundless: plain and coloured glass, enamelled, cut, marbled and inlaid glass (a complex marquetry technique which he launched in 1897), Oriental-inspired cased cameo glass which he so admired in the snuff bottles at the South Kensington (now the Victoria and Albert) Museum in London. All these achievements are part of Gallé's genius and make him the first to express successfully the highest ideals of the Art Nouveau movement in the medium of glass. And when form, decoration and actual technical effect seemed inadequate, then Gallé emphasized his message by the addition of a few poetic phrases and quotations or symbolic prose fragments, and thus created his true *verreries parlantes*. His success was immediate, and the many

exhibitions organized by the Union Centrale des Arts Decoratifs fortunately resulted in many of his best pieces being acquired by the Musée des Arts Decoratifs. He was one of the most influential and spectacular geniuses in the history of glassmaking and he quickly gained many followers and imitators, particularly as regards the later mass-produced cameo glass. Gallé signatures are of infinite variation and respond to the mood of the glass to which they are applied.

One of the earliest studio (as opposed to factory) glass artists was Eugène Rousseau (1827–91), who began as a designer of faience but worked in glass during 1867–85, with his assistant Ernest Baptiste Leveillé to follow in his footsteps, as did another pupil, Eugène Michel. Rousseau was particularly interested in glass texture and colour. His sculptured pieces with crackle glass effects were an attractive novelty, and the experiments with metal inlays and colour streaks are quite striking. Rousseau was a skilful engraver, but his more interesting achievements were directed towards plastic animal and plant forms. An engraved signature may be present, although little identifiable glass appears to be available.

Closest to Gallé in concept and ability is the work of the Daum brothers – Auguste (1854–1909) and Antonin (1864–1930), and that of Muller Frères Lunéville and Landier & Fils, Sèvres. Among the best factories working in the Gallé tradition are St Louis at Münzthal (today Compagnie des Cristalleries de St Louis), signature 'Arsale' (Argental is the French adaptation of Münzthal); Stumpf, Touvier, Viollet & Cie (today Cristallerie de Pantin), signature 'De Vez' after Camille Tutré de Varreux, who was art director of the company; Cristallerie Schneider, signature 'Schneider' or 'Le Verre Français'; Legras & Cie at St Denis, signature 'Legras'; Burgun Schverer & Co. at Meissenthal, who had a secret contract with Gallé (under the leadership of Desiré Christian, 1846–1907, as independent designer decorator), signature 'Verrerie d'Art de Lorraine BS & CO.' Georges de Feure (1868–1928), a very able artist and designer, worked for Fauchon of Paris and produced moulded glass of heavy form and interesting figure detail.

Joseph Brocard (worked *c* 1867–95), who had contributed successfully to the 1867 Paris World Exhibition, revived the exquisite enamelling characteristic of early Islamic glass. His

Below
A double overlay chandelier
with original metal mount,
and a delicate floral pattern.
Daum Frères; *c* 1900; diam
15½in (39.5cm).

fine copies of fourteenth-century Syrian mosque lamps are
often almost indistinguishable from the originals, but most
of his work is signed in brown or red enamel. His later work is
influenced by Rousseau and Gallé, and these rare pieces are
usually enamelled with free naturalistic designs. With the
work of René Lalique (1860–1945), a jewellery designer who
turned from coloured enamels and glass pastes to the glass
material itself, French Art Glass takes on an entirely new
direction with the exploitation of not simply the aesthetic
beauty of glass but also of its possibilities as a functional
medium within the framework of a modern life style.

Lalique, whose first commercial success came with perfume flasks designed for Coty, relied on glass texture,
luminosity and form to achieve his aims, and his exploitation
of the refractory properties and the tensile strength of his
material made him one of the first glass artists to apply his
medium in the field of architecture. This is best expressed in
the chandeliers, fountains and glass doors which he designed
for public places and private houses. The use of colour in
glass was therefore of minor importance to Lalique; the

Left
Emile Gallé is one of the
world's best-known glass
artists; although he also
designed ceramics and
furniture, his work in glass was
a remarkable achievement and
an inspiration to Art Nouveau
designers throughout the world.
Gallé developed many new
techniques for colouring glass,
and especially for carved and
enamelled decoration.
Left to right:
Marqueterie de verre vase,
c 1900; scent bottle with
carved Rose de France
pattern, *c* 1895; cameo vase
with prunus branch, *c* 1890;
'La Têtard' cased and applied
with inscription from Gautier,
c 1900; vase in *verre eglomisé*
with applied decoration,
c 1880–90; 'Les coprins', lamp
blown in two to five layers,
c 1904.

Above
Bowl in transparent greenish
glass with orange inclusions.
François Décorchement;
c 1925; ht 4¾in (12.2cm).
Both handles are decorated with
relief motifs of a snake.

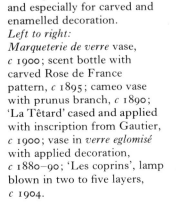

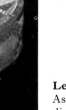

Above
Car mascot in the shape of an
eagle. René Lalique; *c* 1930;
width 3½in (8.8cm).
This amusing piece was
originally mounted on the
radiator of a Mercedes
limousine.

Left
Ashtray moulded in raised
diamond relief around flat rim.
René Lalique; *c* 1920; ht 5¾in
(14.6cm).

Left
'Pierrefonds' double-handled cup in clear and frosted glass. René Lalique; late 1920s; ht 6in (15.2cm).
This is a typical geometrical Art Deco design.

Right
Scent spray with original metal mounts and tassel-covered atomiser, enamelled in black and gilt, and engraved with fluted band. Probably Paris; c 1925; ht 3in (7.5cm).

Above
Bottle of blown glass with stopper, enamelled in brilliant red. Design by Maurice Marinot; c 1920; ht 9$\frac{1}{8}$in (23.2cm).

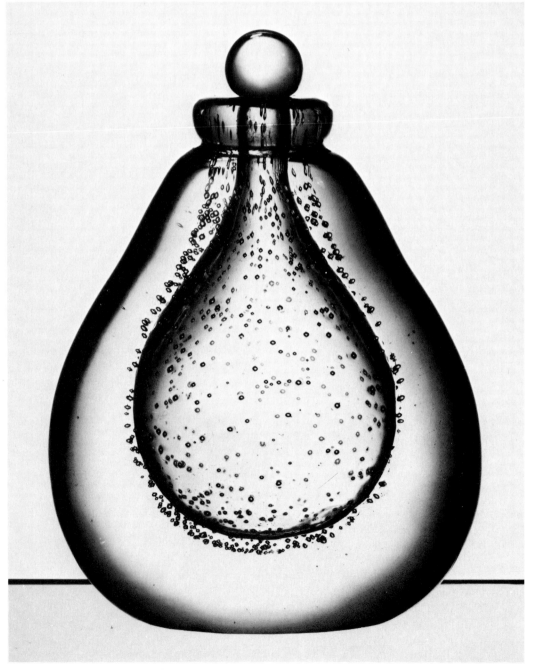

Left
Perfume bottle with stopper, made of clear glass enclosing air bubbles. Designed by Maurice Marinot; c 1931; ht 4$\frac{7}{8}$in (12.3cm).

frosted, subtly opalescent effect achieved by acid or sand blasting, as well as the unique limpid crystal with interior cloudiness are his most interesting achievements. The best in Lalique glass design is the stylised treatment of natural forms, arranged in an exciting geometrical pattern order. Most Lalique pieces are moulded, so there is a large mass-production programme, and many of the early specimens are still reproduced today. Signatures are engraved, or moulded, or even both. After René Lalique's death in 1945, the initial 'R' was omitted from the signature.

Maurice Marinot (1882–1960), a trained painter and a principal follower of the school of Fauvism, exhibited his first lightly enamelled glass in 1912. This early approach soon changed, and after 1922 he preferred his pieces heavy and massive. His expressionist treatment made a striking impact, and his inlaid colours and air bubbles were exceptionally *avant-garde* and appealing to the modern eye. Marinot fashioned every piece himself, from mixing and blowing to the final etching of his signature, and he, perhaps more than any other glass artist, has influenced contemporary studio work.

Pâte de Verre

A very special facet of glassmaking based on ancient techniques was revived in France at the turn of the century by a group of individual studio artists. This technique, termed *pâte de verre*, literally 'glass paste', consists of powdered glass with an added binder which is slowly heated and can be moulded to produce hollow vessels, sculptural forms and plaques. The process is fraught with technical difficulties and many of the pieces which survive in a cracked condition have already been damaged during or after firing or annealing in the studio.

The first Frenchman to experiment in *pâte de verre* was Henri Cros (1840–1907), who made some interesting plaques with mythological themes, using the furnace at the Sèvres porcelain factory. Another ceramist at Sèvres, Albert Dammouse (1848–1926), successfully produced a very fragile *pâte de verre* or *pâte d'email*, akin to a porcelain mass. Dammouse's vessels are beautifully decorated with delicate plant forms in pastel shades of greens, greys, blues and browns. George Despret (1862–1952) worked in a heavier type of *pâte de verre* which was frequently rather sugary in

colouring. Another artist, Ringel d'Illsach, specialised in grotesque masks.

In 1904, Almeric Walter (1859–1942), a ceramist, began to work for Daum, in collaboration with the sculptor Henri Bergé, the artist Victor Prouvé and Joseph Cheret. Walter's *pâte de verre* mass is thicker and more robust and consequently has a higher rate of survival. In 1919, Walter began to work on his own. His pieces are always interesting and usually well modelled. Colour nuances range from green to yellow, red and brown, and on occasion one may find a sweetish pink and a bright blue. The choice of subjects is very varied and includes many figures of the dancer Loie Fuller, plaques, ashtrays incorporating reptiles and marine life, and boxes decorated with flowers or animals.

A less-known artist working in *pâte de verre* was Jules-Paul Brateau (1844–1923), who was largely influenced by Dammouse, but the most subtle and interesting pieces came from the workshops of Gabriel Argy-Rousseau (*b* 1885) and François Décorchement (1880–1971). Argy-Rousseau began with a thinnish *pâte de verre* product, but later made his vessels of a thicker, slightly granular glass texture. His bowls and dishes are always in most attractive colours which are excellently controlled – a most difficult process. Fruit, plant and insect forms often stand away from the vessel surface in high relief, and despite the wall thickness, there is usually a degree of transparent luminosity which relieves any heaviness of form. Décorchement worked at his own furnace at Conches and at first was also much influenced by Dammouse. By 1910, however, his style underwent a change and he developed a thicker and at the same time more transparent material – a *pâte de cristal* – which he utilized for the making of plaques and coloured glass windows. His later, heavier, pieces incorporate polishing and some plain cutting.

Pâte de verre artists almost always sign their work, and each had his own secret technique for producing this fragile glass material.

Between 1907–8 Daum, too, produced window plaques of *pâte de verre* in clear colours. During the 1920s and 1930s Daum still produced some cased and acid-etched colour glass in the Art Deco style. Today they concentrate on luxury glass, frequently in the form of abstract flowing and rhythmic shapes in a pure and limpid crystal. Recently, they have revived *pâte de verre* production and commissioned well-known artists to design their pieces.

Lalique, more successful and costly than ever, is still making glass on similar lines, and there are few French factories that can compete with the supreme quality of their glassmetal. In 1977, René Lalique's son, Marc, died, and the firm continues under the directorship of Marc Lalique's daughter. Baccarat supplies fine and elegant tableware and St Louis are experimenting and producing interestingly patterned cut glass. The workshop and glassblowing school of the Verrerie Biot, near Grasse, is established on the site of an early glassworks, and the glassware produced there is stylish and sensible.

The United States

Glassmaking in the United States began long before the colonies were properly established. As early as 1608 the London Company of Glassmakers were pioneering a new glasshouse, built in the woods near Jamestown, Virginia. It seemed a natural paradise for the new industry; unlimited fuel instead of the constant wrangling with forestry owners in England, good supplies of sand, and river and sea transport to ship the finished products back to the mother country.

Unhappily, both this and a subsequent attempt in 1621 failed miserably. There is no evidence to show if either settlement actually reached the stage of continuous production, and up to the present time, nothing has been found in the area except for a few fragments of green bottle glass. The most common explanation for the failure seems to have been the lack of sympathy between the workers and the management. Both times foreign workers from Bohemia and Italy were brought over with signed contracts; the lure of the open forest land seems to have been more exciting than the prospect of working in what must have been primitive conditions, for an absentee landlord.

Whatever the reasons (and we shall probably never know too much more about this period), both the Virginian furnaces and subsequent attempts to set up glasshouses in Salem, Massachusetts, and New Amsterdam (now New York) suffered the same lack of success.

Early Factories

Finally, in 1739, Caspar Wistar (1696–1752) came to Alloywaystown in New Jersey, and succeeded in establishing the first known glasshouse of record in the colonies.

Wistar had been an immigrant from Germany, who settled in Philadelphia to make buttons. When that business was established and prosperous, he began to look around for a new challenge, and realized that with his connections at home he might be able to introduce a settled and stable community in the growing South Jersey area. Craftsmen were imported from Rotterdam as well as from Germany and Poland, and they concentrated on making practical wares for domestic use in unrefined glass, especially window panes and bottles of all kinds.

Glassblowers are always willing to make a few more ornamental objects, and the glasswork's employees began to use the same green or brown glass to turn out simple, free-blown pieces with a charm and style all their own, today known collectively as South Jersey glass. There are obvious similarities with the northern European *Waldglas*, but they did develop a few unique designs. The most notable is the lily pad with bowls, jugs and goblets blown into a globular shape, and then dipped to pick up a second gather of glass which is tooled up in points all around the original form. Threading was another South Jersey tradition, as well as tooled and applied decoration on handles and finials.

When Caspar Wistar died in 1752, his son took over the factory which by now was a complete community called Wistarberg. It continued to produce simple, good-looking wares until it was sold in 1780.

Henry William Stiegel (1729–85) was a much more colourful character. He called himself 'the Baron' and, like Wistar, his original investment came from a previously

Below
Small bowl and creamer, blown in heavy glass. c 1750–1825; ht of bowl 3½in (8.8cm). Difficult to date because their design was popular for so many years, these shapes were made by glassworkers for themselves and their friends.

Below
Covered jar with swirled flammiform base, and threaded decoration. Norway; c 1756; ht 7½in (19cm). Blowers were hired from all over Europe to work in the growing American factories. Venetian influence came from the north as well as Italy.

successful business, an iron foundry near Shaefferstown, Pennsylvania.

Stiegel began with a fairly modest window and bottle factory near the foundry, in 1763, and he also imported workmen from his home town and district in Mannheim, Germany. Success encouraged him to begin on a second factory, established in 1765 to make better tableware than that in the original range, and his ambition grew to include a third factory in 1769, grandly entitled the American Flint Glass Works. This was intended to be the first American glasshouse specialising in fine tableware of flint glass, both clear and coloured. Perhaps the patriotic Stiegel thought that now that the colonies were really going to be incorporated into a federation, the richer homes would be glittering all through the year with truly American tableware. It seemed possible, and the glass was sold as far away as Boston and New York, while the factory employed at one time over 130 people, an enormous undertaking for the period.

Unhappily the economics had not been quite realistic, and the cost of manufacturing far exceeded the profits. In 1774 the factories were closed. Perhaps it was the timing that was wrong; ten years later Stiegel might have found that his three factories at Manheim, Pennsylvania, were the first home industry in the very new United States.

Stiegel's glass was made in a variety of colours, as well as in clear transparent glass of good quality. The amethysts, blues, browns and greens were rich and deep in tone, and pattern moulded in sophisticated diamond designs for the Eastern seaboard cities. Local neighbours with their strong German background preferred the clear bottles and tumblers with enamelled figures in bright colours, mottoes and garlands, flowers and scrolls. In spite of fragments that have been found, there are very few documented pieces of Stiegel's

Above

Sugar bowl and cover, with applied lily-pad decoration and chicken finial. New York; 1835–50; ht 10⅝in (27cm). Lovely South Jersey pieces like this were made in the Eastern states for 40–50 years.

Right

Two tumblers: *left*, with pattern moulding and engraved band; *right*, with enamel decoration. Possibly from the Stiegel factory at Manheim, Pennsylvania; *c* 1773; ht of taller tumbler 6⅝in (16.7cm). One tumbler was for the sophisticated local middle class, one for the Pennsylvania Dutch population.

Left
A possible reconstruction of
one of John Frederick
Amelung's glasshouses. Drawn
by Richard Stinely; *c* 1790.
Amelung's New Bremen
factory, established in 1794,
started by making window
glass; tableware was added in
1785.

Below
Flask from Amelung's New
Bremen factory, inscribed with
'f. Stenger 1792'.
Ht 6¾in (17.1cm).
This rounded flask is typical of
the glass produced by New
Bremen. The factory closed
three years after it was made, in
1795.

glass – he was not an innovator, and his designs were copies
and adaptations of those made in European and English
glasshouses during the same period. For that reason, most
of this kind of glass is referred to as Stiegel-type.

Another immigrant from Germany, John Frederick
Amelung, came from Bremen especially to build the New
Bremen Glass Manufactory in Maryland. He arrived in
August of 1784 and, after buying land near Frederick, he
built a factory and the necessary houses and community
buildings for the workmen. The New Bremen glasshouse
began by making window glass in a few simple shapes in
clear and green glass, adding tableware in 1785. By the time
production was in full swing in 1787, a village to serve the
factory had been built – homes for 135 people, a community
centre which also served as a church, a school for the
children, and, not unnaturally, a commodious and comfortable house for the Amelung family.

The glass at New Bremen was not always made with lead,
although it was quite good quality. The clear glass had a
slightly smokey, greyish tinge, and there was also a greyish
blue and an amethyst glass. There may have been other
colours, too.

Although there was a considerable Bohemian influence in
Amelung's background, he seems to have been aware that
the Pennsylvania Dutch tradition was slowly losing ground,
and it is quite clear that most of his wares are strongly akin to
English and Irish designs of the earlier part of the century.
The shapes are rather formal, with elegant, capacious
goblets and amply rounded bottles. Decoration was kept to
beautifully handled engraving in order to show off the
quality of the glass, and happily Amelung made many
commissioned pieces for presentation. They give us some
idea of what the other Amelung products looked like.

In spite of Amelung's success, the factory failed to make
money, and a disastrous fire in 1790 almost wiped it out.
By 1795 New Bremen was closed down, and the workmen
dispersed throughout the Midwestern and Eastern states.

At least one group, headed by Albert Gallatin (1761–1840), established a factory in New Geneva, Pennsylvania, in 1798, and almost certainly some of Amelung's experienced men went there, although there are no definitive records to prove this. New Geneva also suffered from the almost intractable job of balancing high cost with low prices, but it managed to stay in business somewhat precariously until 1847, making mainly window and bottle glass. Gallatin had been Secretary of the Treasury from 1803–13, and perhaps his business ability helped the new company to keep afloat.

Amelung, Stiegel and almost all the well-known names in American glassmaking used a great deal of pattern moulding, a process which had been part of glassmking since the first era of blown metal. The gather is expanded inside an open mould, then removed and inflated again to the required size. Ribbing is very common, and the piece is identified by the number of ribs (16-rib, 24-rib, etc) while some pieces, especially bottles and flasks of this period, are made with a diamond, or honeycomb moulding. There is one pattern, a daisy shape within a diamond, which is very rare, and is supposed to have been made in Stiegel's glasshouse. There are variations on that, too.

Nineteenth-century Developments

During the first quarter of the nineteenth century, Ohio became a centre for glassmaking, and there were a number of glasshouses around Zanesville which seem to have a distinctive style. They made covered bowls with a double-dome top and a nice, round fat ball as a finial, and the vases and decorative pieces often had applied handles with pinched decoration, like the winged stems on seventeenth-century Venetian goblets.

Many early American glasshouses experimented with various mixtures containing different amounts of lead oxide. The South Boston Flint Glass Works were the first to make lead glass in New England. South Boston was run by an Englishman, Thomas Cains (1779–1865), one of many who came to the United States in search of relatively easy land purchase and cheap quantities of fuel. Cains then started his own factory called the Phoenix Glass Works in 1821, and it survived until 1870. His designs were heavily influenced by English patterns which had been fashionable at least a hundred years before.

Many of the American glassmakers were influenced by Continental fashions; at the beginning of the nineteenth century, the Bohemian German influence was particularly strong because of men like Stiegel and Amelung and Caspar Wistar. They made the less expensive, enamel-painted wares which the local German community liked so much. Inscriptions in English are the only distinguishing factor and even then, there is no reason to suppose that some families did not prefer to have their loving cup or marriage glass still inscribed with traditional words in their native language. However, as the century progressed, more and more Englishmen came to the new country, and many of the second flood of craftsmen were from England or Ireland. They brought with them the latest fashion in cut and engraved glass, and this was an immediate success, especially along the Eastern seaboard.

Below
Early pattern-moulded pieces, with honeycomb and diamond moulding. c 1770–1800; ht of bowl 6⅝in (16.7cm).
The chequered diamond design on the little salt (c 1790) is often referred to as an Amelung pattern, but there is no evidence that such patterns were not made in other glasshouses.

Blown-mould Patterns in America

Cut glass was expensive – even without the excise tax which had done so much damage in Europe. The high quality of the glass plus the heavy weight of the object itself made the finished pieces dear even for the well-to-do. Pattern moulding had shown that glass could be impressed but as it was necessary to inflate the glass again, the pattern became diffused and soft – perfect for rippled glass and simple shapes, but bearing no resemblance to cut glass in any form. Full-sized moulds were the answer, and blown-three-mould, which was used from about 1815–35, provided the first Anglo-Irish cut glass patterns for the ordinary market. The outlines were still not as sharp as the hand-cut originals, but the designs could be quite complex and the result had a charm of its own.

'Blown-three-mould' is rather misleading, since the mould could be in two, three or even four parts hinged together – 'blown' is the important word, not 'three'. The gather was inserted into the mould, which was hinged so it could be shut, then the object was inflated until it pressed against the sides of the mould all the way round. Blowing usually opened the seams just a little, and there is often a slight bulging seam at that point on the finished article. Finally the glass was removed quickly by opening the mould, and the top and bottom, if necessary, finished off by hand.

There are three basic types of blown-mould patterns:

geometric, arched, and baroque. The geometric patterns are obviously an imitation of the Anglo-Irish cut glass, but the arched and baroque patterns do not appear on other kinds of glass. Baroque in particular is very individual with hearts and flowers, flowing lines and swirling ribbons in all directions.

Many of the blown-three-mould pieces were made in clear flint glass, but there are examples in almost every shade of green, blue and amethyst. Moulds were also used for ordinary bottle glass objects, and they are usually olive green or olive amber in colour.

One point should be noted: in England 'flint glass' was mis-used early in the history of glass to describe the Ravenscroft type of glass using lead oxide. Originally ground flints were tried as a substitute for sand, but were never popular. Nonetheless the name stuck as a synonym for lead glass or glass of lead. In America flints were not tried at all, but the term 'flint' was a quick and easy way of referring to any refined and high quality glass.

All blown-mould pieces can be identified by the pattern on the inside as well as the outside – pressed glass, which occasionally is mistaken for blown-mould glass, has a smooth inner surface.

New England had a number of leading glasshouses, including the Keene (Marlborough Street) Glass Works in New Hampshire, and the New England Glass Company near Boston, Massachusetts. New England was one of the most successful, producing almost every type of glass – blown mould, patterned mould, cut and fine tableware, pressed glass, figured flasks, engraved presentation pieces – the craftsmen were versatile and successful. Unfortunately cheap fuel available to the Midwestern houses meant strong competition and when a strike temporarily closed the plant in 1888, the owners moved the entire place to Toledo and, re-named the Libbey Glass Company, it has remained ever since as one of the leading glass manufacturers in the United States. The glass museum in Toledo has one of the finest collections in the country.

Bottles and Flasks

Bottle and window glass was obviously made in large quantities, since it formed the sound financial bread-and-butter product for most of the larger glasshouses. The basic green tones were complemented by ambers, browns and blues, and some of the early and rare examples from the Midwestern glasshouses are also in a brilliant amethyst.

There is very little to identify the different factories; for example, pattern-moulded flasks were made c 1810–35. The most common effects were variations on diamond and swirled ribbing, almost all with globular bases and long thin necks. They were produced in all sizes, from tiny 2 or 3in (5 or 7.6cm) versions, presumably for medicine or strong brandy, to comfortably capacious examples, 9in (22.9cm) or more in height. The glass is usually soda or lime-based, since lead, or flint, glass was too expensive, and many of the pioneers streaming westward past the settlements in the Ohio and Pennsylvania valleys would need more than one flask.

Some flasks were strengthened by the addition of an extra gather of glass on the body, known as the German half-post

Top
Bowl, blown in pale aquamarine window glass. Made by William Hall at the Washington Glass Works; 1833; ht 5in (12.6cm). Hall blew this simple but lovely bowl for his own household when he worked at Washington which was primarily a window glass factory. It is one of the few documented off-hand pieces of the period.

Above
Compote with silvered glass decoration. Possibly New England Glass Company; c 1850–60; ht 17⅞in (45.5cm). The compote is formed from two pieces, a bowl and a stand, and has been elaborately engraved over the silver plating in a vine and grape motif. See page 192 for the silvered glass process which was one of the most successful techniques of the period.

method. They have now taken on the generic term 'Pitkin flasks', although they were made in many other bottle houses; the Pitkin Glass Works in East Hartford, Connecticut, listed such wares more or less from the time of its establishment in 1783 to around the 1830s.

There were other specialised bottles, of course, for medicines and chemicals of all kinds. Finding examples with labels or moulded trademarks can be an enjoyable and highly profitable field for collectors. Food and drink often came in decorated glass containers, and the varied shapes and sizes and rich, dark, earthy colours have a fascination all their own.

Preserving jars for the homemaker were another mass-produced item. The Mason jar was patented in 1858 and is also now a generic term for all preserving jars and bottles.

Fine lead or flint glass was seldom used for undecorated bottles, but it was perfect for the more ornamental bottle that became so popular in the mid-Victorian period. Only fourteen of the forty bottle houses working in Pittsburgh around 1835 made any lead glass at all, and then they made elaborate shapes in various colour combinations, with milled rings around the top, fancy stoppers, and applied threading.

Historical flasks are also among the winners in collecting appeal, and these were made in blown mould and pressed glass varieties. Bottles were often made for a particular distillery or medicine house, and for that reason are sometimes easier to identify than tableware. They were commonly made from about 1815–70, with many decorative motifs. Some were made for a specific political event, and might show portraits, railway trains, steamboats – all reflections of the busy developing social and economic life.

Almost all historical flasks were made of bottle glass, and so they run the gamut of darkish colours – olive green, olive amber, brown, yellow brown and, just occasionally, a light aquamarine.

Quite often they have the name of the manufacturer or the product itself impressed on the bottle. There is one well-known example with a portrait of Jenny Lind, celebrating her visit to the United States, and the name of Fislerville Glass Works on the base. Another favourite was an Old Cabin Whiskey bottle of 1840, originally made by the Whitney Glass Works.

Many of these blown and pressed bottles have been copied either as novelties or for deliberate fakes. Some are old enough even as fakes to have acquired a certain patina.

Changes in the Mid-nineteenth Century

Deming Jarves (1790–1869) had been the agent for the New England Glass Company from the time it was founded in 1818 until 1825, when he started the Sandwich Manufacturing Company for himself. With additional financial help he ran the re-named Boston and Sandwich Glass Company from 1826–58. Under his management it became one of the most successful glasshouses, employing over 500 people, and burning four furnaces of ten pots each. It won a number of awards for pressed, cut and coloured glassware, and exported up to a fifth of its production to South America and the West and East Indies. The production of such a large glasshouse necessarily included many distinctive patterns, but all the glasshouses copied each other, and fragments found at many sites are remarkably similar. A letter by the agent of the New England Company to a distributor points out that a particular shipment included a quantity of cup plates which they had never made before, and he hoped they would be sold quickly as 'the South Boston Co have already copied our patterns

Above
Salt and small vase, silvered, cased with ruby and cut. Probably Boston and Sandwich Glass Company; c 1860; ht of salt 3in (7.8cm).

Below
Figured flasks, also called historical or pictorial flasks, were popular through most of the 19th century in shapes as varied as their ornaments.

and Mr Jarves will do the same probably'. Attribution to a particular company is really very chancy, except for the few that come with a known 'pedigree' or a shipping label. We know that certain factories made certain patterns, but filching ideas and appealing designs was common practice.

Boston and Sandwich made a wide variety of glassware of every kind, including vast quantities of blown-three-mould patterns, finely cut and engraved glasses, free-blown, 'beehive' bowls and pitchers, lamps, and candleholders, fancy wares with looped applied threading, banks, knobs and salts . . . the list is endless.

Nonetheless they are, and remain, best known for the lacy-patterned pressed glass which became so popular that Sandwich glass has become a generic rather than a specific factory term. John Bakewell of Pittsburgh was one of the first to take out a patent for pressed glass machinery, but Jarves himself soon began the improvements and refinements that increased the potential market from the first, rather poor, imitations of Anglo-Irish cut glass to the unique and individual patterns characteristic of pressed glass at its best.

Popular Designs

By 1830 it had been discovered that stippling the background to a rather simple ordinary design covered the shear mark where the glass was removed from the machine, and created a new lacy effect which was immediately popular. At its best, openwork borders, a more relaxed and naturalistic form of flowers and scrolls, combined with clear and stippled backgrounds to make truly delightful wares. Most were in clear glass, but some coloured glass was used – blues, amethysts, opaque and opalescent white, amber, transparent yellow, and so on.

Some products were marked with the name of the company, some not. And many patterns were copied by other firms, or were indeed copied from them in the first place. The Stourbridge Flint Works in Pittsburgh, the New England Glass Company and the South Boston Glass Company, as seen by the agent's letter, were all making similar pieces, and attribution should be made very carefully.

One of the many advantages of pressed glass was the possibility of putting together various elements to creat new designs. An assortment of candlesticks might be made with similar tops but three or four different bases, giving the buyer a bewildering multiplicity of choice at no extra cost to the manufacturer.

A very popular item for all the companies were cup plates – small saucer-like plates used under tea or coffee cups to keep the cloth from being stained, and also as rests for the cups when tea was poured into another saucer to cool. They were made in such a wide variety of patterns, including commemorative political and topographical pictures, that collecting cup plates has become very popular in the United States, and since they are still inexpensive, except for a few rarities, they are relatively easy to acquire.

The Midwestern glass-producing area, which included Western Pennsylvania, Ohio, West Virginia and Indiana, tried very hard to compete with the flourishing New England companies, and one reference book listed over 1,000 patterns, each table service having up to twenty-five items.

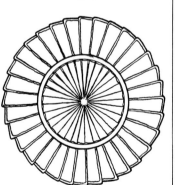

Right
Three 'Mary Gregory' glasses. Unknown factory; c 1860; ht of vase 7½in (19cm).
White enamel figures of Victorian girls and boys were usually painted on pink or green glass.

Left and above
Six pressed glass plate patterns, mostly made between 1830 and 1860. Lacy pressed glass was very popular, and decorative motifs varied immensely (shells, triangles, flowers, etc). There were also commemorative portrait plates for souvenirs, celebration plates for steamship lines, and geometric designs that imitated cut glass.

Above

Candlestick, clear glass. *c* 1860; ht 11in (27.9cm).
Dolphin candlestick, set in square base, the holder in a simple fluted pattern. The nozzles were sometimes sharpened with cutting for the more expensive pairs.

Left above and below

Assorted oil lamps. *c* 1870–1910; ht of top left lamp 5in (12.7cm).
Pressed lamps were an important product. Green and blue colours looked particularly warm and glowing when the bowls were lit. The top three are all variations made from the same moulds.

Right

Pitchers, an essential part of tableware sets, were used for water, milk, and soft drinks like homemade lemonade. The top two examples were blown and tooled by hand; the others show popular pressed glass patterns.

Water sets were one of the most popular products, and were made to match every design or, especially in the finer glasshouses, formed sets of their own. They usually consisted of a large jug or pitcher, a set of tumblers, and a tray. Although intended to hold ice water for the table – a very American habit – they were also advertised as being eminently suitable for milk, fruit juices, lemonades or cider, for serving any time of the day. Early pitchers usually had applied handles but in 1838 Deming Jarves succeeded in designing a machine which would press handle and pitcher together in one operation, and later designs have handles clearly made in one piece with the jug. Cut and engraved pitchers and jugs continued to be made in the better glassworks, decorated with classic patterns, frosted surfaces, or floral engraving. The well-known lily-pad pitcher continued to be made at South Jersey glassworks until well into the second half of the century. Most are on stemmed feet, and are often additionally decorated with threading around the rim. Lily-pad forms were also used for plates, covered sugar bowls and compotes, and although the originals had probably been made in bottle glass as one-off items by workers at the end of the day, they were so popular that lily-pad designs were adapted for fine tableware in high quality flint glass. Many of the delightful covered bowls with lily-pad bases have chicken finials on set-in covers.

Dolphins are a recurrent theme in America. They seem to have been a continually strong selling item, and although used primarily for candlesticks, they often appear with a lovely fishy grin on a number of related pieces made in Pittsburgh and in New England. The Pittsburgh glass-producing area, which actually includes the glasshouses built in the valleys around Pittsburgh on the Ohio and Mongehela rivers, was the first American area to use coal for fuel, and the cheap fuel undoubtedly helped the Midwestern companies to compete with the more aristocratic and older factories on the Eastern seaboard.

One of the prettiest dolphin pieces is the so-called petticoat dolphin compote. It has an unusual flared base, a lovely open ribbed coupé top and the whole is in a very pleasant light peacock blue with the added attraction of an opalescent rim around the top of the coupé. It was made by McKee Brothers in Pittsburgh sometime in the 1860s and it stands only 5in (12.7cm) high. A similar piece was also made in a pale canary yellow. A little candlestick made by McKee also has an unusual base, a scalloped and moulded skirt, and the stick itself is in a shaded opal colour. A much larger pair of dolphins from the same Pittsburgh area carry two elongated lozenge-shaped compotes with lovely openwork sides. Describing these very unusual pieces will suggest that even a shape as commonplace and ordinary as a dolphin base was occasionally made into something really unique, and they are worth looking for. More normally, an entire series of candlesticks carry the dolphin motif, but even here there are variations in the base and candleholder that can indicate a real find. The Boston and Sandwich company made many dolphins and one unusual colour was a very deep electric blue, so shiny that it has been called 'grease-blue'. At least one type was raised on a double platform base, with an added

half-inch in height. Other unusual colours include combinations of opal white and grease-blue socket, a kind of watery white sometimes called 'clam broth', and a clear vaseline yellow.

Covered compote dishes were another particularly popular American shape, perhaps because the warmer summers required protection for food on the table. Sugar dishes were almost always covered, too. Many patterns used a mixture of frosted and plain glass, such as the three-face pattern with masks on the frosted finial, and a frosted stem with a clear dish and cover.

Pillar-moulded glass is another type made during the same period in the Midwestern glass area. The heavy ribs were sometimes edged with a layer of trailed white or contrasting colour. They were very heavy, and are often called 'steamship' or 'riverboat' glasses because the wide base and the weight gave them a great deal of stability.

Lamps were an important product of many American glassworks. They were made most often in a combination of moulded or pressed bases with free-blown tops, and those with oil containers were intended for whale oil. Cut glass lamps were also made for the luxury market, and as the century progressed lamps became more and more elaborate with mercury shades that glowed like silver, and hand-painted scenes.

The Union Flint Glass Works was a small company in Kensington, near Philadelphia. It made a number of semi-commercial wares as well as tableware, and quite a few different kinds of lamps for whale oil and the new 'lamp fluid' which was cleaner than whale oil, but smelt badly.

By the end of the nineteenth century the craze for pressed glass in every form died away and the worst of the novelties were now made in Art Glass and related techniques.

Pressed pattern tableware, on the other hand, seemed to go on forever, and many designs like 'Bellflower' and the 'Horn of Plenty' continued over a long period. Unfortunately, they have also been copied for many years, and here there are a few pointers which may help to distinguish old from new. Fine early examples were made of lead glass, and they have the typical weight and ring. Being old and rounded off, the pattern should not be sharply cut, as it will be when made from new moulds. On the other hand, after the Civil War, when lead glass became more expensive to make, it was reserved for the growing number of quality glasshouses, and much of the pressed pattern tableware was made in soda-lime glass, which was much lighter and more fragile. These period pieces are much harder to distinguish from their originals. Then, too, the imitators have grown more expert as collectors have become more wary, and many new versions have been made from genuine old moulds. Indeed,

Above
Smith Brothers exhibition of lamps and other decorated glass pieces. Probably c 1885. They specialised in painted and gilded lamps and shades of every description, and exhibited regularly at trade shows. The company was based in New Bedford, Massachussetts.

Right
Compotes on footed pedestals were an American addition to the range of decorative tableware. Blown compotes were usually simple, plain or pattern moulded, often with set-in lids (*above right*, and *right*) and knob finials. Pressed glass finials (*far right*) were often much more elaborate.

sometimes these are purpose-made and marked for that reason by a factory that is supplying reasonably priced reproductions for a genuine market.

Of all the popular patterns, 'Bellflower', 'Rose in Snow', 'Lion', 'Wildflower' and 'Westward Ho' were among the most sought-after, then and now, while 'Blackberry' and 'Daisy' and 'Button' in milk glass have still kept their places as firm favourites.

Although the pressed glass products swept the middle range of the market, fine flint wares continued to be produced not only by the larger companies, but also by the smaller firms that specialised in fine quality. Christian Dorflinger's Greenpoint Glass Works in Brooklyn, New York, is a typical example. Specialising in cut engraved glass of the finest metal, it was considered at one time to make the best crystal in the United States, good enough to match that of all but the best Bohemian craftsmen.

As a craftsman from Lorraine, Dorflinger was heavily influenced by European models, but as his factory developed, the interest in simpler delicate designs increased with the fashion. He worked from 1852 until 1915, and one of his factories, in White Mills, Pennsylvania, continued after his death for a while until it closed in 1921. One of his finest achievements was a set of glassware ordered by Mary Lincoln Todd for the White House in 1861.

Above and below
An open compote with an unusually tall foot; cut and cased with ruby panels on dish. The wide foot gives required stability. *c* 1890; ht 6in (15.2cm).
The pressed covered compote *below*, of the same period, is much more traditional.

Left
Pressed glass goblets. *c* 1840–65; ht of 'Bellflower' goblet, *far left*, 6in (15.2cm).
The 'Bellflower' is a perennially favourite pattern. The right-hand goblet shows a 'Lincoln Drape' pattern, made after the assassination of President Lincoln.

Americo-Bohemian Patterns

The Bohemian influence which swept England and Europe was felt in the American glasshouses as well. Cased and coloured glass was used for lamps, candlesticks and decanters. Tumblers and vases were flashed, engraved and gilded in the Bohemian manner, often with scenes of town halls, cityscapes, or vignettes from an important occasion. Not many have been ascribed to a particular factory or decorator – identification is difficult, and unless the scene is obviously American it can be impossible to confirm the country of origin.

Engraved and cut glass of the later period shows much simpler forms, cutting being confined almost always to scalloped edges and bold broad flute and panel patterns.

American cut glass has been neglected for many years; the better pieces were always assumed to have been imported from Bohemia or England. In recent years, the true quality of much American work has finally become obvious, and more research is being done to try and identify the work of individual craftsmen and the smaller houses that specialised in fine wares. Nonetheless, it is worth remembering that the Boston and Sandwich company won a prize for its cut glass in 1838. After the 1876 Exposition in Philadelphia, and especially between 1885 and 1915, Brilliant cut glass was very much in vogue. The glass itself was supplied in thick blocks called blanks, and was cut and decorated in the workshops or by independent cutting firms. The blanks were also imported from abroad. By 1900, there were more than twenty cutting shops in the rather small town of Corning, New York, clustered around the Steuben factory. Obviously most of the shops were found near the glassworks, but there were also cutting shops in cities making up special pieces to order.

Brilliant cut glass has the sharp edges and glassy finish of fine hand-cut crystal. Copies made later were sometimes cut by hand, but the blanks the craftsmen worked on were pressed in order to save both time and money.

Venetian Influences

The Venetian influence was quite strong throughout the history of American glassmaking. Although the majority of the early workers came from the Bohemian and Polish glassmaking centres, rather than Italy, many of the traditional idioms used at Murano found their way to America, sometimes by way of England. A tall bellows-shaped bottle made in the 1850s is decorated with opaque white and red looped trails, marvered in to give a smooth surface, and with threaded spiral decoration, pinched ribbing and ornate feet.

Chain decoration was another device which arrived via England to decorate many American pieces during the nineteenth century. Thomas Cains at the South Boston Flint Glass Works produced many of the chain-decorated plates and decanters, some with two rows of chains around the body. Even whale-oil lamps with pressed feet often had a circle of chain threading around the oil container. In fact, some of the models have threaded spirals all up the entire stem. A money bank, free blown, has looped white threading, an elaborate finial, and a general effect which seems like a clumsier version of a Venetian novelty.

All kinds of looped vases were also made, sugar bowls, creamers, even powder horns, and many were made in the Midwestern glasshouses. They look remarkably like the Nailsea-style glass being made in England.

Very few of the glassblowers attempted to make the lacy stem pieces which the English had copied, but there were certainly some who tried; Nicolas Lutz at the Boston and Sandwich company in the 1880s was supposed to have

Left
Table glass with arched and strawberry-cut panels, floral engraving. Probably Wheeling, West Virginia; c 1860–80; ht of large goblet 6⅝in (16.7cm). In spite of the detail, the effect is of simple elegance rather than the ornate exuberance associated with the Victorian period.

Right
Covered goblet and pitcher in clear glass with mechanically applied threads of ruby colour. Boston and Sandwich Glass Company; c 1875–85; ht of pitcher 8in (20.3cm). Mechanical threading was a marvellous invention which glassworkers exploited to give their pieces a delicate appearance.

made some of the loveliest and most delicate of this style. Strips of twisted *lattimo* are interspersed with clear panels in a covered dish and saucer, while a footed compote in red and white and blue is both brilliant and charming. Other pieces were inspired by aventurine glass, with gold specks picked up on the marver.

Spangled is a term which has been applied to a particular kind of late nineteenth-century glassware, ornamented, usually quite heavily, with assorted flakes of mica or bistite. These were first scattered over the surface of the marver, while the blower made his shape from a parison of glass then rolled the hot glass over the flakes, dipped the form into a pot of clear glass to lock in the pattern, and finished the ornament off in the usual way.

The base metal was almost always opaque, either white or coloured glass, and the spangles could be copper, gold or silver toned. Splashed or spatter glass was made in exactly the same way, but there were no metal flakes; instead, variegated bits of multi-coloured glass were picked up from the marver, and the clear casing was not always added.

The Victorian love of highly decorative fancy bric-à-brac was admirably displayed in these elaborate objects; most splashed and spangled glassware is frilled and ruffled, moulded in ribs or patterns on the body, and finally finished off at rim and foot with handshaped ornamentation. Sometimes an added inner layer of white or coloured glass was used to make the spangles show up even more brightly.

Both kinds of wares were made in England and on the Continent as well as in America, and it is almost impossible to identify the exact source of any one piece, unless it is marked or labelled. Since the ornamentation is so varied, and the decoration depended so much on the individual maker, collectors have to be particularly careful in making attributions – most spangled and splashed pieces are usually described as late nineteenth century, unidentified.

Silvered and Silver Deposit Glass

Silvered glass is another collector's area. Although it was manufactured by a number of firms, the unusual pieces are rare enough to require some effort in finding.

The first American patent was granted to Thomas Leighton of New England in 1855, and he specially requested it for a silvered door knob. The intention was that such a knob would never need polishing, would have the appearance and colour of silver and cost little more than an ordinary porcelain or base metal knob. For the next twenty years at least, silvered articles were produced by many firms and in great variety. There were candlesticks, jugs, pitchers and every kind of tableware. Most of them were blown with double walls, a film of mercury being introduced inside the articles; the glass was then sealed with a plug of plaster, even a small cork, or on the better pieces, a rim of genuine silver. Another company which specialised in such silvered ware was the Boston Silver Glass Company which also mentioned in an advertisement that it would supply silvered curtain pins.

One of the obvious reasons for the popularity of silvered glass was the comparison between the price of such wares and even plated silver. Many small homes and even churches found that they could have an attractive pair of candlesticks for the same money that a tiny dish of silver would cost.

Silvered glass was made in England, too, and in addition to the double-walled invention, a patent for electro-depositing silver on glass had been taken out in 1877. This was quicker and cheaper than blowing double-walled vessels, but as the silver was merely a thin coating on the glass it was liable to chip off and discolour easily. A special variation wasn't silver coloured at all, but a metallic red, blue or green.

In America silver deposit was a very popular technique which reached its fame very quickly. The first processes were developed in the 1880s; by the 1890s it was being made by a number of manufacturers – and it is still being made today. (The modern process involves the use of potassium hydroxide and ammonium hydroxide.) The Alvin Manufacturing Company was one of the silver companies which specialised in silver deposit; others were Reed and Barton, and Gorham.

The designs included fruit, floral and conventional abstract patterns, as well as the curving linear designs which suited the delicate effect of silver deposit so well. The technique was used for decanters of all kinds, claret jugs and glasses, scent bottles, bowls and vases, candlesticks and epergnes, tops for walking sticks and umbrellas, even buttons. Silver deposit patterns were also put onto other surfaces, particularly wood and china (a speciality of the Lenox China Company and Reed and Barton), and also leather and fabric.

Silver deposit was used successfully by many other companies – the H.C. Fry Glass Co. in Pennsylvania produced many opalescent Art Glass pieces with silver deposit decoration as well as coloured glass ornamentation.

John H. Scharling of Newark patented his method of laminating metal in 1893 which also included etching through the finished layer, through metal and glass together. The slightly raised metal pattern was then embellished still further with additional engraving. He used silver and gold in his work. The effect of re-decorating silver deposit wares with additional engraving on the metal was very popular for a period of about twenty years, just before and just after the turn of the century.

Silver Decoration

Silver decorated pieces became increasingly popular, and the deposit method was the only way of making the crystal as ornate as possible. Mounting in silver and gold had always been a way of ensuring that the delicate glass was protected at its weakest points; precious metals and even jewels were added to the original. By the 1890s in America mounting was so popular that even Tiffany had his shimmering Favrile glass encased in silver or gold-plated designs of mermaids and sea creatures, further embellished with aquamarines and pearls. Most everyday pieces were nonetheless beautifully made from specially cut crystal blanks to form vases, large and small bowls, buckets and jugs. The blanks and crystal pieces were made by many of the leading glass companies, including Cambridge, Heisey, Corning and Pairpoint. L. Strauss and Sons of New York were only one of the many companies advertising cut glass for mounting, and again

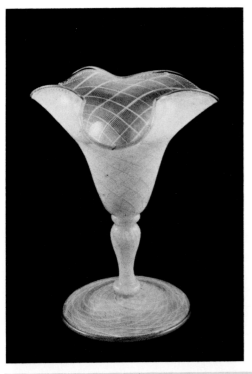

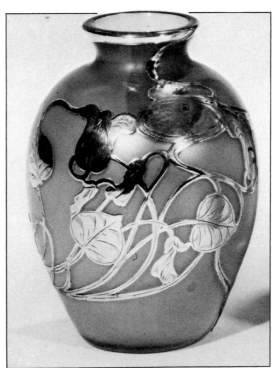

Far left
Vase of threaded glass with
latticino effect. Dorflinger &
Sons, White Mills,
Pennsylvania; *c* 1890; ht 4¾in
(12cm).
The rippled edge with
delicately blue rim to bowl and
foot is typical of the best
Americo-Venetian pieces.
Similar vases were very popular
in England during the same
period.

Left
Silver deposit vase. Lötz,
Austria; *c* 1908; ht 5in
(12.7cm).

Above
Drawing for silvered glass
process. Patented by J. W.
Haynes of Boston Silver Glass
Company, 4 April 1865.

Left
Silver deposit vases. Lötz,
Austria; *c* 1908; ht of tallest
vase 9½in (24.1cm).
Silver deposit and silver overlay
was made in many factories all
over Europe. American
factories developed silver on
glass patterns in rich variety,
and copied the Lötz idea of
silver over iridescent glass.

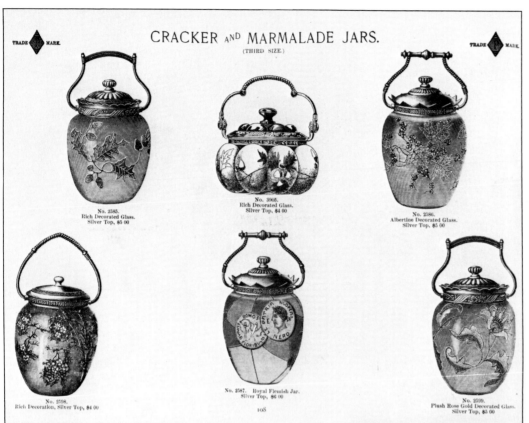

CRACKER AND MARMALADE JARS.
(THIRD SIZE.)

No. 2585.
Rich Decorated Glass.
Silver Top, $5 00

No. 3905.
Rich Decorated Glass.
Silver Top, $4 00

No. 2586.
Albertine Decorated Glass.
Silver Top, $5 00

No. 2598.
Rich Decoration, Silver Top, $4 00

No. 2587. Royal Flemish Jar.
Silver Top, $6 00

No. 2599.
Plush Rose Gold Decorated Glass.
Silver Top, $5 00

105

Left
Page from a Pairpoint catalogue. Mount Washington glass patterns; c 1893.

Right
Two witch balls and stands of aquamarine flint glass with white loopings. South Jersey; 1835–45; ht 23¾in (60.3cm). Some researchers believe that witch balls were made of silvered or reflective glass so that, when hung in a room, their glitter would ward off the evil eye. Other historians think they were sailors' buoys, netted and used to mark floating nets or underwater obstructions. Pairs are very rare, especially with their original stands.

Below
Silver inkwell with glass bottles. Art Nouveau period, c 1890; width 10½in (26.6cm). Glass pieces with silver mounts have always been useful; the metal protects the edges and can be manipulated to form delicate handles and hinged parts.

the objects ranged from the tiny salt cellars and knife rests to inkwells, huge ceremonial punch bowls, and even a presentation piece given by the miners of the Northwest which used gold nuggets to support a cut glass bowl.

The Mount Washington Glass Company had many of its pieces mounted by the next-door Pairpoint Manufacturing Co., which specialised in silver plating. There were sugar bowls and creamers in every conceivable style, cups and saucers, vases and ink stands, toilet bottles and dressing-table sets, cruets and decanters.

Such pieces are much more popular with collectors than they used to be, and good examples are becoming hard to find. Very often, too, the silver shape, which was usually very thin, would be damaged by broken glass, so that really perfect objects in good condition are quite valuable.

There were many silver-mounted pieces made later, especially in the 1920s when there was a revival of simpler shapes and styles. Tall wine glasses in many colours were made with foot, stem, and sometimes the base of the bowl cased in a thin silver-plate form.

An additional form of silver or metal-mounted glass was the making of a metal case, into which the glass was blown. This again was an ancient technique. One of the earliest examples that we know of is blue glass blown into a silver cup with cut-out bosses, so that the glass bulges out in a regular pattern to give the appearance of a silver piece mounted with sapphires. This method was adapted for many of the 'medieval' pieces so popular at the turn of the nineteenth century. Gorham was the original silver company to make use of the jewelled effect in blue, ruby and a rich assortment of ambers, yellows and browns.

Other Unusual Designs
The idea of embedding coins in glass has always been popular. Many early drinking glasses have a contemporary coin encased in the stem or the base of the bowl, and they are very useful for giving a date limit. Of course, there is no way of telling if the glass was made after the date of the coin – many genuinely old examples have still older coins inside – but it does give a date before which the glass could not have been made – at least, not unless someone chose to mint a special coin with a future date on it just for the purpose of confusing modern collectors.

During the late nineteenth century, coin patterns became popular again, and the Central Glass Company of Wheeling, West Virginia, made about twenty-five pieces of tableware

Left above
Compotes and dishes in
Americo-Venetian style.
c 1895; ht of compote 7⅛in
(18cm).
The Boston and Sandwich
Glass Company is best known
for its lacy pressed glass but
they also made delightful
Venetian-style Art Glass.
These free-blown pieces show
dexterity, charm and precision.
The company continued to
make novelties like these
until *c* 1920.

Left
Hanging lampshade in stained
glass with bronze mounts.
Louis C. Tiffany; *c* 1900; ht
5⅞in (14.9cm).
Louis Tiffany was responsible
for innumerable decades of
lampshade designs that copied
his fixtures, particularly
lampshades which were
carefully constructed from
marbled and mottled stained
glass within a bronze
framework. The fruit design
is illustrated, but his
most popular shades were
usually floral.

with real coins embedded in the glass. The government
stepped in after a few months, and production was stopped.
The original platters and dishes are much sought after by
collectors, but a replica produced in the 1960s by the Fostoria
Glass Company can be easily distinguished from the
original, as the 'coins' are all dated 1887. Other coin patterns
did not use real coins, at least in the United States.

Mary Gregory is the name given to a whole group of
probably unrelated glasses, made during the last part of the
nineteenth century, and decorated with white enamel
silhouette paintings of Victorian children. There is a theory
that Mary Gregory was an artist working at the Boston and
Sandwich company, but there are no records which prove
that she painted or designed glassware.

Art Glass
The Mount Washington Glass Company of Bedford,
Massachusetts, called itself the 'Headquarters in America
for Art Glass' and it certainly was responsible for helping to
change the whole trend of American glass away from the
pressed and patterned pieces to the free blown and sometimes violently coloured designs of Art Glass. Between 1880–
1900 companies made every kind of colour in diversified
techniques and often this involved difficult and complicated
processes.

Many of the patents were derived from English originals,
but were adapted or improved by various American inventors. There was enormous rivalry between companies
such as Mount Washington and the Phoenix Glass Works
about the right to make and label such wares with their

Left
Wine glass, spiral cutting on
bowl, cylinder stem and heavy
fluted foot. *c* 1890; ht 4½in
(11.5cm).
Christian Dorflinger's original
factory in Brooklyn was so
successful that he acquired
two other works, and in 1865
established the White Mills
Dorflinger Works in
Pennsylvania.

CROCKERY AND GLASS JOURNAL.

Mt. WASHINGTON GLASS CO.

NEW BEDFORD, MASS., U. S. A.

HEADQUARTERS IN AMERICA FOR ART GLASS WARES.

RICH CUT AND DECORATED.

Semi-Annual Opening Display, 46 Murray Street, New York City.

February 10th to 15th, inclusive.

"DON'T BE TOO FRESH"
·USE THE NEW TOMATO·
·SALT OR PEPPER·
BUY ME FOR ALL SEASONS
THIS·LITTLE·BEAUTY
FOR·SALE·BY·
Mt. Washington Glass Co,
New Bedford, Mass., U. S. A.
46 Murray Street, New York City.

ASSORTED DECORATIONS
IN PERMANENT ENAMEL
COLORS & GOLD
COVERS
QUADRUPLE PLATE
OLD SILVER FINISH
·LACQUERED·
FOR
MARMALADE,
SUGAR,
BON BONIERE,
JEWELRY,
ROSE LEAVES,
Height to top of handle 5½ inches.

Eastern Traveling
Salesman,
H. R. SHIRLEY.

Western Traveling
Salesman,
H. B. WHITNEY.

FOR SALT OR PEPPER—
LARGE SIZE FOR SUGAR—
BON BONS MADE WILD MUSTARD—
AND IN THIS CITY OF
CAPS FOR BON-BONS.

THE SALT OF THE EARTH,
SOLD ALL OVER THE EARTH,
AND IN THIS CITY BY
Mt. Washington Glass Co.
New Bedford, Mass., U.S.A.
46 Murray St., New York City.

New York Agent,
WM. H. LUM,
46 Murray Street.

CRACKER JAR,
ASSORTED DECORATIONS IN
ALBERTINE AND ROYAL
FLEMISH
Permanent Enamel
Colors & Gold.
QUADRUPLE PLATE COVER
·LACQUERED OLD SILVER·
FINISH.
Height to top of handle 9½ inches.

We thank you sincerely for your patronage in 1889, and regret that many orders were necessarily carried over—these will be first on the list for delivery now. Each season we revise and renew the designs on our wares, so that you are sure of getting nothing from us but fresh, bright goods—NO OLD STOCK. The great popularity and large demand for these goods, combined with the care required for their production, and also the scarcity of first-class artists in this line, must be our defense for any delays.

Infringements will have due attention.

SPECIALTIES:

Rich Cut Glassware,   Fine Decorated Lamps, Shades, etc.
Crystal Chandeliers,   The Celebrated Burmese Ware,
Rose Amberina Ware,   Royal Flemish Ware,
Peach Blow Ware.   Albertine Ware.

Mt. Washington Glass Co., New Bedford, Mass., U. S. A.

New York Store, 46 MURRAY ST.

HEADQUARTERS IN AMERICA FOR ART GLASS WARES.

Above
Advertisement for the Mount Washington Glass Company from *The Crockery and Glass Journal*, January 1890.
This advertisement shows that glass marketing was a hard-selling business. The apology for late deliveries is a very modern problem in very polite language.

Left
Peach Blow pitcher. Mount Washington Glass Company; *c* 1888; ht 5¼in (13.3cm). Peach Blow was a soft matt finish, in complete contrast to the elaborate enamelled decoration on many Mount Washington pieces (see advertisement *above*). The simple outlines show off the graduated colours shaded at the fire after the glass had cooled.

popular names. Satin glass was one such example; Benjamin Richardson in England first took out a patent for Pearl Satin Ware, although he carefully termed it a patent for producing 'peculiar Ornamental Effects'.

By 1881 two Americans from Brooklyn had patented almost the exact same process, and the Mount Washington company bought it almost immediately. Meanwhile, in 1886 a Mr Webb of Phoenix patented his own version, but although it had some improvements the principle was the same as Richardson's. Not one of the subsequent patents (and there were many others) even mentions Richardson.

Finally, Frederick Carder at the Steuben Glass Works in Corning, New York brought his own *Verre de Soie* with air traps onto the market.

These are all good reasons for being very careful about attributing to one man, or even one company, this outburst of achievement. In fact, many similar articles were being made in France and Bohemia, with the basic pearl or satin finish ornamented with painted and gilded designs.

It had also been discovered that re-heating certain kinds of glass could produce a rich and varied shading, which was extremely popular with the larger customers. A variety of colours and shades was achieved, and all called different names – Rose de Bohème, Yellow de Bohème, Pearl Satin, Blue Pearl and so on.

Jade Glass

Jade was another very popular Art Glass product. Glass had been used to imitate expensive jade pieces as early as the fourth century BC especially in China. The Egyptian glassmakers specialised in making 'jade' which was so like the true stone that even naturally occurring discolourations could be copied, and such pieces would stand up to very close inspection until they were handled.

The Venetians repeated the Egyptian and Oriental formulae, but they preferred the marked and striated stones, and it was the Chinese in the eighteenth century who kept up the tradition of 'jade' bottles and bowls, often elaborately carved in their own right, and marvellously true to the original in colour and texture. Finally, in the nineteenth century, the brilliantly coloured Bohemian glasses started the craze for gemstone imitations all over again, and with the new technical mastery of the period, both English and American craftsmen began to develop all kinds of intricate formulae which resulted in the most amazing array of Art Glass pieces.

Jade glass had already been made by Stevens and Williams in Stourbridge, and when Frederick Carder came to America, Steuben began to make many varieties of Jade glass objects. Carder often cased the basic Jade with a translucent white alabaster layer, and engraved a design through the top to let the Jade show through.

Oxides were added to the basic soft white glass to make up the many colours of natural jade, and the result was a soft, 'soapy' appearance which was remarkably effective, and seemed to glow, especially if it was finished off with a satin surface. Some pieces were also given a dull surface to increase the dense appearance. A pink-toned Jade glass was also very popular – it was sold under the trademark of Rosaline.

Carder and Steuben

Frederick Carder was born in 1863 in England, and he began his career as a glass technician and designer very early, studying in Stourbridge where he grew up, until he went to work for Stevens and Williams as a young man of seventeen. He was classified as an apprentice for many years, but his talents and skill brought him a considerable reputation among the glassworkers and craftsmen.

Stevens and Williams were well known for their cut glass

Left
Ewer in Islamic shape. Frederick Carder; 1920; ht 13in (33cm).

Above
A cameo berry bowl of opal glass. Made at the Mount Washington Glass Company, mounted by the Meriden Silverplate Company, Connecticut; c 1885; ht 7in (17.7cm).
The silver-mounted jars on the opposite page are obviously related to this very similar piece with its florid decoration.

Left
Plate cut in the Russian
pattern, of the Brilliant
period. T. G. Hawkes & Co.,
Corning, New York; *c* 1906;
diam 13⅜in (34cm).
There were many cut glass
companies in Corning that
probably relied almost entirely
on the very fine blanks made
by Steuben.

Right
Vase made with the Intarsia
method of inlaid coloured
patterns. Frederick Carder,
Steuben; 1920s; ht 6½in
(16.5cm).

Below left and right
Two Favrile vases. Louis
Comfort Tiffany; *c* 1906; ht of
left-hand vase 12⅞in (32cm).

in the late Victorian style, and Carder's early designs are not particularly unusual or inspired. However, over the next twenty years, he became more and more interested in the techniques and ideas of the Art Nouveau movement in France, and he studied with Emile Gallé to learn his principles and the theories behind the Ecole de Nancy.

The use of colour was something that fascinated Carder, and he began to experiment with various glasses and methods. The cameo glass made by Northwood was increasingly popular, and Carder became well known for his ornamental pieces in delicate cameo designs. By the turn of the century, American glass seemed to be more experimental and more exciting than the English factory production, and when Carder was asked to go to upstate New York he decided to make the move permanent. In 1903 he and his family went to Corning and he began to work on making heavy blanks, to be cut and engraved by T. G. Hawkes & Co. Carder's interest in designing was too great to be suppressed, and soon he, Hawkes and other craftsmen founded the Steuben Glass Works to make Art Glass of all kinds. Many of his first productions are Italianate in both general style and overall detail. As late as 1930, Carder was producing a few pieces of Intarsia glass, where the coloured pattern, with or without *millefiori*, was laid into the surface of the glass between two layers of clear glass – a remarkable achievement. The designs and techniques which Carder had been studying all his life culminated in an outburst of creative work that produced some of the loveliest and most original Art Glass in America. He specialised in creating new and different colourings, in all kinds of patterns, and using many combinations of modern and traditional techniques. Some of the glasses made famous by Carder and Steuben are Alabaster, Aurene, Cintra, Cyprian, Diatreta, Florentia, Intarsia, Jade, *Verre de Soie*, *pâte de verre* and *cire perdue*.

Carder went to every period in history for inspiration; there are Etruscan vases, Roman lamps, Italian *millefiori* bowls, Bohemian engraving and northern *Römers* complete with prunts and threading. He also used controlled bubbles to create the impression of the earlier, light soda glass with its many seeds and imperfections. Steuben became known as one of the greatest experimental glasshouses in the country, but for many years its fame was overshadowed by the Louis Tiffany studio which was firmly associated in the minds of collectors and connoisseurs with Art Nouveau, stained glass lamps, and beautiful iridescent glasses of all kinds. In fact, Carder and Tiffany were producing much the same sort of work during the first quarter of the twentieth century, and many of their pieces are almost indistinguishable. It's probably impossible to say at this stage who was copying whom, but it is certain that by the 1930s the great period of Tiffany glass was over, while Steuben, re-organized and inspired by the newer designs coming from Germany and Scandinavia, took on another lease of life. Gradually Steuben has become the leading glasshouse in America, making fine quality commercial tableware as well as supremely beautiful individual pieces of crystal, many with superb engraving.

There is very little or no coloured glass now, and the

Below
Tall prism-cut obelisks.
Steuben; 1970s; ht 15⅝in (39.9cm).
Carder's influence remained extremely strong at Steuben, but his experiments with colours and shapes were not fashionable during the Scandinavian-influenced 1940s–70s. The very simple shapes and clear crystal prisms of the 1970s are best expressed in this pair of obelisks.

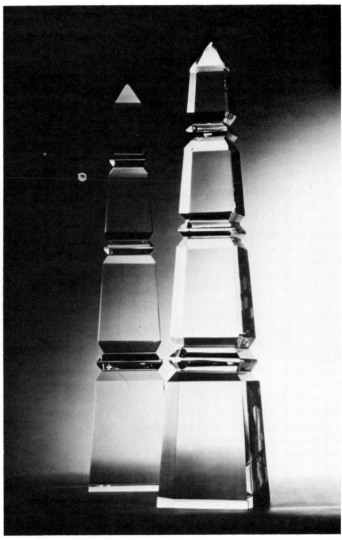

crystal is remarkably clear and consistently of a pure limpid colour. Carder remained as art director until 1933, but he continued to work there occasionally after his retirement, and was an important teacher and contributor to the art of glassmaking until his death in 1963.

Louis Comfort Tiffany

Tiffany is a name known throughout the glass world for magnificent iridescent glassware, stained glass lamps and other lighting fixtures, often combined with leading and bronze.

Louis Comfort Tiffany was an American artist, the son of Charles Lewis Tiffany a well-known New York jeweller.

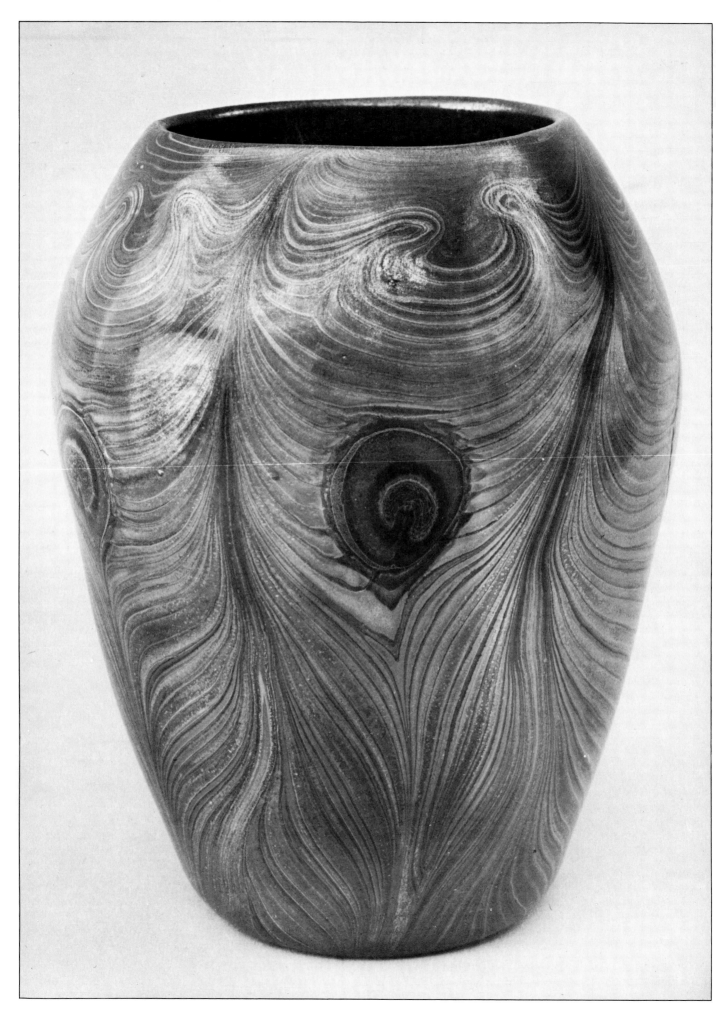

He travelled to Paris in 1868 to study with Bailly and other painters of the period, and although he realized soon enough that his talents as a painter were somewhat limited, he continued to paint in oil and watercolour for most of his life. In 1879 he finally decided to concentrate on interior design, and he founded Associated Artists. Samuel Colman who was the first president of the American Watercolour Society, Mrs Candace Wheeler – also a founder of the Society of Decorative Art – and Lockwood de Forest, another painter, were all involved in this attempt to co-ordinate the many crafts of the period into decorative schemes for homes, offices and even churches.

Tiffany himself was very much influenced by the entire Art Nouveau movement in France, and particularly by the inspiration derived from Japanese art. Charles Tiffany's leading designer collected all kinds of Oriental art, and Louis started some of the collections which were to be incorporated into his designs for wallpapers and fabrics.

He was also inspired by Gallé's work in France, and in 1885 he decided to concentrate on glass. He founded the first Tiffany Glass Company in Corona, Long Island, especially for glass windows and lighting fixtures. It became Tiffany Glass and Decorating Company in 1892. The famous Favrile glass, an iridescent glass with a metallic lustre, was registered in 1894 and that, together with his display at the Chicago World's Fair of 1893 and the Paris Exposition of 1900, firmly established his reputation.

A division of his company, called Tiffany Furnaces, was run by Arthur Nash; and Tiffany Studios in New York was established in 1900 to act as the main outlet for his design and decorative work in North America.

In Europe his designs were sold through the well-known Salon d'Art Nouveau, run by Samuel Bing.

At the same time, Tiffany took over his father's jewellery business in 1902, and he also made a wide range of small pieces of glass and silver as decorative ornaments and personal jewellery of all kinds. Sometimes small glass jewels were used in various settings, but also on glass objects.

In 1919, Tiffany began to withdraw from the business he had founded, although he was involved to some extent until 1928, when he withdrew all financial support and the use of his name. He died in 1938.

There were many special formulae which were made by the Tiffany company; some were particular kinds of Art Glass, such as aquamarine, Paperweight, damascened, and a version of Venetian *reticello* called *vetro di trina*.

One of the more important aspects of Tiffany's work is the lamps, usually with bronze bases in various naturalistic forms, and shades of stained glass in floral and insect patterns. The best known is perhaps the type known as wisteria which was actually based on a design by Curtis Freshel. The lamp base forms the vine, with the shade patterned after the hanging lilac wisteria blossoms in a wavy, irregular shape.

Other shades were used as chandeliers, mostly in bowl form, in Tiffany's favourite rich colours.

Tiffany Studios designed stained glass windows which were enormously popular with the turn-of-the-century aristocracy who were building comfortable mansions in New York, Chicago and many other major cities.

Tiffany also made church windows with biblical scenes and landscapes. Another typical window of the period (*c* 1915) is actually a portrait of the man who commissioned the

Left
Favrile vase with elaborate peacock feather design. Ht 11in (27.9cm).

Right
Three vases in agate glass. Ht of small vase 3½in (8.8cm). All vases on this page by Louis Tiffany; *c* 1880–90.
Tiffany's great contribution to glassmaking was the use of intrinsic colour rather than superimposed decoration. Compared to the work of Emile Gallé (see page 174), heavily cased and carved, his Art Nouveau glasses were blown in the simplest shapes to show off the iridescence and depth of a remarkable range of jewel-like colours.

work, and had it installed in his Madison Avenue mansion.

Other objects produced by the Studios included paper knives, jars, carved cameo vases, glass tiles, photograph frames, humidors – everything for the home that could be made in bronze and decorated with glass. Most of the glass was made in some form of Favrile, but occasionally other types were used – the Cypriote vases have an uneven, pitted surface with lustre trails. Most of the shapes of Tiffany glass objects were simple, relying for their effect on the spectacular colouration and iridescence of the glass itself. A mark of Tiffany's influence is the number of copies made today, especially of his lamps and chandeliers, in everything from modern glass to cut-out plastic.

Tiffany was also responsible for teaching other glass-makers about the production of Art Glass. One of the companies which was founded by two ex-Tiffany workers was the Quezal Art Glass and Decorating Company in Brooklyn, New York.

The two men, Martin Bach and Thomas Johnson, established Quezal in 1901, and the trademark was intended to represent the quezal bird, a South American bird with brilliant and colourful plumage, which presumably represented the opalescent and iridescent Art Glass which the company specialised in making until it closed, in 1925. Most of the Quezal glassware was vases and lamps, again in simple rounded or fluted shapes, sometimes with wavy rims. The decoration was in the glass itself, in various metallic lustre colours, and almost always based on leaf or flower designs. Many of the Quezal glasses are marked.

Other companies included the Handel company of Meriden, Connecticut, who made many table lamps with painted shades; and Victor Durand Jr's Vineland Flint Glass Works founded in 1897 in Vineland, New Jersey. Vineland made a number of individual Art glasses, including Ambergris and Peacock Feather, and its decorative effects often included pulled threads and trails.

After Durand's death in 1931, the factory was merged into another company, and stopped making most of its Art Glass products.

Twentieth-century Trends

By the end of the nineteenth century, the American glass manufacturers had turned away from the more elaborate pressed glass patterns. Art Glass, both blown and pressed, stayed popular until roughly the beginning of World War One. Cut glass was also staging a comeback, particularly in the Brilliant and deep cutting which was typical of the period. But this kind of glass was very expensive. As the century began to reach its second decade, the economic situation in the country began to change, and the first shadows of the Depression stretched across the post-war celebrations.

Continual mechanical advances had finally resulted in machinery which could make glass tableware and holloware completely automatically, without the need for hand-finishing which had occurred with all the previous pressed glassware.

Depression glass, so-called because it was made during the 1920s and 30s and up to the American entry in World War

Right
Yellow cameo vase with silvered design. Made by Frederick Carder, founder of Steuben Glass Works; c 1880; ht 14in (35.5cm).
Cameo-cut glass had become a newly developed fashion in the 1880s. The very complex and difficult cutting methods used by John Northwood to make his copy of the Portland Vase, and by Frederick Carder and others working on classical pieces of all kinds, had been superseded by cheap imitations made with the acid etching process. Eventually designers learned to use acid etching as a technique in its own right to make, quickly, delicate and intricate patterns which would be almost impossible to carve by hand.

Left and above
Two flower-form vases. Louis Tiffany; late 19th century; ht of left-hand vase 18½in (46.9cm). These delicate 'flowers' are very fragile. They were made as decorative pieces rather than useful vases, and many are now chipped at the rim. Frederick Carder made similar pieces at about the same time. There was always a certain amount of rivalry between the two glassmakers, until Tiffany's retirement.

Two in 1941, was a product of this complete automation; it was very cheap, and sold in places like the Five and Ten Cent stores and cheap department stores. Many of the patterns were made in complete dinner services with matching serving pieces. Some collectors have concentrated on trying to make up complete services in each pattern, but it is more common these days to concentrate on specialist areas, and look for the more unusual pieces, like cookie jars, butter jars, punch sets, etc. The colours of Depression glass are usually basic – pink, green, clear and in varieties of brown and blue. The patterns can be quite simple, like 'Adam Orblock', or elaborate like 'Fiesta', made of a white opal glass with applied coloured bands. Occasionally, a pattern tried to imitate the lacy pressed patterns – 'Lace Edge' has an openwork border on the plates and sugar bowls.

Kitchenware and barware were important additions to the everyday use of glass, as such pieces could be turned out in huge quantities and very cheaply. In addition, the growth of refrigerators suddenly plunged the whole kitchenware world into the twentieth century, with refrigerator storage dishes in various sizes, nests of boxes, flour and sugar canisters, caddies for dry goods, bottles and jars, etc. Even grapefruit and citrus fruit squeezers made of glass have become collectors' items. They were produced by a variety of companies, especially McKee and Jeanette. They were made in the usual colours of clear crystal, pink, green, etc but the opal and opaque colours are now quite rare, and bring relatively high prices.

The use of ovenproof glass also inspired many cheap additions to the kitchen range, especially casseroles and baking dishes, although sets of mixing bowls to use with eggbeaters are not easy to find.

There were also decorated pieces made with pictures of such people as Shirley Temple, or Tom and Jerry cartoon figures. Many of these are becoming quite rare, since they were often discarded when the children of the house grew up.

Some special items such as punch bowl sets and serving pieces combined metal holders. Again, the clearer colours are the most common, opal, dark and opaque versions being comparatively unusual.

Depression glass is from an interesting time in American history, because for the first time cheap useful wares were widely available to anyone with a limited income. Some of the patterns are reflections of better kinds of glassware, and many of the manufacturers were making much better tableware for the more discriminating end of the market. Nonetheless, although artistic merit is not very high, Depression glass has its place, if chosen carefully, as a stage of industrial development.

The colours are bright and cheerful, and factories kept clear enough records for us to be able to attribute products to the major manufacturers. The choice of design, pattern and colours is a guide to everyday taste in the 1920s and 30s. The major factories were Federal, Macbeth Evans, Jeanette, Hazel Atlas, Hocking, Indiana and McKee.

Modern American glass has gone through many changes since the Depression. The return of prosperity encouraged a number of factories to produce fine quality lead glass. Sidney Waugh at Steuben was largely responsible for a very distinctive style of wheel-engraved crystal on clear backgrounds. He worked on many presentation pieces, now in museums throughout the world.

Pairpoint Manufacturing Company, and Libbey Glass Company of Toledo, were among the other innovators – Libbey developed a series of Americana glasses, and Pairpoint also produced sets based on traditional patterns. Many other firms re-created some of the more popular Art Glass colours of the 1880s, using modern designs with original formulae.

After World War Two, glassmaking took a very different turn. Studio glass suddenly became a viable field for artists who preferred to work on their own. The huge glass factories of the past, with their teams of anonymous workers, concentrated on the more commercial tableware, while named artists used hot and cold glass techniques in dozens of different ways. Rods and tubes could be re-heated and shaped over a gas-oxygen flame, lampworkers revived the art of paperweights. Some of the finest work today is being produced in America by artists such as Keith Varino and Robert Benchman. Harvey K. Littleton, Dominick Labino and Andre Billeci were pioneers and teachers, a source of inspiration for artist-craftsmen all over the world. Today brilliant colours and experimental, often humorous, objects are almost a trademark at international exhibitions where many young glassworkers get their first chance to show what the new American tradition is all about.

Canadian Glass

Canadian glass manufacturers were generally clustered in the Great Lakes district and specialised in pressed glass tableware as well as commercial glass.

Many American mould manufacturers supplied Canada through the waterways and canals – one Pittsburgh company shipped $40,000 worth of the latest patterns across the border in 1885 alone. For that reason, identification of Canadian pieces is often difficult, and must rely on invoices, manufacturers' records, and so on.

Most of the best crystal made in the twentieth century came from the Corning area, which was close to the Canadian border and was sometimes decorated in small engraving workshops in Canada. A treasured presentation, the Great Ring of Canada, designed by Donald Pollard and Alexander Seidel, was made at Steuben to commemorate the Canadian centenary.

During the past fifteen years, a number of small studios have grown up in Canadian cities, particularly in Toronto and on the West Coast in Vancouver. They have tried to emphasize the Canadian aspect of their work, and although some turn out banal and uninteresting tourist versions of maple leaves and Eskimo carvings, a few have begun to develop an individual and exciting approach to studio glass.

Left
Fruit cup in green bubble glass with bucket bowl, ornamented with threading and prunts. Steuben; 1930s; ht 4½in (11cm). Carder drew inspiration from every period and every style to create new designs.

The Far East

Japan

Oriental glass has had a long history in the art world, but its reputation has been based on relatively few types: painted or jewel-coloured snuff bottles, and carved double-overlay vases. Although Japanese glass in particular is almost entirely unknown in the West, some very unusual kinds of glassware are found only in Japan.

There is still considerable doubt about the early history of Japan, and comparatively little is known about the cultures which existed during the Jōmon period (10,000–250 BC). As far as we can tell, little if any native glassmaking was attempted, although a few carefully preserved artefacts found on excavated sites were probably imported from western Asia. During the following centuries, the crafts developed gradually, and signs of a much more sophisticated culture appear – pottery was improved enormously by the use of the wheel, and bronze and iron founding was an important step in providing the people with domestic and religious articles of usefulness and beauty. The numbers of actual glass objects were still painfully few, and those seem to have been mainly beads which have been found in many colours, ranging from pale blues and greens to dark purple.

Beads have played a vital role in the growth of Japanese glass – they were used constantly as ornaments, inlays, decorative additions to other materials, and as barter or a type of currency for the payment of taxes.

There are many kinds of beads, some made by coiling molten glass around a wire, other types produced from short lengths of glass tubing, softened and shaped in the fire. Many of the opaque, browny-red beads have been found throughout Asia as well as in Japan, so the knowledge of production seems to have been fairly widespread, if fairly primitive.

So far there has not been enough evidence to pinpoint a glass factory site, but beads such as these could have been made by many craftsmen working in their homes, with equipment that was little more complicated than a charcoal fire and a few tools.

Nara Glassmaking

With the coming of Buddhism, there was a corresponding flowering of all the crafts; the Nara period which began around the seventh century AD introduced many artisans to the importance of achieving and maintaining high standards of craftsmanship in the production of even small and ordinary articles for everyday use. The government set up what can be called official centres of design and manufacture – glassworkers would have come under the *imono-no-tokoru*, or the casting office. Aside from the production of the inevitable beads, one of the features of Nara glassmaking was the *shari-tsubo*, glass vessels which were ceremoniously buried beneath Buddhist shrines, and which could be filled from above with offerings from the monks or any worshipper.

The Nara period was like an early Renaissance as far as Japanese culture was concerned, and it was unhappily followed by a period of unrest which destroyed most of the settled crafts. Glassmaking was totally neglected during the long centuries afterwards. Some mirrors and beads must have continued in production, and there are a few coarse bottles which indicate an attempt at reviving the craft, but

Right
Pair of decanters, free blown, cased and cut. Seiyu-ku Kan factory, Satsuma, Japan; *c* 1857; ht 10in (25.4cm).

Below
Vase decorated in the cloisonné technique. Japan; probably late 19th century; ht 6in (15.2cm).

except for the occasional find, almost all the glass dating from the Middle Ages was imported from China or western Asia, and even these pieces are few and far between.

Finally, at the beginning of the seventeenth century, Portuguese, Spanish and Dutch traders, fighting between themselves (and with the Japanese from time to time) began to bring foreign glasses to Japan. Starting with the introduction of bottles, flasks, and practical equipment of various kinds, they encouraged those Japanese who retained some knowledge of the craft, either through literature, or through the work of Chinese artisans who settled in Edo and Nagasaki, to begin to develop their own industry.

Influence of the Middle Classes

This period of re-growth was encouraged by the rise of the middle classes, who enjoyed many of the more vigorous arts, and greatly added to the cultural life by commissioning decorative objects for themselves and their homes. The feudal lords of the time, according to one missionary, would welcome gifts of sand-timers, eye glasses, bottles containing confections, and glass vessels of all sorts. By 1811, Sir Thomas Stamford Raffles, lieutenant governor of Java, could write home that 'the Japanese are passionately fond of cut glass of every description. A variety therefore should be sent from a plain cut glass rummer to a magnificent lustre. Coloured and plain liqueur bottles, glasses and ornamental smelling bottles are in great request . . . plate and window glass . . . astronomical and optical instruments, looking glasses . . .'. It would be extraordinary if this sudden discovery of the multiple uses of glass had not stimulated the Japanese to develop their own industry more vigorously.

Traditionally, the artistic culture of Japan had centred around ceramics, weaving, painting and metalwork, although of course there had also been a great interest in cloisonné, and the glassy enamels used by the metalworkers. But skill was hard to come by; the craft itself was as secretive as any medieval guild in Europe – information was handed down from father to son, or at most, to a chosen disciple or two, who in turn would pass on the knowledge to his own successor. And the artisans who did know their craft had the best reasons for trying to keep their trade confidential – this new, marvellous material which could be used for so many exciting things was almost a monopoly of a small group of glassblowers in Nagasaki and some of the other major cities, and they had no reason to encourage rival shops.

It must have been very difficult to go beyond the fairly simple production of ornaments, beads and other small items, and it was obvious that the workers depended greatly on foreign textbooks and forms to copy from imported pieces. The production of fine quality glass took some time to evolve, but the Japanese were determined students, and by 1863 Sir Rutherford Alcock, who was the first British minister to Japan, wrote home that '. . . they have attained no small skill in manufacturing glass for themselves, in great variety, although I am not aware whether they have attempted window glass, but lamp chimneys, ground glass shades, bottles cut and moulded – these they can manufacture at about English prices, and scarcely, if at all, inferior in material or workmanship.'

Nagasaki was one of the main centres of glass production – they made beautiful inlay pieces for lacquer work, mirrors and cloisonné, and a special toy called pokon-pokon which was a flexible funnel. Thin and pliable, it gave a ringing sound when blown. Made in clear or coloured glass, the toys were sometimes decorated in bright enamel patterns, and a rather wistful traveller in the nineteenth century recalled years later the soft Nagasaki summer nights, and the children hopping alongside their mothers, holding their pokon-pokons.

There were hair and comb ornaments of all kinds in the glassworkers' shops. Many of the larger combs had inset panels of cut glass, and the patterns and shapes varied from region to region. These were articles of considerable prestige – more popular were the long hairpins ornamented with a brightly coloured ball or twisted bead dangling from the head. Pipes were made with metal bowls, and glassblowing pipes themselves were made of glass, and sometimes decorated with delicate gilding or engraving.

Shiny balls were hung from the ceiling to scare off flies, and probably as ornaments, too – one of the more charming customs of the old feudal lords was to decorate their rooms with goldfish bowls hanging from the ceilings, so that in the hot days of summer you could lie back and watch the glittering fish swim slowly in the green water.

The glassmakers also made thousands of *biidori-e*, glass plaques painted with landscapes or engraved with designs. These were used by themselves, or more commonly inset into furniture, paper walls, lacquer trays, combs, fans, and all sorts of objects. Another device was a variation on the quail cages which many Japanese hung up outside their homes, as we would have canary cages. The framework was of cane or metal, but the rods were often made of glass.

Osaka was well known for its mirrors and of course its beads, while the glasshouses in Kyoto concentrated on beads and small pieces for inlay work. Edo, now called Tokyo, had had glassmakers for many centuries – a Dutch traveller mentioned seeing a glass factory in 1691, but the first known craftsmen, Gennojo and his son Hanbei, worked mainly in the eighteenth century. Woodblock prints of the period advertise glass factories, and illustrate their wares for potential customers.

Other types of Glass

Edo craftsmen made lanterns, *biidori-e*, lamps, mirrors, eye glasses, and by the end of the nineteenth century, a great variety of cut glass bowls, vases and tableware. Even *netsuke* were sometimes made of glass, and glass *inro* were sold, too, although presumably the conservative Japanese gentleman would have preferred the traditional (and lighter) lacquer. Other charming products were miniature wine and tea sets made for the Doll Festival, and *shari-tsubo* for the temples.

Of all the glassmaking regions during this period, Satsuma province was probably the most important. Namiakira Shimatzu was a feudal lord who appreciated the proper use of skilled craftsmanship, and under his patronage the glass factory was greatly enlarged. During his lifetime, the variety and quality of the Satsuma wares were almost unique – cut glass bowls of a particular successful light red, cased and cut

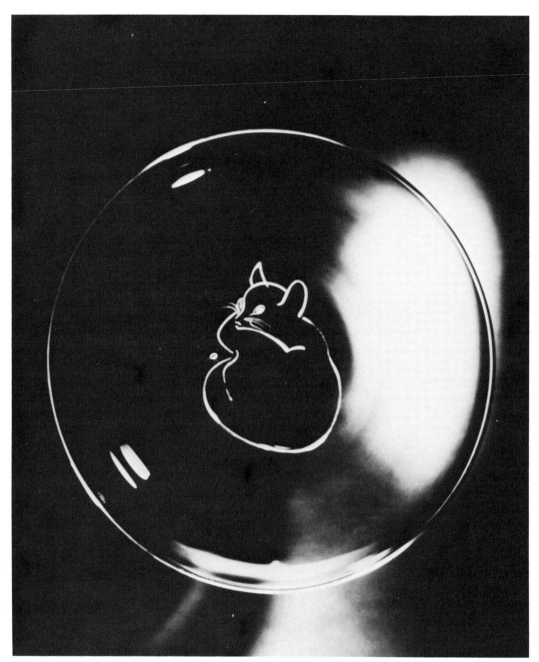

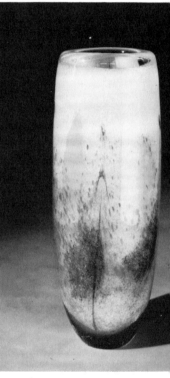

Left
'The Cat', an engraved plate
designed by Isamu Noguchi.
Made at Steuben, America;
1940; diam 10in (25.5cm).
Noguchi's design combines the
best of spare, linear Oriental
drawing with the clarity of the
finest lead crystal. Most of
Noguchi's work is international
and highly original, but this
small plate is very much a
part of the classic Japanese
tradition.

Below
Vase of tall simple shape, with
encased enamel decoration.
Toshichi Iwata, Tokyo;
c 1954; ht 11⅜in (29cm).

glass in many colours, particularly the popular red or blue, platters with gold decoration and tea bowls of all kinds, moulded tableware, bottles, and even the first Japanese production of flat plate glass.

After Namiakira's death in 1858, and the destruction of the industrial area by British warships in 1863, glass production declined and finally died out. In the new capital city of Tokyo the first modern glass factory was built – the Shinagawa Glassworks. It finally closed down after a very chequered career, but nonetheless it was the start of modern glass-making in Japan.

Today there are many modern glasshouses, and glass-making is a very important industry, even though the larger number of the factories concentrate on making products for commercial and industrial use. One of the important artistic craftsmen was Satoishi Koshiba, who worked in *pâte de verre* and glass mosaic murals, founding the company that still concentrates on architectural decoration.

Toshichi Iwata was also a painter, and his very light-hearted and lively pieces are collector's items, although his glassworks also produce an enormous range of well-designed but commercial glass.

Fukyoka Art Glass Company is another leading commercial glasshouse, making an unusual version of three-layered glass which combines soda and lead-glass layers in unique pieces.

These are, of course, only a few. Many individual workers have joined the growing number of artist-craftsmen who work in the medium of studio glass, acting both as designers and glassmakers. In every modern exhibition, young and talented Japanese glassmakers are clearly showing that glass has become a medium of expression throughout the world, and the old divisions of Western and Oriental art have only partial relevance to contemporary craft.

China

It has always been an extraordinary aspect of glass history that the Chinese, who were supreme in the creative art of the potter, the metalworker, the woodcarver, and the print-maker, have been relatively uninterested in glassmaking.

Pre-eighteenth Century

Traditionally, glass was first made in China around 400 AD; there are some artefacts found in Han tombs (200 BC–220 AD) which show that the Chinese knew about the value of glass, but there is so far no evidence to show that craftsmen actually worked within the imperial borders. The finest work was undoubtedly imported from Syria and Persia along the silk caravan routes, and the early history remains entirely con-jectural until the reign of K'ang Hsi (1661–1722).

The young Manchu emperor was very susceptible to Western influences, as well as being an ardent and generous patron of the arts. According to Dr Bushell, one of the modern historians writing at the turn of the century, K'ang Hsi established a number of imperial workshops in 1680 which included clock and watchmakers, enamellers, and a glasshouse. The Jesuit Society had become increasingly influential in Chinese cultural life, and the emperor's friendship with a Netherlands missionary led Dr Bushell to believe that these workshops were managed, if not staffed, by craftsmen from Europe, most probably from the Nether-lands. The Dutch glasshouses were producing fine *façon de Venise* glass, and many of the Venetian characteristics can be seen in the forms and decorations of those few remaining Chinese wares which date from this period.

A possible confirmation of this theory is the fact that all these early pieces, without exception, show some degree of crizzling or glass sickness, and many of the pieces are so badly flawed that they seem to sweat, and actually produce a film of sour-smelling moisture. Perhaps the native glass-workers had not yet achieved the degree of skill that would enable them to produce the right proportions and the best ingredients for their glass. Western glasshouses learned fairly quickly how to cope with this glass sickness, but the Imperial furnace had more trouble, and crizzling remained a constant trouble to the Chinese manufacturers for many years. Peking glass of this period is sometimes blue or yellow-brown, or originally clear, but now so marked with cracks that the entire surface is greyed or powdered in various striations and pittings.

Shapes of this period are beautifully simple and typically Chinese: slim jars, usually with slightly bulbous bases, fluted and plain bowls of incredible elegance, simple stand-ing cups, and perfectly plain brush pots. Another Chinese characteristic which links these Peking wares is a plain ball finial on jars and covers, often of blue glass, set simply on top of a little cushion. All the forms seem adapted from porcelain originals, although one or two later examples are rather more Venetian in appearance. There is one *ku* vase with a slender waist which even has a typically Western milled ring around the centre.

Patterns are brocade-like entwined dragons and scrolls, foliage and flowers, usually moulded or engraved in diamond point, although sometimes decoration is referred to as

Below
Bottle. China; reign of Ch'ien Lung 1736–95; ht 9⅞in (25cm). This bottle is made of blue and white lacquered glass; the carved floral decoration is typical of the period.

wheel engraved. There are two foot forms which seem to be typical of the factory at Peking; the first is a curved rim, something like a cup upside down, which can also be seen in the contemporary bowls made by Ravenscroft in his Savoy glasshouse. The second foot was a piece of coiled cane, laid on the glass and overlapping at one point.

Sometimes the foot is ground down slightly to make a flat surface for the bowl or glass to stand firm on. One additional reason for assuming the masters and chief supervisors were from the Netherlands lies in the engraving. Diamond point as done by the Venetians consisted of long, even strokes, while the Dutch used short scratching strokes to create the pattern. A bowl from this period engraved in diamond point shows clearly that the Dutch method was used.

In the past few years, as more and more work has been done on the history of Chinese glass, a number of pieces have been compared, and the results seem to bear out the theory

Above
Snuff bottle. China; 18th
century; ht 2¼in (5.7cm).

Right
Chinese snuff bottles varied as
much in shape as in design.
Carved lotus leaves, interior
painting of magpies, and
single overlay decoration are
shown here.

that there was basically a single glasshouse or group of
furnaces working under the same master craftsman during
the latter part of the seventeenth century, and probably the
first quarter of the eighteenth. The extant pieces are remarkably similar in texture and in having a lesser or greater degree
of glass sickness, in simplicity of outline, and the use of a few
simpler Western techniques.

At the present time, it seems possible to assign all the
known objects to the Imperial glasshouse, around 1680–
1740. A later date might be possible for some, but an earlier
period, except within the usual range of ten or twenty years,
is unlikely.

Eighteenth Century and After

After K'ang Hsi's death, and that of his son, Yung Cheng,
the Emperor Ch'ien Lung (1736–1795) came to the throne.
He moved the centre of glass production to Po-shan-hsien in
the province of Shantung. The move was apparently
prompted by a valuable and convenient source of supply of

sand and potash which was used in China as the flux instead
of soda ash or lead oxide. Po-shan is on the edge of a moun-
tainous area where deposits of coal gave ample fuel for the
hungry furnaces, and easily mined deposits of quartz were
available to be pulverized and melted into batches of
reputedly fine quality glass.

In any case (according to a visiting missionary, Rev.
Alexander Williamson), by 1870 glass seems to have been
regarded as an old established craft in the region, with a
number of furnaces in and around the main settlement,
supplying dealers in Peking with window glass, bottles of
various sizes, moulded cups of every description, lanterns,
beads and ornaments, as well as rods of plain and coloured
glass sold in bulk, presumably for lampworkers and decorative additions. Peking does seem to have continued as the
source of fine glassware, because a note is made of dealers
who sell the Po-shan glass 'as if it were made in Peking'. But
as there is not enough documentation on the relative production of the Peking–Po-shan glasshouses, glassware of this
period is considered together.

Ch'ien Lung glass falls into three main categories: plain
glass, clear or translucent, colourless or tinted; cased glass,

carved in cameo or relief, sometimes intaglio; and glass made to imitate other materials – stone or stoneware, porcelain, tortoise-shell, horn, jades, etc. There is not always a clear demarcation line between the three groups; an opaque white vase may be so near to porcelain that even an expert might be fooled until he touched it. Enamelling and engraving styles also occur on all the glasses.

The first category consists of bowls, vases, plates, and drinking vessels (the *kendi* related to the Spanish *porró*, with a long neck and a spout at the side). The glass was often mould blown, with the simple but supremely satisfying decoration we have come to associate with the finest Chinese art. Wheel-cut decoration was common, either as crisp relief patterns or to sharpen the outline of feet and rims, or perhaps to add the reign mark. Prism-type cutting, which was becoming popular in the West, was not apparently used. Occasionally objects seem to be made with the Muslim market in mind – a *kendi* in deep red transparent glass is decorated with a Persian-inspired gilt scrolled band, and at least two or three others of the same period have moulded or painted inscriptions in Arabic. The colours were amber, greens, blues, and purples, the shapes simple and pleasing.

A sub-group was made in opaque glass, and imitated porcelain either accidentally or on purpose. The colours were clear and powerful, in particular a brilliant yellow, which was always an imperial colour in China and was the preferred royal colour of the Ch'ing Dynasty as well as being a symbol of prosperity. These objects are often breathtakingly perfect in outline; bowls, vases and incense burners may well have been used in court rituals. Relief carving was almost always in the same colour, with the exception of one pair of vases in cased glass with a middle layer of sepia brown, revealed only in delicate intaglio-cut panels.

The cased glasses themselves form a unique and very striking group. The terms 'flashing' and 'casing' can be used interchangeably, although most writers use flashing to indicate a much thinner layer of glass, easily scratched away, something like the black top surface of scraperboard. For that reason the Chinese glass referred to here is more properly termed 'cased', since the layer is often quite thick, and is usually cut away with the wheel. Glass vessels can be cased in two layers or, by an expert craftsman, in three or even four. Sometimes the layers are clearly visible at the rim, although this can be obscured by an added mouth cap.

The background colour from which the shape was first blown was usually white or a pale colour. Sometimes the clear ground was frosted to give an ice glass effect; this could also be colourless or yellow. The top layer was often dark blue, red, or a particularly rich garnet colour. The decoration, all-over patterns of entwined vines, flowers, and lotus leaves, appeared on everything from tiny snuff bottles to whole altar sets of incense burner and candlesticks, as well as jars of all kinds, plaques on carved wood screens and other decorative objects.

The snuff bottles were made throughout this period, then suffered a decline, were revived in the nineteenth century and again in the mid-twentieth century. They are very hard to date; many fine craftsmen worked in traditional styles,

Above left

Mirror painting of the interior of a house. China; 19th century; ht in frame 36in (91.4cm).
Many kinds of mirror paintings were produced during the 19th century, some of individual people, but often of complicated interior scenes such as the example shown here. They are often a tribute to the fine work of the artist rather than the glassmaker, since the mirror was used simply as a canvas. However, a particularly bright background was obviously considered more attractive than paper or silk.

Above

Double snuff bottle. China; 19th century; ht 2⅜in (5.9cm). Made of clear glass; one can see the shadows of the two small spoons attached to the cork of the stoppers. Using a fine-pointed bamboo pen, the artist painted the interior walls of the bottle.

Left
Snuff bottle. China; 19th
century; ht 2½in (6.3cm).
This enlarged photograph of a
typical painted snuff bottle
shows that the detail can be
quite crude – especially in
19th-century examples.

Right
Large bowl of green glass,
moulded and pressed with
radiating ribs and a circular,
smooth centre. Peking, China;
19th century; diam 10in
(25.5cm).
The Chinese, whose supremacy
in the art of porcelain and
pottery has never seriously
been questioned, were quite
late in appreciating the quality
of glass. A common factor in
Chinese glass is its resemblance
to porcelain; it is often opaque,
and moulded and painted in
ceramic styles. Nevertheless,
they did make some
interesting transparent glass.
This large bowl from the
Imperial Factory at Peking is
fitting testimony to their skill.

with patterns copied for hundreds of years from old models.
In any case all date marks in the East, unlike hallmarks on
silver or metal, need bear no resemblance to the actual date
of manufacture. They were often added as indications of
style rather than attempts to deceive, and an artist would
give the name of a master craftsman of another era as a
tribute. Although they are sometimes useful as final corrobo-
ration, they should not be regarded as prime factors: a
Chinese date mark will tell you that the piece cannot be
older than its mark, but it may be a good deal later.

Wares in the final group were made as deliberate imitations
of other materials, and include moulded vases, carved bowls,
incense burners and so on. The Romans and Venetians had
both specialised in this kind of *trompe l'oeil*, and the Chinese
followed tradition with jade, splashed colours, chalcedony,
aventurine (brown glass splashed with gold and multi-
coloured flecks), marble, shell, horn, stone and so on. Here
the collector must be very careful; much similar glass was
made in the nineteenth century in the West, especially in
those simple Oriental forms chosen to resemble Chinese
porcelain and stoneware. It is very difficult to separate
Oriental and Western examples of this type of ware.

Painted Glass

The painted wares are very different; they took advantage
of the porcelain perfection of opaque white glass surfaces as
backgrounds to fine painting. They are relatively early,
coming from the period before the manufacture moved from
Peking to Po-shan, and show the beautiful enamel painting
which was characteristic of porcelain vases during the same
period. The style is known as Ku-Yueh Hsuan, and includes

scenes of the changing seasons, 'European' landscapes,
flowers, birds, and so on. The engraved date marks or seals
are sometimes painted in blue enamel on the base, and the
actual manufacturer or the names of the artists are still
unknown. Snuff bottles were painted as well as carved,
particularly in reverse; that is, the painting was done on the
interior of the bottle, after it was annealed, with tiny brushes
inserted through the narrow mouth. A date mark may be
added but must be viewed with the same caution as all such
marks. Snuff bottles form a collector's paradise all on their
own, and may be made of stone, jade or crystal as well as
glass. The painted ones are all clear glass, of course, or the
work would not be visible.

Little is known about Chinese glass today, except that
there has been a growing market for paperweights made in
imitation of French designs in both glass and plastic; but
lately some really good examples have come on the market,
and perhaps the factories will use their new skills to return
to distinctive Chinese patterns.

For the collector or the student of glass, one of the great
advantages of Chinese glass is that so much remains to be
discovered. The literature on the subject is so far almost non-
existent except for a few courageous writers who are willing
to explore almost unknown territory. It is not easy to learn
about current findings in China itself in order to corroborate
theories and disprove other assertions. As exhibits from the
great storehouse of Chinese treasures begin to travel to
other parts of the world, it is hoped that new discoveries and
recent findings will help to establish as much background as
possible for one of the least-known aspects of Chinese art.

Scandinavia

The earliest traces of glassmaking in the northern countries date from the sixteenth and seventeenth centuries. In Jutland, in Denmark and in southern Sweden, archaeologists have uncovered remains of primitive glass furnaces and fragments of their products, dating from *c* 1550 to 1650. Documentary evidence shows that these early forest houses were staffed with German glassblowers and financed by royal or noble patrons, who wanted windows for their manor houses and drinking glasses for their tables. The furnaces appear to have been worked only seasonally. During the sixteenth century, small teams of Venetian glassmakers worked for short periods in Copenhagen and Stockholm, but nothing of what they produced has been preserved.

A continuous production of glass in Sweden began in *c* 1580, when a glasshouse was set up at Bryggholmen in Stockholm. It enjoyed royal privileges, was staffed by Germans and existed until *c* 1640, when the privileges were taken up by Melchior and Gustaf Jung, father and son. With the help mainly of Italian glassmakers, the Jungs ran glasshouses in various places in Stockholm and also in Finland (then a Swedish province) until 1695. No existing glass can be identified as products from either the Bryggholmen enterprise or from any of the Jung factories.

Left
Magnificent crowned goblet in Venetian style, the entwined initials forming the elaborate stem. One of a group made at Kungsholm Glasbruk, Sweden; *c* 1725–50; ht 18⅛in (46cm).

Page 218
Footed bowl of clear glass, painted in a geometric overall pattern, primarily deep pink, purple and black and yellow with gilded outlines. Possibly decorated at home by an inexperienced outworker. Russia; *c* 1880; ht 9in (22.9cm).

Page 219
Covered bowl of clear glass, enamelled mainly in red, blue and black with considerable gilding. The geometric design encloses medallions showing mythological figures and animals. Almost certainly made in an eastern Russian factory for the Oriental market. Russia; *c* 1900; ht 8½in (21.5cm).

Above
Decanters of the *Zirat Fladske* type. Gjövik Glasverk, Norway; 1830–40; ht 10⅝in (27cm). With their patterns of stripes and blobs of glass laid on the body, these decanters are unusual because the decoration is in coloured glass.

Left
Cone-beaker in olive-green glass with folded rim. Excavated at Hablingbo, Gotland, Sweden; 7th century AD; uneven ht 8⅛in (20.6cm).

Sweden also provides the earliest non-excavated, preserved glass of undoubted Scandinavian origin: a small group of covered goblets, made of clear glass with the stems manipulated into fantastic shapes, obviously by Italian glassmakers. They were made at the Kungsholm Glasbruk in Stockholm, founded in 1686 by an Italian, Giacomo Scapitta, and a small team of workmen proficient in the making of glass *à la façon de Venise*. Scapitta and his friends soon disappeared, but the glasshouse was soundly based financially, the craft had rooted at Kungsholm, and the glasshouse remained active until 1815. Venetian details can be traced in Kungsholm products until well into the eighteenth century, but as the century proceeded, German styles became increasingly noticeable and finally dominant.

Skånska Glasbruket at Henrikstorp in Scania (1691–1760) produced engraved glass in a charmingly rustic style, which in some cases is more original than that of the sophisticated Kungsholm products with their international character. Göteborg Glasbruk in Gothenburg (1761–1808) was renowned for its stylish neoclassical models, many of them made in deep blue or opaque white glass and decorated with cutting, engraving and gilding.

The year 1742 saw the foundation of the Kosta factory, in the heart of Småland. In this region some of the old forest furnaces have been found, and eventually Småland was to become Sweden's most productive glassmaking district, always with Kosta at the heart of developments. Kosta has remained active to this day, but its early products were modest and without original character.

From 1397 until 1814 Denmark and Norway were united under one crown, with Copenhagen as the joint capital. We know of no glassmaking activities in the twin kingdoms from the end of the old forest glassmaking in Denmark in *c* 1650, until the middle of the eighteenth century, when a sizeable and lasting glass industry was established in richly forested Norway.

Eighteenth-century Developments in Norway

The plans for a glass industry in Norway were conceived in Copenhagen in 1739 and tentatively put into practice in 1741 at Nöstetangen near Drammen. The crucial years in the factory's history are 1754–66, when the industry was directed by a Norwegian officer, Caspar Herman von Storm. In the early years, Nöstetangen and the other glasshouses which he founded in other parts of Norway, were staffed exclusively by German workmen. Von Storm was, however, very much aware of the revolutionary developments in techniques and styles which were taking place in England, and he set out to model the production of table and luxury glass at Nöstetangen on what was being done there. In 1755 he managed to produce lead crystal of an English type at Nöstetangen, and in the same year his agents lured James Keith from his Newcastle glasshouse to come and work at Nöstetangen together with his workmate, William Brown. James Keith remained in Norway to the end of his days, retiring from active work in 1787. At Nöstetangen he introduced the Anglo-Venetian style with its fine furnace-worked details for more elaborate products, as well as a number of drinking glass models copied directly from England, with stems of baluster form or with inlaid air or enamel twists.

The strongest artistic impulse at Nöstetangen was, however, lodged in the engraver Heinrich Gottlieb Köhler. From the style of his preserved engraved work (which is in many cases signed), it is clear that he was trained in Silesia, and there is some evidence to suggest that he was a pupil of the famous Warmbrunn master-engraver Christian Gottfried Schneider. Köhler left Silesia after the war with Prussia and made his way to Copenhagen, where he can be traced from 1746 onwards. He produced some fine work for the royalty and nobility from 1752, with the title of *Hofglasschneider* (Court Engraver). From the mid-1750s he settled at Nöstetangen, where he headed a workshop with a fairly large staff. One apprentice at least, Villas Vinter, was trained to a great degree of proficiency as an engraver. For his Norwegian customers of rich merchants and landowners, Köhler produced a proud series of goblets, engraved partly in a conventional, allegorical style, but partly with pictures of buildings and landscapes as he saw them around him. He also designed specially elaborate models to be made to order. The most famous product of Nöstetangen is three large chandeliers, designed by Köhler and blown by James Keith, made in the Venetian style, of clear, blue and manganese red glass, for the rococo interior of the church at Kongsberg. In 1770 Köhler left Nöstetangen and for a few years he worked as a freelance in Oslo. Finally he returned to Copenhagen, where he must have ended his days.

In 1779 the crystal production of table glass and decorative pieces in Norway was moved to Hurdals Verk, where neoclassical elements were introduced into the repertoire, and where by *c* 1800, models in pure Empire style were being made in dark blue and opaque white glass. In 1809 the production was moved to Gjøvik Verk. Some of the old models were retained, and at least one interesting new genre was introduced, the *Zirat Fladske*, which belongs to the 1830s. Long-necked decanters of globular or rectangular bodies are ornamented with strips and blobs of glass, which in exceptional cases are coloured, in freely composed patterns. Sometimes the strips form letters or even dates, which in all known cases are within the 1830s. Waisted gurgling-bottles were also made with this kind of *Zirat* at Gjøvik. Production at Gjøvik was stopped in 1843, by which time the factory had shrunk into a small and provincial establishment, catering mainly for local customers.

Glasshouses were first set up in Finland in the late seventeenth century, and many new foundations followed during the eighteenth century. Most famous is the factory of Notsjö (Nuutajärvii), founded in 1793 and still active today. But in those early days, Finland's glasshouses, Notsjö included, produced nothing but simple tableware, utilitarian household and chemists' glass.

The Nineteenth Century

The nineteenth century saw great changes in the glass map of Scandinavia. As the great factories in Britain, France and Belgium invented new technical methods of making more and better glass, and as the general demand for glass increased, the Scandinavians also expanded and modernized their industries to meet the new conditions.

Top
Goblet, wheel engraved with
the god of love, names of
gentleman and lady and
inscription. Kungsholm
Glasbruk, Stockholm; *c* 1700;
ht 8⅝in (22cm).

Above
Wine glass. Nöstetangen
Glasverk, Norway; *c* 1775; ht
6⅞in (17.4cm). Deep round
funnel bowl engraved on one
side with a rococo cartouche
and a coronet with initials.

Right
Engraved goblet in clear glass.
Nöstetangen Glasverk,
Norway; *c* 1760–70;
ht 9⅞in (25cm).

In Sweden, Kosta emerged as the country's largest and most up-to-date factory, especially from 1830 onwards, when a new management transformed the old forest house into a modern industrialized enterprise. In 1810 a glasshouse had been set up at Reijmyre in Östergötland, and it soon developed to equal Kosta in size and efficiency. Throughout the period and until the time of World War One Kosta and Reijmyre dominated glassmaking though there were dozens of other glasshouses in Sweden, mostly concentrated in Småland. Industrialization led to a great uniformity and internationalization of styles. Pressed glass was made from the 1840s, partly from moulds hired or borrowed from abroad, while during the latter part of the century, great stress was laid on cutting in complex Brilliant style. A few cased glass and enamelled models were specially designed at the Swedish factories, but no great originality in style or technique can be discerned in Swedish nineteenth-century glass. Some tasteful Art Glass was being made at Kosta and Reijmyre from the 1890s onwards, in the style of Emile Gallé, designed by the painters Gunnar Gunnarson Wennerberg (1863–1914) and Alfred Wallander (1862–1914) and by the architect Ferdinand Boberg (1860–1946) – much of it signed in the Gallé manner.

In Norway we find a similar development. In 1852, the old bottle-house of Hadeland was re-organized and refitted to produce tableware and decorative glass in modern techniques and styles, and from that day to this, Hadeland has been Norway's chief producer of such goods. During the 1850s a Bohemian artist, Robert Gube, arrived at the factory. He produced some exquisite engraved work as well as enamelling of quality, some of it signed. Pressed glass was made from 1855 onwards, while engraving, cutting and acid etching were practised with proficiency. From 1855–60, a series of good cased glass tankards were made, with geometrical patterns cut through the coloured casings on to the clear ground in the Bohemian manner. Some were engraved to order and fitted with silver covers. In 1911, A. E. Boman, a Swedish technician, experienced in the making of Gallé-style vases, produced a group of vessels in this manner.

In Finland, and particularly at Notsjö, similar developments took place. But in 1857 an interesting interlude began, unique in Scandinavia. In that year, a team of French and Belgian glassmakers was called in, led by Charles Bredgem,

who mastered some of the more complex Venetian techniques, particularly filigree glass. Some Notsjö models, still preserved, show an attractive use of inlaid work in coloured glass, simplified but unmistakably Venetian varieties of glassmaking skills.

During the nineteenth century Denmark entered the glassmaking stage again after an interval of almost 300 years: in 1825 Count Christian Danneskiold Samsøe set up a glasshouse on his estate at Holmegaard on Seeland, to exploit a large peat bog on the land. Holmegaard prospered and is still active, though now its production is based on modern fuelling methods. During the nineteenth century. the factory produced good quality table glass, much of it closely modelled on Continental fashions or perhaps slightly simplified.

From the 1830s onwards, many small glasshouses sprang up in various parts of Denmark, some shortlived, others of one or two generations' duration. They produced table glass and decorative ware in modest forms, with some use of tinted glass and with a strong flavour of neoclassical or Biedermeier styles. In 1847 a new factory was founded at Kastrup near Copenhagen, initially to satisfy the ever-growing demand for bottles from the Danish breweries. Kastrup also produced tableware, and from the 1880s good pressed glass was being made there. Kastrup became a stimulating competitor for Holmegaard.

Twentieth-century Developments

Soon after the outbreak of World War One, the Scandinavians struck out on completely new and original lines in glassmaking, with Sweden as the great creative force.

During World War One, as part of their new design programme to improve the quality of industrial goods, the Swedes encouraged factories to engage artists as designers, and in 1916 Orrefors, founded in 1898 as a modest producer of utilitarian glass, asked two painters, Simon Gate (1883–1945) and Edward Hald (b 1883) to join the factory as resident, full-time designers of Art Glass. Both of them took to glass as if by inspiration, and when Swedish glass was shown to the world at the Paris Exhibition in 1925, it became clear to everyone that a new nation had entered the world of fine glassmaking. Orrefors showed some graceful free-blown glass, but it was their engraved glass which had the most spectacular success.

Right
Vases of Graal glass. By Edward Hald for Orrefors, Sweden; 1936; ht of small vase 8½in (21.5cm).
Themes like seaweed and fish harmonised easily with the fluidity of Graal, and 'Fish Graal' in many varieties became very popular.

Below
Vase. By Gunnar Wennerberg for Kosta, Sweden; 1899; ht 4¾in (12cm).
The Art Nouveau pattern of lilies is set against a background matted by acid etching.

Left
'Europa and the Bull', Graal glass vase. By Vicke Lindstrand for Orrefors, Sweden; 1937; ht 10¼in (26cm).

Below
Graal glass vase. By Vicke Lindstrand for Orrefors, Sweden; 1937; ht 7½in (19cm).
With its jazzy rhythms, the motif has a marked period character.

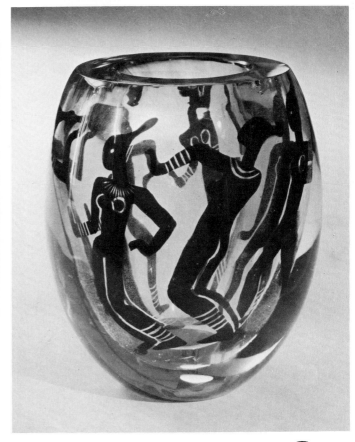

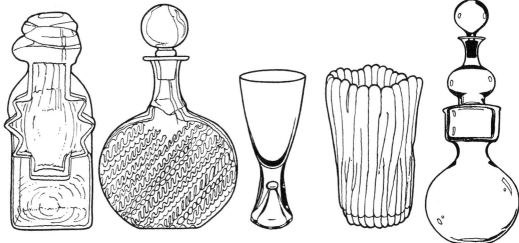

Left and right
Swedish and Finnish designs, typical of the many kinds of glassware made 1940–70.

Above
'Washing', engraved vase. By
Vicke Lindstrand for Kosta,
Sweden; 1951; ht 10⅝in
(27cm).
The grace of the figure, and the
varied engraved surface
patterns, give great charm to
this piece.

Far right
'The Beak Vase'. By Per
Lütken for Holmegaard,
Denmark; 1971; ht 16⅛in
(41cm).

Gate's grand classical models owed an obvious debt to
Lobmeyr in Vienna, but possessed a force and vitality which
was something new and stimulating, while Hald's witty
and spirited pictures of modern life represented something
of a revolution in engraving. Their most original contribution was, however, Orrefors Graal glass, with coloured
patterns and pictures inlaid in the glass. The starting point
for Graal (invented in 1916) was Gallé's standardized cased
glass vases with clinging flower patterns, which since c 1890
had become the accepted form of Art Glass the world over.
But while Gallé's cased glass was finished off by etchers and
engravers working on the cold glass, Orrefors Graal received
its final form in the heat of the furnace. This gave to Graal
motifs a fine mobility which was something quite original.

The Graal technique was developed and varied during
the 1920s, and during the 1930s the related technique,
Ariel, was created. Here enclosed air bubbles were organized
into patterns and figures. Vicke Lindstrand (b 1904, at
Orrefors 1928–40) and Edvin Öhrström (b 1906, at Orrefors
1936–47) both had a hand in its creation, and practised it
with skill and artistry. A proud series of massive pieces in
Graal and Ariel now followed, with a most fascinating inter-
play of reflections and refractions inside the massive vessels.
Lindstrand was also a prolific designer of motifs for engraving, with perhaps the most popular of all, 'The Shark
Killer' (1937), to his credit. The last of the great Orrefors
colour techniques was created by Sven Palmqvist (b 1906,
at Orrefors from 1928), and the jewel-like richness, the
depth of the inlaid patterns and the mosaic-like appearance
fully justify the name given to it of Ravenna. It was invented
during the late 1940s, and must be seen as the climax of
technical inventiveness at Orrefors.

Parallel with these exploits at Orrefors, Elis Bergh (1881–
1954, at Kosta from 1929) revived the old technique of
cutting in a modern spirit. Edvard Strömberg (1872–1946),
a chemist, and his wife Gerda (1879–1960), a designer,
produced bowls and vases of absolute simplicity of form
and perfection of material – noble representatives of the
purist tendencies noticeable in much Swedish design of
the period. Strömberg started at Kosta, worked at Orrefors
for a time, and in 1928 he and his wife moved to Eda.
In 1933 they set up their own glasshouse, Strömbergshyttan,
in the Småland forests.

After the war a new generation of young designers came
to Orrefors, Ingeborg Lundin (b 1921, at Orrefors from
1947) giving perhaps the most interesting contribution in
her abstract designs for engraving and in free-form compositions. At Kosta, Vicke Lindstrand worked as head
designer from 1950. From 1953 he was joined by Mona
Morales-Schildt, and it was perhaps here that the greatest
inventiveness and artistic creativity in Sweden could now
be found. At less ambitious factories like Gullaskruf and
Reijmyre, much excellent design work was being done for
simpler techniques.

The first to rebel against the stylishness and restraint of
the Swedish art glass tradition was Erik Höglund (b 1932).
In 1953 he became attached to the Boda factory, where he
began producing primitive, roughly shaped vessels with

decorations in furnace work or engraving, often using un-refined glass in bottle-glass colours. Another innovative designer, Bertil Vallien (b 1938), won a scholarship to the United States. When he came back in 1963 and joined the factory of Åfors, he began making glass as a free art form, and Sweden was set on the course of studio glass.

The rich glassmaking *milieu* in Sweden has attracted many foreign studio glassmakers, while young Swedes travel widely – and so, in studio glassmaking, the old national lines are becoming blurred. Ann Wärff (b 1937 in Lübeck), has lived and worked in Sweden for twenty years. She won the European studio glass competition at Veste Coburg in 1977. She works spontaneously with coloured glass, letting the glass in action lead her along, often with fanciful and inspiring results. She also designs tableware for Kosta.

Immediately after the war, the Finns emerged as great art glassmakers. The ground had been prepared during the 1930s by the work of Henry Ericsson (1898–1933) and Arttu Brummer (1891–1951), both working for Riihimäki in engraved, cut and textured glass. A real pioneer was a pupil of Brummer's, Gunnel Nyman (1909–48), whose graceful designs were soon recognized for their originality. She decorated her pieces with simple cutting or sand blasting and her 'folded' models are elegant, even poetic, works of art. She worked for all the leading Finnish factories, Nuutajärvi (Notsjö), Karhula-Iittala and Riihimäki.

During the 1950s and 1960s, Tapio Wirkkala (b 1915) and Timo Sarpaneva (b 1926) were the most strikingly inventive of a group of very fine glass designers. Some of their models from that time are still in production at Karhula-Iittala. Unique in style are the Savoy vases, designed in 1937 by the architect Alvar Aalto (1898–1976), and still in production at Karhula-Iittala. With their freely undulating lines in asymmetrical form, they have undoubtedly been inspired by Aalto's laminated bentwood chairs of the same period.

In Denmark, Holmegaard engaged the architect, Jacob E. Bang (1899–1965), as a full-time, resident designer, and from 1928–41 he re-created the factory's table glass reper-toire and designed a series of more ambitious models. The techniques are simple, the lines pure, revealing the thinking of an architect. From 1957 onwards, he worked for Kastrup,

Above
Vase. By Gunnel Nyman for Riihimäen Lasi, Finland; 1946; ht 9in (23cm).
The vase shows a complex combination of furnace work and engraving.

Above
Vase of clear glass. By Timo Sarpaneva for Iittala, Finland; 1954; ht 13in (33cm).

Left
Bowl. By Sigurd Persson and Lise Bauer for Kosta, Sweden; 1974; ht 4⅞in (12.3cm).

Right
Spoon in delicate metalwork of *plique-à-jour* filled with green and blue glass. Length 4½in (11.4cm).
A delightful example of combined craftsmanship, this metalwork spoon with glass was probably made in northern Europe as part of a set. Boxed sets of coffee spoons in enamelled and engraved gilded silver were very much in fashion during the late 19th century.
But glass examples of any period are very rare, and so far this fascinating novelty is unique.

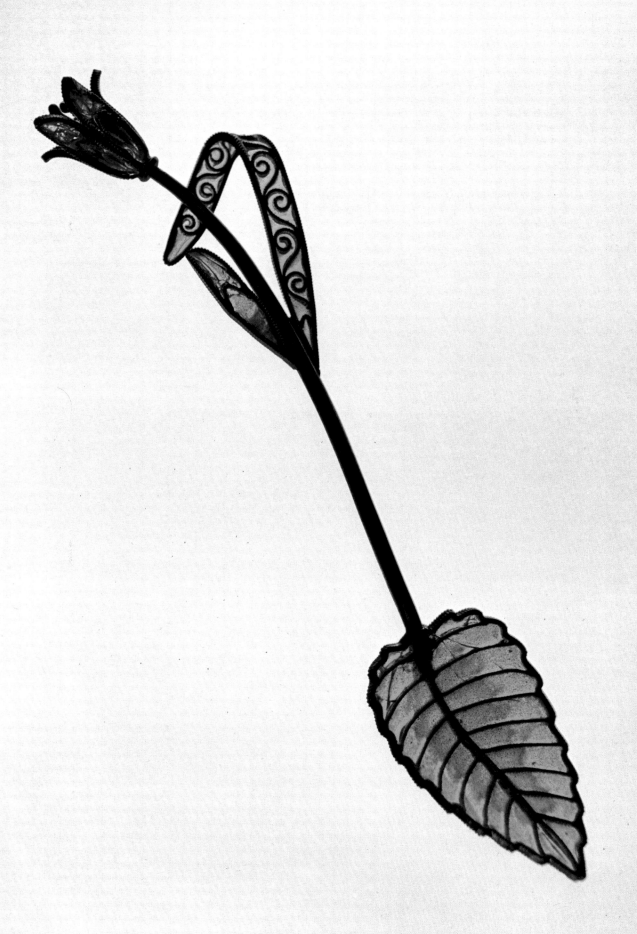

where several younger designers did sporadic work, some of it excellent. At Holmegaard, Bang was succeeded by Per Lütken (b 1916), who struck out on his own line, exploiting and stressing the fluidity of the material.

The Danish factories have never gone in for engraving in a big way, though Elving Runemalm from Orrefors worked for Holmegaard from 1934 to 1941. Åse Voss Schrader learned glass engraving from the great German master, Wilhelm von Eiff. From 1936 until well into the post-war period, she worked freelance in her workshop in Copenhagen.

Among the many young designers now working in glass in Denmark, Jacob Bang's son, Michael (b 1944), has designed for the Holmegaard-Kastrup daughter factory in Odense, a series of lamps and sets of tableware which are original in conception, good to use and delightful to look at. Each piece is a different colour, creating a beautiful harmony. Studio glass also has its practitioners in Denmark, with Finn Lynggaard (b 1930) as the most prominent name.

Apart from some good designs by Arne Lindaas (b 1924) at Magnor, Hadeland has, throughout the period, been the leading producer of table glass and decorative ware in Norway. Their first full-time designer was Sverre Pettersen (1884–1959), appointed in 1928 and succeeded in 1940 by the sculptor, Ståle Kyllingstad (b 1903). After the war a permanent design studio was set up in the factory itself. Willy Johansson (b 1921) is the son of a glassblower and himself proficient in the craft, as well as being a trained and talented designer. He has worked at Hadeland since 1936, except during his training period in Oslo. His approach is essentially Functionalist, and he has produced many excellent models, and won several international prizes.

There are many other creative people who have worked for Hadeland. Herman Bongard (b 1921, at Hadeland 1947–55) used black or coloured spirals and patterns inside thick, clear glass. Arne-Jon Jutrem (b 1929), who studied with the painter, Fernand Léger, has worked on and off for the factory from 1950. He works with textured glass and plastic decoration on the surface of the glass. Gerd Slang (b 1925) had a spell of eight years, starting in 1963, at the factory. The present team consists of Johansson, Gro Bergslien Sommerfeldt and Severin Brørby.

Benny Motzfeld (b 1900) worked at Hadeland from 1955–67 and, after a short period at Randsfjord Glassverk, she now has her own glasshouse at the crafts centre PLUS in Fredrikstad. She instructs a team of two glassblowers who have worked with her for many years. She has experimented with metal netting and glass fibre in openweave enclosed in the glass and also uses coloured enamels and oxide effects with fine understanding and poetic imagination.

The new generation of artists is exploring the outer reaches of the sculptural potential in glass. This was reflected in the 1979 glass exhibition organized by the Corning Museum of Glass, where exhibits by independent artists ranged from new Graal bowls (Gunnar Cyren, b 1931) to complex abstract designs by Lars Hellsten (b 1933) and Jan Johannson (b 1942). These artists all do work for Orrefors; Hellsten also for Skrufs. Delightful primitives by freelance Ulrica Hydman-Vallien (b 1938) for Kosta-Boda were also outstanding.

Above
Two vases, engraved with flowers. Orrefors, Sweden; 1970s; ht of left-hand vase 7¾in (19.6cm).

Right
Table lamp of opaque white glass with a brown casing on the shade. By Michael Bang for Odense glass factory, Denmark; 1971; ht 11in (28cm).

Right
Glass engraved with heron. By Mats Jonasson for Royal Krona, Sweden; c 1975; ht 7in (17.7cm).

Left
Vase of massive glass with inlaid patterns of air bubbles. By Benny Motzfeldt, PLUS Studios, Norway; 1974; ht 5½in (14cm).

International Studio Glass

In the centuries since glass was first mass-produced, the exact line between designer and artisan has never been easy to draw. Historical records have been vague on the respective parts played by the chemist evolving formulae, the designer exploring new techniques, and the craftsman at the fire. Presumably during the very early centuries, all three were combined in one person, probably with the patron/customer playing an important part by defining his particular needs. As blowing complicated glasses came to require the work of a team, the individual contributions became more specialised; just as one member of the team was responsible for bringing small blobs of glass to the master blower, so decorators worked more in particular arts. Anthony de Lysle engraved in diamond point, James Giles' workshop painted in enamels and gilding.

There were always some brilliant creative men who spanned all the talents, but until the end of the nineteenth century, most glassmaking had settled down to a highly specialised, industrialized craft. The most individual results were obtained only in embellishing already completed glass objects, an artistic effort that was often carried out away from the glasshouse.

Towards the end of the nineteenth century a new attitude, fuelled by the Arts and Crafts movement, arose among many talented painters and designers who became very interested in the medium, and were used to working primarily for individual clients rather than mass manufacturers. The popularity of the new craftsman-oriented ideology ensured that the work they produced, although largely made by established glasshouses, found a ready market. Gradually a search began for ways of simplifying the difficult industrial process. However, it was not until after the Second World War that many new materials and techniques could be exploited.

In 1962 Dominick Labino, a scientist and artist, first succeeded in developing a new formula for glass which could be melted in a small kiln that held enough material for a single individual or a small team. In the same year Harvey K. Littleton built a small kiln for using Labino's glass at the University of Wisconsin, and began the first course in studio work. Three years before, the Corning Museum of Glass had organized the first major exhibition of international contemporary glass, and the jury had noted that a number of the larger glass companies had begun to sponsor small studios within their factories, for one-off pieces and a growing number of glass sculptures which treated the material as suitable for pure rather than applied art.

Today, in the United States alone, over a hundred universities and colleges have studio glass courses, often in their Fine Arts departments, and America has become the most important centre for the innovation and encouragement of studio work.

Littleton and Labino also encouraged the growing movement in Europe and Japan spearheaded by Erwin Eisch of Germany and Sybren Valkema of Holland, who both became instrumental in establishing European seminars and classes. Sam Herman of the United States went to London and the Royal College of Art; his students included Asa Brandt of Sweden, who returned to her home country to set up her

own workshop, and Pauline Solven of Britain. In 1969 Herman, Solven and Graham Hughes set up The Glasshouse in London to operate as a centre and communal kiln for English artists, and in that same year the first exhibition of American and European studio glass was held at the Boymans van Beuningen Museum in Rotterdam. It included pieces by all the leading workers, including Eisch, Herman, Littleton, and Marvin Lipofsky.

With this, the movement began to grow rapidly, and exhibitions inspired contributions and experiments throughout Europe and the United States. Today most craft centres have a full complement of studio glass exhibits, some of them marvellously inventive and exciting; and most established glass factories continue to increase their efforts to hire individual artists to work on studio pieces. Steuben, Orrefors and Rosenthal are only three of the best manufacturers, and studio glass is an increasingly profitable part of their production.

Glass sculpture has developed rapidly, and artists and

Left and below

Left, green goblet, freely blown and sturdy rather than elegant. England; *c* 1960; ht 7¼in (18.4cm).
Below, a realistically detailed *pâte de verre* relief panel, made by Paul Gardner while working with Frederick Carder. 1930s; ht 18in (45.8cm).
Far below, lighthearted teapot, with a touch of fantasy typical of many young experimental groups. *c* 1973; ht 3¼in (8.3cm).

glassblowers also specialise in architectural work, stained glass, relief panels, paperweights – even portraits.

In 1979 Corning decided to repeat their major show of the 1950s, and 'New Glass 1979' has already been exhibited in Toledo, Ohio, Washington D.C., New York and San Francisco.

Exhibitors included 196 individual artists/craftsmen/designers, and factories in 28 countries. Over 700 other entrants sent in work – an extraordinary example of the profound and remarkable change that has occurred in this most traditional of crafts. For the first time in the history of glassmaking the fine art of glass, whether made by an artist, a team or a factory, has taken a lead in contemporary crafts, while the industry as a whole seems to have settled for technical development and mechanical innovation.

Another obvious change is the design and choice of subject. Twenty years previously most exhibits had been functional, but the 1979 exhibition was clearly on the side of abstract images, even on useful objects such as bowls and jugs, and included many sculptural pieces of purely non-representational imagery.

The use of non-blown plate glass, laminated glass, and even glass 'rocks' on a bed of sand (Jon Kuhn) has been yet another innovation.

For the first time, studio pieces far outnumbered industrial designs; and came from everywhere in the world, including Japan where a major group of artists has emerged in recent decades.

'New Glass 79' can be regarded as a miniature history of studio glass in the last twenty-five years, with exhibits by some of the movement's major figures. Labino's magnificent paperweight rises in multiple overlaps of clear rosy fountains. Eisch, whose sagging gold telephone enlivened the first Corning show, contributed five macabre fingers with appropriately sinister decoration; and Pavel Hlava of Czechoslovakia, one of Herman's pupils in that first Royal College course, contributed a totally abstract globular sculpture that reflected the very latest trends. He works at Rosenthal Studio House, while Willem Heesen, chief designer at Leerdam, has his own studio where his more traditional blown vase was made.

Stained glass panels by Hans Gottfried von Stockhausen and Robert Kehlmann are effective and tranquil, but a wiry study of two cows in white lampwork on green plastic turf is entirely new and entirely delightful (Jamie L. Conover). A very strong example of the continuing fascination that the old traditions retain is the plate by Laura Santillana, at 26 the youngest member of one of the great Venetian glass-working families; it is made of fused mosaic canes in a technique dating back to pre-Roman times.

Obviously no one exhibit can be said to speak for the entire craft on a world-wide basis; even the examples from the United States, where over eighty exhibits were made, do not include any from a number of very fine glassmakers who, for one reason or another, either did not submit work, or were not chosen by the jury. The same reservation must be expressed about the selection from Czechoslovakia and Germany, the second most important new centres for contemporary work.

Nonetheless, 'New Glass 1979' has proved that studio glass has achieved a major place in the craft world, and will surely mark 1979 as being as important to our contemporary world of art as the Great Exhibition of 1851 was to the Victorian age.

Some of the post-war idealism about strictly one-person studios may have begun to evaporate – the technical achievements of the large glass companies can be utilized to help find new ways of handling more individual production. A number of traditional factories have hired young artists to work not only on their own, but also within the streamlined glasshouses to help develop modern appreciation of the best commercial glass products. Perhaps the best results in the future will come from that traditional co-operation between art and craft which has given us so much pleasure in the past.

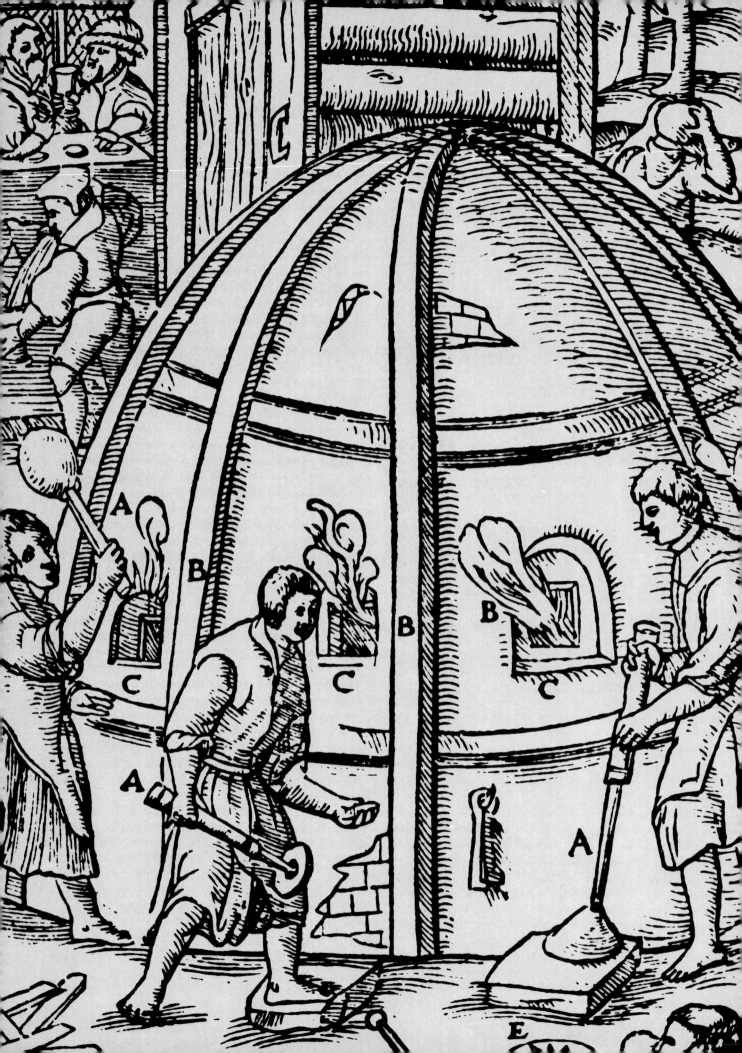

Part Two

Techniques

Glass Melting

None of the major developments in glass production could have been achieved without the sciences of chemistry, physics and engineering. These have given us an understanding of the nature of glass, the way in which it is formed and its physical and chemical properties. Research and development in combustion of fuels, heat transfer, furnace construction and new refractory materials, have enabled the glass industry to make great progress.

The temperature at which raw materials fuse to produce glass is between 1300–1500°C, depending on the composition of the glass required and the raw materials used. Achieving such a high temperature was a serious problem for the pre-nineteenth-century glassmaker, and consequently most old glass is softer, with a higher proportion of alkali than glass produced today. High-alkali glasses have a lower resistance to atmospheric attack and that is why they may be covered in a white film, or show the flaking surface symptomatic of glass sickness.

The old glassmaker had to be content with solid fuel in the form of wood or coal and had no means of achieving a high temperature by re-using the heat from the waste gases of combustion. The methods of heat regeneration and recuperation rectified this and today all furnaces operate one of these two heat recovery systems and solid fuel has been replaced by the more versatile oil or gas.

Furnaces and Fuels

Two ways of melting glass are used: pot melting and tank melting. The first is used for a small quantity of handmade glass, including lead crystal, and the second for large-volume production of flat glass, bottles, mass-produced domestic glassware, glass fibres and large volume lead crystal glass.

Pot furnaces are mainly of the recuperative type. This relies on a large chamber through which the hot waste gases are conducted to the atmosphere. This chamber is constructed of refractory bricks and has refractory or metal tubes through which air, needed for the combustion of fuel, is led into the furnace. On the outward journey the hot gases pre-heat the combustion air in the tubes and thus higher temperatures and fuel savings are achieved.

For small-volume production the pot furnace has the advantage that the glass can be melted in a number of pots, made of refractory clays, and thus several types of glass can be melted at the same time. Often the furnace is circular with the mouths of pots, from which gathering is done, facing outwards, giving access to the glass.

For large scale automatic production, tank furnaces are exclusively used. These consist of a larger rectangular bath, known as the melting end, connected by a narrow channel at the bottom of the tank to a much smaller semi-circular bath, known as the refining or working end. These furnaces are capable of producing anything between 20 and 450 tons of bottle glass and 1,000 tons or more of flat glass per day. Normally there is a series of oil or gas burners along each side of the furnace and the firing is done alternately from each side for twenty minutes each.

These furnaces are invariably of the regenerative type. When the firing is done from the left-hand side, the flame sweeps across the top of the glass from left to right, and the waste gases are exhausted through a large refractory chamber, known as the regenerator, packed with refractory brickwork situated on the right-hand side. While the waste gases find their tortuous way between the brickwork, they give up a large proportion of their heat to it, which is held until the process is reversed and the firing is done from the right-hand side. The combustion air is then drawn into the furnace over the pre-heated brickwork and the heat is extracted by the air and returned to the furnace. Again high temperatures and substantial fuel savings are achieved. The whole furnace is covered by a refractory brick arch – the crown.

From the working end protrude the forehearths. The glass flows into these troughs or forehearths to be prepared for entry into the feeding mechanism. The raw materials (batch) are fed automatically at the back of the furnace and are melted as they move towards the front. Only well-melted glass from the bottom of the tank can pass through the narrow channel, called the throat, into the working end where it is refined and made into the final product.

Until the mid-1950s the predominant fuel was producer gas made on the plant from coal. This was a fairly low calorific-value fuel made by blowing air and steam through a glowing bed of coal and converting the carbon into carbon monoxide and the steam into hydrogen. The production of the gas and its firing caused considerable atmospheric pollution and its use has now been completely eliminated in favour of heavy fuel oil and natural gas.

The glassmaking process starts in the batch house. Gone are the days of the craftsman weighing out his secret raw materials in proportions only known to himself and mixing them by hand. It is now a highly mechanized fully automatic process from the moment raw materials are brought to the glassworks by road, rail or sea to the moment they are fed into the furnace as batch.

Glass Compositions

The main raw materials for soda-lime-silica glass used in bottle glass, flat glass and cheaper quality domestic ware are: sand (silica), limestone (calcium carbonate), feldspar (alumina compounds), dolomite (calcium and magnesium) and cullet (broken glass). Other raw materials like salt cake (sodium sulphate), sodium nitrate, selenium, cobalt, chromium oxide, sulphur, carbon, iron, etc, are used in smaller quantities for refining, colouring and decolourizing.

The raw materials have to be as near pure as possible, especially when colourless glass is required; the iron impurity in sand and limestone is the glassmaker's greatest enemy. Sand with a very low iron content has to be used and, although sand is the most common mineral in the earth's crust, deposits of suitable glassmaking sands are not abundant. Many glassmaking sands have to be chemically purified and even then the glassmaker has to resort to decolourization in order to prevent an objectionable green tint. Decolourizing takes advantage of the fact that green, red and blue, being complementary colours of the spectrum, cancel each other out to give a colourless appearance. To counteract the green which comes from the iron, mainly in the sand, the glassmaker adds to his batch a small amount of selenium, which colours it red, and a small amount of

Above
Illustration from an engraving
on glass manufacture. France;
16th century.
Sand is the primary ingredient
of glass. Impurities will give the
molten glass its colour, and
also affect the translucency and
clarity of the finished product.
In this illustration workers are
raking the sand over the boards
while another man at the left
shovels up dirt and foreign
particles.

Right
Illustration from *De Re
Metallica*. Italy; 14th–15th
century. Glassmaking has
changed very little in the past
300 years. This medieval
furnace (B) would be
recognized by any modern
craftsman.
A – The blow-pipes or irons.
C – The openings through
which the molten glass is
gathered onto the pipes and
the pontil irons.
D – Pincers used to shape the
cooling glass, open up the lips.
E – Partmoulds used to shape
the first gather.
The foreman, bottom left, is
reckoning up the day's work,
while completed glasses cool on
the bed of sand at the right.
The merchant or pedlar, top
right, is leaving with his pack,
and the landlord and customers
at the tavern, top left, are
putting the glasses to good use.

237

cobalt, which gives it a blue tint. The result is really a muddy-grey colour, but to the eye it appears colourless. There is, of course, a limit to the intensity of green above which decolourizing cannot successfully be achieved.

A few typical soda-lime-silica glass compositions are as follows:

	Bottle glass colourless (flint)	Bottle glass amber*	Window glass	Lamp bulb glass	Domestic glassware
SiO_2 (silica)	72.1%	72.5%	72.0%	72.9%	70.5%
Na_2O (sodium oxide)	13.6%	14.4%	14.3%	16.3%	16.5%
Al_2O_3 (alumina)	2.0%	2.0%	1.3%	2.2%	2.5%
Fe_2O_3 (iron oxide)	0.06%	0.1%	0.06%	0.06%	
CaO (calcium oxide)	10.4%	10.2%	8.2%	4.7%	5.5%
MgO (magnesia)			3.5%	3.6%	3.0%
K_2O (potassium oxide)				0.2%	1.2%
B_2O_3 (boric oxide)				0.2%	
Others (sulphur, cobalt, etc)	0.7%	0.8%	0.6%		

*Amber colour is achieved by the combination of iron and sulphur which, due to reduction by carbon, forms iron sulphides.

The silica content is almost the same for all of them. Some of the calcium oxide in the bottle glass has been replaced by magnesium oxide in the window and lamp bulb glass. The variation in composition, although apparently small, is essential for the different physical properties required for these glasses to make them more suitable for the processes for which they are intended.

Lead oxide had been used in glazes in ancient times but a true lead glass was perfected in the seventeenth century by George Ravenscroft. In trying to eliminate cracking and clouding of glass (crizzling) caused by the then necessarily high proportion of alkali, Ravenscroft added lead oxide to his raw materials. This gave the glass a lower fusion point, a longer span of viscosity at which the glass could be manipulated and, above all, a very high refractive index resulting in its exceptional brilliance.

Lead glasses can have a variety of composition with the lead content varying from a very small percentage to more than forty per cent. Thus a typical composition of full lead crystal glass is:

SiO_2 (silica)	55.55%
PbO (lead oxide)	33.00%
K_2O (potassium oxide)	11.00%
Fe_2O_3 (unavoidable, unwanted iron oxide)	0.025%

It should be noted that potassium has replaced sodium and there is no calcium at all.

A lower quality lead glass can consist of:

SiO_2 (silica)	66.00%
PbO (lead oxide)	15.5%
K_2O (potassium oxide)	9.5%
Al_2O_3 (alumina)	0.9%
CaO (calcium)	0.7%
BaO (barium oxide)	0.5%
Na_2O (sodium oxide)	6.0%
B_2O_3 (boric oxide)	0.6%

It is quite evident from the foregoing that there is no hard and fast rule as to what a glass composition should be. The composition is adjusted to suit the product to be made.

The third, large group of glasses is known as boro-silicates. Typical compositions include:

SiO_2 (silica)	76.2%	80.0%
Al_2O_3 (alumina)	3.7%	2.5%
CaO (calcium)	0.8%	
Na_2O (sodium oxide)	5.4%	4.5%
B_2O_3 (boric oxide)	13.5%	12.2%

Here again are two widely differing compositions, but both are used for heat-resistant glassware. Boro-silicate glasses have a much reduced coefficient of expansion, a higher softening temperature and better resistance to chemical and atmospheric attack. They are therefore used for cooking ware, chemical apparatus, industrial applications in chemical plants, and medical equipment requiring frequent sterilization and where it is important that nothing should be leached out of the glass which could be harmful to the patient. The low coefficient of expansion enables the glass to be heated to a very high temperature and then cooled rapidly, as it must be in oven-to-table glassware.

Glass breaks when tension is applied to its surface. It is almost impossible to break it in compression. When a piece of glass has been heated throughout, as a dish which has spent some time in the oven, and is then suddenly cooled, the outer surface tends to contract, but is prevented from doing so by the inside which holds hot food and remains hot. Severe tension is developed on the surface which leads to inevitable rupture if the coefficient of expansion is high. In the case of boro-silicate glass, the contraction of the outer surface is so small that it is insufficient to create stress in excess of the breaking point. Obviously, the thicker the glass, the greater is the temperature gradient, and the greater the stress. This is the reason why electric light bulbs, which are not made of heat-resistant glass, are so thin as to be able to survive very sudden temperature changes.

Structure of Glass

It has been mentioned before that glass is a liquid and not a solid. There are several methods of ascertaining this; the simplest begins by questioning the nature of glass's transparency. The property of transparency can indicate either that glass is a single crystal or a liquid. However, when glass is cracked or broken, it can be seen that the fracture has no tendency to travel in one direction more than another and this would demonstrate that the glass is not likely to be a single crystal. It must therefore be some sort of liquid. Its transparency indicates that there are no internal surfaces of a size approaching the wave-length of visible light.

A test which would indicate that glass was a non-crystalline super-cooled liquid could be carried out by heating it to a temperature at which viscosity is reduced sufficiently to enable a movement of atoms; and on gradual cooling crystals would form, causing it to lose the property of transparency. Highly sophisticated scientific methods have to be used to unlock the secrets of glass's precise structure.

Right
Ceiling from Governor Samuel Tilden's house on Gramercy Park, New York. Installed c 1901 and still intact.

Flat Glass

Left
Mirror. Bilbao-type made in southern Europe; ht 49in (124.5cm).
By the 19th century, mirrors were exported from England and France to be mounted in carved frames in various studios throughout Europe.

Page 240
'*Rencontres du visible et de l'invisible.*' Window designed by Jean Cocteau, made by Dr Oidtmann Studio, West Germany. It was made for the village church at Chapelle des Simples, France. 1958; ht 38½in (98cm).

Page 241
Interior window from Governor Samuel Tilden's Gramercy Park house. c 1901.

The ancient glassmakers had two ways of producing flat glass. They either cast it from a crucible or pot containing molten glass on to a metal table and then rolled it to the required thickness, or they used a method which was in principle the same as that used for hollow glassware. The second method produced crown glass which can be seen in windows of many historic buildings today. To make crown glass, the glass-blower gathered a large gather at the end of his blow-pipe and blew a very big glass bubble. He then removed the bubble from the blow-pipe, transferred it on to a rod and then spun the rod at a high speed allowing the centrifugal forces to open, flatten and spread the bubble. He was then left with a large disc, approximately one metre in diameter, at the end of his rod. He cut the disc off and placed it in an annealing kiln. Once the disc was annealed, it was cut into smaller diamonds, or later into squares, for use as window glass. Only small pieces of glass could be produced by this method and this may account for small window panes in ancient buildings. The centrepiece of the disc was called the 'bull's eye' and is often found in glass in old buildings. This method was practised up to the nineteenth century.

Cylinder Glass

As larger window panes were needed, new methods were developed and the next stage still used the principle of glassblowing. Instead of blowing a large bubble which would then be flattened by centrifugal force, the glassblower blew a long cylinder of glass. The more glass he could get into his gather, the longer and thicker would be the cylinder, and to achieve this the glassmaker gathered the glass from a pot, started blowing and by rolling (marvering) and shaping the gather, he was able to collect more glass and again shape it and blow it gently. Having produced a sizeable cylinder, he then swung it in a pit to elongate it. Both ends of the cylinder

Above
Two drawings of early windows: *top*, a Georgian sash window set in wooden frames; *above*, a typical diamond pane lattice casement, side hung and set in lead.
Crown glass was sometimes called Normandy because the best Norman sand made the clearest and brightest window glass. Even when the cheaper and more convenient cylinder method was developed, crown glass was more highly regarded for its clarity and extra lustre, until the development of sheet glass in c 1830 completely demolished the older methods. One glass-making area produced seven million square feet of crown in the 1830s, but by the 1860s they produced none at all.

Left
View of a candy store. New York; 1901.
By the 1900s flat glass was so readily available it covered almost every surface in newly-fitted shops, and was used for elaborate, multi-shelved display units.

Above and below
Two details of pub glass.
London; 1850s.

Above 19th-century development of leaded window, based on lattice and stained glass.

were cut off, it was then cut longitudinally and placed in a re-heating furnace. As the cylinder was heated, it softened and, with the help of metal rods, was opened out and flattened into a large sheet of glass. Sheets of up to two metres square were made but the quality was very poor indeed, although it is often considered quaint by us today. The glass was full of bubbles and blisters, its thickness was not uniform and it had many marks caused by the tools used for flattening it. Nevertheless, it was a reasonably efficient way of producing large pieces of glass.

As is usual in the history of glass, there were attempts at imitating the mouth-blown and manual methods. As recently as 1903 Lubbers and the American Window Glass Company developed a method for the mechanical blowing of cylinders many times larger than mouth-blown cylinders. Cylinders up to fifteen metres in length and one metre in diameter were produced. These enormous test-tube-like objects were cut into sections, flattened, annealed and, finally, cut into stock sizes. The cylinder method was widely practised up to the early 1920s, when it was displaced by the more efficient method of drawn glass.

The replacement of the cylinder method by the flat drawn process resulted in a staggering increase in production efficiency and a reduction in the number of flat glass producing plants. In the United States the number of plants was reduced from a hundred in 1899 to a mere sixteen in 1929. As with all processes imitating a hand process, the cylinder method was only a transition between hand operation and an entirely new mechanical concept.

Flat glass produced by drawing, though of infinitely higher quality than any glass made before, did not have a perfectly flat surface. In order to produce non-wavy plate glass, it had to be cast and the surface had to be ground and polished. A great step forward was made when Pilkington Brothers of St Helens, Lancashire, developed a twin grinding and polishing process for plate glass. In this, the glass was ground and polished simultaneously on both sides as it emerged from the annealing lehr.

It was Pilkington Brothers who in 1959 revolutionized flat glass production by the introduction of the float process. In this a ribbon of glass is floated onto a bath of molten tin. The result is a perfectly smooth, polished surface of glass of almost any width, length and thickness. It does away with grinding and polishing and produces glass of the highest quality. One furnace can produce a thousand tonnes of glass a day. The process is now rapidly replacing all other means of flat glass production, and is operated throughout the world under a licence from the British inventors.

Mirrors

Looking glasses have been known since ancient times, made from highly polished metal discs, but the first substantial evidence of metal-backed glass mirrors dates from around the twelfth century. They were probably made first in Lorraine which was noted for its flat glass. Such early examples were small, the reflective backing made with tin, lead, or an amalgam of other metals. Metal was also usually used for the frame.

Convex mirrors were made during the fifteenth century

Right
Detail of stained glass window.
England; *c* 1890.

by the Nuremberg glassmakers. A metallic mixture was blown into hot glass globes to coat the interior. After cooling, the globes were cut into pieces and framed – the first of a fashion which became popular in Regency England.

By the end of the seventeenth century, Venice and France supplied large quantities of fine mirrors to an eager market. The Venetians used the split cylinder method until the perfection of cast glass in France.

During the Art Deco period it seemed that almost every room was reflected in peach and smoky mirror panels. A remarkable bathroom for Tille Losch included an entire wall of mirrored glass with an inset fireplace. Sand blasting was used to create texture, replacing acid etching which was impractical on large surfaces.

Today, decorative treatments have reached new heights, and mirrors can be marbled, smoked, coloured or plain, painted or even printed.

Stained Glass

The technique of making stained glass is a fascinating art. A microscopic examination of twelfth-century red and blue glasses shows alternate coloured and clear layers, as though they were not properly mixed. Whether deliberate or not, this produced a wonderful richness of colour variation in each piece. Later, from the thirteenth century, a more intense colour could be made and layered or flashed over the parison of clear glass by dipping it into a separate pot. Part of the surface was laboriously rubbed away with sand or a grinding agent to reveal the bottom layer. The technique today is accomplished by a masking agent and hydrofluoric acid. Any lines or slight imperfections in the sheets are blessings in disguise, for they catch the light and make the glass sparkle.

The process of making sheet glass by hand is known as the 'antique' method. Most stained glass windows are still made from handmade sheets, either pot antique (made in one pot and therefore single coloured), or layered flash antique.

The factors that affect the design of a window have been accepted by stained glass artists for more than ten centuries: the overall size of the window, openings, interesting columns in the line of sight, and, outside, any nearby buildings or trees. Above all, because a window transmits light, it is dramatically changed by that light.

A preliminary small, coloured drawing shows what the finished window will look like. Once the design is accepted, a full-scale drawing is made, with an overlay to show the shape and position of each piece.

Cutting used to be done by running a hot iron slowly along the proposed line of fracture; a crack would follow the iron. Today, a scratch or score is made with a small steel wheel mounted in a handle; bending or tapping the glass along the mark causes it to break.

Most windows have painted details over the coloured and plain pieces. The paint is a mixture of very soft glass ground with metallic oxides to make a black or brown powder. (The red colour on the back of some Victorian windows is iron oxide which shows black against the light.) The powders are mixed with oil, or gum and water, although an ancient formula recommends honey instead of gum to render the paint thick enough to stay on the brush, as well as to prevent flaking. Silver chloride or nitrate mixed into a paste with pipe clay is also used as enamel, staining the glass yellow. (According to a romantic story, a thirteenth-century glass-maker inadvertently dropped a silver button onto molten glass, turning it yellow.)

The painted pieces are re-heated at a temperature that will melt the surface, but not cause the glass to flow and distort the cut shape; the paints and enamels sink just into the surface.

The lead glazing bars, H shape in section, are now made in moulds and milled to exact sizes. Originally they were made by pouring molten lead over reeds laid in a box with tiny gaps between them. Each reed provided a hole through the lead sheet for a half section.

Today, stained glass utilizes many totally new materials, and often completely different designs. One example is slab glass. An inch thick, it is cut into approximate shapes either with a hammer over an anvil made by fixing a large chisel edge into lead or a log of wood, or with a special tungsten steel-tipped hammer. The edges are faceted like a diamond to make them sparkle. These pieces are held together with concrete or modern resin-reinforced stone and form structures of considerable strength but of enormous weight. They make windows that can let in a great deal of light, but lack the subtleties of design found in painted windows.

Paperweights

A Venetian writer, Sabellico, referred in 1494 to little balls of glass with all sorts of flowers, and we know from Apsley Pellatt (1849) that the Venetians decorated such spheres with herringbone patterns of small slices arranged in colourful sequence. Some balls seem to have been drilled, and were probably intended as a kind of pendant or elaborate bead for the centre of a necklace. By the sixteenth and seventeenth centuries, hundreds of designs were made into drawn-out rods for *millefiori* slices, and even more elaborate filigree patterns were twisted and spiralled to form the intricate *reticello* and *vetro di trina* for stems, edgings and whole cups and platters.

Paperweights became overwhelmingly popular from the 1840s onwards as items which sold in quantity through stationery stores, and corner shops, often for remarkably low prices. We associate them most commonly with the *millefiori* technique which was used to decorate most of the weights made during the classic period, the 1840s and 1850s. In fact, *millefiori* work is one of the basic techniques, which also include lampwork, and enclosure or incrustation. The latter is the simplest of all, with the glass moulded and shaped around an already manufactured form such as a cameo or a miniature figure. Filigree canes were also used.

Millefiori

Rods were first made in Mesopotamia, as relatively simple drawn canes marvered into the surface of cast or moulded vessels. By the pre-Roman era they were complicated layers of glass in different colours and different shapes. Sometimes bowls were made entirely of simple, layered, round slices, laid in a mould and heated until they fused. Other rods were twisted as they grew thinner, so a rope effect was created. These were the first filigree canes, and instead of being sliced they were used as short lengths within the bowls, or laid around the rim to form a beading. The same filigree was used to create an enormous variety of twist-stem glasses during the eighteenth century.

Mosaic plaques were also decorated with shapes and figures made by the *millefiori* process, and incorporated into wall panels and jewellery. *Millefiori* continued to be used sporadically, and when Venice became the centre of glass-making in the fourteenth century the technique was revived. It was finally elaborated and perfected in the great nineteenth-century French crystalleries, for paperweights and related objects such as decanters, perfume bottles, etc.

The *millefiori* paperweight consists of tiny glass 'flowers' arranged in a variety of designs and encased in clear glass. Each flower is the cross-section of a thin multi-coloured glass rod, which has been cut into short pieces approximately 10mm long. Glass is gathered in several layers from pots of molten glass containing different colours. The first layer is gathered on the end of an iron pipe and rolled into a solid cylinder. The second colour, gathered on top, is marvered again and the operation is repeated until the required number of layers is obtained. The cylinder is moulded into a star shape, with layers of multi-coloured glass, and a star-shaped cross-section. Next, the star cylinder is drawn into a long thin rod. The thickness of the rod depends on the speed with which it is drawn, and the design.

Right
Left to right, garland with Clichy rose; butterfly and clematis; concentric with ribboned edge; crown swirl; radial; single flower, cased and faceted; muslin swirl; flat bouquet; concentric torsade

Once the rods are cooled and annealed they are cut into the required slices. The long rods are sometimes called canes.

It is important to remember that the glassmaker will be fusing these rods into the body of a different glass and consequently, to prevent undue stresses in the final article, all the glasses used must be compatible especially with regard to their ability to expand and contract.

The cooled rods are arranged in the desired pattern inside a shallow straight-sided iron pan the same size as the finished weight. This operation is done by hand and the artist has the opportunity of creating a variety of patterns. The finished pattern is called a set-up.

One of the glassmaking team places the pan in the furnace to pre-heat it and then gathers some clear glass on the end of an iron rod and pours it over the top of the *millefiori* pattern. The iron rod remains attached to the glass. The pan is removed with a gentle tap and the glass is re-heated in the furnace and shaped into a *millefiori* disc. The disc, still attached to the iron rod, is passed to the next glassmaker who gathers another layer of glass on to it. He shapes the glass into the final paperweight with the help of a wooden paddle or a pad of wet paper. The paperweight is knocked off the iron rod into a bed of sand, annealed and finished off by hand grinding to remove the punty mark left where the glass was attached to the rod.

Lampwork

Lampwork has been used from the earliest period to form figures or models as well as handles, finials, and so on. In seventeenth-century France, lampwork figures were often set in elaborate landscapes, and Nevers seems to have been the centre for such scenes. Tiny figures, of animals in particular, were often used as enclosures in paperweights, but there are also many lampwork flowers, baskets, ships, etc, set inside weights with or without *millefiori* and filigree background decoration. Once the group is set up on the ground, it becomes the base of the paperweight just as the *millefiori* set-up is finished off. Lampwork could be done away with the glasshouse itself. Miniature animals and other tiny decorative pieces made with glass rods, a single burner and a few simple tools, are still made that way at stalls and fairgrounds.

Enclosures

Any introduced object coated in clear glass is an enclosure. The original inspiration may have come from double-walled glasses enclosing painted or gold-leaf decoration, but the technique works equally well for cameos or sulphides laid on a flat base and topped by a domed glass.

French Paperweights

The result of all this experience over the centuries meant that by the nineteenth century the climate for full-scale development of this art form was just right. The Renaissance

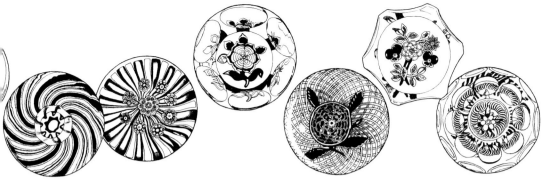

Venetian ballweights which Sabellico mentioned were haphazard and random collections of bits and pieces of coloured rods, figures, filigree chunks and so on, thinly covered with glass. This remained the pattern for Italian weights even through the nineteenth century. From the end of the eighteenth century German and Bohemian glass-makers had been experimenting with all kinds of colours and shapes, producing bottles, buttons and pieces of jewellery. In France, research was being done into the variety and type of filigree glass, going back to the best Venetian work – Georges Bontemps, a director at Choisy-le-Roi Glassworks, was a well-known maker, and the author of a still highly regarded book on that subject.

By the middle of the century, the classic format for paper-weights had established itself in the French factories, and later was copied all over the world: a low, convex design, carefully arranged rather than simply thrown together, en-cased in a rounded dome which both protected the design and added a magnifying effect, and with a flat base. There were many other objects made – bottles and decanters, furni-ture and cabinet knobs, inkwells and trays, boxes and glass, vases, door stops – the list is endless. Nonetheless, it was in the simple paperweight shape that the great factories made their most successful and spectacular examples. St Louis, Baccarat and Clichy were rivals for this unexpected popular success, and they competed with each other to make the most complicated, the most difficult and the most artistic weights imaginable. Today, although many of the best weights are clearly from one or other of the factories, there are other examples whose origin is unknown. Sometimes, even the country is a matter for speculation.

Air and Coloured Glass Designs

A popular design of paperweight is one in which the glass appears to be full of large air bubbles. Badly melted glass often has bubbles in it, but these are not uniformly large and are not distributed in a regular pattern, so obviously the bubbles in the paperweight must have been introduced by design. This is accomplished by placing the first gather in a mould with protrusions making indentations in the glass. As a second layer is gathered, air is trapped in these indenta-tions thus producing the desired effect.

Many designs today utilize coloured glass swirls and streaks within the weights to form abstract or symbolic patterns, with or without the controlled use of air bubbles.

Twentieth-century Weights

Modern paperweight makers include Paul Ysart who worked in mostly traditional styles at various Scottish glass-houses; Caithness in Scotland, which is well known for its modern weights such as the planet series; and Charles Kaziun, and Paul Stankard in America.

In the last ten or fifteen years, there has been a revival in

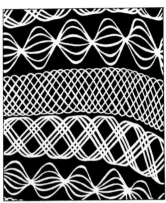

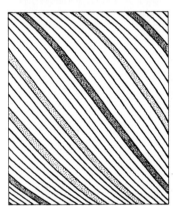

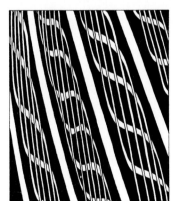

studio glass which has moved away from the purely innova-tive and has begun to re-interpret some of the fine traditional techniques in the interest of modern glassmaking.

There is no doubt that part of the reason for this is curio-sity. Many of the classical paperweight techniques have remained difficult if not impossible to copy, and skilled craftsmen always enjoy pitting their wits and ingenuity against accepted 'classical' standards.

Then there is now the growing independence of the lone glassmaker. Paperweights can be made relatively easily by one man or a small team. The set-ups can be prepared separately while the crystal is melting for the covering layer; and using rods, *millefiori* slices, enclosures and cameos as well as air bubbles and small amounts of coloured glass, a remarkable variety of effect can be achieved within the limits of a small studio or workshop.

The beauty of a paperweight does not rely entirely on the pattern encased in it but also on the outside decoration. Shapes are produced by grinding away large chunks of glass to create facets at varying angles or by engraving or etching artistic designs.

Major Paperweight Styles

For ease of identification, paperweights are largely described by pattern, and a brief resumé of the most popular kinds are as follows:

The problem is to keep the swirls close together over the base as they radiate outwards. These lovely patterns were almost all made by Clichy. Marbries give a true kaleidoscope effect, with the ribbons, twisted from flat to edge, making marvellous, shimmering geometric 'mirror' effects.

Garlands

Garlands of *millefiori* canes are interwoven in a particularly lovely way. The best were made by the Clichy factory, with occasional fairly mundane efforts by one of the other factories. Most of the garlands are made in the larger size, so smaller examples, under 2in (5cm) in diameter, are likely to have been cut down – a fact for collectors to bear in mind. Cut down weights of all kinds can usually be spotted by a very thin layer of glass around the design or an uneven layer

Close Millefiori

These are most like original Venetian spheres – the *millefiori* canes are scrambled together, seemingly in a random pattern. They cover the entire base of the weight, and with magnification of the dome seem to fill the weight completely with literally hundreds of tiny flowers, and occasionally an odd shape or two. They can sometimes be identified by a particular cane which is known to have been used by a specific factory – an animal silhouette cane for example, or one which actually incorporates an initial and date. There are quite a few dated B (for Baccarat) 1848, but other dates are more scarce. Close *millefiori* were made by Clichy and St Louis, as well as by almost all the paperweight factories in Europe.

Spaced Millefiori, Carpet Grounds and Chequers

These are all variations of the geometrically arranged *millefiori* weight, and they provide one of the most varied and appealing of all the weight patterns. Simple spaced weight designs allow each cane to be surrounded by clear glass or set against a 'carpet' of filigree or lattice work. Sometimes a variety of large and small canes is used, sometimes they are in concentric circles or reflecting patterns like a kaleidoscope of infinitely varied, brilliantly coloured flowers. A particularly lovely Baccarat example is a double gourd bottle which has a base of close *millefiori*, a second bulb of spaced *millefiori* and a stopper of a lampworked flower – very rare and *very* effective. There are literally thousands of variations that are possible within this range; some of the largest and most impressive weights use only two kinds of canes, usually with white, and a single coloured motif; many were made by George Bacchus in England.

Swirls and Marbries

Swirls are another geometric form, depending on ribbons of glass swirled out from a central cane, in Clichy often a rose.

which suggests either an inept workman or a damaged piece cut down to where the chip or damage was cut away.

Crowns

Crown weights are hollow blown, with the canes and filigree in ribbons and twisted ropes billowing out from a central cane or motif at the top, and swirling down around the sides to a narrow base. St Louis made these their special trademark, and some even had a little stand to match. The New England Glass Company in America did very well with crown weights; it is likely that their best examples may have been made by French craftsmen working in their factory near Boston.

Mushrooms and Baskets

Mushrooms are another unusual shape, often interpreted as a bouquet or posy, such as one very rare and beautiful example made at Clichy which actually had white 'slats' around the sides to represent the basket, and a gilt handle fitted across the top for carrying. The base and sometimes the rim of the basket was often wrapped in a twisted ribbon rope, known as a torsade. They were made by all the French factories, as well as Bacchus in London, and by unknown factories in Bohemia.

Sometimes the entire shape is enclosed within the weight and it becomes a central pattern inside the dome instead of forming the weight itself. When the rounded top of the basket shape has a stem narrowing down to the foot, it becomes a mushroom.

Overlays and Facets

In addition to manipulation within the weight, there were two other ways of decorating the finished object. When the dome of glass is cut into facets, it multiplies the reflections and gives an extra sparkle, or kaleidoscope effect. Sometimes the weights were completely cased in one or two colours, usually white underneath, covered by apple green, turquoise, pink or blue. The overlay or casing was cut away in 'windows' very carefully placed so that the central decoration appears in each facet like a bouquet of flowers in a window. The lily could be gilded even further with gold engraving or painting on top of the coloured surface. Overlays are more likely to chip than plain weights and should therefore be examined very carefully.

Flowers

Single sprays of lampworked flowers were made at Clichy, but they were also made at St Louis and the American

Below
A range of paperweights: swirls, crowns, flat flowers, fruit, bouquets, close *millefiori*, sulphide portrait.

factories at New England, and Boston and Sandwich. The flowers themselves may or may not resemble real flowers, but the art was to arrange them as prettily as possible, either on a clear base, or a carpet of lattice work, or very occasionally a coloured ground. The lampwork can be in itself the identifying feature for attribution – leaves were made in a certain form at one factory and in a different shape at another. Baccarat, for example, has only two kinds of leaves no matter what the flower, and St Louis has one. Mount Washington weights often show the veining which was produced by the same type of clamp which was used to form both parts of the flower – the petals as well as the leaves. Dahlias made at St Louis and Baccarat seem to fill the entire weight. At other times a smaller flower is centred inside a ring of *millefiori* canes or, at Clichy, a ring of miniature flowers.

Flowers come in many forms; the simplest are the flat single sprays or flower heads in the usual paperweight shape, with a plain or undecorated ground. There are also floral bouquets laid flat on a clear or latticework base, sometimes with three or more flowers, and a butterfly as well. Occasionally Clichy laid the flowers on an opal plaque instead of inside a dome weight. Then there are three-dimensional flowers, of which the most spectacular is the Milleville Waterlily, made in America at Whitall, Tatum and Company in a special crimp which gives an extraordinary appearance like groping fingers to the half-closed flower. These were actually made much later than the 'classic' paperweight period – in about 1910.

Many American companies concentrated on making three-dimensional floral weights where the image extended quite far up inside the weight. There was always the danger of trapping air bubbles between the tiny parts of the lampwork and the covering blob of clear glass, but bubbles were sometimes part of the design like dewdrops on the edge of a petal.

Upright bouquets were made in sheaves or in baskets and some very remarkable results were achieved with naturalistic effects.

Fruit

Fruit designs are another delightful novelty made during the classic period, and revived recently. Some are arranged formally – a single pear or a bunch of grapes in the centre of the weight. Some spill across the weight, like strawberries or cherries, occasionally laid on a lattice ground as if just tossed in a basket. Whole weights in the shape of apples and pears were made at New England. These were copied from the St Louis examples by a process of blowing and casing the desired shape in layers of subtly tinted glass until a three-dimensional soft appearance was obtained. The American versions were made later than the French ones – towards the end of the nineteenth century.

Reptiles

There were other novelties – the most numerous being the reptile group. These consisted of salamanders and snakes in various coiled positions, stalking around between leaves, or simply curled up on top of an elaborately decorated ball weight, which was often encased or gilded. Moulded lizards were made at St Louis and their effect was very similar to the effect of the relief decoration on Emile Gallé's vases at Nancy.

Sulphides, Portraits and Cameos

These were made of a special clay, moulded and fired and then enclosed within a simple weight, sometimes decoratively cut on the outside to reflect even more light. Historic portraits and scenes are the most interesting.

Sulphides were first developed in France, but the most popular in England were made by Apsley Pellatt (1791–1863) of London. He called them crystallo-ceramie, and used them in vases, tumblers, lamps and plaques. Bakewell's in Pennsylvania were the most successful American sulphide manufacturers.

There were all kinds of other designs. Plaques were made of overlaid wafers cut away to form decorative designs, usually in one or two colours and shaded like cameos. Sometimes steel dies were dusted with fine white glass powder to make a picture, then covered by the clear glass; the die was then knocked off and a base added afterwards. There were miniature water scenes with swans floating beside a pool, birds nesting, butterflies perched on the edges of flowers, insects hovering – dozens and dozens of individual designs made by most of the major factories, and copied in various degrees of excellence in England, America, Bohemia and later in China.

Bottles

The process of making a bottle – the most common of all glass products – has an interesting history, going back to ancient times. It starts with the early sand-core process which was replaced by the blow-pipe, then using the blow-pipe principle, the semi-automatic process was developed and refined to the highly mechanical and automated fast production of today.

As a result of the introduction of glassblowing, bottles became cheap articles made in quantity, and commercial bottlemaking spread rapidly through the Middle East and the Roman Empire. Large bottles were used for wine, oil and many other liquids. They were usually simple, blown in a mould, with little or no decoration. Tiny bottles were also made, some blown into elaborately carved moulds, some free blown in graceful or fanciful shapes.

Since the ancient glassmaker could not achieve high melting temperatures the glass was, unavoidably, high in alkali content and thus of poor quality. Most examples found today show signs of atmospheric attack in the form of an iridescent film, scaling and layering. The extent of this corrosion helps the scientists determine their age.

The invention of the blow-pipe enabled the glassmaker to gather a blob of glass at the end of a pipe and blow a bubble which he could then shape by means of very primitive tools into a bottle. The process used today is based on this principle. The first shape was, and is, known as the blank or parison. The parison is much smaller than the final shape, but of much thicker glass. The parison was re-heated and the bottle was finally blown from it. (Bottlemakers later used moulds made either from iron or wood which were kept from burning by frequent dipping in water.)

The neck of the bottle, intended to receive the stopper or some other form of closure, was made last. The finally shaped bottle was cut off from the blowing pipe and the neck was finished off. The top of the bottle neck was thus known as the finish. Today, in the modern bottlemaking process, the top of the neck is made first but this has not prevented the bottlemakers from retaining the word 'finish' to describe this part of the bottle.

Nineteenth-century Developments

Towards the end of the nineteenth century, innumerable patents were produced all trying to imitate this process by mechanical means; eventually out of all these ideas semi-automatic bottle production was born. This was made possible once the inventors had realized that automation could only be achieved if the mouth-blown process was reversed – that is, the finish was made first. Thus the following process was developed: the blow-pipe was abandoned and the glass was gathered at the end of an iron rod. The gatherer then allowed the glass to flow into a parison mould, at the bottom of which was the 'finish' or 'ring' mould with a little metal plunger sealing the opening through which the air would be blown. When enough glass had been allowed to flow in, the stream was cut off by a pair of hand shears. A baffle plate was placed over the top of the parison mould and compressed air was blown upwards. A bubble started and the glass was blown up against the baffle plate and mould walls. The glass parison was thus completed. It already had

Bottles are often compared and contrasted in terms of use rather than date.

Above
Three sealed wine bottles. England; the centre one dates from 1771, the two others are early 18th century; ht of centre bottle 10¾in (27.3cm).

Left
Decanter of clear glass, engraved on the wheel. Inscribed 'Success to the Waterford Volunteers'. Rib-moulded base, three annulated rings at the flared neck, and a plain stopper. Ireland; 1782; ht 10¼in (26cm).
These early decanters were simple and beautifully balanced. There was no real difference in style between English and Irish glass at this period.

Left
Decanter, cut with reeded corners and wheel-engraved picture. Marked 'The Bushmill Old Distillery, County Antrim, Ireland'; c 1790; ht 11¼in (28.5cm).

Right
Pictorial flask, mould blown with sailing ship. Midwestern glasshouse, America; 1815–17; ht 7⅛in (18.1cm).
Two 'promotion' bottles: the rare Irish example, and the American flask mass-produced for a commercial and inexpensive market. Original pictorial flasks were pleasantly shaped and decorated – later the quality of both glass and design degenerated. Today there are many outright fakes and copies.

Left
Assortment of silvered glass
tableware, some with bands of
painted roses. America; late
19th century; ht of tall vase
8⅜in (21.2cm).

Below left
'Brilliant' cut glass. America;
late 19th century; ht of ewer
12¾in (32.4cm).

In spite of their technical
excellence, the elaborate sets
of tableware on the left are
less popular with collectors
than the simple, commercially
made flask on page 251.

the completed finish on it, but it was then in a neck-down
position. It had to be inverted, suspended by the finish in
the final mould and blown, again by compressed air, into the
final bottle shape. Thus mouth-blowing was eliminated,
craftsmanship in shaping the parison was dispensed with,
shaping of the finish was no longer needed, and production
speed was increased. Some of these machines could make as
many as 200 small bottles in an hour. This could be compared with present production speed, well in excess of 300
bottles per minute. This process was and still is known as the
'blow and blow' process.

Around the same time another process, known as the
'press and blow' process, was invented. The gather was once
again put into a mould, but this time the parison was
pressed out within the mould by means of a large plunger.
The parison was then transferred to the final mould where
it was blown into the required shape. There was, however,
one link missing – the glass had to be fed into the mould by
hand and until this problem could be overcome, no full
automation was possible.

Automation

Many attempts were made at imitating the operation of
the gatherer. At last came the development which completely changed bottlemaking. It was, of course, the automatic glass-feeding device known as the feeder. Essentially,
it is a simple system which consists of a long trough, made of
refractory (heat-resistant) materials, connected to the front
end of a glass-melting tank furnace. This trough, known as
the forehearth, is there to prepare the glass by ensuring its
uniformity of temperature and viscosity, before it enters the
actual feeding mechanism. The importance of correct
conditioning of the glass at this stage cannot be over-
stressed, as on it depends the success of the bottlemaking
operation. The glass then enters the feeding mechanism,
which consists of a round basin at the bottom of which is a
hole called the orifice ring. A large-diameter, refractory,
rotating tube, capable of being raised or lowered, is suspended vertically just above the orifice ring. This tube,
known as the sleeve, controls the rate of flow – the nearer it
is to the orifice ring, the smaller is the amount of glass
able to flow through. Inside the sleeve is a reciprocating
refractory plunger. A stream of glass is allowed to flow down
through the orifice ring, and as the plunger moves down,
it forces extra glass through the orifice, so thickening the
stream. We can thus imagine a stream of glass with regular
thickenings flowing out of the orifice ring. Underneath the
orifice ring there is a pair of automatic shears which split
this stream into 'gobs' of glass, each gob being a bottle in the
making. The gobs are then dropped into the parison moulds
waiting below the feeder, and the process as described
previously is done automatically. Dropping two gobs at one
time into two waiting parison moulds is today the normal
practice. So-called triple-gobbing is currently becoming
more and more common and even quadruple-gobbing is
being practised.

Several bottlemaking machines are in existence, but by
far the most important one, which has almost replaced all
others, is the IS machine. It is not certain whether the IS

Right
Carbonated beverages were
always difficult to bottle.
Each of these patented bottles
had a glass marble or stopper
which rolled away from the
opening when the bottle was
tilted, and back over the
opening when it was held
upright.

stands for the initials of the inventors, Ingle and Smith, or for Independent Sections machine, which, in fact, it is. This machine can be operated on the 'blow and blow' or 'press and blow' process. It can consist of anything between a single section and ten sections, each section being a machine in its own right, synchronized with a feeder mechanism, other sections and any process taking place after the bottles leave the machine.

It can operate single, double, triple or even quadruple gobs. The higher the number of moulds filled at one time, the higher the production speed and the more complex becomes the synchronization problem. Any section can be stopped independently of all others, moulds can be changed on it or adjustments made while the other sections continue in normal production. Almost any size of bottle, from very small cosmetic to large five-litre bottles can be produced; its versatility is almost limitless.

Narrow-neck bottles are normally made by the 'blow and blow' process while the 'press and blow' process is generally reserved for the production of wide-mouth jars, although the faster 'press and blow' process is used more and more for narrow-neck bottles. The gob or gather has to be of a precise predetermined weight and shape and of uniform temperature. The outside shape of the bottle follows the shape of the mould cavity, but the weight of glass controls the bottle's volume, so that the more glass there is in a bottle of a given shape and outside dimensions, the smaller is its capacity. There are various ways of controlling the shape and weight of the gather, but the most important one is the sleeve's ability to be raised or lowered. By raising it, more glass is allowed to flow through the orifice ring; lowering has the opposite effect. The position of the shears, diameter of the orifice, glass temperature and speed and length of the stroke of the plunger are also factors which can control the weight and shape of the gather.

Why is it necessary to have the gather at a uniform temperature? We already know that the higher the temperature of the glass, the lower is its viscosity and the easier it is to blow. It is then obvious that the hot parts of the gob will be blown out first, leading to thin spots in the bottle. Bottle strength depends on the glass distribution and modern methods of accurate temperature control of the gob have enabled glassmakers to produce lighter and cheaper bottles.

Left
A variety of smaller commercial bottles. Europe; 19th century; ht 3in–6in (7.6cm–15.2cm). Bottle glass was almost always dark not only because it was cheaper, but in order to protect the contents from light. Pharmaceutical bottles often had measurements of some kind moulded into the shape to avoid accidents if the label was lost (*far left column, second and fourth pictures*). Cosmetic bottles (*far left, top*) were sometimes very elegant, and suitable for re-use.

Another method of gathering glass uses a vacuum for sucking the glass into the parison mould. The mould is dipped into glass which rushes into the mould to fill the vacuum. There is, however, the problem that every time the parison moulds dip into the glass they make it too cold and stiff to be 'vacuumed' in by the next set of moulds. This is overcome by having a large rotating pot which ensures that hot glass is always available while the chilled glass is taken away for re-heating. The advantage of this method is that the parison is always of the right weight and therefore more accurate capacity control is possible. This method is now seldom used for bottle production, but is still used for tumblers, wine glasses and other domestic blown glassware.

cooled at any speed without permanent strain being left, but the rate of cooling is limited by the temporary stresses developed during cooling, which could cause the article to break.

The annealing is done in a tunnel, approximately 30 metres long, in which the temperature is closely controlled, called the lehr. The articles are carried down the lehr on a steel mesh continuous belt. Annealing can take anything between forty-five minutes to several hours, depending on the types of ware being annealed. After being annealed, all bottles undergo a stringent, mainly automatic inspection before they are packed or put on pallets and despatched.

Over the last decade tremendous progress has been made

Left and above
Modern commercial bottles.
Milk bottle (ht 8⅛in, 20.6cm), preserving jar, mould-patterned coffee jar and canister.
England; c 1970s.
Dark glass is generally considered unacceptable today – modern bottles are intended to show off the contents in shops rather than protect them at home. It is understandable from a commercial viewpoint, but not so satisfactory for long storage. In spite of mass-production, variations do occur – the base of the jar is pleasantly irregular.

All glass has to be annealed. If a glass article, irrespective of the way in which it was produced, is allowed to cool down freely, internal stresses are developed, which inevitably lead to its spontaneous breakage. The surface of an article sets very quickly, while the inside is still in a state of lower viscosity. The inner layer contracts during cooling, exerting a force on the already set layers. The result is non-uniform areas of tension and compression in various parts of the article. This is prevented by a process known as annealing. In this the glass is brought to a temperature just sufficient for flow to take place. It is held at this temperature (normally around 600°C) until the whole article has reached it throughout. It is then cooled slowly to a temperature at which no further flow can take place. After this the article can be

in the field of lightweight glass containers. The term 'lightweight container' is often taken to mean that it is made of some mysterious lighter glass. In fact, the same glass is used for lightweight and standard weight bottles, but as a result of much research, and improvements in production methods, a more uniform glass thickness throughout can now be maintained and bottle designs are made with lightness in mind. Thus bottles of half the weight of their predecessors are produced without any loss of strength. A recent development of coating containers with tin chloride before annealing, and organic compounds after annealing, has given the surface a lubricity which protects the containers from scratching and bruising. Glass is an extremely strong material, but it breaks mainly because of damage to its surface.

The Chemistry of Colour

The ancient glassmaker knew that by adding certain substances to glass's raw materials, coloured glass could be produced. It is certain that he knew *what* happened, but not *why*; he was therefore unable to control the colour with the same accuracy as his modern counterpart. Today, we know the theoretical principles governing the development of colours and can achieve quite remarkable results. Control of colour comes with knowledge of the factors which govern the addition of certain materials to the batch.

Two basic factors affect the colouring power of certain substances and these are the nature of the atoms and the action of chemical and electrical forces. In glass colourants only inorganic substances are dealt with, thus the nature of the atom is the more important factor. The various materials which can give colour can themselves be colourless or intensely coloured, depending on their state of valency (how many links are available for combining with other atoms), and thus a clear demarcation line between colouring and colourless substances cannot be drawn. It is, however, well known by glass technologists that certain compounds which contain an element with more than one valency give a more intensive colour when this element is in its lower state of valency, while other elements can give the opposite result. This knowledge is used in decolourizing glass which must inevitably, contain a small percentage of iron impurity. In its low state of oxidation iron, in the form of ferrous iron, gives an objectionable bluish-green tint to the glass, whereas in its higher state of oxidation as ferric iron, it gives a less objectionable yellowish-green tint which is capable of being masked by the addition of the complementary colours, blue and red. To ensure that most of the iron impurity is in its ferric state, oxidizing agents like sodium nitrate are added to the batch in small amounts. The oxidation of iron is known as chemical decolourizing while the masking of the green by blue and red is called physical decolourizing, and is achieved by the addition of cobalt and selenium.

Above
Vase of purples and reds in extremely light soda glass. Israel; *c* 1978; ht 12in (30.4cm). The surface of modern soda glass is matt and slightly rough, so the colouring becomes the most important and immediately attractive eye-catcher.

Left
Bowl of blown glass in an iridescent feather pattern. Lötz, Austria; *c* 1900; ht 10¾in (27.3cm).
Looped patterns have always been extremely popular. Combed and marvered, trailed or inlaid, or worked into the molten glass itself as here, they have appeared in all kinds of glassware from ancient Egyptian bottles to modern studio pieces.

Above
Bowl of blown glass in a striped iridescent pattern. Tiffany (marked LCT), America; *c* 1900; ht 4½in (11.4cm).
At the turn of the century, glassmakers experimented with iridescence and shaded colours. Tiffany was the pace-setter.

Iron

In addition to being an undesirable impurity, iron is a very useful and powerful colouring agent. In its highest state of oxidation in the form of hexavalent ferrates it could, in combination with barium, give bluish-red glasses, but these would have to be melted under high oxygen pressures and cannot be produced in practice. This fact illustrates the wide colour range obtainable with iron. In its metallic form iron cannot remain in equilibrium with glass and can be disregarded, but its divalent (ferrous) and trivalent (ferric) forms are of practical interest.

In its reduced condition iron, in combination with chromium, is used for the manufacture of green bottle glass of the shade found in wine bottles, but in combination with sulphur, iron sulphides are formed giving a dark amber colour. Sulphur and iron by themselves would not give the required amber colour, and a reducing agent in the form of carbon powder is added to the batch. The shade of amber can be controlled within narrow limits by varying the amounts of coal added in relation to the already existing iron impurity and carbonaceous matter in the raw materials.

Manganese

Manganese compounds are some of the oldest used for the colouring of glass. Purple Egyptian glass discovered at Tel-el-Amarna, produced around 1400 BC, was found to contain this element. In its low state of oxidation manganese is colourless, but at the same time it is a strong oxidizing agent and has sometimes been used for decolourizing purposes to oxidize the iron. It gives a reddish tint in its higher state of oxidation. In modern glassmaking manganese has been replaced by sodium nitrate and selenium in decolourizing.

Its main colouring function is to produce purple glasses similar in colour to that of a solution of potassium permanganate crystals. The purple colour is caused by the trivalent manganese, but in its divalent state, which cannot be completely eliminated, it imparts only weak yellow or brown colours which are responsible for the green or orange fluorescence of manganese glasses.

Chromium

One of the most powerful colouring materials is chromium. Its use in dark green glass production only dates to the beginning of the nineteenth century as the element itself was not discovered until 1795. Before it was available, iron oxide was used for producing this glass. The material can be introduced into glass either in the form of chromic oxide or potassium dichromate, the latter being a more convenient form. The material is such a powerful colouring agent that in large amounts it produces black glass.

Chromium is not easily soluble in glass and chromic oxide may form chromates which remain in the glass as undissolved black specks. The inadvertent introduction of chromium ore into a tank furnace can cause very serious problems with black specks. In the glassmaking area of St Helens in Lancashire, a warning system is in operation, which ensures that if any of the several glass manufacturers finds chromium black specks in his glass, the whole area is alerted and a joint investigation is instituted to discover their origin. On one occasion, it was found that some railway wagons delivering limestone to the glassworks had previously been used for chromium ore transportation, and minute quantities of the ore, which were not swept out, had found their way into the glassworks and ruined several days of production.

Potassium chromate is yellow and this colour can be imparted to certain glasses. To produce emerald green glass in which a yellowish cast has to be avoided, the addition of arsenic or tin oxide is necessary.

All chromium glass, irrespective of the state of oxidation of the chromium, has a high transmission in the red part of the spectrum and the material should therefore never be used as a major colourant for a green signal glass as the two colours will cancel each other out. The main colourant for these glasses should be copper with small additions of chromium as a colour modifier.

The manufacture of chromium aventurine, now rarely produced, is of historical interest. The aventurine effect is caused by the formation of fairly large plates of chromic oxide which crystallize out from the melt. During blowing these crystals orient themselves nearly parallel to the glass surface and their reflections give a glittering effect. Best results are achieved in heavy lead glasses.

It can be seen that, although chromium is associated mainly with green glass, colours from yellow through bluish-red, red to dark green or even black can be achieved in combination with other oxides. If mixed crystals of chromium oxide and aluminium oxide are produced and the furnace atmosphere is controlled so that either oxidizing or reducing occurs, the following results can be obtained: with a crystal mixture of 5 per cent chromic oxide and 95 per cent aluminium oxide, under oxidizing conditions the colour would be red, and under reducing conditions, bluish-red; with a crystal mixture of 30 per cent chromic oxide and 70 per cent aluminium oxide, under oxidizing conditions the colour would be bluish-red, and under reducing conditions, green. In a crystal mixture of over 50 per cent of chromic oxide, the colour would be green irrespective of oxidizing or reducing conditions.

Copper

Another powerful and versatile colouring agent is copper, whose use in colouring glass and glazes goes back to ancient times. The famous Egyptian blue, which was popular in the Roman Empire, derived its colour from a copper compound. The Egyptians managed to produce blue colours by the use of copper and iron. Copper-coloured glasses were found at Tel-el-Amarna.

Copper greens and blues are not difficult to produce, although the behaviour of copper in a silicate melt is rather complicated. As mentioned before, copper is used extensively in producing green signal lens glasses.

The art of using copper for ruby glasses reaches far back into ancient times, but their successful manufacture depends on so many factors that they are the most difficult of all coloured glasses to make. They are produced by the colloidal dispersion of metallic copper.

In contrast, copper staining of glass is a relatively new process developed by Friedrich Egermann of Haida, Bohemia, c 1832. The technique of red etching requires two or sometimes three firings. It is a process in which the copper ions migrate into the surface of the glass. Only glasses of certain compositions can be treated in this way, and potash-containing glass is most suitable for this purpose.

Cobalt

The most powerful blue colourant is cobalt which gives rich blues, particularly in potash-containing glasses, but can give shades of pink in a boro-silicate glass and green with iodides.

We have no definite knowledge as to where and when cobalt was first used as a colourant, but references to the use of cobalt in church stained glass windows in the twelfth century have been found. One scientist reported that a piece of glass discovered in Tutankhamen's tomb was found to be coloured by this material. Before cobalt was used for colouring glass, it was known for producing blue colours on pottery glazes. Ming Dynasty (1368–1644) Chinese porcelain and the earlier Tang Dynasty (616–906) vases were decorated with cobalt blue.

In general, the addition of cobalt will produce a blue colour and its intensity depends on the base glass. The deepest blues are obtained with potash-containing glasses and careful adjustments to the base glass can produce other colours. Only very small quantities are used for physical

decolourizing. The quantity is so small that it must be introduced into the batch mixed with sand, as the minute amount of cobalt, if introduced by itself, would have no chance of being uniformly distributed throughout the batch. The sand thus acts as a pre-mixed dilutant. In fact all physical decolourizing agents are used in such small quantities that it is normal to pre-mix them with sand to enable better handling and better dispersion throughout the batch.

Nickel

Although sometimes used for the production of smoky-coloured glasses and in conjunction with cobalt for de-colourizing lead crystal, nickel is not an important colouring agent. When introduced into lead crystal it gives a purplish colour which compensates for a yellowish tint produced by other constituents. Depending on its state of oxidation, it can also produce yellowish tints.

Uranium

Uranium gives rise to a prominent yellow colour and is used for the production of the so-called 'Anna' yellow in some Bohemian glasses. In a very high lead-containing glass (with 71 per cent lead oxide), it gives a deep red colour. In view of the unusual composition of the required base glass, it cannot be used as a colouring agent for commercial red glass.

Non-metallic Elements

Of the non-metallic elements – sulphur, selenium, tellurium and phosphorus – the first two are the most important colouring agents.

Sulphur has already been mentioned as a colourant in combination with iron and carbon for the large-scale manufacture of amber glass, the colour of which can vary from very light straw to deep reddish-brown or even black. Under the strongly reducing conditions created by the carbon, iron polysulphides are formed and these give the required depth of colour. For a given quantity of sulphur and iron, the formation of polysulphides depends on the amount of carbon present. In boro-silicate glasses containing a high proportion of boric oxide, sulphur can produce a pure blue colour and, in combination with calcium in almost any glass, it gives deep yellows.

Cadmium sulphides, which have a deep yellow colour, are often used for the production of enamels and glazes. Since cadmium is a strongly toxic metal, national legislation to limit its migration from domestic utensils and glassware into food already exist. For EEC legislation in preparation, the final limit of migration is likely to be no more than two parts per million of lead and no more than two parts per ten million of cadmium, when tested under strictly controlled conditions, that is 2mg per litre of test solution of lead and 0.2mg per litre of test solution of cadmium.

In some sulphide glasses the colour does not develop immediately and has to be 'struck' by raising the already melted and cooled glass to a temperature at which the colour suddenly appears. 'Striking' is a well-known phenomenon used for making gold ruby glasses.

Selenium is one of the most important colouring agents for making pink and red glasses. Being a non-metallic element, selenites, selenates and selenides of metallic elements are formed, but most of these are colourless and it is

Above
Two vases, the left mounted in bronze. Lötz, Austria; *c* 1910; ht of left-hand vase 14½in (36.8cm).

the free selenium atoms which give the pink colour so important for decolourizing. On the other hand, it is the selenide which produces deep red colours.

If increasing amounts of selenium are added to a cadmium sulphide glass, its pure yellow colour changes to orange and finally to a brilliant red known as selenium ruby. Depending on the composition of the base glass and furnace atmosphere, ruby glasses can develop their colour on melting or the colour has to be 'struck' by re-heating the cooled glass.

Metal Atoms

Colours produced by metal atoms are caused by the dispersion of metals in the glass. The three most important metals used for this purpose are gold, silver and copper.

The invention of gold ruby glass dates back to 1685 when Andreas Cassius published his work, *De Auro*, in which he described for the first time the method of producing a red precipitate of stannic acid with gold, which later became known as the 'Purple of Cassius'. The high price which this glass commanded and the efforts needed to produce it could hardly be justified by its beauty. It was the mysticism connected with gold which was responsible for the demand.

The preparation of red ruby glasses is still based on Cassius's discovery and is achieved by the precipitation of metallic gold by a mixture of stannous and stannic acid. The tin has to be present in the two chloride forms because the stannous chloride has to act as a reducing agent to bring about the formation of the metallic gold. Depending on the composition of the base glass, the ruby colour can develop during cooling, or the glass may have to be re-heated to 'strike' the colour. The production of gold ruby is complicated and expensive, and is used only when special properties are needed.

Silver Staining of Glass

The silver-yellow obtained by surface staining involves a new principle different from those described for producing coloured glasses. The phenomenon of staining is based on a property of silver ions whereby they are able to replace some of the alkali ions of the glass at a temperature below the softening point. The silver ions can diffuse into the glass to be reduced to elementary silver when reacting with other ions like iron or arsenic.

Opal Glass

Glass is a non-crystalline, super-cooled liquid, and crystallization or devitrification causes it to lose its transparency. It should therefore be possible to induce a controlled amount of crystallization to make it opaque or opal. By slow cooling glass from its low viscosity state, or not super-cooling it, crystallization would take place without the help of opalizing agents. However, if fluorides are added they form nuclei for crystal formation even with a normal cooling cycle. Varying amounts of sodium or potassium fluoride are added to the batch for varying degrees of opacity.

To produce closely controlled colours is a complicated technology and one cannot help but admire the ancient glassmaker who was able to produce the most wonderful colours without today's scientific knowledge.

Left and above
Two goblets of clear glass, both Swedish; *left, façon de Venise* 'crown' goblet of soda glass, *c* 1675, ht 18½in (46cm); *above*, potash glass goblet with cover, *c* 1650, ht 11in (27.9cm). Both goblets show how much colour there can be in clear glass.

Below left
Opal glass ewer, painted in grisaille. Wordsley Glassworks, W. H., B. & J. Richardson. England; *c* 1850; ht 9in (22.9cm).

Below
Opal glass ware. Boston and Sandwich Glass Company; *c* 1870; ht of pitcher on right 7⅝in (19.3cm).
Opaque white glass is easily made but opal glass is much more unstable and therefore relatively rare. The surface should have the soft matt appearance of alabaster.

Right

Celery vase. Ireland; 1780s;
ht 11⅜in (28.8cm).

Left

Oil lamp with matching vases,
in transparent ruby glass
cased in opaque white.
Bohemia; *c* 1850–70; ht of
lamp 22½in (57.1cm).
Many of the most popular
Bohemian patterns were made
in ruby glass, overlaid in white,
and sometimes also gilded and
painted.
Occasionally there were two or
three layers on top of the base,
and the 'windows' cut through
to the bottom layer were
bevelled so that all the layers
showed around the edges.
Lamps were particularly well
suited to casing, since the
reflected light showed up the
elaborate cutting and the
contrast between the transparent base and opaque top.
The most popular cutting
shapes were porthole and leaf,
as these three pieces show, but
there were also clover and
quatrefoil patterns, curling
vine stems, and flower heads.
Casing was very fashionable
during the 19th century, but
had been used since early
Roman glassmaking; cameo
glass begins with a cased base,
the top layer being cut away
in subtle and complicated
designs. This type of glass was
revived in the late 19th century
with the success of Art
Nouveau; cased glass was used
to create unusual and subtle
shades based on thin and thick
layers of up to three or four
different colours.

Casing

Many cut glass vases, bowls or wine glasses are decorated
with several colours of glass. This effect is achieved by a
similar process to the one used to make the *millefiori* rods.
Several layers of glass of different colours are gathered and
marvered in between each gathering. The composite gather
is then blown into the required article and the finished piece
is decorated by grinding a pattern. The depth to which the
glass is ground away reveals the colour of glass hidden underneath the surface.

To produce, for example, an opal cut glass vase with red
decoration, the glassmaker first gathers red glass on the end
of his blow-pipe, blows a small bubble and marvers it. He
then moves to the opal glass pot and covers his original
gather with a layer of the opal glass. He marvers the composite gather and proceeds to blow the vase in a mould. The
annealed vase is then cut to show the red decoration by
grinding the opal glass to a depth where the red glass shows.

One of the problems in this process is to ensure that the
glasses used are of compatible coefficients of expansion. If
they are not, stresses will develop after annealing and these
will inevitably lead to cracks.

Cold Glass Decoration

Cutting and Engraving

There are only a few methods of decorating cold glass: cutting and engraving; and painting and gilding.

Cutting is apparently the oldest method. Alexandrian workshops were known through the Middle East for their fine workmanship, developed from their experience of hardstone and gem cutting. By the time of the Roman Empire, shallow wheel cutting was widely known, and series of shallow grooves and hollows were built up into simple but very attractive patterns.

A more delicate and complex method was based on sculpture. Tools similar to those used in cameo work were employed by glass sculptors to create pieces of exceptional artistry and beauty. The most famous examples are the Portland Vase and the Lycurgus Cup, both extraordinary creations by any standard. The Cup and others in a group of glasses known as *vasa diatreta* are also masterpieces of complex cutting. The glass was thickly blown in one layer, or more as in the Portland Vase, but instead of cutting away the background just enough to leave the design in relief, the geometric design of either lettering or latticework was cut almost completely away from the background, leaving only a few struts to hold the 'cage' to the base cup.

Types of Engraving

During the period after the Roman Empire, glass in Europe was decorated almost entirely by hot manipulation, while the Alexandrian workshops continued to produce fine cut glass work, with lapidary tools. Gradually, the development of Venetian *cristallo* provided a surface too fragile for any serious incisions, and such engraving as was practised was done using a diamond point to scratch designs on the surface.

Left
Modern miniatures from all over the world. Tubes and rods are blown into fantastic shapes to make very collectable souvenirs.

Page 262
Looped flasks. Nailsea Glassworks, England; late 18th–early 19th century; length of gimmel flask 7⅛in (18cm).
These flasks were originally very inexpensive, made as fairings for country market days, and as bright souvenirs. The transparent gimmel flask can stand; the other three must be laid down. The green flask, of a later date than the others, has been decorated with threading on a machine. This invention, in 1876, became so popular that by 1880 factories in England, Europe and America were all making threaded glassware in large quantities.

Page 263
Scent bottle from 'Claire de Lune' series, enamelled in black. France; 1882; ht 4¼in (10.7cm).

Below
Small wine glass with simple facet-cut stem. England; c 1760; ht 4¼in (10.7cm). Early cut patterns were shallow and fairly simple. This typical glass was cut on the stem only. Heavier glasses were cut on the base of the bowl and under the foot.

Left and below
Two simple examples of early 19th-century cutting. The celery vase shows the straight horizontal and vertical fluting that was to develop into flashy, brilliant, step-cut designs. Ht 9in (22.9cm).

Left
Detail from a ceremonial goblet for the Glassmakers' Guild. England; c 1810. Note the difference in technique between the fairly simple, flat engraved sprays just visible on either side, and the three-dimensional effect of the glass-house scene engraved in relief.

Below
Detail of early 19th-century cutting. Ireland; c 1810. The extra-wide turned-in rim of this little jug was cut in simple step-cut prisms, over a body of strawberry diamonds, each point cut into a tiny star.

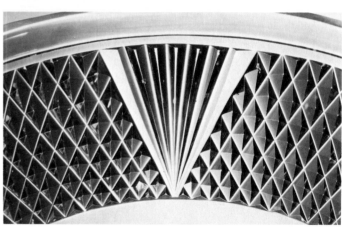

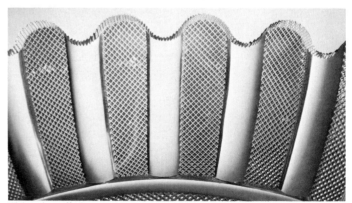

Centre and above
Details of more elaborate cutting in the mid-19th century. *Centre*, diamonds and fan; *above*, fluted panels of tiny diamonds. Diamonds tended to become smaller and more precise during the century, forming texture rather than pattern.

Although the best work is charming representational drawings were rather crude except for those of the Dutch engravers who later became the foremost artists in Europe, using the diamond point technique. They also developed stippling, a lighter version of diamond point in which the design is made up of hundreds of tiny dots, much as in the *pointilliste* paintings of nineteenth-century France. Both diamond point and stippling have continued as glass engraving techniques; a small number of modern glass artists have made world-wide reputations with their work.

Wheel engraving could only develop after the formula for potash glass replaced the fine soda glass perfected by the Venetians. In Bohemia during the sixteenth century, potash glass was heavy, and clear enough to be worked as if it was rock crystal. (Crystal and all other gemstones were in demand all over Europe, to be carved, worked, inlaid, engraved, or generally decorated in elaborate and precious mountings.) Many workmen recognized this quality in the new glass, and a number of engravers constantly experimented with different kinds of wheels and techniques. Caspar Lehman, who worked at Prague for Emperor Rudolf II, is generally credited with being the first to establish the re-birth of an old technique in a new guise with the use of lapidary wheels. Only one glass is known to be signed by Lehman, but he was appointed special artist to the emperor's court for his efforts. See page 99.

Cameo and intaglio techniques worked on clear glass were carefully derived from those of traditional rock crystal engraving, and their crisp detail and swirling asymmetrical scrolls show baroque Bohemian art at its finest. For the next 150 years, Bohemian wheel engraving remained a symbol of perfection for the engraver as sculptor.

Cutting Techniques

At the end of the seventeenth century, the new lead glass perfected by George Ravenscroft inspired another development in glass cutting techniques. Lead glass was particularly heavy, and its refracting properties were soon apparent. Glasscutters began to experiment with heavier wheels which made deeper sharper cuts in the glass, and allowed the light to sparkle as if seen through prisms. Until the tax on glass weight in 1745, there was no limit to the amount of glass used in any one object (and blanks were substantial enough to allow cutting all over the glass). After the Act, it became uneconomical to use so much material, and lighter shapes meant that deep cutting was restricted to stems and the bases of bowls, while shallow patterns were developed to decorate the lighter parts. Free trade was granted to Ireland from *c* 1780 to 1825, labour was considerably cheaper, and many factories continued to use the heavier blanks.

After the repeal of the Act in 1845, cut glass was again made with deep facets in glittering patterns, often with coloured accents.

By the middle of the nineteenth century, Bohemian coloured glass had become increasingly popular, often cased with two or three layers over clear glass, and cutting became more like the original cameo work – based on showing off relief patterns rather than reflecting light and glitter. Finally, at the turn of the century, the linear patterns and colours of Art Glass and Art Nouveau demolished the cut crystal industry entirely. Today modern designers have begun to appreciate the qualities of cut and engraved glass, and the new patterns that are evolving may borrow techniques from almost every period of glassmaking.

Above
Engraved glasses with typical 18th-century designs. *c* 1730–1800; ht of glass on right 5¾in (14.6cm).
Most wheel engraving of the finest quality was done during this period by Dutch or Bohemian craftsmen. Flower sprays or simple vine borders were made in many workshops in England and America, but elaborate scenes and complicated armorial patterns were generally attributed to Continental engravers.

Below
Three examples of later 19th-century cutting.
Left, a cased vase, its ruby top layer cut through to the clear base. Royal Brierley factory, England; *c* 1870; ht 12¾in (32.4cm).
Centre, a cameo vase with the top layer carved away to form a three-dimensional cameo effect.
Right, a goblet with elaborate bowl, cut and engraved in panels, on a comparatively simple stem.

Mass-production Techniques

Acid etching or engraving was an attempt to provide cameo and relief patterns at economical prices. The principle of etching had been known for centuries, but it became generally used only in the nineteenth century. A more recent development is sand blasting, an American process which can be commercially used, much as acid etching. The design is coated with a protective layer and the exposed surfaces are blasted with a high-pressure sand gun, which abrades them quickly and smoothly, leaving a matt, dull finish that contrasts with the smooth gleam of the covered part.

Modern Cutting Processes

The process of cutting glass in what are known as traditional patterns is still based on older engraving techniques, but

Left
Detail of candelabra; the bent wire hooks for the cut drops show at the top. England or Ireland; c 1790–1810.
Relies more on the fashionable neoclassic urn shape than on elaborate detail.

Above
Engraved designs from 18th and early 19th-century pieces. Most were floral or leafy derivations, sometimes surrounding a special vignette or a set of initials. Symbols were also popular, ranging from a Jacobean portrait to masonic insignia, or a simple spray of hops and barley for an ale glass or tankard.

Above
Goblet. American cutting factory in the Midwest area. c 1815–40. When American cut glass became popular it first followed the Anglo-Irish tradition of heavy glass and all-over patterns. James Robinson in Pennsylvania and George Dummer & George Dummer Lyman in Jersey City were only two known glassmakers who turned out cut glass in pleasant variety. A very typical border pattern was based on a shallow roundel with a rayed fan motif, and was found on decanters, glasses, celery vases, etc. Unfortunately few documented pieces are available, and too many patterns were copied from abroad to attribute individual pieces with certainty.

the practice is different. Today's wheels are much larger and rougher than those used in previous centuries. The process begins with marking out the design. The designer has drawn a pattern, combining the basic motifs – square-ended, hollowed and V-shaped – in a way which suits the style of the blank, the designer's concept and the cutter's skill.

The quality of the glass must also be considered. If the factory making the blank shape is known to produce top quality lead glass with few imperfections, the designer can give his imagination free reign. If it is slightly imperfect material, the design may have to be adjusted. For a new pattern, the designer will probably work with the cutter doing the prototype. When they have both approved the blank (often made by a different factory), and made any alterations they think necessary, the actual cutting can begin.

First, the design is marked on the blank, usually in a mixture of red lead and turpentine, although felt-tip markers are sometimes used. Then the wheel is chosen – the cutter has a choice of three, each with a different edge. The flat-edged wheel will make a square-ended cut. The convex-edged wheel will make a hollowed cut, and the mitre-edged wheel will make a sharp V-shape on the glass. Traditionally, these first roughing-out wheels were made of stone. Some today are made of steel, or carborundum, or copper.

A hopper suspended above the wheel contains sand and water mixed to a fine paste. This drops on to the surface as the wheel turns, providing the abrasive to cut into the glass blank. The wheel revolves by a foot pedal, now electrified; the cutter holds the blank against the underside of the wheel. This first rough cutting is done very quickly. A finer wheel is used to finish off the rough cutting and make the edges smooth and sharp. The fine wheels have three versions side by side, that correspond with the rough wheels. No sand is used during the second part of this operation; pure water provides the only lubricant. The finishing wheels come in varying sizes from a few inches to a few feet, and it is during their use that the real skill of the cutter is employed. Finally, the glass is polished, either by hand or chemically.

Hand polishing requires the cutter to switch to yet another set of wheels. These are wooden, and are used with a very fine abrasive such as jeweller's rouge. A final polish is given with felt wheels and more rouge. When the finishing is done chemically, the process is the same as that used in acid etching; the entire piece is dipped into a mixture of hydro-fluoric and sulphuric acid, which eats away the top, abraded layer and leaves a brilliant shiny finish over the entire piece. This method is always used for particularly fine and fragile pieces, but the old wheel polish is still occasionally found useful when the designer wants some variation in the groove, to add depth and shadows to the finished work.

When the prototype is finished, the designer and cutter examine the piece again, and discuss any difficulties. They may spend a good deal of time on a detail which can be altered. Once accepted the pattern goes into production.

Although wheel-cutting shops are noisy and dirty, they do not require the conditions of a glasshouse. For that reason, many glass-decorating shops with cutting rooms have no factory, and buy their blanks from suppliers.

Enamelling

Enamels, which are really very low melting-point glasses, were known even long before glass was ever produced; stones were glazed with enamel and used as pieces of jewellery. Vases and bottles were decorated with strands of coloured glasses which were probably what we would consider glazes or enamels. This is not really surprising since the craftsman, whose most serious problem was to create a high temperature, used materials which would fuse easily.

Then, as glass came to be used on its own, enamel colours were restricted to linear decoration, painted on after the glass was made, then re-fired carefully for as short a time as possible – just enough to fuse the enamel onto the surface, not enough to distort the glass.

The muffle kiln, traditionally used for enamelling glass, encloses the objects and heats gradually to the firing point. A more modern kiln is the continuous firing triple kiln; the three sections are kept at different temperatures, the lowest for pre-heating, the central for firing and the top for cooling and annealing. The glass is moved manually from one chamber to another. This method is generally quicker but more dangerous – the firing chamber must be watched carefully, since the firing may take only a few minutes.

Historically, glass enamellers have been decorators rather than glassmen, working outside the furnace area. Enamellers decorated pottery or glass almost interchangeably. In England there were a number of professional enamellers including the Beilby family, Michael Edkins and James Giles. In Staffordshire, painting on opaque white glass was also popular during the 1770s.

In German-speaking countries and the Low Countries highly skilled artists were popular. Johann Schaper (1621–70) specialised in *Schwarzlot* and a restrained colour range. Samuel Mohn (1762–1815) and his son Gottlob Samuel Mohn (1769–1825) ran a factory at Dresden.

Schaper had invented some transparent enamels in *c* 1650,

Above
Bride's Bottle. America; 18th century; ht 4½in (11.4cm). Early, fairly crude enamelling. These Bohemian-style bottles were made throughout central Europe, and in the Midwestern glasshouses of America for the Pennsylvania Dutch market.

Above
Zwischengoldglas beaker with scene of Lunardi's ascent in a balloon. Russia; early 19th century; ht 5¾in (14.6cm). A totally different technique – delicate fine enamelling, suitable for the aristocratic table.

and the Mohns revived the use of this medium in *c* 1810. As most early enamels had been opaque, their introduction greatly extended the scope of painted decoration.

Other countries employed various enamelling techniques, depending on the changing fashions, glass shapes and their suitability for painted ornament.

Modern concern with clear and self-coloured glass, cutting and engraving, has almost completely ousted surface decoration. In addition, hand-painted enamelling is affected by constant machine washing, and most modern enamelling is restricted to commercially made wares.

Commercial Enamelling

Enamel labels are applied to bottles and domestic glassware is often decorated by a pattern produced by vitreous enamels. Most of the work is done by machinery.

We are familiar with multi-coloured labels on bottles. To produce these a finely ground vitreous enamel, suspended in a liquid medium and made into the consistency of thick paint, is squeezed on to the bottle through a silk or more often a very fine wire mesh screen. Each colour has to be applied separately, but the machines have a registering device which ensures that the colours are always applied in exactly the right position to give the desired pattern. The bottle generally has a registering 'pip' to help to position it in the machine. The bottle is pressed against the underside of the screen which rotates the bottle as it moves along. At the same time a squeegee moves along the top of the screen pushing the enamel through it. The suspension medium for the enamel is such that it has to be kept warm, but it solidifies on touching a cold bottle. It is thanks to this property that the need for drying is dispensed with and colours can be applied immediately after each other. The labels are fired on to the bottles in a special enamelling lehr.

The difference between an annealing and enamelling lehr is that the former has a hot zone at the point where the ware is fed into it and is used for gradual cooling, while the latter starts with a cold zone and the bottles are gradually heated to a temperature of around 550°c, at which the enamel fuses into the glass, and are then gradually cooled as in an annealing lehr. The result is a label which forms part of the glass.

The screens are produced by a photographic process. The silk or wire mesh is coated with a light-sensitized layer of gelatine which is exposed to ultraviolet light through a negative, in very much the same way as photographs are enlarged. The negative, however, has to have a positive picture on it as this process, unlike the photographic process, reproduces the same picture as on the negative. Where the light impinges on the gelatine coating it makes it insoluble in water while the unexposed portions remain soluble. After exposure, the screen is washed in warm water which removes the unexposed portions allowing the enamel to be squeezed through the uncovered sections of the screen. It is necessary to have a separate screen for each colour.

Tableware and casseroles are more often decorated by transfers which have the complete design printed on a paper backing which is removed from the article. These are applied and fired in the special enamelling lehr. A large range of colours is available to the decorator.

Gold Decoration and Gilding

There are a number of forms of gold decoration: the use of gold leaf, enclosed by two layers of clear glass; gold leaf or powder mixed with a fixative of some kind, painted on as an enamel and fired; and gold leaf applied to the surface with a semi-permanent fixative, without subsequent firing.

The first method is obviously permanent as long as the glass layers remain intact. Roman and Egyptian flasks were decorated with gold leaf layered bands and cut-out decorations within double bowls; mosaic tiles were often made of such layered pieces; and the same technique was used by Bohemian craftsmen in their *Zwischengoldglas* pieces.

Most gilding is done by the second method, the gold being mixed with any number of fixatives, including honey, white of egg, mercury, etc. The thick liquid is painted or brushed on, and the decorated glass is fired again in a low temperature kiln. It may be combined with other enamel colours, or used alone. The gold is dull when it comes from the kiln but can be highly burnished, and with some care is very longlasting.

Cold gilding is a more impermanent method, which requires the gold leaf to be laid over some sort of oil or gum on the glass and simply dried. It is very fragile, easily rubbed or washed off, and was generally used on cheaper objects. 'Fancy' Victorian cut glass ware was often gilded in this way and the pattern can be seen because of the fixative, even when the gold has rubbed off.

Above and right
Two 19th-century bottles, both enamelled and gilded. *Above*, English, 1847; *right*, American, ht 13in (33cm).

Tableware

Lead glass has a longer working range and is therefore more versatile than other glass. Although the composition of lead glass can vary widely there are three main types of lead glass: the highest quality with at least 30 per cent lead, which even today is made into articles entirely by hand; lower quality with about 24 per cent of lead; and the cheapest with about 10 per cent of lead. The latter two can be produced by hand or by machine.

Normally lead glass is melted in pots holding between 500 and 750kg of glass. The pots are of the closed type design, which means that the glass does not come into contact with combustion gases in the furnace. This is important since combustion gases often have reducing properties which could reduce the lead component into black, metallic lead. However, in recent years, for large volume production, tank furnaces are also being used and the chemical reduction is prevented by ensuring that only oxidizing flames come into contact with the glass, or by using electricity for melting. The glassmakers producing stemmed wine glasses work in a team of four. The first man is the blower and it is his job to produce the bowl. He pre-heats the end of a long blowing iron, dips it into the surface of the molten glass and by rotating it in the glass gathers just enough to produce the bowl. To accomplish this, simply by judgement, requires a very high degree of training and skill. He then blows a bubble and afterwards shapes the glass by rolling it, still held at the end of the blowing iron, on a metal plate called a marver. This process is equivalent to that of making a parison for bottle blowing but it is done by hand without the help of a mould. Two halves of a blow mould with a cavity in the shape of the final bowl are closed around the parison. The blower then blows his parison to its final shape, while

Above
Table service in clear glass. Designed by Philip Webb for William Morris, made by Powell & Sons, Whitefriars, London; c 1860; ht of tall glass 5in (12.7cm).

Below
An international group of blown table pieces. c 1940–70. The left-hand white wine glass is Czechoslovakian, and quite inexpensive. The right-hand red wine glass, by Baccarat, is a classic shape and extremely fragile; ht 6⅜in (16.2cm). Cutting during the Scandinavian Modern period was usually restricted to stems, and the bases of bowls.

continuously rotating the blowing iron.

If we examine an ordinary bottle we shall discover vertical seams on either side. These seams are where the two halves of a hinged mould came together. A two-piece hinged mould is also used for making a wine glass but no seams are to be found anywhere. How is this then achieved? The answer is very simple: the mould is kept wet with water and the heat of the mould produces steam which forms a cushion on which the glass is rotated during blowing.

The blowing iron, with the bowl still attached, is then passed to the head man of the team, called the servitor, whose job is to add the stem and foot to the bowl. The third man in the team, known as the bit gatherer, gathers a small amount of glass from the pot and takes it to the servitor, who with primitive tools and sophisticated skill shapes the stem. Having completed the stem, he receives another piece of molten glass from the bit gatherer and makes the foot.

The foot is flared out by rolling the iron pipe with the bowl, the stem and the glass for the foot at the end of it on the arm of a glassmaker's chair and shaping it with a flat piece of wet wood. The completed article is then broken off from the blowing iron and taken by the fourth man to the annealing lehr to be annealed and finished off afterwards. The articles can then be hand decorated by cutting or engraving. Jugs, fruit bowls and vases are also made by hand.

The same method is used for hand production irrespective of the type of glass used. It is a part of the glassmaker's skill to adjust his methods to accommodate the various properties of his glass. Lead glass has a long working range, which means that its viscosity remains more constant over a wider span of temperature than the viscosity of other glasses. He can therefore take longer over shaping an article made of lead glass than of, say, soda-lime-silica glass. Boro-silicate glass has a higher softening point than other glasses so a higher temperature is needed to work it. The glassmaker makes all these adjustments using his skill and experience with no instruments to guide him.

Making tableware by hand is not only a very skilful job, but also a time-consuming one. The vast quantity of glassware used in everyday life at home, in restaurants and bars could not possibly be made by the hand method described above, and today practically all the cheaper quality tableware is machine-made by a fully automatic process.

Automatic Machine Production

Whereas the method of fully automatic bottle production only partly imitates hand operation, modern engineers and technologists have, so far, been unable to invent a method which does not exactly follow the method used by the skilled glassmaker. Let us first examine how thin-walled tumblers are made and then look at the more complicated automatic production of stemmed wine glasses.

From the glass-melting tank furnace protrude the fore-hearths to condition the glass. Each forehearth supplies glass to a large, continuously rotating machine. Feeding of the glass to the machine is done by suction. This idea is similar to the vacuum method used for bottle production except that the glass is not sucked into a parison in which it is blown, but into a cavity which is in the shape of a gather to be placed on top of a spindle, which can be compared to a glassmaker's blowing iron. This operation is done by means of a ram (moveable arm) with two cavities connected to a vacuum line at its end. The ram moves to the forehearth and just dips into the glass. Glass is sucked into the cavities, lifted out and on its way back to the machine, a knife blade cuts

Below
Vase by Burtles, 1880s;
pressed glass swan by Selby,
Gateshead, 1879, ht 3¾in
(9.5cm).
Pressed glass novelties for the
table were made by dozens of
factories, who all copied
each other's patterns.

Right
Three Art Deco glasses –
coloured bowls in amber and
green, set on chrome stands.
America; 1930s; ht 6½in
(16.5cm).
Chrome was widely used
during the Art Deco period.
This vari-coloured set is more
delicately made than most
contemporary examples.

Left
'Bellflower' table glasses.
America; 1880s; ht of tumbler
3⅛in (7.9cm).
Many pressed patterns were
made over long periods of
time. 'Bellflower' has always
been extremely popular, and
copies made today are often
bought as genuine antiques.

Right
Modern pressed glass tableware.
Ht of 'Coca-Cola' glass 8¼in
(20.9cm).
Commercial glass today is
colourful and attractive. These
tumblers and beer glasses are
mass-produced for everyday
use, with a wide variety of
decoration. The 'wine label'
tumbler is a copy of a
homemade glass cut from the
base of a wine bottle – an
example of recycling
reproduced.

274

off a ribbon of glass trailing from it, leaving the required amount of glass in the cavities. The two lumps of molten glass are placed on top of the waiting spindles. There is no rotating pot as on a suction bottle machine and the problem of chilling the glass is overcome by a radial movement of the ram, which pushes the cold glass away from the point from which the next set of gathers will be collected. The machine then continues to imitate the glassmaker. The spindles rotate and a puff of air starts a bubble. The rotating spindles, with the glass at the top, slowly turn through a semi-circle from a vertical up position to vertical down and so enables the glass to become elongated to the correct parison shape. The parisons are then enclosed in the blow moulds. The blow moulds are kept wet and the spindles continue to rotate while the final blowing is done. The moulds then open, the article is released and the top is burnt off by very fierce small flames. The articles are pushed into an annealing lehr at the end of which they are inspected, packed and despatched.

The automatic production of stemmed ware also imitates the hand process. The bowl is made on one machine in exactly the same way as the tumbler described above while the stem, complete with foot, is pressed out on another machine. The bowl and the stemmed foot are then brought together and fused. The two machines are kept next to each other so that both the parts to be joined are quite hot when they are brought into contact, but they are not sufficiently hot to achieve the fusion without the help of oxygen-enriched gas flames.

A technique of producing stemmed glasses on one machine only is now widely used. In this the stem is formed as the moulds close around the parison. Some better quality machine-made tableware is decorated by automatic glass-cutting machines. This often resembles cut crystal although it lacks the brilliance of real lead crystal glass.

Plates, dishes, cups, thick tumblers – in fact any products which are of a shape which can be retrieved from a mould without the need for the moulds to be opened are normally pressed. Pressing can be done manually or automatically. In the hand process, the gatherer gathers the glass on the end of an iron rod from a pot or the forehearth of a glass tank furnace and runs it into a mould. When the press operator feels that enough glass has entered the mould, he cuts off the flow with a pair of shears, introduces a plunger in the shape of the article into the mould and applies very high pressure to it by means of a long lever. After the glass has set, the article is pushed out by a small plunger at the bottom of the mould and is taken away for annealing. Pressing is a one-stage operation carried out in a single mould which has to be cooled in order to prevent adhesion between the glass and the mould iron.

The mould and the plunger often have decorative patterns engraved in them, but this creates the problem that the pattern may prevent the finished article from being released from the mould, and composite moulds consisting of two or more sections become essential. Composite moulds lead to rather objectionable mould marks, but these can be hidden in the pattern or removed by fire polishing.

Machine pressing is, in principle, the same as manual pressing except that the gatherer is replaced by an automatic feeding device, as used for bottlemaking, and the single mould is replaced by a number of moulds carried on a large rotating table. The table does not rotate continuously, for each mould stops underneath the feeding mechanism to receive its charge of glass, and then moves on to the next stage where a hydraulically operated plunger presses the glass. After the glass has set, it is removed and taken away for annealing. Pressing is used in the manufacture of a wide range of items, including car headlamps, television tube screens, high-voltage electrical insulators and optical lenses.

Utility Glass

Optical Glass and Lenses

There are several hundreds of optical glasses of various compositions. Each of these has the composition adjusted to give it a particular property for a specific purpose. This could be colour, light absorption in a limited or wide range of the spectrum, refractive index, photochromic properties, or any combination of these.

The raw materials used for optical glass have to be exceptionally pure. Special high quality sand has to be used to avoid a green tint from iron impurity. This can be made from quartz rock low in iron content such as can be found at Loch Aline in Scotland. The rock, which has an iron content as low as 0.006 per cent, is crushed into sand and can be further purified by chemical method to a level of 0.001 per cent iron. Optical glass must also be of exceptional homogeneity and to achieve this the molten glass is stirred either by mechanical means or by strong currents of glass set up by hot spots inside the melt. This is done by passing an electric current through the molten glass.

In general terms optical glasses can be divided into two categories: flints and crowns. These can be subdivided into: extra dense flints with a high lead content and a high refractive index; dense flints with a high lead content and a high refractive index; light flints with a moderate lead content and refractive index; extra light flints with a low lead content and refractive index.

Crown glasses range from soda-potash glass with a low refractive index through crown flint with a little lead, light barium crown with some barium, dense barium crown which is high in barium content, extra dense barium crown with a very high barium content, lanthalum crown down to boro-silicate crown with a low refractive index.

The refractive index can vary from 1.75060 for extra dense flint through 1.6511 for extra dense barium flint and 1.54110 for light barium crown to 1.51700 for boro-silicate crown with a host of other refractive indices in between.

Until the 1950s optical glasses were melted in pots. Lens blanks were then made either by casting in moulds or pouring between rollers to produce a glass ribbon. In the 1950s ophthalmic colourless glass was produced in a tank furnace from which a ribbon of glass was formed. The ribbon, when cooled and annealed, was then cut into pieces which were re-heated and moulded into lens blanks.

More recently a new method has been developed which has enabled the ophthalmic pressings to be made directly from a stream of glass melted continuously in a tank furnace. This is now used by all the major optical lens glass manufacturers throughout the world.

Quality control has to be extremely rigorous. All bubbles which are generated during melting have to be eliminated by a refining process and the composition has to be constant to impart the desired optical properties. Homogeneity must be strictly observed as any striae (streaks of glass of different composition and thus different refractive index) would make it unacceptable for lens production.

Forming is done in a way similar to that used for pressing of domestic glassware. Gobs of molten glass are dropped into a mould and are automatically pressed. The moulds are made of cast iron or heat-resistant steel. The shape of the blank is defined by the contour of the mould and the concave and convex surfaces are made by the plungers used for pressing. Once they have been formed, the lenses are passed through an annealing lehr or are collected in large containers which are then placed in an annealing furnace with an accurately controlled heating and cooling cycle. The process is a continuous one, working twenty-four hours per day throughout the year, exactly the same as in bottle, tableware and flat glass manufacture.

As recently as 1964 the development of photochromic light-sensitive glass by Corning Glass in the United States opened a new vista for optical glass. This was followed by the introduction of a light-sensitive spectacle lens in 1968.

Photochromic materials are those which, on exposure to light, darken, but they differ from photographic materials because the process of darkening is a reversible one, that is they revert to their original colour when removed from the influence of light. This phenomenon is achieved by the introduction of silver halide microcrystals formed by precipitation and subsequent heat treatment at a temperature between the strain point temperature (at which flow is just beginning) and the softening temperature (at which glass can be moulded).

The glass can be made light sensitive to different portions of the spectrum and thus if it is required that it should darken in the range between 300 and 400nm wave-lengths, silver chloride is used in the batch. If the photosensitive range is required to be between 300 and 650nm, silver chloride in conjunction with silver iodide would be used. When photochromic glasses were first developed, their reaction to light exposure was rather slow, but recently improvements have been made which render these suitable for use instead of sun glasses with the advantage that they perform as normal lenses at low light intensity.

Two compositions of photochromic glasses are below:

SiO_2 (silica)	52.4%	51.0%
Na_2O (sodium oxide)	1.8%	1.7%
Al_2O_3 (alumina)	6.9%	6.8%
B_2O_3 (boric oxide)	20.0%	19.5%
Li_2O (lithium oxide)	2.6%	2.5%
PbO (lead oxide)	4.8%	4.7%
BaO (barium oxide)	8.2%	8.0%
ZO_2 (zirconium oxide)	2.1%	4.6%
Ag (silver)	0.31%	0.30%
Br (bromine)	0.23%	0.11%
Cl (chlorine)	0.66%	0.69%
CuO (copper oxide)	0.016%	0.016%

Basically these two glasses are very similar, but the very small difference in bromine gives them specific and different photochromic properties.

Photochromic lenses are used for indoor and outdoor activities but fused multifocal lenses cannot be made from such glass, as the temperature at which the fusing has to be done would destroy their photochromic property.

Lenses can be toughened in a similar way to flat glass, but the method of chemical toughening by ion exchange is

Above
Culpeper-type monocular
microscope. England; mid-19th
century; ht 11in (27.9cm).

Left
Brass binocular microscope.
Swift and Sons, England; late
19th century; ht 17in (42.1cm).

more widely practised. In this hot lenses are dipped in a bath of molten potassium nitrate and the large potassium ions are made to replace some of the smaller sodium ions from the glass surface, thus creating a layer of compression on it. This method, though tried, has not been very successful on a commercial scale in bottle toughening.

With some optical glass it was found that the replacement of sodium ions by lithium ions gave even better results.

Spectacles

Sheet glass is usually the starting raw material for spectacle lens production. The sheet is marked out and cut into pieces, each one to become a lens. The pieces are then placed in a rotary heating furnace, are heated to a softening point and are pressed to the required surface curvature by dies and plungers. They are then annealed and emerge ready for further processing. When only moderately large quantities are needed it is possible to use pre-formed gobs which do not require preparation before moulding, and wastage due to cutting is avoided.

Spectacle lenses fall into two main groups – single vision and multifocal. The mass-producer must be able to offer a range of finished or partly finished lenses, which will cater for the majority of day-to-day needs which, unfortunately, can run into thousands of different combinations; but a high percentage of single-vision lenses can be produced from a large, but manageable, range.

The lenses will have to be cut in accordance with a prescription issued by the ophthalmologist who will use the diopter (D) as his unit for measurement. The power of a lens in diopters is the reciprocal of its focal length in metres $\left(\frac{1}{\text{focal length (m)}} \right) = \text{D}$. Thus a lens of 200mm focal length has a power of 5D and one of 100mm focal length, 10D.

Multifocal lenses are normally either of one-piece or fused construction. A very large variety of combinations is possible, but by means of grouping a few basic lens combinations, the range which can be supplied for final grinding to satisfy individual prescriptions can be quite manageable.

Most single-vision lenses have one spherical surface and the other either spherical or toroidal – volume formed by rotating a sphere about an axis which does not pass through its centre. To cover a range of about 1,000 items by a minimum number of variables it is common practice to have ten spherical and an equal number of toric shapes. The final preparation to suit each prescription is done by grinding and polishing.

Bifocal Lenses

The human eye becomes less flexible with age and reaches the stage when it cannot re-focus on close objects. Even a person with normal vision may find difficulty in seeing clearly at a distance of 500mm and some form of correction by spherical lenses becomes essential.

Left
Quarter-plate tropical camera.
Sanderson, England; c 1915–19.

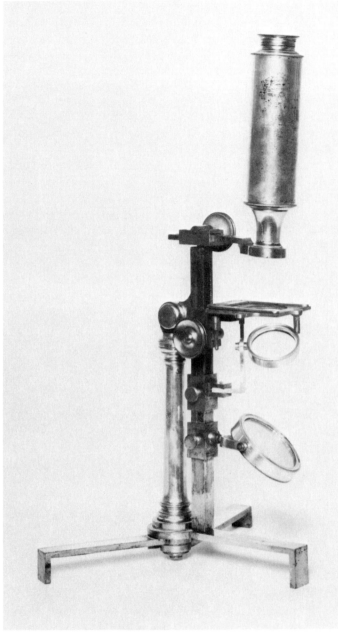

Above
Brass pillar microscope. J.
Smith, England; c 1843; ht
16in (40.6cm).

Above
Modern Contax RTS with Carl
Zeiss Tele-Tessar lens.

The obvious solution, to have two focal lengths on the same lens, occupied the minds of ophthalmologists for many years and early attempts at joining two lenses with Canada Balsam and other attempted techniques proved abortive. In the 1890s Borsch succeeded in the USA in producing a bifocal lens by fusing a segment of high density flint glass on to a crown glass blank, giving an effect similar to a modern bifocal lens.

Today the main lens of a fused bifocal type consists of a standard crown glass with a selected piece of flint glass fused to it. Here again the problem of matching the coefficients of expansion of the two glasses to prevent permanent stresses developing on annealing is essential. The difference in the focal length of the segment as compared with the main lens is by virtue of its different refractive index.

There is, however, another way of obtaining the same results from a single piece of glass. In the early part of this century, British lens maker A. H. Emerson developed a method of grinding two separate areas of different power on the same blank. This type of bifocal is known as solid or one-piece. It has the advantage of dispensing with the hot process of fusing and the lens is made of crown glass throughout, which is harder than flint glass and has a better scratch resistance.

This development was then followed by a further one in which the small segment was replaced by a larger area of the reading portion obtained either by fusion of two glasses or grinding from a one-piece lens. This type of spectacle has now become very popular and is generally known as the 'executive'. The most recent innovation in this particular field is one of a graded lens on which there is no distinct dividing line but the power changes gradually from top to bottom of the glass.

Grinding of Lenses

The finishing of lenses is done in three stages: roughing, smoothing and polishing.

The grinding machine consists essentially of a rotating base and a grinding spindle. The spindle, which carries the grinding tool, can be set at a predetermined angle to give the correct curvature. Water and medium-grade grinding powder are fed on to the lens and the grinding is done by fast rotation of the spindle. The grinding material used today is aluminium oxide which seems to have completely replaced the earlier used corundum, but grinding tools impregnated with industrial diamond chips are also used. For smoothing, a similar machine is used but the grinding medium this time is a fine-grade grinding powder.

The principle of polishing is to generate very localized frictional heat sufficient to make the surface flow to a polished condition. For polishing, various materials, one of which is a mixture of cerium oxide powder in suspension, can be used.

Latest developments in lens technology have been in the field of surface coatings of several layers to reduce or even eliminate unwanted light reflection.

The ophthalmic industry has made tremendous strides over the last few decades but further innovations are bound to be forthcoming in the future.

Toughening Glass

Glass has tremendous compressive strength by virtue of the fact that, being a non-crystalline material, it has no lattice structure. When compressive forces are applied to other materials there is sliding within their lattice structure but this cannot take place in glass. The compressive strength of glass is in fact so high that it has never been measured accurately.

In its pristine state (that is, molten glass untouched and unexposed to the atmosphere), glass also has a very high tensile strength of the order of 7000 MN/m^2 (1,000,000lb per square inch) but, unfortunately, pristine glass does not exist in practice and this high value is only a theoretical one. In reality, as soon as glass is exposed to atmosphere or is formed into an article, minute sub-microscopic flaws develop in its surface and reduce its strength to around 70 MN/m^2. After it has been handled, its strength is reduced further to some 35 MN/m^2, so that only 1/200th of its original strength remains.

As the compressive strength is extremely high, in practice glass will break in tension only. When a glass article is put under load or is subjected to an impact, tension develops in some part of its surface and it is there that it breaks. If the surface could be put in a state of compression before the

A well-annealed, stress-free glass is heated to a temperature just above the annealing point – one at which the viscosity is reduced to a level at which flow can take place. The surfaces are then rapidly chilled and 'frozen'. At this stage there are no stresses since the inside of the glass, which is still plastic, can accommodate the linear contraction of the surfaces. On further cooling the inside becomes rigid again and continues its process of linear contraction while the previously frozen surfaces, being cold, do not contract any more and are placed in a state of compression.

The chilling of the surfaces is done by means of air jets arranged in a pattern – that is why one can sometimes see a pattern on a car windscreen when the light falls on it at a certain angle. The glass is in a state of disturbed stress balance and when the outer surface is penetrated all the glass shatters into small fragments, as is often seen on a broken car window. Because toughened glass shatters when fractured and loses its transparency, the tendency has lately become to replace it in car windscreens by laminated glass, consisting of two or more sheets of plate glass with transparent plastic interlayers. Such glass is no stronger than ordinary plate glass, but when fractured, it is held together by the plastic interlayer thus preventing injury.

article were to break, the compression would have to be overcome and sufficient tension applied for fracture to occur. It is this principle which is used in producing toughened plate glass for car windscreens, shop windows, or toughened domestic glassware like plates, cups and tumblers.

If a piece of glass were heated uniformly on both sides, the outer surface would tend to expand but would be prevented from doing so by the cold inner layer and a state of temporary compression on the outside would be created, while the inside would be in tension. Under these conditions the glass would not break and as long as the temperature did not reach that at which flow could occur, it would revert to its original state on cooling. If this stress pattern could be induced permanently, we would have glass which was some ten times stronger than when normally annealed. This, in fact, is precisely what is achieved in toughened glass.

Above left
Eye baths in thick glass, blank and cut. Ireland; c 1780; ht 3¾in (9.5cm).
Thick clear blanks of English lead glass, much stronger than any previous formula, were an early form of toughened glass.

Above
Modern toughened glass: various forms of Pyrex and toughened kitchen glass. Ht of kilner jar 4⅛in (10.4cm).

Right
Water jug of 'Vitrified' and enamelled glass. Made by W. H., B. & J. Richardson, Wordsley, Stourbridge; c 1848; ht 9¼in (23.5cm). Toughened glass could be fashionable and beautiful, as well as practical.

Light Bulbs

The advent of the electric lamp called for vast quantities of glass bulbs. In the early stages these could only be produced on the rather slow suction machine, but in 1926 the Corning Ribbon machine came to the rescue with a production capacity starting at 400 bulbs per minute which has now been increased to well over 1,000 per minute.

In this machine a ribbon of glass, approximately 25mm wide, flows out from the forehearth of a glass melting tank furnace. The ribbon is passed between two cooled rollers. One of these is plain and the other has indentations in the shape of discs. A ribbon of glass discs, roughly 10cm apart and connected by a thin strip of glass, is placed over a metal belt with holes, approximately 25mm in diameter, spaced at 10cm intervals. The machine is synchronized so that each disc is placed above a hole. As the belt travels, the hot glass begins to sag through the holes and the automatic making of the parison thus begins.

A continuous belt carrying blowheads moves above the ribbons and another carrying blow moulds below it. All three belts are synchronized. As the sagging of the glass commences, a blowhead comes above it and very low pressure blowing begins. As the ribbon moves on, the parison is formed and is then enclosed by a rotating wet mould on the belt below. Blowing continues in the mould, the mould opens and the completed bulb is cut off from the ribbon, dropped on a conveyor belt and carried to be annealed. It is interesting to note that the mould itself rotates to prevent mould marks. The glass being very thin and uniform can be annealed very quickly and at such high production speeds very few machines can supply the world with light bulbs.

Glass Fibres

Glass fibres are increasingly in demand because of their thermal, sound and electrical insulating properties, their inertness, heat resistance and strength. Their use in reinforcing plastics is widespread, but their use in reinforcing concrete has only recently been developed. In the past, the chemical attack of concrete on glass fibres rendered them unsuitable for this purpose. Many unsuccessful attempts were made at producing concrete which would not attack glass but recently a scientific paper written in 1917 by the late Professor W. E. S. Turner and his co-worker Violet Dimbleby, dealing with a special glass extraordinarily resistant to alkali attack, was resurrected and formed the basis for a special glass-fibre-reinforced concrete.

Glass fibres were first produced mechanically in 1908 by the Gossler process. Cullet (broken glass) was melted in a small tank and the glass was allowed to flow through a perforated disc. The fibres were drawn and wound on to a drum. A similar method was previously used by glassblowers in the eighteenth century.

There are three processes for making fibres for yarn and for glass fibre wool, which can be spun into fabrics. In the first method, glass marbles are fed into an electrically heated platinum crucible with a perforated base through which the glass is allowed to drip; it is then drawn, spun and wound on to a drum.

In the fibre-wool-making process, glass is allowed to flow in streams from the furnace through perforated platinum bushes, and the streams are blasted by a jet of steam which breaks the glass into fine fibres. The fibres are then sprayed with a binding agent, formed into a mat of specified thickness, cut into lengths, formed into bales and packed ready for despatch.

The third process relies on the action of centrifugal forces to break a stream of glass into fine fibres. The stream of glass flows from a forehearth of a glass melting tank on to a rapidly spinning disc. The principle is the same as that used in producing candy floss. The glass fibre wool is then sprayed with a binding agent and made into insulating mats.

Tubes and Rods

Glass tubing and rods are often needed in special glasses or colours and are therefore made by hand in small quantities. There is, however, a vast market for them in the electrical, medical and chemical industries and all the supplies for these are machine-made.

Drawing tubing by hand is a fascinating and skilful process. The glassmaker gathers the glass from a pot or a tank on the end of a blowing iron. He then rolls it on a metal plate into a thick cylinder. He re-heats the gather and enlarges it by repeating the operation. He blows a bubble into it and rolls it again. His assistant attaches an iron rod to the bottom of the cylinder and the blower draws the thick cylinder into a tube, blowing into it while drawing. The outside diameter, the wall thickness and the length are all determined by the glassmaker's skill. Rods are made in the same way except that no blowing is required.

In the automatic process, using the Danner machine, glass flows from the tank over a rotating hollow mandrel (tube). As the glass is drawn mechanically, air is blown into it to maintain the correct bore. The outside diameter, bore and wall thickness are governed by the size of the orifice through which the molten glass is allowed to flow, the air pressure used for blowing and the rate of drawing.

Tubing for different purposes requires a variety of glass compositions. Boro-silicate glass is used where thermal and chemical resistance are needed. For electronic components the coefficient of expansion has to match the glass to which the tube is to be joined and often be of similar expansion to metals to be sealed into it. There are hundreds of different compositions of glass, each designed with a particular property for a specific purpose.

A large proportion of tubing is used in the manufacture of ampoules, vials, thermometers, etc. For these the tubing has to be of exceptional dimensional accuracy. The tubing is automatically cut into the required lengths and is manipulated mechanically with the help of oxygen-enriched flames into whatever form is required.

Right Argon light bulb, used for flash and special effects.

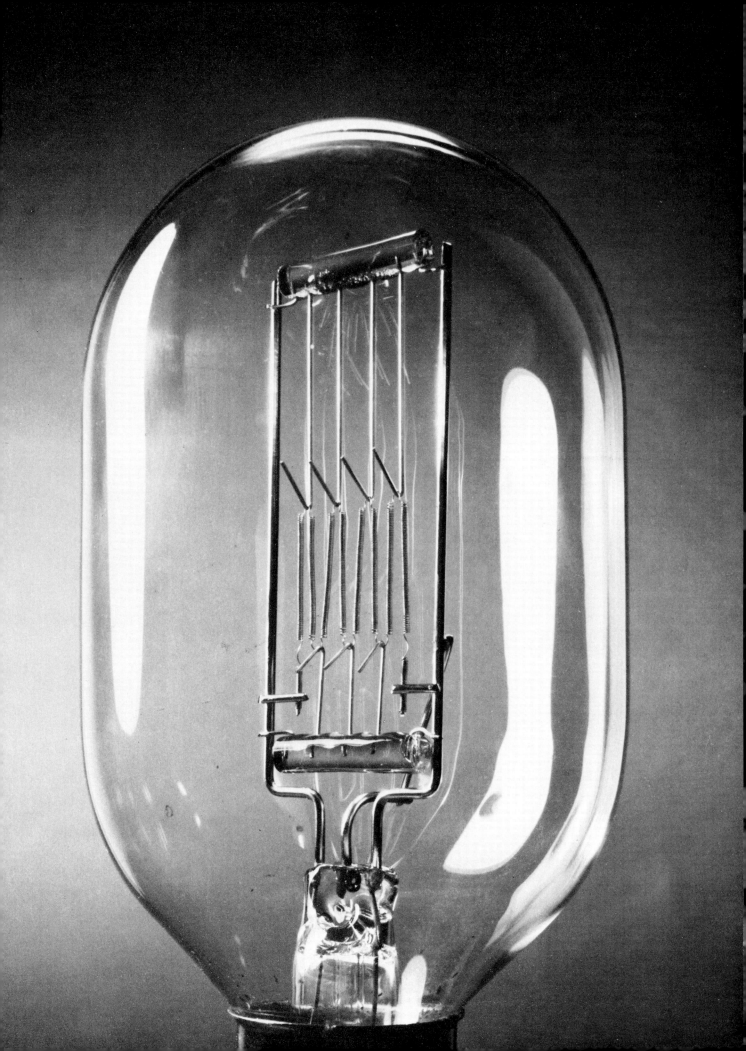

The Future

The last two or three decades have seen tremendous progress in the science of glass technology. Probably the most important development has been the Pilkington float process for plate glass manufacture. For the first time in the history of flat glass it can be manufactured at a much increased output with perfectly flat surfaces without grinding. This process is rapidly replacing all other processes and it is quite possible that the next decade will see the complete disappearance of all other flat glass manufacturing processes. Whether a new, faster and better method for flat glass manufacture will evolve remains to be seen; at this moment in time it looks as though it would be difficult to improve on the float process.

Photosensitive glass has made great strides for both window glass and optical lenses. Its ability to change colour rapidly to accommodate changes in light intensity is by no means perfect and calls for more research. Optical glasses of new compositions are always being developed and new coating materials for lenses to eliminate reflection are also being researched.

Coloured glasses, which previously needed a tankful of glass of a given colour, can now be produced from a tank of colourless glass which can be coloured in the forehearth. This adds flexibility to production with no extra furnaces. The technique is available and fairly widely practised, but improvements are needed.

The container industry has undergone a revolution in the method of producing lighter and stronger articles. Weights of bottles of the same size and strength have been reduced to about a quarter of those of their counterparts ten years ago. Surface treatment has played an important part in this development. New methods of treatment which depend on ion exchange on the surface are being developed. The glass container industry is under heavy pressure from competitive materials like cans, plastics and paperboard and it is essential that its products should become as light, as cheap and as strong as possible. There is also strong pressure from the environmentalist lobby for all glass containers to be made re-usable. The glass industry has to produce one-trip products that are more economical to finance than their returnable counterparts. To this end vast glass recycling schemes are being operated.

Glass manufacture is an energy-intensive process. Efforts to save energy are being made by designing and building more efficient furnaces with better insulation. The development of refractory materials for furnace building, which can withstand higher temperatures and are more resistant to corrosion, have revolutionized the industry. Only twenty years ago the life of a tank furnace was only about twelve months whereas today seven years is to be expected. Better refractories enable better thermal insulation and, no doubt, in another ten years furnaces lasting ten years or more, working at higher temperatures and using less fuel, will be in general use.

Fossil fuels are in limited supply and eventually atomic energy for producing electricity could replace all other forms of energy. The fact that glass, although a very good electrical insulator at atmospheric temperature, becomes a conductor at elevated temperatures, when movement of the ions

Willis, Faber & Dumas office building. Ipswich, England; designed by Foster Willis Associates; completed 1975. Award-winning building; the exterior is of solar-tinted toughened glass and concrete.

becomes possible, has already been utilized in electric melting of glass and boosting to achieve higher outputs from furnaces. So far, the price of electricity has prevented a widespread use of electric melting except in areas where hydro-electric power makes this possible. In electric melting the energy is put right into the glass and not to the top surface of the bath as in conventional fuel firing. Further research into this melting process may produce results which will make electric melting more widespread.

In the domestic glassware field, decoration of crystal glass by fully automatic methods is likely to be developed and the price of these articles should be reduced without their aesthetic value being lost. The same applies to automatic crystal glass production. As much as one must regret the possible disappearance of an ancient craft, highly skilled labour is becoming progressively rare and more costly, and consequently may have to be replaced by machines.

Glossary

Acid etched
A registered name of a form of Art Glass consisting of two layers and two colours of cased glass. Developed by Frederick Carder in the US *c* 1932, the design is made by acid etching as opposed to carving.

Acid etching

Decorative technique which involves covering glass with an acid-resistant protective layer, scratching on a design, and then applying hydrofluoric acid to etch the pattern into the glass.

Acid polishing
A technique to give cut glass a polished surface by dipping it in a hydrofluoric acid bath.

Air twist

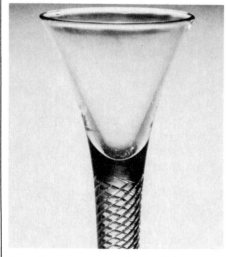

A major stem type of the 18th century which came to perfection in the 1740s. A solid blob of clear glass is indented with metal prongs, which are rapidly withdrawn. The space is covered quickly on the top with more glass, leaving a bubble of air rather elongated in shape inside the glass. This is then drawn out while the air bubble becomes longer and thinner. Twisting the rod as it is pulled will result in any number of spiral patterns, created simply by the air rather than opaque or coloured glass which is used to make colour twists. Air twists are almost impossible to make in elaborate shapes, so that most air twist stems are simple with one or two knops at the most. Sometimes air and opaque glass were used together to make combination stems.

Annealing
A process that toughens glass and eliminates internal stress by heating and gradual cooling in an annealing oven or lehr.

At-the-fire
Re-heating a glass item at the glory hole, to allow re-working or additional blowing into a larger or new shape.

Aventurine

Coloured glass combined with flakes of gold (15th century), or crystals of copper (from 17th century) giving the glass a lustrous sheen.

Baluster

The stem of an English drinking glass, adopted from the pillars that support staircase handrails. Some are inverted, some pure, and others have knops, internal tears, bubbles, etc.

Barilla
A plant that grows in the salt marshes near Alicante in Spain, and in some other areas of the Mediterranean region. It has dark blue-black berries, and dull green leaves. The bushes are collected into piles and burned to make a special kind of soda ash which is used in glassmaking as an alternative to potash. In Spain the plant was always considered of especially high quality, and European and English glass-makers in the 15th and 16th centuries imported shiploads of *barilla* for their furnaces. After the advent of lead glass, *barilla* became much less important, and today chemical soda has largely replaced the plant for commercial use.

Basal rim
A foot ring found on some paper-weights, basically to protect the base from constant wear and accidental chipping.

Basket
A basket made of glass; or a funnel-shaped decoration surrounding some paperweight motifs.

Batch
A mixture of various raw ingredients placed in the pot, which when melted produces glass. A batch usually includes a proportion of broken glass known as cullet.

Blank

A piece of solid glass before being cut into the desired shape or pattern.

Blowing

Process of blowing air through a metal tube or blow-pipe in order to shape the molten glass blob on the end.

Blow-pipe

A hollow metal tube used to gather molten glass from the pot and then to blow air through in order to shape the glass.

Cameo

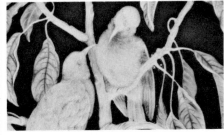

Two or more layers of cased glass in two or more colours, the outer of which is carved on a wheel. The effect was to create a raised design in low or high relief similar to cameo-carved stones; imitations were made by using moulds or controlled acid baths. Known to the Egyptians and Romans, this technique was also used by Emile Gallé and Thomas Webb. The Portland Vase is the most notable example of cameo glass.

Canes

Thin clear or coloured glass rods used for *millefiori* or mosaic glass, and for making cotton twist or opaque twist decoration.

Carpet ground

Close-packed ground of identical canes used as a background or foil for a design.

Cartoon

In stained or mosaic glass, the design in tracing paper for planning and laying out the individual pieces that make up the completed picture.

Cased

Glass made of two or more layers of different colours. Produced by the Romans (Portland Vase), popular in Bohemia and England in the mid-19th century and later fashionable in the United States. The outer layer(s) were cut away in patterns to allow the colours beneath to show according to the design and effect desired. In paperweights, casing was used to create 'windows' to see into the decorative centre-piece.

Chair

A bench with flat arms at either end used by gaffers while making glass; also a team or 'shop' of glassmakers. Not used often today.

Chequer, checker

'Chequerboard' paperweight design with regularly spaced canes separated by a horizontal grid of filigree canes.

Clichy rose

Rose-like cane favoured by the Clichy factory, but imitated by others.

Colour ground

Background of transparent or opaque colour on which designs are placed.

Colour twist

Coloured spiral threads in the stems of English drinking glasses, mostly *c* 1735–75. Continental examples often have poor colours. Rare, and therefore often faked or heavily restored.

Combing

A decorative effect of wavy, feathery or zig-zag designs, made by applying coloured threads to the object in straight lines, then stroking up or down with a special comb and marvering the threads into the surface.

Concentric

Tightly packed or separated circles of canes about a common centre.

Cotton twist (US)

Describes all twists of opaque white glass.

Cords

Defect consisting of slight striae on the surface of flint glass.

Cracking off

Process of removing an object from the pontil. After it has cooled by scoring, as opposed to shearing, the pipe is gently knocked and the object falls into a sand tray or a V-shaped holder used by the assistant.

Cristallo

Italian soda glass, developed around the 14th century, made with *barilla*, pale yellow or clear in colour. A main characteristic was extreme 'softness' or ductibility, so that it could be worked quickly into fantastic shapes. *Cristallo* was comparatively transparent for its period, hence the name; thin, brittle, and suitable only for diamond point engraving, trailings and filigree decoration.

Crizzling (crisselling)

Defect in glass that looks like a mass

of fine cracks; due to imbalanced ingredients in the batch. Prevalent before the late 17th century but remedied *c* 1676 by George Ravenscroft. It still occurs by accident.

Crown weight
Hollow-blown paperweight.

Cruciform
Term to describe glass, mostly bottles, made in the shape of a cross.

Crystal, full and lead
Full '*cristal supérieur*' contains 30% lead; half lead contains 24%.

Cullet
Broken scraps of glass which are melted with a new batch; constitutes $\frac{1}{4}$ to $\frac{1}{2}$ of a batch and saves on fuel (it melts faster) and on expensive ingredients. Not usually used for coloured glass because of possible imperfections.

Cusp
A point at which two branches of a curve meet and stop. A centrally placed pointed stem knop.

Domed feet

These were mostly used in 17th and 18th-century glasses, especially large goblets and sweetmeats. They also kept the early rough pontil marks from scratching the table.

Drawn stems
Some stems such as air twist or opaque twists are cut from longer lengths of decorated glass and attached at either end to bowl and foot. Drawn stems are simply made – when the bubble for the bowl is formed, a pontil takes up the glass at the top of the bowl, and the thicker blob at the end of the blow-pipe is pulled in such a way as to draw out the stem to the required length. Most drawn stems are solid, but they can be made with a hollow core as in some champagne glasses. Drawn stem glasses usually have simple round, oval shaped, or trumpet bowls.

Enamels

Longlasting decoration using vitreous enamel paints, fired to fix the colours in a muffle kiln. See 'Enamelling' page 269.

Encased overlay
Single or double overlay design, further encased in clear glass.

Filigree
Clear cane with twisted glass rods or embedded threads of glass that form a very fine network pattern. Also known as 'lace' or 'muslin'.

Fire polishing
Re-heating a finished piece at the glory hole in order to remove tool marks; removes the dull surface. Sometimes replaced in modern glass with acid polishing.

Flammiform
A decorative effect in the form of a flame, usually at the termination of wrythen moulding.

Flashed, flashing
A thin coating of different-coloured glass, visible in section and much thinner than a casing or overlay.

Flat bouquet
Design in which flowers and leaves (or canes representing flowers) have been placed flat, parallel to the base of the weight.

Flint glass
Another name for lead glass; called 'flint' because the original experimenters used powdered flints instead of lead oxide. Also the American term in the 19th century for fine glass.

Fluting

Vertically cut decoration in long narrow sections, usually wheel cut but sometimes moulded.

Flux
A substance added to the basic ingredients to help stabilize the batch. The most well-known fluxes are soda (Venetian glass), potash (Bohemian glass), wood ash (forest glass) and lead oxide (lead crystal). Another use was in mixing enamel colours; the addition of a flux made it possible for the enamels to melt and fuse into the surface before the object itself melted.

Folded foot

The edge of the foot is turned under, making a sturdy double rim on which the glass could rest. Folded feet were particularly important for fragile soda glass. As lead glass became popular they gradually disappeared. A rare type of 19th-century lampworked glass has feet folded over. Folded rims were made for much the same purpose, for protection against damage.

Foot

The part of a glass object (other than its base) on which it rests.

Frigger

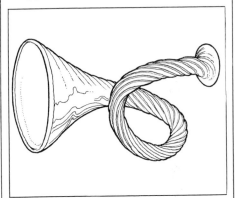

A traditional term for any small glass object made by the craftsman for his own use, either as decoration, a present for the family, or as something to sell to neighbours or friends. They were made 'after hours', usually using up the glass left in the pots at the end of the working day, and so were sometimes called end-of-day glass.

Many areas reserved special days for workmen to parade their pieces through the streets. A prize was awarded to the most original piece. See also **Off-hand**.

Gadget

A special rod with a spring clip on the end that grips the foot of the just made glass while the worker trims off the rim, softens the lip, or otherwise puts the finishing touches to the rest of the piece. It was developed to take the place of the pontil and to avoid leaving a mark on the foot. A simple plunger closes the clip to hold the glass, and pulls out to release it when the workman is ready to drop the glass into the sand bed before it goes into the annealing oven.

Gadrooning

A decorative band originally derived from a popular silver form made of moulded, applied or deep cut sections of reeding. Used on many Venetian glasses, jelly glasses and on the lower part of the bowls of some drinking glasses.

Gaffer

The head glassmaker of a team, sometimes called the master blower.

Gather

A blob of molten glass attached to the end of the blow-pipe, pontil or gathering iron, prior to making the glass object. The gather is formed by dripping and twirling the pipe in the pot until a blob begins to form.

Gilding

The use of gold on glass in one of two ways: (a) gold leaf or powder mixed with a fixative, painted or brushed on and fired, and then burnished; (b) the design painted with a fixative, gold leaf laid on top and dried.

Another method of gold decoration has gold leaf enclosed in two layers of clear glass. Dating from ancient times, the technique was also used in Bohemian *Zwischengoldglas* pieces.

Glory hole

A small-sized opening in the side of the furnace used basically for inserting cooling objects to re-heat without melting or destroying the shape.

Ground

The decorative background on which a paperweight design sits. It may be flat, domed, of single opaque or translucent colour or highly detailed with many canes.

Hand pressed

Glass made in a hand-operated press, as opposed to machine pressing.

Holloware

The term used as in metalwork for all containers as opposed to flat objects; drinking glasses, bowls, jars, bottles, etc.

Hollowed

Generally a design term referring to a concave surface, such as a hollowed diamond or thumbprint.

Ice glass (verre craquelé: broc à glaces)

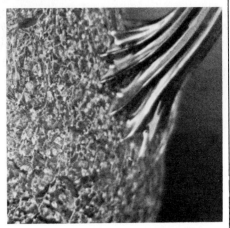

Decorative glassware with a rough outer surface. The French terms refer to two Venetian techniques of ice glass, revived in the 19th century.

Intaglio

Decorative engraving or wheel-cut designs below the surface; the reverse of cameo.

Jasper
Mottled ground composed of small particles of glass usually in two colours imitating jasperstone.

Kick

A conical indentation at the base of a glass or bottle which adds to its strength. Also used to surround the pontil mark so it would not damage the surface of a table.

Knop
A knob or bulge in the stem of a glass, either hollow or solid; there are many variations on knop shapes.

Lampwork

Making glass objects at-the-lamp or by using a small flame, like a Bunsen burner. Miniatures of all kinds, too small to be manipulated at the fire, are made by lampwork from already prepared rods or thin canes. Paperweight patterns are also assembled on a mould at-the-lamp from prepared chips and cane slices, before being enclosed at-the-fire.

Latticino (sometimes latticinio)

Lacy-looking glass made of embedded opaque white rods forming the pattern.

Lattimo
Opaque white glass (*latte* – milk).

Laub-und-Bandelwerk
Decorative pattern of leaf and floral strapwork (German term).

Lehr
The annealing oven for all kinds of glassware. It usually has a moving base, which travels more or less slowly through controlled loss of heat until the objects can be taken out at the other end. The rate of speed can be adjusted to the type of glass.

Liners

Early silver dishes became pitted and damaged by salt; today glass liners protect the metal, which is often designed in openwork patterns to show off the glass colours. Blue is the most popular.

Magnum
Paperweight over $3\frac{1}{4}$in (8.3cm) diameter.

Marver

An iron table on which the gather is rolled into an evenly shaped mass. It can also be used to embed trailings into the surface as the glass is rolled. The marver is also used as a pick-up surface when working in pellets of coloured glass or a paperweight set-up.

Merese

A flattened ring or collar usually between the stem and bowl or the stem and foot of a wine glass, although it may be used anywhere along the stem.

Metal
Molten or cold glass – the actual material; used mainly by English writers to distinguish the material from the object. Sometimes confusing to new collectors.

Milled ring

Vertical grooves similar to those found around the rim of a coin have been used to decorate collars, footrims and trailings.

Millefiori
Means 'a thousand flowers'. Many slices of coloured glass canes are embedded in clear glass, in floral-like designs. Also the technique for using such canes.

Millefiori canes
Canes are made in elaborate *millefiori* patterns by encasing moulded shapes and even sometimes small figures of animals or birds in concentric layers of differently coloured glass. The canes are originally quite thick, but when the design is finished they are heated again, and then drawn out by two

men walking away from each other until the rod is many feet long and no thicker than a pencil. This is laid in specially made forms on the floor to cool and harden. It is then sliced very thinly into hundreds or thousands of pieces, and used to form paperweights, door knobs, door stops, bottle bases and all other kinds of *millefiori* decoration. The canes are given their name from the flowerlike effect of the vividly coloured slices scattered inside the glass.

Miniature
Any paperweight not over 2in (5.1cm) diameter.

Mitre cut

Glass cut with a sharp groove on a V-edged wheel. Also mitre corners.

Moil
The waste glass left on a blow-pipe or pontil; used in making cullet. It is knocked off after every making, into a collecting bin.

Mould
The wooden or iron form used to shape glass. Pattern or half moulds are used before the glass is entirely expanded. Full or three-part moulds are used to give identical same-size shape to the glass.

Moulded glass

Blown glass ornamented or given its final body shape by the use of moulds.

Mounted glass

Fragile edges can be protected with metal mounts; pewter was sometimes used, but during the 18th and 19th centuries silver was much more common. Damaged pieces can also be mounted to display bowls or fragments which would otherwise be useless. Gold was also used to mount glass, especially small boxes and objets d'art. Hallmarks can help to establish the forward date, but the glass may be older than its marked mount.

Muffle kiln
Low temperature kiln used for re-firing glass to fix enamelling and gilding.

Mushroom weight (tuft)
Vertical, spreading mushroom-shaped bundle of *millefiori* canes, arranged in a close or concentric design and nearly always encircled near the base by a spiral torsade.

Nipt diamond waies
Diamond-shaped network decoration made by nipping together ribs or trailings of glass threads. A Venetian design, but a Ravenscroft term (*c* 17th century).

Notched

A V-shaped cut or folded edge especially in cut glass.

Novelties

A generic term for small pieces. Handmade novelties were produced by lampworkers and blowers, while Victorian fireplaces often displayed pressed glass novelties of all kinds. Miniatures have always been collectable – animals, ships, books and hats, even complete sets of pitcher and water glasses for doll houses. Some novelties such as paperweights were intended for a purpose as well as decoration; rolling pins holding cold water were extremely practical for pastry-making, and are now made in toughened glass.

Off-hand (US)

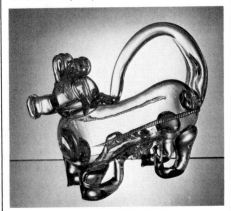

Hand fabricated, usually used to indicate objects made for pleasure, or not as part of the normal working production. See also **Frigger**.

Opaque twist

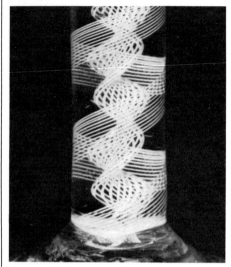

White or coloured opaque rods twisted into lacy patterns and drawn out into thin rods for decorative stems or working into the body of the glasses. Cotton twist in America.

Overlay

The outer edge of cased glass. Double overlay glass consists of two outer layers of different colours. American – usually used as a synonym for cased glass.

Parison (paraison)

Balloon of molten glass, formed when the glassmaker blows through the blow-pipe and expands the gather.

Pâte de verre

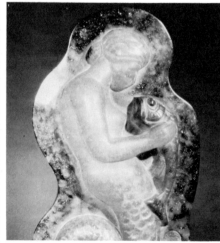

Literally means glass paste. Made by grinding glass into a powder, melting it and then putting it into a mould.

Pedestal

Raised on a tall stem. Also a type of stem previously called Silesian in England.

Pinched trailing

A decorative pattern made by applying bands or threads of glass in lines and then pincering them together into a wavy motif. Similar to nipt diamond.

Pontil, punty

The solid shorter iron which is an essential tool for glassblowers. The pontil is used to take off expanded objects from the blowing iron and allow the top to be finished. As it cools, the glass solidifies, and it is knocked off the iron leaving the pontil mark. The rough mark was considered the sign of handmade glass, but since the 19th century it has often been ground flat.

Pot

A crucible made of fire clay in which the batch of glass ingredients is heated before being transferred to the furnace. There are many kinds of pots; open, closed, and small ones for coloured glass, sometimes called skittles. A pot will last from 3 to 6 weeks before it starts to break up and has to be replaced.

Pot arch

The furnace in which the pot itself is fired before being transferred to the furnace for glass melting.

Pot ring

A fire-clay ring which floats on the surface of an open pot. Although the glass may be moving in the pot because of the heat, the ring keeps the glass within it comparatively still. The gatherer always puts his pipe within the ring to be sure the glass is as free from bubbles and impurities as possible.

Pot settling

Transferring the pot from the pot arch to the melting furnace.

Potash glass

Potash was used as the major flux in some kinds of glass, particularly *Waldglas* in Germany and Bohemia. It was obtained by burning beechwood or burning the residue of wine. It was harder than soda glass and more brilliant in tone, so it could be engraved and cut on the wheel much more satisfactorily. Potash glass is still used today and is also an ingredient in lead glass.

Pressing

Molten glass is poured into a mould which forms the outer surface. A plunger, lowered into the mass, leaves a smooth centre with a patterned exterior. Flat plates and dishes are formed in a base mould; an upper section folds down to mould the top, something like a waffle iron. Fine pressed pieces are often finished by hand to obliterate the mould marks, and may be difficult to distinguish from cut glass.

Printy, printie

The opposite of prunt, a print in a hollow or below the surface pattern, usually a shallow circle or oval.

Prunt

A blob of glass, rounded, pointed or irregularly shaped, applied as a decoration. They have been made in almost every country. Often a crimp or stamp was applied, so the prunt had a 'strawberry' top or was moulded as a lion or a mask.

Reticulated

Manipulated trails of glass which appear as an open network or 'knitting'. Originally a 16th to 18th-century Venetian technique, also used in friggers and Nailsea-type novelties.

Rib mould

A pattern mould for bowls, bottles, etc marked in more or less heavy vertical ribbing.

Rigaree

A trailing in which the ribbon of glass is impressed into parallel notches, like a ruffled collar. Generally an American term.

Rod

A solid stick of glass; a group of rods make up cane decoration.

Schmelzglas (German)

Opaque marbled glass imitating stones, e.g. agate, chalcedony, etc.

Seeds

Tiny air bubbles in the glass, indicating an underheated furnace. Also impurities caused by flecks of dust or dirt.

Sickness

A glass which is not properly tempered or annealed is said to be sick. It usually shows in tiny random cracks, flaking and eventual disintegration. Some early glasses were so badly affected that they actually 'weep' and feel damp to the touch.

Soda glass

Glass consisting of soda as the alkali rather than potash. It is brownish or yellowish and lacks resonance but is easier than lead to manipulate. Venetian *cristallo* was a soda glass. The soda was traditionally obtained by burning *barilla*, a seashore plant (known also as glasswort).

Stave

Rectangular rod used as an enclosure for a design.

Stones

Specks found in batches which must be removed.

Striae

Undulating marks on glass due to uneven furnace temperature, or sometimes made by tools as the glass is rotated.

Sulphide

A relief medallion or cameo made of clay-silica paste, enclosed in paperweights, bottles or even glasses. Apsley Pellatt (1791–1862) was the major English glassmaker who used sulphides.

Swirl

A type of paperweight in which rods of two or more colours radiate spirally downwards from a top central cane.

Taker-in

An apprentice who assists the gaffer, especially by taking the finished ware to the lehr.

Tazza

A (usually wide) cup, or serving plate, with or without handles, mounted on a stemmed foot. *Tazze* were used as dishes for cakes, fruit, etc, as well as bases for tall epergnes made up of smaller tiers.

Tear

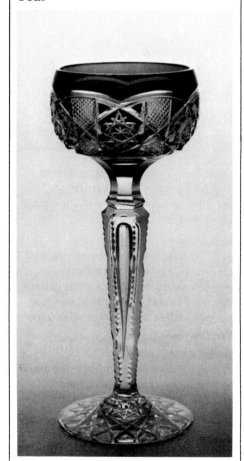

A drop-shaped air bubble enclosed in the glass, often in the stem.

Tessera

Small, usually square, piece of flat glass used to build up a mosaic picture or pattern.

Thread

A thin trail of glass used as decoration. The hot glass is dropped on to the object and rotation allows the trail to spiral around the desired place, in any pattern.

Torsade

Filigree ring of opaque white and/or coloured threads, frequently of complicated pattern, used as a low set border for mushrooms and upright bouquets.

Trailing

The action of applying threads of glass in decorative patterns.

Two- and three-part glasses

Two-part glasses are made with drawn stems, the bowl and the stem being made in one simple piece, with an added foot.

When the stem is made separately, the glass becomes a three-part glass (*top right*). They are often more elaborate than drawn or two-part

glasses since the process allows more easily for decorative bowls and complicated stem shapes. However, there are simple plain-stem shapes which are occasionally made in three parts in order to give a wider 'set' to the bowl, especially if the design requires a slender stem that does not swell towards the top, as any drawn stem shape will do.

Upright bouquet

A vertically placed floral design.

Vermicular collar

A slender, wavy ring around the stem or the bottom of the bowl of a glass, or around the neck of a bottle. It is trailed off by the workman, and gets its name from the worm-like shape. Vermicular collars are sometimes used around a tall stem to provide a lip for the fingers to hold the glass securely.

Verre eglomisé

So-called after a French mirror and picture framer, Glomy (*d* 1786). Silver or gold foil was applied on the reverse, cut or engraved in a pattern, and then backed usually with a red, blue or black ground.

Also loosely used to describe a type of *Zwischengold* decoration, used in jewellery and medallions.

Wear marks

These are tiny usually almost invisible scratches on the base or foot which indicate normal wear and tear over the years.

Wear marks can be produced artificially by rubbing a new glass over a rough surface to create marks, but these give themselves away by being too regular and evenly divided. On the other hand, glasses which were bought for ceremonial or religious purposes may have been kept in a cabinet for most of their ownership, and would show very few signs of wear, even if they were genuinely old.

Wheels

Cutting wheels developed from lapidary equipment. Large stone and steel wheels are used for deep cuts, smaller copper wheels for engraving.

Wrythen moulding

Sometimes mistakenly called flammiform, wrythen decoration is vertical ribbing which has been softened and swirled to encircle the rising shape of the glass. It is most often seen on small, low-stemmed ale glasses, and the pattern may extend to the top of the glass, or stop just below the rim. When there is a clear edge to the glass, it is called flammiform, since the swirls end irregularly in a flame-shaped pattern, hence the confusion.

Glass Museums

ADRIA, ITALY
Civic Museum

AMSTERDAM, HOLLAND
The Rijksmuseum

BALTIMORE, MARYLAND, U.S.A.
Baltimore Museum of Art
Maryland Historical Society
Walters Gallery

BARCELONA, SPAIN
Instituto Amatller de Arte Hispanico
Museum of Art

BATH, ENGLAND
The American Museum
The Holburne of Menstrie
Museum of Art
Victoria Art Gallery

BEDFORD, England
Cecil Higgins Museum

BEIRUT, LEBANON
Archaeological Museum of the
American University of Beirut

BENNINGTON, VERMONT, U.S.A.
The Bennington Museum

BERLIN (WEST), GERMAN FEDERAL
REPUBLIC
Dahlem Museum

BOSTON, MASSACHUSETTS, U.S.A.
Fine Arts Museum

BRISTOL, ENGLAND
The City Art Gallery

BROOKLYN, NEW YORK, U.S.A.
The Brooklyn Museum

BRUSSELS, BELGIUM
Royal Museums of Art and History

BUDAPEST, HUNGARY
Hungarian National Museum

BURNLEY, LANCASHIRE, ENGLAND
The Towneley Hall Museum and
Art Gallery

CAMBRIDGE, MASSACHUSETTS, U.S.A.
Botanical Museum, Harvard
University

CAMBRIDGE, ENGLAND
The Fitzwilliam Museum

CANTERBURY, ENGLAND
The Canterbury Museum

CARDIFF, WALES
National Museum of Wales

CHICAGO, ILLINOIS, U.S.A.
Art Institute of Chicago

CINCINNATI, OHIO, U.S.A.
The Cincinnati Museum of Art

CLEVELAND, OHIO, U.S.A.
Cleveland Museum of Art

COBURG, GERMAN FEDERAL REPUBLIC
Kunstgammlungen der Veste Coburg

COLOGNE, GERMAN FEDERAL
REPUBLIC
Kunstgewerbemuseum
Romisch-Germanisches Museum

COPENHAGEN, DENMARK
Rosenborg Castle

CORK, IRELAND
Cork Public Museum

CORNING, NEW YORK, U.S.A.
The Corning Museum of Glass

DEARBORN, MICHIGAN, U.S.A.
Henry Ford Museum and
Greenfield Village

DEERFIELD, MASSACHUSETTS, U.S.A.
Historic Deerfield Village and
Museum

DELFT, HOLLAND
Museum Prinsenhof

DUBLIN, IRELAND
The Civic Museum
The National Museum

DUSSELDORF, GERMAN FEDERAL
REPUBLIC
Museum of Dusseldorf

EDINBURGH, SCOTLAND
National Museum of Antiquities
Royal Scottish Museum

EXETER, ENGLAND
The Royal Albert Museum

FLORENCE, ITALY
National Museum
Pitti Gallery

FRANKFURT, GERMAN FEDERAL
REPUBLIC
Museum fur Kunsthandwerk

GLASGOW, SCOTLAND
Glasgow Art Gallery and Museum

THE HAGUE, NETHERLANDS
Municipal Museum

HELSINKI, FINLAND
National Museum of Finland

HUDDERSFIELD, ENGLAND
The Tolson Memorial Museum

KABUL, AFGHANISTAN
Kabul Museum

LAWRENCE, KANSAS, U.S.A.
The University of Kansas Museum
of Art

LENINGRAD, RUSSIA
Hermitage Museum

LEWISBURG, PENNSYLVANIA, U.S.A.
Packwood House and Museum

LONDON, ENGLAND
The British Museum
London Museum
Science Museum
The Victoria and Albert Museum

MADRID, SPAIN
Instituto de Valencia de Don Juan
National Archaeological Museum

MANCHESTER, ENGLAND
City Art Gallery

MANCHESTER, NEW HAMPSHIRE,
U.S.A.
The Currier Gallery of Art

MELBOURNE, AUSTRALIA
National Gallery of Victoria

MILAN, ITALY
Poldi Pezzoli Museum

MILLVILLE, NEW JERSEY, U.S.A.
Heaton Historical Association and
Village

MURANO, ITALY
Museo Vetrario

NAPLES, ITALY
Capodimonte National Museum and
Gallery

NEWCASTLE-ON-TYNE, ENGLAND
The Laing Art Gallery and Museum

NEW ORLEANS, LOUISIANA, U.S.A.
The Isaac Delgado Museum of Art
The New Orleans Museum of Art

NEW YORK, NEW YORK, U.S.A.
The Hispanic Society of America
The Metropolitan Museum of Art

NORWICH, ENGLAND
Strangers Hall

NOTTINGHAM, ENGLAND
Castle Museum and Art Gallery

OXFORD, ENGLAND
Ashmolean Museum

Glass Periodicals

Paris, France
Cluny Museum
Decorative Arts Museum

Philadelphia, Pennsylvania,
U.S.A.
Burholme Park Museum
Philadelphia Museum of Art

Pittsburgh, Pennsylvania, U.S.A.
The Historical Society of Western
Pennsylvania

Poznan, Poland
National Museum at Poznan

Prague, Czechoslovakia
Museum of Decorative Arts

Preston, Lancashire, England
The Harris Museum and Gallery

Rome, Italy
National Museum of Rome
Vatican Museums

Rotterdam, Netherlands
Boymans-Van Beuningen Museum

St Helen's, England
Pilkington Museum of Glass

St Louis, Missouri, U.S.A.
City Art Museum

Saint Paul, France
Maeght Foundation

Sandwich, Massachusetts, U.S.A.
Sandwich Glass Museum

Sheffield, England
Society of Glass Technology
Weston Park Museum

Stockholm, Sweden
National Museum

Sturbridge, Massachusetts, U.S.A.
Old Sturbridge Village and Museum

Sydney, Australia
Nicholson Museum

Tokyo, Japan
National Museum of Tokyo

Toledo, Ohio, U.S.A.
Antique and Historic Glass
Foundation
The Toledo Museum of Art

Toronto, Canada
Royal Ontario Museum

Washington, D.C., U.S.A.
Hillwood Museum
The Smithsonian Institution

Antiques
Antique Collector
Antique Dealer's and Collector's
    Guide
Antiques Journal
Apollo
Australian Bottle Review
Bulletin of the National Early
    American Glass Club
Ceramics Monthly
The Connoisseur
Country Life
Crafts
Craft Horizons
Glass
Glass Art Magazine
The Glass Circle
The Glass Club Bulletin
Hobbies
International Bottle Trader's
    Gazette
Journal of Glass Studies
Old Bottles and Treasure
    Hunting
Old Bottle Magazine

Bibliography

America

AMAYA, Mario
Tiffany Glass, New York: Walker & Co., 1967; London: Studio Vista, 1968

AVILA, George C.
The Cairpont Glass Story, New Bedford, Mass: Reynolds-De Walt Printing Inc., 1968

BARRETT, Richard Carter
Blown and Pressed American Glass, Manchester, Vermont: printed privately, 1964

BARRETT, Richard Carter
A Collector's Handbook of American Art Glass, Manchester, Vermont: Forward's Colour Productions Inc., 1971

BARRETT, Richard Carter
Identification of American Art Glass, Manchester, Vermont: printed privately, 1964

BELKNAP, Eugene M.
Milk Glass, New York: Crown, 1949, N E 1959

BUTLER, Joseph T.
American Antiques 1800–1900, New York: Odyssey Press, 1965

CHIPMAN, Frank W.
The Romance of Old Sandwich Glass, Sandwich, Mass: Sandwich Publishing Co. Inc., 1932

CONSENTINO, Geraldine and STEWART, Regina
Carnival Glass: A Guide for the Beginning Collector, New York: Golden Press, 1976

COPPEN-GARDNER, Sylvia
A Background for Glass Collectors, London: Pelham Books, 1975

Corning Museum of Glass
Glass from the Corning Museum of Glass, Corning, New York, 1965

DANIEL, Dorothy
Cut and Engraved Glass, 1771–1905, New York: M. Barrows and Co., 1950, 6th ed. 1965

DAVERIO, Paul J.
Louis Comfort Tiffany, Lausanne: Galerie des Arts Décoratifs S.A., 1974

DAVIS, Pearce
The Development of the American Glass Industry, Cambridge, Mass: Harvard University Press, 1949

DORFLINGER, William
'The Development of the Cut Glass Business in the United States', a paper given at the meeting of the American Glass Association of Flint and Lime Glass Manufacturers, held at Atlantic City, July 25th, 1902.

DREPPERD, Carl W.
Primer of American Antiques, New York: Doubleday & Co., 1944

DREPPERD, Carl W.
ABC's of Old Glass, New York: Doubleday & Co., 1949

DYOTT, T. W.
An Exposition of the System of Moral and Mental Labor Established at the Glass Factory of Dyotville in the County of Philadelphia, Philadelphia, Pennsylvania: printed privately 1833

FIELD, Anne E.
On The Trail of Stoddard Glass, Dublin, New Hampshire: William L. Bauhan, 1975

FLORENCE, Gene
.The Collector's Encyclopaedia of Depression Glass, Paducah, Kentucky: Collector Books, 1977

FREEMAN, Larry
Grand Old American Bottles, Watkins Glen, New York: Century House, 1964

FREEMAN, Larry
Iridescent Glass (intro. by Frederick Carder), Watkins Glen, New York: Century House, 1956

GARDNER, P. V.
The Glass of Frederick Carder, New York: Crown Publishers Inc., 1971

GROVER, Ray and Lee
Art Glass Nouveau, Rutland, Vermont: Charles E. Tuttle, 1968

HAND, Sherman
The Collector's Encyclopaedia of Carnival Glass, Paducah, Kentucky: Collector Books, 1978

HARRINGTON, J. C.
Glassmaking at Jamestown, America's First Industry, Richmond, Virginia: Dietz Press, 1952

HARTLEY, Julia M.
Mills Glass Collection at Texas Christian University, Fort Worth: University Press, 1975

HEACOCK, William
The Encylopaedia of Victorian Coloured Pattern Glass, Marietta, Ohio: Richardson Printing Corp., 1974–1977

HERRICK, Ruth
Greentown Glass, Grand Rapids, Michigan: printed privately, 1959

HUME, Ivor
Glass in Colonial Williamsburg's Archaeological Collection, Williamsburg, Virginia: Williamsburg Press, 1969

HUNTER, Frederick William
Stiegel Glass, Boston: Houghton Mifflin Co., 1914
N E by Helen McKearin, New York: Dover Press, 1967

INNES, Lowell
Early Glass of the Pittsburgh District, 1797–1890, Pittsburgh, Pennsylvania: Exhibition at Carnegie Museum, 1949

INNES, Lowell
Pittsburgh Glass, 1797–1891, Boston: Houghton Mifflin Co., 1976

JARVES, Deming
Reminiscences of Glassmaking, Boston, Mass: Eastburn's Press, 1854
2nd rev. ed. New York: Hurd & Houghton, 1965

JEFFERSON, Josephine
Wheeling Glass, Mt. Vernon, Ohio: Guide Publishing Co., 1947

JENKINS, Dorothy
A Fortune in the Junk Pile, New York: Crown Publishers Inc., 1970

KAMM, M. W.
Pitcher Books, Numbers 1–8, Grosse Point Farms, Michigan, 1939–54 published by the author

KLAMKIN, Marian
The Collectors' Guide to Depression Glass, New York: Hawthorn Books, 1973

KNITTLE, Rhea M.
Early American Glass, New York:
The Century Co., 1927, Garden City,
New York, 1948

KOCH, Robert
*Louis C. Tiffany's Glass – Bronze –
Lamps*, New York: Crown Publishers
Inc., 1971

KOCH, Robert
Louis C. Tiffany, Rebel in Glass, New
York, Crown Publishers Inc., 1964,
1966, 1971

LANAHAN, Jack
*Frederick Carder and his Steuben
Glass, 1903–1933*, West Nyack, New
York: Dexter Press, 1966

LANMON, Dwight P.
'The Baltimore Glass Trade, 1780–
1820', *Winterthur Portfolio V* (1969)
pp. 15–47

LEE, Ruth Webb
Antique Fakes and Reproductions,
Northborough, Mass: published
by the author, 1950

LEE, Ruth Webb
Early American Pressed Glass,
Wellesley Hills, Mass: published by
the author, 1946, 1960

LEE, Ruth Webb
Sandwich Glass, Framingham Centre,
Mass: published by the author, 1939

LEE, Ruth Webb
Victorian Glass, Northborough,
Mass: published by the author, 1944

LEE, Ruth Webb
American Glass Cup Plates, Northborough, Mass: published by the
author, 1948

LINDSAY, Bessie M.
American Historical Glass, Vermont:
1967

LINDSAY, Bessie M.
Lore of Our Lane Pictured in Glass,
Vols. *1 & 2*, Forsyth, Illinois, 1948

McCLINTON, Katharine M.
Collecting American Glass, New York:
Gramercy Publishing Co., 1950

McKEARIN, George S. and Helen
American Glass, New York: Crown
Publications, 1948

McKEARIN, George S. and Helen
*Two Hundred Years of American
Blown Glass*, New York: Doubleday,
1950; New York: Crown
Publications, rev. ed. 1966

McKEARIN, Helen
Bottles, Flasks and Dr. Dyott, New
York: Crown Publishers Inc., 1970

McKEARIN, Helen
*The Story of American Historical
Flasks*, Corning, New York: The
Corning Museum of Glass, 1953

Maryland Historical Society
Amelung Glass: An Exhibition,
Baltimore: The Maryland Historical
Society, 1952

Metropolitan Museum of Art
*19th Century America: Furniture and
Other Decorative Arts, a Special
Exhibition*, New York: The Museum,
1970

METZ, Alice H.
Early American Pattern Glass,
Westfield, New York: Guide
Publishing Co., 1958

MILLARD, S. T.
Goblets, Topeka, Kansas: Central
Press, 1938

Also: *Goblets II, c* 1940

MILLER, Everett and ADDIE, R.
*The New Martinsville Glass Story,
Book II, 1920–1950*, Manchester,
Michigan: Rymack Printing, 1975

MILLER, Robert W.
Mary Gregory and Her Glass, Des
Moines, Iowa: Wallace Homestead,
1972

MILLFORD, Harriet N.
'Amelung and His New Bremen
Glasswares' *Maryland Historical
Magazine, XLVII* (March, 1952)
pp. 1–10.

MUNSEY, Cecil
*The Illustrated Guide to Bottle
Collecting*, New York: Hawthorn
Books Inc., 1970

NEUSTADT, Egon
The Lamps of Tiffany, New York:
Fairfield Press, 1970

PALMER, Arlene M.
*The Wistarburgh Glassworks: The
Beginning of Jersey Glassmaking*,
Alloway, New Jersey: Alloway
Township Bicentennial Committee,
1976

PAPERT, Emma
*The Illustrated Guide to American
Glass*, New York: Hawthorn Books
Inc., 1972

PEARSON, J. Michael and Dorothy,
*American Cut Glass for the
Discriminating Collector*, New York:
Vantage Press, 1965

PEARSON, J. Michael and Dorothy
*A Study of American Cut Glass
Collections*, Miami Beach, Florida:
published privately, 1969

PERROT, Paul N., GARDNER, Paul V.
and PLANT, James
*Steuben: Seventy Years of American
Glassmaking*, New York: Praeger,
1974

PETERSON, Arthur
400 Trademarks on Glass, Takoma
Park, Maryland: Washington College
Press, 1968

REVI, Albert Christian
American Art Nouveau Glass, New
York: Thomas Nelson & Sons, 1968

REVI, Albert Christian
American Cut and Engraved Glass,
New York: Thomas Nelson & Sons,
1965

REVI, Albert Christian
*American Pressed Glass and Figure
Bottles*, New York: Thomas Nelson
& Sons, 1964

REVI, Albert Christian,
*Nineteenth Century Glass: Its
Genesis and Development*, New York:
Thomas Nelson & Sons, 1959,
rev. ed. 1968

RIVERA, Betty and Ted
*Inkstands and Inkwells, A Collector's
Guide*, New York: Crown, 1973

ROCKWELL, Robert F.
*Frederick Carder and His Steuben
Glass, 1903–1933*, Corning, New
York: privately printed, 1968

ROSE, James H.
The Story of American Pressed Glass of the Lacy Period, Corning, New York: Corning Museum of Glass, 1954

Sandwich Glass Museum
Sandwich Glass Museum Collection, Sandwich, Mass, 1969

SCHWARTZ, Marvin
Collector's Guide to Antique American Glass, Garden City, New York: Doubleday & Co. Inc., 1969

SPILLMAN, Jane S.
Glassmaking: America's First Industry, Corning, New York: The Corning Museum of Glass, 1976

SWAN, Frank,
Portland Glass, Des Moines, Iowa: Wallace-Homestead Book Co., rev. ed. 1969

THOMPSON, James H.
Bitters Bottles, Watkins Glen, New York: Century House, 1946

Toledo Museum of Art
Libbey Glass, a Tradition of 150 Years, Toledo, Ohio: The Museum, 1968

Toledo Museum of Art,
The New England Glass Company, 1818–1888, Toledo, Ohio: The Museum, 1963

TOULOUSE, Julian H.
A Collector's Manual of Fruit Jars, Camden, New Jersey: Thomas Nelson, 1970

VAN RENSSELAER, Stephen
Early American Bottles and Flasks, Peterborough, New Hampshire: Transcript Printing Co., 1926

VAN TASSELL
American Glass, New York: Gramercy Publishing Co., 1950

WARMAN, Edwin G.
American Cut Glass, Uniontown, Pennsylvania: privately printed, 1954

WATKINS, Lura W.
American Glass and Glassmaking, New York: Chanticleer Press, 1953

WATKINS, Lura W.
Cambridge Glass 1818–1888, Boston, Mass: Marshall Jones Co., 1930, reprinted 1953

WATSON, Richard
Bitters Bottles, New York: Thomas Nelson & Sons, 1965, supplement, 1968

WEEKS, Joseph D.
Report on the Manufacture of Glass (Census of 1880), Washington D.C. 1884

WILLEY, Harold E.
Heisey's Deep Plate Etching, Etched and Carved, Pressed and Blown, Handmade Glassware, Des Moines, Iowa: Wallace Homestead, 1973

WILLIAMS, Lenore W.
Sandwich Glass, Bridgeport, Connecticut: 1922

WILSON, Kenneth M.
Glass in New England, rev. ed. Sturbridge, Mass: Old Sturbridge Village, 1968

WILSON, Kenneth M.
New England Glass and Glassmaking, New York & Toronto: Old Sturbridge Inc. & Thomas Y. Crowell, 1972

WILSON, Kenneth M., 'The Glastenbury Factory Company' *Journal of Glass Studies, Vol. V*, 1963, pp 116–123

Ancient

ASHMOLE, B.
'A New Interpretation of the Portland Vase', *Journal of Hellenic Studies*, 1967, pp 1–17

BARAG, D.
'Mesopotamian Glass Vessels of the Second Millennium B.C.', *Journal of Glass Studies, IV*, 1962, pp 9–27

BIESANTZ, Hagen
'Rätsel Portlandrase'. *Werkzeitschrift Jenaer Glaswerk Schott & Gen., Mainz*, 1965, No. 3, pp 6–13

CHARLESWORTH, D.
'Roman Square Bottles', *Journal of Glass Studies*, 1966, pp 26–40

CHIRNSIDE, R. C. and PROFFITT, C. M. C.
'The Rothschild Lycurgus Cup: An Analytical Investigation', *Journal of Glass Studies, V*, 1963, pp 18–23

CLAIRMONT, C. W.
The Excavations at Dura-Europos, Final Report IV, Part V, The Glass Vessels, New Haven: Dura-Europos Publications, 1963

Corning Museum of Glass
Glass from the Ancient World, the Ray Winfield Smith Collection, a Special Edition, Corning, New York: The Museum, 1957

DALTON, O. M.
'The Gilded Glasses of the Catacombs', *Archaeological Journal LVII*, 1901, pp 225–53

HARDEN, D. B.
Roman Glass from Karamis, University of Michigan Studies, Ann Arbor, 1936

HARDEN, D. B.
'Snake-thread Glasses Found in the East', *Journal of Glass Studies*, 1934, pp 50–55

HARDEN, D. B.
'The Rothschild Lycurgus Cup: Addenda and Corrigenda', *Journal of Glass Studies, V*, 1963, pp 9–17

HARDEN, D. B.
Vasa Murrina, Journal of Roman
Studies, XXXIX, 1949, and XIV
1954.

HAYES, John
*Roman and Pre-Roman Glass in the
Royal Ontario Museum*, Toronto:
Royal Ontario Museum, 1975.

HAYNES, D. E. I.
The Portland Vase, London: The
British Museum, 1964.

ISINGS, C.
'A Fourth Century Glass Jar with
Applied Masks', *Journal of Glass
Studies*, 1964, pp 59–63

ISINGS, C.
Roman Glass from Dated Finds,
Groningen, Djakarta: J. B. Wolters,
1957

ISINGS, C.
Roman Glass in Limberg, Netherlands:
Wolters-Noordhoff, 1971

MARIACHER, Giovanni
*Italian Blown Glass from Ancient
Rome to Venice*, London: Thames
and Hudson, 1961

MOREY, C. R.
*The Gold-Glass Collection of the
Vatican Library*, Citta del Vaticano,
1959

NEUBURG, F.
Glass in Antiquity, London: Art
Trade Press, 1949

OLIVER, A., Jr
'Late Hellenistic Glass in the
Metropolitan Museum', *Journal of
Glass Studies*, 1967, pp 13–33

OPPENHEIM, A. Leo, and others
*Glass and Glassmaking in Ancient
Mesopotamia*, Corning, New York:
The Corning Museum of Glass, 1970

PINDER-WILSON, R.
'Cut-Glass Vessels from Persia and
Mesopotamia', *British Museum
Quarterly*, 1963, pp 33–9

PLINIO, *Naturalis Historia*, (sec. I d.
C.), ediz. Moderna, Rome, 1946

SALDERN, Axel von
Ancient Glass in the MFA, Boston:
New York Graphic, 1968

SMITH, R. A.
'A Roman Glass Flask from Rich-
borough', *British Museum Quarterly*,
1932–33, pp 11–12

ZECCHIN, L.
'Vetri al Museo di Adria', *Giornale
Economico*, Venice, 1956

Canada

BIRD, Douglas and Marion
*A Century of Antique Canadian Glass
Fruit Jars*, Ontario & London:
printed privately, 1971

BLANCHE, Alice
Manitoban Stained Glass, Winnipeg:
University of Winnipeg Press, 1970

Dominion Glass Company Ltd.
Catalogue of Blown Tumblers,
Montreal: Herald Press, 1915

Dominion Glass Company Ltd.
Druggists' Glassware, Montreal:
Dominion Glass Co. Ltd., n.d.

Dominion Glass Company Ltd.
Lamp Chimney Catalogue, Montreal:
Dominion Glass Co. Ltd., n.d.

Dominion Glass Company Ltd.
Packers' Glassware, Montreal:
Dominion Glass Company Ltd., n.d.

MACLAREN, George
Nova Scotia Glass, Halifax: Nova
Scotia Museum, 1968

PIERCE, Edith C.
*Canadian Glass. A Footnote to
History*, Ontario: Ryerson Press,
1954

RUSSELL, Doris S.
*A Heritage of Light; Lamps and
Lighting in the Early Canadian
Home*. Toronto: University of
Toronto Press, 1968

SPENCE, Hilda and Kevin
A Guide to Early Canadian Glass,
Toronto: Ryerson Press, 1961;
Ontario: Longmans Canada, 1966

STEVENS, Gerald F.
Canadian Glass, 1825–1925,
Toronto: Ryerson Press, 1967

STEVENS, Gerald F.
Early Canadian Glass, Toronto:
Ryerson Press, 1960, reprint, 1967

STEVENS, Gerald F.
Early Ontario Glass, Toronto: Royal
Ontario Museum, 1965

STEVENS, Gerald F.
The Edith Chown Pierce and Gerald Stevens Collection of Early Canadian Glass, Toronto: Royal Ontario Museum, 1957

UNITT, Doris J. and Peter
American and Canadian Goblets, Peterborough, Ontario: Clock House, 1970

UNITT, Doris J. and Peter
Bottles in Canada, Peterborough, Ontario: Clock House, 1972

UNITT, Doris J. and Peter
Canadian Silver, Silver Plate and Replated Glass, Peterborough, Ontario: Clock House, 1970

UNITT, Doris J. and Peter
Treasury of Canadian Glass, Peterborough, Ontario: Clock House, 1969

Collecting

BACON J. M.
English Glass Collecting for Beginners, London: Penrith, 1942

BUTTERWORTH, Lionel M.
The Manufacture of Glass, London and New York: I. Pitman, 1948

CHARLESTON, Robert J. (ed)
Glass Circle: Papers for Collectors, London: Unwin Bros., 1972, 1975

CURTIS, Tony
Glass: Antiques and Their Values, New York: Lyle Publications, 1976

DOUGLAS, Jane
Collectible Glass, London: Longacre, 1961

DREPPERD, Carl W.
First Reader for Antique Collectors, Garden City, New York: Garden City Books, 1946

EVERS, Jo
The Standard Cut Glass Value Guide, Paducah, Kentucky: Collector Books, 1975

GARDNER, Sylvia
Background for Glass Collectors, London: Pelham, 1975

GROS-GALLINER, Gabriella
Glass: A Guide for Collectors, London: Muller, 1970

HAMMOND, Dorothy
Confusing Collectibles, Leon, Iowa: Mid-America Book Co., 1969

HUGHES, George Bernard
English Glass for the Collector, 1660–1860, New York: MacMillan; London: Lutterworth, 1958

LAVERICK, A. (ed)
European Glass Directory and Buyer's Guide, London: Industrial Newspapers, 1976

TURNBULL, George,
Price Guide to English Eighteenth Century Drinking Glasses, Detroit: Gale, 1973

WARD, Lloyd,
Investing in Georgian Glass, London: Barrie Cresset, 1969

WEBBER, Norman W.
Collecting Glass, New York: Arco, 1973

WILLS, Geoffrey
Antique Glass for Pleasure and Profit, London: Orbis Publications, 1972

England, Scotland and Ireland

AITKEN, William C.
Glass Manufacturers of Birmingham and Stourbridge, Birmingham, 1851.

ASH, Douglas (ed.)
Dictionary of British Antique Glass, London: Pelham, 1978

ASH, Douglas
How to Identify English Drinking Glasses and Decanters, 1680, 1830, London: G. Bell, 1962

ASHDOWN, Charles H.
History of the Worshipful Company of Glaziers of The City of London, London: Blades, 1919

BARKER, T. C.
Pilkington Brothers and the Glass Industry, London: Allen & Unwin, 1960

BATE, Percy
English Tableglass, New York: Charles Scribner's Sons, 1905

BEDFORD, John
Bristol and Other Coloured Glass, London: Cassell, 1964; New York: Walker, 1965

BEDFORD, John
English Crystal Glass, New York: John Walker and Co, 1966

BICKERTON, L. M.
An Illustrated Guide to Eighteenth Century English Drinking Glasses, New York & London: Great Albion Books, 1972

BLES, Joseph
Rare English Glasses of Seventeenth and Eighteenth Centuries, Boston: Houghton Mifflin Co., 1925

BOWLES, W. H.
History of the Vauxhall and Ratcliff Glasshouses and Their Owners, printed privately *c* 1926

BRADFORD, Betty
Victorian Table Glass, London: H. Jenkins, 1976

BUCKLEY, Francis
The Birmingham Glass Trade, 1740–1833, Sheffield: Society of Glass Technology, 1927.

BUCKLEY, Francis
History of Old English Glass, New York: Dingwell-Rock, 1925

BUCKLEY, Francis
Old London Drinking Glasses, Edinburgh: Ballantyne Press, 1913

BUCKLEY, Francis
Old London Glasshouses, London: Stevens & Sons, 1915

BUCKLEY, Wilfred
The Art of Glass. Illustrated from the Wilfred Buckley Collection in the Victoria & Albert Museum, London, 1939

BUCKLEY, Wilfred
Diamond Engraved Glasses of the Sixteenth Century, London: Ernest Benn Ltd., 1929

BUTTERWORTH, Lionel M.
British Table and Ornamental Glass, London: L. Hill, 1956

Chance Brothers & Co. Ltd.
100 Years of British Glass Making, 1824–1924, London: Chance Bros, 1924

CHARLESTON, Robert J.
English Glass, London: Victoria & Albert Museum, 1977

CLARKE, Harold G.
The Story of Old English Glass Pictures, 1690–1810, London: Courier Press, 1928

COOPER, William,
The Crown Glass Cutter and Glazier's Manual, London: Simpkin, Marshall, 1835

CRELLIN, J. K. and SCOTT, J. R.
Glass and British Pharmacy, 1600–1900, London: Wellcome Institute of the History of Medicine, 1972

CROMPTON, Sidney (ed)
English Glass, London: Ward Lock, 1967; New York: Hawthorn, 1968

DAVIS, Derek C.
English and Irish Antique Glass, London: Barker, 1964; New York: Praeger, 1965

DAVIS, Derek C.
English Bottles and Decanters, 1650 – 1900, New York: World Publications, 1972

DAVIS, Derek C. and MIDDLEMAS, K.
Coloured Glass, London: Jenkins, 1968; New York: Clarkson N. Potter, Inc., 1968

DAVIS, Frank
Early 18th Century English Glass, London: Hamlyn, 1971

DILLON, Edward
Glass, New York: G. P. Putnam's Sons, 1907

DRAKE, Maurice
A History of English Glass-Painting, London: T. W. Laurie, 1912

EBBOTT, Rex
British Glass of the 17th and 18th Centuries, London: Oxford University Press, 1971

ELVILLE, E. M.
English and Irish Cut Glass 1750–1950, London: Country Life, 1953; New York: Charles Scribner's Sons, 1951

ELVILLE, E. M.
English Tableglass, London: Country Life, 1951; New York: Charles Scribner's Sons, 1951

FLEMING, John Arnold
Scottish and Jacobite Glass, Glasgow: Jackson Son & Co., 1938

FRANCIS, Grant R.
Jacobite Drinking Glasses, London: Harrison & Sons, 1925

FRANCIS, Grant R.
Old English Drinking Glasses, Their Chronology and Sequence, London: Herbert Jenkins, 1920

GILLINDER, William T.
'Treatise on the Art of Glass Making, containing 272 Practical Receipts', Birmingham, England, 1894

GODFREY, Eleanor S.
The Development of English Glass-making, 1560–1640, Chicago: University of Chicago Press, 1957; London: Oxford University Press, 1975

GUTTERY, David R.
From Broad-Glass to Cut Crystal; A History of the Stourbridge Glass Industry, London: L. Hill, 1956

HADEN, Henry J.
Notes on the Stourbridge Glass Trade, Brierley Hill, England: Libraries and Arts Committee, 1949

HALLEN, Arthur W.
*French 'Gentlemen Glassmakers';
Their Work in England and Scotland,*
Edinburgh: T. & A. Constable, 1893

HARDING, Walter
Old Irish Glass, Liverpool: Liverpool
Printing, 1930

HARTSHORNE, Albert
Old English Glasses, London & New
York: E. Arnold, 1897; New York &
Boston: Brussel & Brussel, 1968

HAYES, John
*The Garton Collection of English
Table Glass,* London: Her Majesty's
Stationery Office, 1965

HAYNES, E. Barrington
Glass Through the Ages, Harmonds-
worth: Penguin Books, 1948

HONEY, William B.
English Glass, London: Collins, 1946

HONEY, William B.
*Glass: A Handbook & Guide to the
Victoria and Albert Museum
Collection,* London: The Victoria
and Albert Museum, 1946

HORRIDGE, W.
*The Rose and Emblems on Jacobite
Drinking Glasses,* London:
Transactions of the Circle of Glass
Collectors, No. 56

HUGHES, George Bernard
*English, Scottish and Irish Table
Glass from the Sixteenth Century to
1820,* New York: Bramhall House,
1956; London: B. T. Batsford, 1956

HUGHES, George Bernard
*English Glass for the Collector,
1660–1760,* London: Lutterworth
Press, 1958

JANNEAU, Guillaume
Modern Glass, London: Sir Isaac
Pitman and Sons, 1918

KENYON, George H.
*The Glass Industry of the Weald
(1350–1620),* Leicester: University
Press, 1967

LAGERBERG, Theodore C.
British Glass, New Port Richey,
Florida: Modern Photographers,
1968

LLOYD, W.
Investing in Georgian Glass, London:
Barrie & Rockliff, 1969; New York:
Potter, 1969

MARSON, Percival
Glass, London: Sir Isaac Pitman and
Sons, 1918

O'LOONEY, Betty
Victorian Glass, London: Victoria
and Albert Museum, 1972

PELLATT, Apsley
Glass Manufacturers, London:
B. J. Holdsworth, 1821

PELLATT, Apsley
Curiosities of Glassmaking, London:
David Bogue, 1844, 1849; Mon-
mouth, England: Ceramic Book Co.,
1969

PERCIVAL, MacIver
The Glass Collector, New York:
Dodd, Mead & Co., 1919

POWELL, Harry J.
Glassmaking in England, New York
& London: MacMillan & Co., 1923

POWELL, Harry J.
*Principles of Glass-Making, Together
with Treatises on Crown and Sheet
Glass,* London: G. Bell, 1883

RAMSEY, William
*History of the Worshipful Company
of the Glass Sellers of London,*
London: T. Connor, 1898

ROHAN, Thomas
Old Glass Beautiful, English and Irish,
London: Mills & Boon, 1930; New
York: Dial Press, 1931

Royal Scottish Museum
English Glass, Edinburgh: Royal
Scottish Museum, 1964

RUSH, James
The Ingenious Beilbys, London:
Barrie & Jenkins, n.d.

SEABY, W. A.
Irish Williamite Glass, Belfast:
Ulster Museum, 1965

SEABY, Catriona and BOYDELL, Mary
*Irish Glass: from the 18th Century to
the Present Day,* Limerick, Ireland:
City Art Gallery, 1971

SIMON, André Louis
*Bottlescrew Days; Wine Drinking in
England During the 18th Century,*
London: Duckworth, 1926

Sotheby & Co.
English and Continental Glass (sale
catalogue) London, 1965

STANNUS, Mrs. Graydon
'Old Irish Glass', London:
Connoisseur, 1920

Steuben Glass
British Artists in Crystal, New York,
1954

THORPE, William A.
English Glass, London: A. & C.
Black Ltd., 1949; 3rd ed. 1961

THORPE, William A.
A History of English & Irish Glass,
2 volumes, 1929, Boston: Hale,
Cushman & Flint, 1929

THORPE, William A.
English and Irish Glass, London:
Medici Society, 1927

TURNBULL, George
*The Price Guide to English 18th
Century Drinking Glasses,* Wood-
bridge, Suffolk: Baron, for the
Antique Collectors Club, 1970;
supplement, 1973

VINCENT, Keith
Nailsea Glass, Newton Abbot: David
& Charles, 1975

WAKEFIELD, Hugh
Nineteenth Century British Glass,
London: Faber & Faber Ltd., 1961,
1970; New York: Yoseloff, 1961

WAKEFIELD, Hugh
Victorian Glass, London: Circle of
Glass Collectors, 1958

WARREN, Phelps
Irish Glass: The Age of Exuberance,
London: Faber & Faber Ltd., 1970;
New York: Scribner, 1970

WEBBER, Norman W.
Collecting Glass, Newton Abbot:
David & Charles, 1972; Melbourne:
Lansdowne, 1973

WESTROPP, Michael
Irish Glass, Philadelphia: J. B.
Lippincott Company, 1920

WESTROPP, Michael
*'Irish Glass. An Account of Glass-
Making in Ireland from the 16th
Century to Present Day',* Dublin:
Royal Academy Proceedings, Vol.
29, 1911

WILKINSON, Oliver N.
Old Glass, Manufacture, Styles, Uses,
London: Benn, 1968; New York:
Philosophical Library, 1968

WILKINSON, Reginald
The Hallmarks of Antique Glass,
London: Richard Madley, 1968

WILLS, Geoffrey
*Antique Glass for Pleasure and
Investment*, London: Gifford, 1971;
New York: Drake, 1972

WILLS, Geoffrey
Candlesticks and Lustres, London:
Guinness Signatures, 1968

WILLS, Geoffrey
Chandeliers, London: Guinness
Signatures, 1968

WILLS, Geoffrey
Commemorative Goblets, London:
Guinness Signatures, 1968

WILLS, Geoffrey
*The 'Country Life' Pocket Book of
Glass*, London: Country Life, 1966;
as *The Collector's Pocket Book of
Glass*; New York: Hawthorn, 1966.

WILLS, Geoffrey
Drinking Glasses, 2 parts, London:
Guinness Signatures, 1968

WILLS, Geoffrey
18th Century Coloured Glass,
London: Guinness Signatures, 1968

WILLS, Geoffrey
Enamelled and Engraved Glass,
London: Guinness Signatures, 1968

WILLS, Geoffrey
English and Irish Glass, 16 parts,
London: Guinness Signatures;
Garden City, New York: Doubleday,
1968

WILLS, Geoffrey
Ewers and Decanters, London:
Guinness Signatures, 1968

WILLS, Geoffrey
Glass, London: Orbis, 1972

WILLS, Geoffrey
Irish Glass, London: Guinness
Signatures, 1968

WILLS, Geoffrey
Modern Glass, London: Guinness
Signatures, 1968

WILLS, Geoffrey
Novelties and 'Friggers', London:
Guinness Signatures, 1968

WILLS, Geoffrey
Table Wares, London: Guinness
Signatures, 1968

WILLS, Geoffrey
Victorian Glass, 2 parts, London:
Guinness Signatures, 1968

WILLS, Geoffrey
*English Glass Bottles for the
Collector*, Edinburgh: John
Bartholomew & Son Ltd., 1976

WILMER, Daisy
Early English Glass, London:
Lipcott Gill, 1910

WINBOLT, Samuel E.
*Wealdon Glass, The Surrey-Sussex
Glass Industry*, Hove: Combridges,
1933

WINSTON, Charles
*An Inquiry into the Difference of
Style Observable in Ancient Glass
Paintings*, Oxford University Press,
1867

YOUNG, Sidney
*The History of the Worshipful
Company of Glass-Sellers of London*,
London, 1913

YOXALL, James H.
*Collecting Old Glass, English and
Irish*, London: Heinemann, 1916

France

ARNOLD, Hugh
*Stained Glass of the Middle Ages in
England and France*, New York:
Macmillan, 1956

APPLEGATE, Judith
French Art Glass, Boston: Museum
of Fine Arts, 1975

AVRAY, M. C.
Cristal de France, Paris: 1967

BARRELET, James
*La Verrerie en France de l'Epoque
Gallo-Romaine à Nos Jours*, Paris:
Librairie Larousse, 1935, 1953

BLOUNT, Henry
French Cameo Glass, Des Moines,
Iowa: Wallace Homestead, 1971

FILLON, Benjamin
L'Art de Verre Chez les Poitevins,
Niort, 1964

FRÉMY, Elphège,
*Histoire de la Manufacture Royale
des Glaces de France*, Paris, 1909

GROVER, R. I.
European Art Glass Nouveau,
Rutland Ut.: Tuttle, 1967

LE VAILLANT DE LA FIEFFE, O.
Les Verreries de la Normandie,
Rouen, 1873

McCAWLEY, Patricia M.
*Antique Glass Paperweights from
France*, London: Spink & Son, 1968

McCLINTON, Katharine
Lalique for Collectors, New York:
Scribners, 1975

ROSSER, James
*The Radiance of Chartres; Studies in
the Early Stained Glass of the Ca
Medrae*, New York: Random House,
1965

Saint Louis Glass Factory
Cristal de France, Paris, 1967

SHERRILL, Charles H.
Stained Glass Tours in France,
London: John Lane, 1908

VON WITZLEBEN, Elizabeth
Stained Glass in French Cathedrals,
New York: Reynal & Co., 1968

General

ARCHER, Douglas
Glass Candlesticks, New York:
Collector Books, 1975

ARWAS, Victor
Glass : Art Nouveau to Art Deco,
New York: Rizzoli, 1977

BEARD, Geoffrey
International Modern Glass, London:
Barrie & Jenkins, 1977

BEARD, Geoffrey
Modern Glass, London: Studio Vista,
1968

The British Museum
Masterpieces of Glass, London: The
Museum, 1965

BUCKLEY, Wilfred
European Glass, Boston: Houghton
Mifflin Co., 1926; London: Ernest
Benn, 1926

BURTON, John
*Glass, Handblown, Sculptured,
Colored*, Philadelphia, London, New
York: Chilton Book Co., 1967

CHAFFERS, William
*Catalogue of the Collection of Glass
formed by Felix Slade*, London:
British Museum, 1871

Corning Museum of Glass
*A Decade of Glass Collecting :
Selections from the Melvin Billups
Collection*, Exhibition, Corning,
New York: The Museum, 1962

Corning Museum of Glass
*Glass from The Corning Museum of
Glass : A Guide to the Collections*,
Corning, New York: The Museum,
1955

Corning Museum of Glass
*Glass Drinking Vessels from the
Collection of Jerome Strauss and the
Ruth Bryan Strauss Memorial
Foundation*, Corning, New York:
The Museum, 1955

Corning Museum of Glass
*Glass 1959 : A Special Exhibition of
International Contemporary Glass*,
Corning, New York: The Museum,
1959

DAVIS, Derek and MIDDLEMAS, Keith
Coloured Glass, London: Barrie &
Jenkins, 1968

DAVIS, Derek Cecil
Glass for Collectors, London:
Hamlyn, 1971

DAVIS, Frank
Antique Glass and Glass Collecting,
London: Hamlyn, 1973; New York:
International Publications, 1974

DAVIS, Frank
*Continental Glass : From Roman to
Medieval Times*, London: Barker,
1972

DAVIS, Frank
The Country Life Book of Glass,
London: Country Life, 1966

DIAMOND, Freda
The Story of Glass, New York:
Harcourt, Brace, 1953

DILLON, Edward
Glass, London: Methuen, 1907;
New York: G. P. Putnam's, 1907

DOUGLAS, Ronald W. and FRANK,
Susan
A History of Glassmaking, Henley-
on-Thames: Foulis, 1972

DRAKE, Wilfred James
*A Dictionary of Glasspainters and
'Glasyeis' of the 10th to 18th Century*,
New York: Metropolitan Museum,
1955

DUTHIE, Arthur L.
Decorative Glass Processes, London:
Constable, 1908; New York: D. van
Nostrand, 1911

ELLVILLE, E. M.
The Collector's Dictionary of Glass,
London: Country Life, 1961

ENGLE, Anita, comp.
Readings in Glass History, Jerusalem:
Phoenix, 1973

FIELD, Kate
The Drama of Glass, Toledo, Ohio:
1899

FOSSING, Paul
Glass Vessels before Glass-Blowing,
Copenhagen: Ejnar Munksgaard,
1940

FRANKS, Augustus W.
*Guide to the Glass Room in the
British Museum*, London: British
Museum, 1888

GANDY, Walter
*The Romance of Glass-Making. A
Sketch of Ornamental Glass*, London:
S. W. Partridge, 1898

GARNIER, Édouard
*Histoire de la Verrerie et de
l'Émaillerie*, Tours: 1886

GROS-GALLINER, Gabriella
Glass : A Guide for Collectors,
London: Muller, 1970; New York:
Stein & Day, 1970

GROVER, Ray and Lee
European Art Glass Nouveau,
Rutland, Vermont and Tokyo:
Charles E. Tuttle & Co., 1967

HARDEN, Donald B.; PAINTER, K. S.;
PINDER-WILSON, R. H. and TAIT,
Hugh
Masterpieces of Glass : A Selection,
London: The British Museum, 1968

HAYES, E. Barrington
Glass Through the Ages, Harmonds-
worth, England: Penguin Books Ltd.,
1959

HOLLOWOOD, A. Bernard
Pottery and Glass, London: Penguin,
1947

HONEY, William B.
*Glass : A Handbook for the Study of
Glass Vessels of All Periods and
Countries and a Guide to the Museum
Collections*, London: Ministry of
Education, 1946

JANNEAU, Guillaume
Modern Glass. Translated by Arnold
Fleming. London: The Studio Ltd.;
New York: William E. Rudge, 1931.

JOHNSON, Stanley
Collecting Old Glassware, London:
Country Life, 1922

JULLIAN Philippe
*The Triumph of Art Nouveau ; Paris
Exhibition 1900*, New York:
Larousse, 1974

KAEMFER, Fritz and BEYER, Klaus
Glass : A World History. Translated
and revised by Edmund Launert.
London: Studio Vista, 1966;
Greenwich, Connecticut: New York
Graphic Society, 1967

LABARTE, J.
Les Arts Industriels, Paris, 1875

LABINO, Dominick
Visual Art in Glass, Dubuque, Iowa:
William C. Brown, 1968

LARDNER, Dionysus,
*The Manufacture of Porcelain and
Glass*, Philadelphia, 1832

LEWIS, J. Sydney
Old Glass and How to Collect It,
London: Laurie, 1916; Philadelphia:
Lippincott, 1916

McGRATH, Raymond and FROST,
Albert
Glass in Architecture and Decoration,
London: Architectural Press, 1937

MARIACHER, Giovanni
*Glass from Antiquity to the
Renaissance*. Translated by Michael
Cunningham, London: Hamlyn,
1970

MARIACHER, Giovanni
L'Arte del Vetro, Milan: 1954

MIDDLEMAS, Robert Keith
Antique Glass in Color, Garden City,
New York: Doubleday, 1971

MIDDLEMAS, Robert Keith
Continental Coloured Glass, London:
Herbert Jenkins, 1968

MOORE, N. Hudson
Old Glass, European & American,
New York: Frederick A. Stoles Co.,
1924

NESBITT, Alexander
*A Descriptive Catalogue of The Glass
Vessels of All Ages in the South
Kensington Museum*, London: Eyre &
Spottiswoode, 1878

NEUBURG, Frederic
Glass in Antiquity, London: Art
Trade Press, 1949

NEWMAN, Harold
An Illustrated Dictionary of Glass,
London: Thames & Hudson, 1977

O'DONNELL, Erica
Glass, London: Ginn, 1964, 1970

PAYTON, Mary and Geoffrey
The Observer's Book of Glass, London
and New York: Frederick Warne &
Co. Inc., 1976

PERROT, Paul N.
A Short History of Glass Engraving,
New York: Steuben, 1974

PHILLIPS, Phoebe (ed)
*The Collector's Encyclopedia of
Antiques*, New York: Crown, 1973;
London: Pan, 1978

POLAK, Ada
Glass: Its Tradition and Its Makers,
New York: Putnam, 1975; as *Glass:
Its Makers and its Public*, London:
Weidenfeld & Nicolson, 1975

POLAK, Ada
Modern Glass, London: Faber; New
York: Yoseloff, 1962

POWELL, Chance and Harris
The Principles of Glass-Making,
London: 1883

ROBERTSON, R. A.
Chats on Old Glass, London: Benn,
1954; revised edition London:
Constable, 1969; New York: Dover,
1969

ROGERS, Frances and BEARD, Alice
5000 Years of Glass, New York:
F. A. Stokes, 1937; Philadelphia:
Lippincott, 1948

ROSENHEIM, Walter
Glass Manufacture, London: 1908

SAUZAY, Alexandre
*Marvels (or Wonders) of Glass-
Making of All Ages*, London: S.
Low, Marston, 1869; New York:
Scribners, 1870. New title: *Wonders
of Glass & Bottle Making in All
Ages*, Fort Davis: Frontier Press,
1969

SAVAGE, George
Glass, London: Weidenfeld &
Nicolson, 1965; New York: Putnam,
1965; N E London: Octopus Books,
1972

SAVAGE, George
Glass and Glassware
London: Octopus Books, 1973

SAVAGE, George
Glass of the World, New York:
Galahad Books, 1975

SCHMIDT, Robert
Das Glas, Berlin: 1912, 2nd ed. 1922

SCHRIJVER, Elka
Glass and Crystal, 2 volumes, New
York: Universe Books, 1964;
London: Merlin Press, 1963

SHIPLEY, Sylvia
*Handbook of Glass, Exhibition 'Glass
Through Time' Oct.–Nov. 1944*,
Baltimore: Museum of Art, 1944

SIMON, André (ed)
*Wine Trade Loan Exhibition of
Drinking Vessels Catalogue*, London:
Vintners Hall, 1933

SKELLEY, LeLoise D.
Modern Fine Glass, New York:
Richard R. Smith, 1937

SLADE, Felix
*Catalogue of The Collection of Glass
formed by Felix Slade*, London:
privately printed, 1871

SLOVILLE, Warren C.
Revolutions in Glassmaking,
Cambridge, Massachusetts: 1948

STENNET-WILLSON, R.
The Beauty of Modern Glass, London:
The Studio Ltd., 1948; New York:
Studio Publications, 1948

Toledo Museum of Art
*Art in Glass: A Guide to The Glass
Collections*, Toledo, Ohio: The
Museum, 1969

VÁVRA, Jaroslav R.
Das Glas und die Jahrtausende,
Prague: Artia, 1954

VOSE, Ruth Hurst
Glass, London: Connoisseur, 1975;
New York: Hearst, 1976

WAUGH, Sidney
The Art of Glass Making, New York:
Dodd, Mead, 1937

WEISS, GUSTAV
The Book of Glass, New York:
Praeger Publishing Co., 1971;
London: Barrie & Jenkins, 1971

WEYL, Woldemar A.
Coloured Glasses, London: Dawsons,
1960

WILKINSON, R.
The Hallmarks of Antique Glass,
London: Richard Madley, 1968

Germany

CHARLESTON, R. J.
'The Monogrammist HI: A Noteable German Engraver', *Journal of Glass Studies IV*, 1962, pp 67–84

HETTES, Karel
'Venetian Trends in Bohemian Glassmaking in the 16th and 17th Centuries', *Journal of Glass Studies V*, 1963, pp 39–52

KLESSE, Brigette
Glas, Catalogue of the Kunstgewerbe Museum der Stadt Köln, 1963

PESTOVA, Zuzana
Bohemian Engraved Glass, translated by Arnost Jappel for Paul Hamlyn, London, 1968

RADEMACHER, Franz
Die Deutschen Gläser des Mittelalters, Berlin, 1933

SALDERN, Axel von
German Enamelled Glass, New York: Crown, 1971

SCHMIDT, Robert
Das Glas, Berlin, 1912

SHERRILL, Charles H.
Stained Glass Tours in Germany and Austria and the Rhinelands, London: John Lane, 1927

VYDRA, Josef
Folk Painting on Glass, Prague: Artia, n.d.

Holland and Belgium

BUCKLEY, Wilfred
Notes on Frans Greenwood and the Glasses that He Engraved, London: E. Benn, 1930

BUCKLEY, Wilfred
Aert Schouman and the Glasses that He Engraved. With a supplementary note on glasses engraved by Frans Greenwood. London: 1931

BUCKLEY, Wilfred
D. Wolff and the Glasses that He Engraved. With a supplementary note on a glass engraved by Frans Greenwood. London: Methuen 1935

CHAMBON, Raymond
L'Histoire de la Verrerie en Belgique, Brussels: Librarie Encyclopédique, 1955

GELDER, H. E. van
'Achttiende – eeuwse glassnijders in Holland', *Oud-Holland*, 73, 1958, pp 1–17, 90–102, 148–155, 211–219

HUDIG, Ferrand W.
European Glass by Wilfred Buckley, London, 1926

HUDIG, Ferrand W.
Das Glas. Mit besonderer Berücksichtigung der Sammlung in Nederlandsch Museum voor Geschiedenis en Kunst in Amsterdam, Vienna, 1923

SCHMIDT, Robert
'Die gerissenen und punktierten holländischen Gläser', *Der Cicerone*, 1911, p. 817 ff

Italy

APOLLONIO, Umbro
Baldinelli, Rome: Edizioni d' Arte Moderna, n.d.

BOVINI, Giuseppe
Ravenna. Translated by Leonard Von Matt, New York: Abrams, 1971

Corning Museum of Glass
Three Centuries of Venetian Glass, a Special Exhibition, Corning, New York: The Museum, 1958

FRANCESCHINI, Felice
'Die Glasindustrie in Italien', *Glastechn Berichte* 27, 1954, pp 166–9

HETTES, Karel
Old Venetian Glass. Translated by Ota Vojtisek, London: Spring Books, 1960

MARCHINI, Giovanni
Italian Stained Glass Windows, London: Thames and Hudson, 1957

MARIACHER, Giovanni
Italian Blown Glass from Ancient Rome to Venice, London: Thames and Hudson, 1961

VOLBACH, Wolfgang F.
Early Christian Mosaics; From the Fourth to the Seventh Centuries: Rome, Naples, Milan, Ravenna, New York: Oxford University Press, 1943.

Oriental

BLAIR, Dorothy
A History of Glass in Japan, Tokyo:
Kodansha International Ltd. and
Corning: The Corning Museum of
Glass, 1973

KATO, Koji
Glassware of the Edo Period.
Translated by Fumio Tanaka,
Tokyo: Toku ma Shoten
Publishing Co., 1972

LAMM, Carl J.
*Oriental Glass of Medieval Date
Found in Sweden*, Stockholm:
Wahlstrom & Widstrand, 1941

MOSS, Hugh M.
Snuff Bottles of China, London:
Bibelot Publications, 1971

PERRY, Lilla S.
Chinese Snuff Bottles, Rutland,
Vermont: C. E. Tuttle, 1960

SCHMOEANZ, Gustav
*Old Oriental Gilt and Enamelled
Glass Vessels Extant in Public
Museums and Private Collections*,
London: G. Norman & Son, 1899

Toledo Museum of Art
*Exhibition of East Asiatic Glass; An
Exhibition of Glass from Regions of
Asia*, Toledo, Ohio: The Museum,
1948

Paperweights

BEDFORD, John
Paperweights, New York: Walker &
Co., 1968; London: Cassell and Co.
Ltd., 1968

BERGSTROM, Evangeline H.
Old Glass Paperweights, Chicago:
Lakeside Press, 1940; London: 1947

BERGSTROM, John Nelson
*Glass Paperweight Symposium
Lectures, June 27-30, 1976*, Neenah,
Wisconsin: Bergstrom Paperweight
Research Center, Bergstrom Art
Center and Museum, 1976

BROTHERS, J. Stanley
'The Miracle of Enclosed
Ornamentation', *Journal of Glass
Studies IV*, 1962, pp 117-126

CLOAK, Evelyn C.
*Glass Paperweights of the Bergstrom
Art Center*, New York: Crown
Publishers, Inc., 1969; London,
Studio Vista, 1969

CLOAK, Evelyn C.
'A Glossary of Paperweight terms'.
Antiques, 65, No. 4, April 1969, pp
559-63.

ELVILLE, E. M.
*Paperweights and Other Glass
Curiosities*, London: Country Life,
1954.

GAYLE, Mary Redus
*Glass Paperweights from the Estelle
Doheny Collection*, Ephrata,
Pennsylvania: Science Press, 1971

HOLLISTER, Paul
*The Encyclopedia of Glass Paper-
weights*, London: 1970; New York:
Clarkson N. Potter, Inc., 1969

HOLLISTER, Paul
*Glass Paperweights; An Old Craft
Revived*, Scotland: William Culross
& Son Ltd., 1975

HOLLISTER, Paul
*Glass Paperweights of the New York
Historical Society*, New York:
Clarkson N. Potter, Inc., 1974

HOLLISTER, Paul
*Glass Paperweights at Old Sturbridge
Village: the J. Cheney Wells
Collection*, Sturbridge, Massa-
chusetts: Old Sturbridge Village,
1969

HOLLISTER, Paul
'Outstanding French and American
Paperweights in the Wells Collection',
Antiques, 89, No. 2, February 1966,
pp 265-269

HOLLISTER, Paul and LANMON,
Dwight P.
*Paperweights: Flowers Which Clothe
the Meadows*, Corning, New York:
The Corning Museum of Glass, 1978

IMBERT, R.
French Crystal Paperweights, Paris:
Art and Industry, 1948

JOKELSON, Paul
Antique French Paperweights,
New York: privately printed, 1955

JOKELSON, Paul (ed)
*Bulletin of the Paperweight Collectors
Association*, Scarsdale, New York,
1954

JOKELSON, Paul
*Sulphides: the Art of Cameo
Incrustation*, New York: Thomas
Nelson & Sons, 1968

JOKELSON, Paul
*One Hundred of the Most Important
Paperweights*, Scarsdale, New York:
privately printed, 1966

LEGGE, J. M. D.
'More Glass Paperweights', *Antique
Dealer and Collectors Guide*, 19, No.
11, June 1965, pp 62-65

LEGGE, J. M. D.
'Old Glass Paperweights', *Antique
Dealer and Collectors Guide*, 19, No.
10, May 1965, pp 41-43

McCAWLEY, Patricia K.
*Antique Glass Paperweights from
France*, London: Spink & Son, 1968

McCAWLEY, Patricia K.
Glass Paperweights, London: Charles
Letts, 1975

MacKAY, James
Glass Paperweights, New York:
Viking Press, 1973

McKEARIN, George S. and Helen
American Glass, New York: Crown
Publishers, Inc., 1948

MANHEIM, F. J.
A Garland of Weights, New York:
Farrar, Straus and Giroux, 1967

MANNONI, Edith
Sulfures et Boules Press-Papiers,
Paris: Editions Ch. Massin, n.d.

MELVIN, J. S.
*American Glass Paperweights and
Their Makers,* revised edition; New
York: Thomas Nelson, Inc., 1970

SELMAN, Laurence and Linda
Paperweights for Collectors, Santa
Cruz, California: Paperweight Press,
1975

SMITH, Francis E.
American Glass Paperweights,
Wollaston, Massachusetts: The
Antique Press, 1939

VULLIET, Andre
*A Message from Baccarat about
Paperweights,* New York: Baccarat
Inc., 1967

WILSON, Kenneth M.
New England Glass and Glassmaking,
New York: Thomas Y. Crowell Co.,
1972

Russia

KACHALOV, N. N. and VARGIN, V. V.
'Antike russische Gläser', *Glass and
Ceramics (Russian),* 1954, pp 11–13

Scandinavia

ANDERBJÖRK, Jan Erik
*Schwedische Glasanfertigung während
400 Jahren, Annales du 6ᵉ Congres de
l'Association pour l'Histoire du Verre:*
Cologne, *1973*

ANDERBJÖRK, Jan Erik och Nisbeth,
Åke, *Gammalt glas,* Uppsala:
ICA-förlaget, 1968

ANNALA, Vilho
Notsjö glasbruk 1783–1943, Helsinki:
1943

BERNSTEN, Arnstein
En samling norsk glass, Oslo:
Gyldendal Norsk Forlag, 1962

CHRISTIANSEN, G. E.
*De gamle priviligerede norske
glassverker og Christiania
Glasmagasin I–III,* Oslo:
H. Aschehoug & Co., 1939

Catalogue to the Coburger Glass
Prize, Kunstsammlungen der Veste
Coburg, 1977

Danish Glass 1814–1914. The Peter
F. Heering Collection. Victoria and
Albert Museum catalogue, London:
1974

LARSEN, Alfred, RIISMOLLER, Peter
and SCHLÜTER, Mogens
Dansk Glass 1825–1925, 2nd revised
edition, Copenhagen: Nyt Nordisk
Forlag Arnold Busck, 1974

LASSEN, Erik and SCHLÜTER, Mogens
Dansk glas 1925–1975, Copenhagen:
Nyt Nordisk Forlag Arnold Busck,
1975

LIE, Inger-Marie
Hadelands-glass 1850–1900, Oslo:
C. Huitfeldts Forlag, 1977

Modernt svenskt glas
Dedicated to Edward Hald on his
60th birthday and written by Erik
Wettergren, Edward Strömberg and
others, Stockholm: Jonson &
Winter AB, 1943

NIILONEN, Kerttu
Finskt glas, Helsinki: 1964

Notsjö Glasbruk
Price list from 1882, facsimile
edition), Notsjö: 1969

OPSTAD, Lauritz (ed)
Glasskunstneren Benny Motzfeldt
(with an English summary),
Kunstindustrimuseet i Oslo, 1973

POLAK, Ada B.
Gammelt norsk glass (with an English
summary), Oslo: Gyldendal Norsk
Forlaf, 1953

POLAK, Ada B.
*The manufacture of glass à la facon de
Venise in Scandinavia*, Annales du 2^c
Congres des 'Journées Internationales
du Verre', Leyden, 1962

POLAK, Ada B.
Modern Glass, London: Faber &
Faber, 1962

POLAK, Ada B.
Glass, its makers and its public,
London: Weidenfeld & Nicolson,
1975

RIISMÖLLER, Peter, JEXLEV, Thelma
and SCHLÜTER, Mogens
*Dansk glas i Renaessancetid 1550–
1650.* Copenhagen: Nyt Nordisk
Forlag Arnold Busck, 1970

SEITZ, Heribert
Aldre svenska glas (with an English
summary), Stockholm: Nordiska
Museet, 1936

STEENBERG, Elisa
Svenskt 1800–talsglas, Stockholm:
1952

Spain and Portugal

BARLER, Edwin A.
*Spanish Glass in the Collection of the
Hispanic Society of America*, New
York: G. P. Putnam, 1917

FOLCH Y TORRES, Joaquim
*El Tresor Artistic de Catalunya. Els
Antics Vidres Catalans Esmaltats*,
Barcelona, 1926 (Quaderns de
Divulgacio Artistica de la 'Gaesta
de les Arts', Serie B. Secció IV).

FROTHINGHAM, Alice W.
Barcelona Glass in Venetian Style,
New York: Hispanic Society of
America, 1956

FROTHINGHAM, Alice W.
*Hispanic Glass, with examples in the
Hispanic Society of America*, New
York: Hispanic Society, 1941

FROTHINGHAM, Alice W.
Spanish Glass, New York: Thomas
Yoseloff, 1964

RIAÑO, Juan F.
'Essay on Spanish Art', reprinted
from the catalogue of Spanish Works
of Art in the South Kensington
Museum, London, 1881

RIAÑO, Juan F.
The Industrial Arts in Spain, London:
South Kensington Art Handbooks,
1879

ROBINSON, J. C. (ed)
*Catalogue of the Special Loan
Exhibition of Spanish and
Portuguese Ornamental Art*, London:
South Kensington Museum, 1881.

SHERRILL, Charles H.
*Stained Glass Tours in Spain and
Flanders*, New York: Dodd, Mead,
1924

TATLOCK, R. R.
Spanish Art, London: Burlington
Magazine Monograph, 1927

Stained Glass

ARMITAGE, E. Liddall
*Stained Glass, History, Technology
and Practice*, Newton, Mass: C. T.
Branford, 1959

AUBERT, Marcel
Le Vitrail en Fránce, Paris:
Larousse, 1946

BERNSTEIN, Jack W.
Stained Glass Craft, New York:
Macmillan, 1973

CLOW, Barbara and Jerry
Stained Glass: A Basic Manual,
Boston: Little, Brown, 1976

CULLENBINE, Carol W.
Stained Glass Reflections, Palo Alto,
Calif: Hidden House, 1976

DIVINE, J. A. F. and BLACHFORD, G.
Stained Glass Craft, New York:
Dover, 1972

DUNCAN, Alistair
*Leaded Glass: a Handbook of
Techniques*, New York: Watson-
Guptill, 1975

DUVAL, Jean-Jacques
*Working with Stained Glass:
Fundamental Techniques and
Applications*, New York: Thomas Y.
Crowell & Co., 1972

FRENCH, Jennie
*Glass-Works; the Copper Foil
Technique of Stained Glass*, New
York: Van Nostrand Reinhold, 1975

FRODL-KRAFT, Eva
*Die Glasmalerie: Entwicklung:
Technik: Eigenart*, Vienna: Anton
Schroll & Co., 1970

GICK, James L.
Patterns for Stained Glass, Laguna
Hills, Calif: Future Crafts Today,
1977

HAHNLOSER, Hans R. (ed)
Corpus Vitrearum Medii Aevi,
Basel: Birkhäuser Verlag, 1956

HAMILTON, Alice Blanche
Manitoban Stained Glass, Winnipeg:
University of Winnipeg Press, 1970

HAMILTON, Walter J.
The Technique of Making Leaded Glass Ornaments, Silver Spring, Md.: Hamilton Studio, 1971

HILL, Robert and HALBERSTADT, Jill and Hans
Stained Glass : Music for the Eye, Oakland, Calif: Scrimshaw Press, 1976

ISENBERG, Anita and Seymour
How to Work in Stained Glass, Philadelphia: Chilton Book Co., 1972

ISENBERG, Anita and Seymour
Stained Glass : Advanced Techniques and Projects, Radnor, Pennsylvania: Chilton Book Co., 1976

ISENBERG, Anita and Seymour
Stained Glass Lamps : Construction and Design, Radnor, Pennsylvania: Chilton Book Co., 1973

JOHNSON, James Rosser
The Radiance of Chartres, New York: Random House, 1965

JUDSON, Walter W.
Introduction to Stained Glass : A Step-by-Step Guide, Los Angeles: Nash Publishing, 1972

LAYMARIE, Jean
The Jerusalem Windows. Translated by Elaine Desautels. New York: Braziller 1967

LEE, Lawrence
The Appreciation of Stained Glass, London: Oxford University Press, 1977

LEE, Lawrence; SEDDON, George; STEPHENS, Francis
Stained Glass, New York: Crown Publishers, Inc., 1976

LIPS, Claude
Art and Stained Glass, New York: Doubleday, 1973

LLOYD, John G.
Stained Glass in America, Jenkintown, Pennsylvania: Foundation Books, 1963

LUCIANO
Stained Glass Window Art, Palo Alto, Calif: Hidden House/Flash Books, 1974

McGRATH, Raymond
Glass in Architecture and Decoration, London: The Architectural Press, 1961

MARCHINI, Giovanni
Italian Stained Glass Windows, London: Thames and Hudson, 1957

METCALF, Robert and Gertrude
Making Stained Glass, New York: McGraw-Hill, 1972

MOLLICA, Peter
Stained Glass Primer, Volumes I & II, Berkeley, Calif: Mollica Stained Glass Press, 1977

NEWTON, R. G.
The Deterioration and Conservation of Painted Glass : a Critical Bibliography and Three Research Papers, London: Oxford University Press, 1974

O'BRIEN, Vincent
Techniques of Stained Glass : Leaded, Faceted and Laminated Glass, New York: Litton (Van Nostrand), 1977

PIPER, John
Stained Glass : Art or Anti-Art, London: Studio Vista, 1968

RACKHAM, Bernard
The Ancient Glass of Canterbury Cathedral, London: Lund Humphries, 1949

READ, Herbert; BARKER, J. and LAMMER, A.
English Stained Glass, New York: H. N. Abrams, 1960

REYNTIEN, Patrick
The Technique of Stained Glass, New York: Watson-Guptill, 1967

RIGAN, Otto B.
New Glass, San Francisco: San Francisco Book Co. Inc., 1976

ROTHENBERG, Polly
Creative Stained Glass ; Techniques for Unfired and Fired Projects, New York: Crown Publishers, Inc., 1973

SEWTER, A. Charles
The Stained Glass of William Morris and His Circle, Vol I, New Haven: Yale University Press, 1974

SEWTER, A. Charles
The Stained Glass of William Morris and His Circle – A Catalogue, vol 2, New Haven: Yale University Press, 1975

SIBBETT, Ed, Jr.
Stained Glass Pattern Book, New York: Dover, 1976

SOWERS, Robert
'The Lost Art. A Survey of One Thousand Years of Stained Glass,' *Problems of Contemporary Art*, No. 7, New York: George Wittenborn Inc., 1954

SOWERS, Robert
Stained Glass : An Architectural Art, New York: Universe Books Inc., 1965

Stained Glass Association of America
Story of Stained Glass, 6th edition, St. Louis, Missouri: Stained Glass Association of America, 1970

STETTLER, Michael
Swiss Stained Glass of the Fourteenth Century from the Church of Koenigsfelden, New York: Batsford, 1949

TWINING, Ernest W.
The Art and Craft of Stained Glass, London: Isaac Pitman & Sons Ltd., 1928

VOIGT, Robert J.
Symbols in Stained Glass, St. Paul, Minnesota: North Central, 1957

WAYMENT, Hilary
The Windows of Kings College Chapel, Cambridge, a Description and Commentary, London: Oxford University Press, 1972

WHALL, C. W.
Stained Glass Work, London: Sir Isaac Pitman & Sons Ltd., 1920

WOOD, Paul W.
Stained Glass Crafting, New York: Sterling Publishing Co., 1971

Studio Glass Crafts

ANDERSON, Hariette
Kiln-Fired Glass, Philadelphia:
Chilton Book Co., 1970

BARBOUR, R.
*Glassblowing for Laboratory
Technicians,* Oxford: Pergamon
Press, 1968

BERLYE, Milton K.
*The Encyclopedia of Working with
Glass,* Dobbs Ferry, New York:
Ocean Publications, 1968

BURTON, John
*Glass : Philosophy and The Modern
Hand-blown, Sculptured, Colored,*
Philadelphia: Chilton Book Co., 1967

Crafts Advisory Committee
Working with Hot Glass, Papers
from the International Glass
Conference, September 1976,
London: The Committee, 1977

DUTHIE, Arthur L.
Decorative Glass Processes, London:
A. Constable and Co., 1919

FLAVELL, Ray and SMALE, Claude
Studio Glassmaking, New York: Van
Nostrand Reinhold, 1974

FRASER, B. Kay
*Creative Bottle Cutting : Art and
Functional Projects from Old Bottles,*
New York: Crown Publishers, Inc.,
1972

GROVER, Ray and Lee
Contemporary Art Glass, New York:
Crown Publishers, Inc., 1975

HEDDLE, G. M.
*A Manual on Etching and Engraving
Glass,* London: Alec Tiranti, 1961

Huntington Galleries
*New American Glass : Focus West
Virginia,* Huntington, West Virginia:
The Galleries, 1976

KINNEY, K
Glasscraft, Philadelphia:
Chilton Book Co., 1962

KULASIEWICZ, Frank
*Glassblowing : The Technique of Free-
blown Glass,* New York: Watson-
Guptill; London: Pitman Publishing,
1974

KULASIEWICZ, Frank
*Offhand Blown Glass as a Contem-
porary Craft,* Ann Arbor, Michigan:
University Microfilm, 1972

LITTLETON, Harvey K.
Glassblowing, New York: Van
Nostrand Reinhold, 1971

LITTLETON, Harvey K.
Glassblowing – A Search for Form,
New York: Van Nostrand Reinhold,
1972

NORMAN, Barbara
Engraving and Decorative Glass, New
York: McGraw-Hill, 1972

SCHULER, Frederic
*Flameworking : Glassmaking for the
Craftsman,* Philadelphia: Chilton
Book Co., 1968

SCHULER, Frederic and Lilli
*Glassforming : Glassmaking for the
Craftsman,* Philadelphia: Chilton
Book Co., 1970; London: Pitman
Publishing, 1970

STANWORTH, J. E.
Physical Properties of Glass, London:
Oxford University Press, 1950

Technical

ANGUS-BUTTERWORTH, L. M.
'Glass', *A History of Technology,*
Volume IV, Oxford: Oxford
University Press, 1958

BARFF, F. S.
Glass and Silicates, London, 1876

CORNISH, Derek C.
*The Mechanism of Glass Polishing ; A
History and Bibliography,* Chisle-
hurst, Kent: British Scientific
Instrument Research Association,
1961

DOUGLAS, R. W.
'Glass Technology', *A History of
Technology,* Volume IV, Oxford:
Oxford University Press, 1958

GERSPACH
L'Art de la Verrerie, Paris, 1885

Glass-Making Dictionary, (English–
German – Polish) revised edition,
New York: Heinemann, 1974

HARDEN, D. B.
'Glass and Glazes', *A History of
Technology,* Volume II, Oxford:
Oxford University Press, 1957

HUMPHRYS, Leslie George
Glass and Glassmaking, Oxford:
Blackwell, 1961

JANSON, S. E.
*Descriptive Catalogue of the
Collection Illustrating Glass
Technology,* London: Science
Museum, 1969

London Science Museum
*Glass Technology : Descriptive
Catalogue,* London: Science
Museum, 1969

MARSON, Percival
Glass and Glass Manufacture,
4th ed London: Pitman Publishing,
1949

MOREY, George W.
The Properties of Glass, 1938, New
York: Reinhold Publishing Co.,
rev. ed. 1958

NESBITT, Alexander
*Catalogue of Glass, Slade Collection,
Notes on the History of Glass
Making,* London, 1871

PHILLIPS, Charles J.
Glass : Its Industrial Applications,
New York : Van Nostrand Reinhold,
1960

PHILLIPS, Charles J.
*Glass : The Miracle Maker. Its
History, Technology and Applications*,
New York : Pitman Publishing, 1941

SHAND, E. B.
Glass Engineering Handbook, New
York : McGraw-Hill, 1958

TOOLEY, F. V. (ed)
Handbook of Glass Manufacture, 2
volumes, New York : Glass
Publishing Co., 1960

TURNER, William E.
'Studies of Ancient Glass and
Glassmaking Processes', Journal of
the Society of Glass Technologists 38
(1954) pp 436–46; 40 (1956) pp
162T–86T; 40 (1956) pp 227T–
300T; 40 (1956), pp 39T–52T

TURNER, William E.
'The Technical Study of Ancient
Glass. A Review of Progress and A
Plan for The Future', *Glastechn
Berichte 32k*, 1959, pp VIII/57
VIII/58

WYATT, Victor
*From Sand-core to Automation. A
History of Glass Containers*, London :
Glass Manufacturers' Federation,
1966

WYMER, Norman
Glass ; It's Made Like This, London :
J. Baker, 1964

Venice

BIRINGUCCIO, V.
De la pirotechnia, Venezia, 1540

CECCHETTI, B.
Della filatura e tessitura del vetro,
Venezia, 1867

CECCHETTI, B.
*Sulla storia dellárte vetraria
Muranese*, Venezia, 1865

FIORAVANTI, L.
Dello specchio di scientia universale,
Venezia, 1572

GASPARETTO, A.
'Decorazione a smalto su vetro
islamica e veneziana', *Giornale
Economico*, Venezia, 1953

GASPARETTO, A.
*Il vetro di Murano dalle origini ad
oggi*, Venezia, 1958

GASPARETTO, A.
'Nuove ipotesi sulle origini della
vetraria veneziana', *Ateneo Veneto*,
1953

GOZZI, G.
Del vetro, Venezia, 1794

MARIACHER, G.
Antichi lampadari vitrei veneziani,
Venezia, 1957

MARIACHER, G.
'I vetri della raccolta Maglione
presso il Museo Vetrario di Murano',
Giornale Economico, Venezia, 1954

MARIACHER, G.
Three Centuries of Venetian Glass,
Corning, New York : Corning
Museum of Glass

MOSCHINI, G. A.
Guida per l'isola di Murano, Venezia,
1808

ZANETTI, V.
Delgi specchi di Venezia, Venezia,
1877

ZANETTI, V.
Il Libro d'oro di Murano, Venezia,
1883

Index

315

Acknowledgements

Our grateful thanks to illustrator
Christopher Evans for his beautifully
detailed drawings, and to the many
museums, companies and
individuals, including those listed
below, who provided us with
illustrations. Where relevant,
photographers or photographic
libraries are given immediately after
the source.

Archives Photographiques, Paris/
The Bridgeman Art Library 99tr;
Blandford Press 254; British
Museum 20c, 21tl, 21br, 22t, 22c,
23t, 23b, 28, 33, 34, 35, 36t, 36b,
37l, 37tr, 37br, 38, 39tr, 39bl, 40,
43r, 43b, 44t, 44b, 45l, 45r, 46, 47,
58t, 61t, 73r, 121l, 128, British
Museum/The Bridgeman Art
Library 123r; Christies, London 61c,
62, 66br, 67b, 73l, 74br, 96b, 99l,
106, 108–9cb, 120, 121, 124tr, 127r,
127r (detail), 175tl, 176tl, 193tr,
193bl, 258; Cinzano 27t, 27b, 32, 41,
42, 59, 60, 69, 70, 71, 74tl, 74bl and
back cover cr, 76tl, 79b, 91, 96tr,
101t, 101b, 113, 119cr, 119br, 135,
138, 156, 223bl, 290bl; CNAM,
Musée des Techniques, Paris/The

Bridgeman Art Library 170r; The
Bridgeman Art Library 132t, 132b,
133l, 142b, 146br, 146tr, 149b, 151t,
171cr, 172, 191, 201r, 234/5, 237t,
237r, 250t, 250c, 259tr, 259tl, 259b,
270, 272, 281, 286tl, 289ct; The
Corning Museum of Glass, New
York 20t, 20b, 79c, 80r, 93, 97l,
107l, 108t, 108 2nd d, 108 3rd d,
108b, 109tr, 109br, 110t, 110 3rd d,
110b, 117t, 117b, 143c, 171t, 180r,
198 (both), 201l, 202tl, 203, 207,
210t, 210b, 212l, 212r, 233b, 251,
269r, 291bl, 291tr, 292bl, 292r; The
Corning Museum of Glass/The
Bridgeman Art Library 68l, 179b,
179t, 180l, 182b, 183, 194tl, 200tl,
271, 286tl; The Corning Museum of
Glass/Walter Parrish 181, 189t;
Dartington Glass 154bl, 289cb,
290tl; Derek Davis 61b, 72, 133r,
137, 139l, 266tl, 143t, 286r, 292c,
293c, 293tr, 294br, 266tl; Derek
Davis/Wallace Heaton 267t, 290cl,
267t; Direzione Civici Musei, Venice
66bl, 75t, 78tl, 79t; John Donat 284–
5; Editions Graphiques 116, 158,
160; Editions Graphiques/The
Bridgeman Art Library 127tl; Focal
Press 279b; Martin Harrison 49, 51,
55, 129r, 240 and back cover l;
Haworth Art Gallery 205; Hispanic
Society of America 83, 84, 85, 86;
Lucinda Lambton 244t;
Metropolitan Museum of Art, New
York 53, 289tr; Metropolitan

Museum of Art/The Bridgeman Art
Library 204; Museum of the City of
New York/Fotofolio 243; National
Arts Club, New York/Martin
Friedman 239, 241; New York
Historical Society/The Bridgeman
Art Library 178r, 206l; Nordiska
Museet 223tl; Orrefors 225cr; The
Packwood House Museum 186
(both), 195, 252t, 253b, 256br, 260,
269l; Walter Parrish 193tfl; Patent
Office, USA/The Bridgeman Art
Library 193br; Photographic
Records Ltd 265l, 268r; Pilkington/
The Bridgeman Art Library 68r,
76r, 107ct, 107r; Private collections
10–11, 12, 78c, 81, 92, 102t, 107cb,
114 (both), 119tl, 142c, 144t, 159,
187, 189b, 194b, 197, 202tr, 218,
219, 220, 221tr, 225tr, 225tl, 227,
228l, 229, 233t, 263, 287tl, 289br,
291ct; Private collections/The
Bridgeman Art Library 95, 97br,
188, 214cr; Private collections/
Hawkley Studios 16, 27c, 39br, 78tr,
80tl, 80bl, 127bl, 133c, 134b, 139tr,
139br, 140cr, 140cl, 140t, 141l, 141r,
142t, 144t, 154t, 230, 231t, 231b,
232, 255, 256tr, 256tr, 280r, 286bl,
286c, 287ct, 287cb, 288l, 290cb,
290ct, 291cr, 293bl, 293ct, 294bl,
294cb; Private collections/Graham
Portlock 2–3, 4–5, 29, 30, 94, 103,
104, 115, 125, 126, 136, 147 and back
cover, 148, 196, 208, 262, 264, 272–
3, front cover; Private collection/

Lane Stewart 140bl, 144bl, 144br,
145l, 190, 217, 250b, 280l;
Riihimaen Lasi
Oy, Helsinki 228t; Royal Brierley
Glass 267b; Smithsonian Institution,
Washington DC 182t; Smithsonian
Institution/The Bridgeman Art
Library 200bl; Sotheby's Belgravia
15, 50, 52, 277r, 277l, 278, 279t,
294tl; Sotheby's Belgravia/Wallace
Heaton 153t; Sotheby's Belgravia/
The Bridgeman Art Library 152c,
292tl; Sotheby's Zurich 118, 119tr;
Sotheby Parke Bernet & Co.,
London 166t, 166b, 167tr, 169, 248–
249; Spink & Co 157; Sundahl AB
226l; Teigens 225cl; Teigens/The
Bridgeman Art Library 178b;
Maureen Thompson Ltd, 82, 261;
Maureen Thompson Ltd/Graham
Portlock 9, 185; Gabriel Urbanek,
Prague 63, 66tr, 66tl, 74tr; Victoria
& Albert Museum, Crown Copyright
31t, 31b, 87l, 87r, 88, 89t, 89b, 97l,
102b, 122, 123l, 146l, 150, 151b,
173, 176bl, 176–7, 202b, 213, 214tl,
215, 216, 223r, 228r, 228c, 256bl,
259c, 288c, 291br; Victoria and
Albert Museum, Crown Copyright/
The Bridgeman Art Library 67t,
75b, 76bl, 98, 100, 109tl, 110 2nd
from t, 111l, 111r, 129l, 145r, 151t,
153b, 171c, 171b, 270, 272, 281; A.
Vigliani & Figli 58b; Waterford
Crystal Ltd 143b, 154br; Ole
Woldbye 231c.

(b = bottom; c = centre; t = top; l = left; r = right; d = down; f = far)